TO: Wanda Scott

THE COMMON FOE & RACIAL DIVIDE OF AMERICA

*It's a pleasure to endorse this
Book to a Woman who embraces the
principles and values of God's creation
and Universal Laws
that govern All Mankind
for
the Unity and Love of
"All"*

*Thanks James L. Webb
2016
Peace and Love
Always.*

THE COMMON FOE
& RACIAL DIVIDE
OF AMERICA

JAMES L. WEBB
A Winning Traditions Production

Printed in the United States of America.

ISBN: 978-159571-452-7
Library of Congress Control Number: 2009936598

Edgewood Press
205 Fifth Avenue
Tarentum, PA 15084

Table of Contents

Preface

The Unsung Heros and their Constitution

They were brought here from a faraway continent, a land known as the "cradle of life" that once housed the greatest civilization on this planet, a land that gave the world wisdom and knowledge and a legacy of a heritage that influence the world through its succession of supreme dynasties since the beginning of time. They were brought here in chains, shackled together and forced to endure one of the most horrific journey ever suffered by human beings since the beginning of creation. A defenseless people sold and kidnapped into slavery here in America. Upon their arrival they were branded, beaten, traumatized, and physically and psychologically dehumanized and forced into providing free labor and services for white people across this nation for over 250 years. These people deprived of any social or outside life turned to God and their spirituality for only the Creator could have kept them strong enough to endure and overcome the white man's wrath and abuse. A great part of their bondage survival was that they became humble and forgiving and rose up to be some of the strongest able-bodied people of this country, with their faith in God they knew their day would come.

These strong men and women made the economic growth of these white people soar across the nation, the banking system brought and sold them as assets and collateral, making them into the wealthiest money control systems in America. The plantation owners became some of the richest people in the country, the cotton, rice and tobacco industries made billions and billions of dollars out of their free labor, where are the reparations owed to the relatives of these slaves? The Japanese were given reparations for being placed in camps in California for 3 years during World War II, they did no work for anyone, and were deprived of their freedom for 3 years, and got their reparations approved. Blacks provided 250 years of free labor, no freedom and received nothing. I hope the lawyers continue to pursue this travesty of prejudice action by the powers that be, if the Constitution and Bill of Rights applied to Japanese, why not to the Black Americans, this is about fairness, of which this country is supposed to be built upon as a nation, let them show the country and the world that fairness. One of the major banking systems have apologized and given grants and scholarships to blacks some years ago and I applaud them for acknowledging the role of which these slaves played in their system of things. The Wachovia bank is one I read about some years ago, I say to them thanks for making a difference in a time when we are trying to right the wrong that was done. The American banking systems are the enormous wealth profiteers of the nation's finances, as they brought and sold slaves nationwide for hundreds of years; they must recognize their obligation to honor the debt they owe to these black people who they bought and sold as property into some of the most shameful circumstances ever inflicted upon a race of people. Slaves were herded into auction areas, stripped of their dignity, dehumanized before slave owners, banking salesmen and purchased, examined, handled and evaluated and then sold. Families were often torn apart, an account of such a sale, there was this slave mother, her husband already sold, was left alone with her 3 male children, 11, 9, and 5 years of age. She was purchased, someone else had bought 2 of her boys and the 5 year old was put up for bidding, she became horrified that she would be totally devastated of all of her children, so she broke free from the holding area and ran over to the man who had bought her, fell to her knees pleading for him to purchase her last son. She was kicked upon and abused by him for several minutes before he had her dragged back into the holding area, bleeding and screaming for God's help. This was a common scene as it was always to separate the children from the parents for easier indoctrination of these youthful children. These banks and other major corporate businesses who still reap this wealth today need to be identified and pursued for their retribution and compensation for their evil deeds of the past. I hope there will be a concerted effort to identify and follow up on these businesses and corporations and hold them accountable. If there's any wealth made from that period of time that manifested into any major financial gain, there's a PRICE they should pay today, we don't want to leave any business behind. Whatever Wachovia bank did to rectify the past should totally be expected from all others.

Acknowledgments

All praise to GOD for allowing this book to happen. It was a tremendous spiritual journey with Him, where I recieved the enlightenment of my true purpose in this system of things, as I traversed the path of life, back to that darkness from where I came. A journey that gave me an inner strength and true understanding of knowledge and wisdom, to accomplish my dream to reach out to the people of our nation and world, with Peace and Love for all Mankind.

First I owe my mother, Ruth Harrison my sincere gratitude for her tenacity and fortitude, love and patience in raising me and struggling as a single mother, yet influenced me to excell in all endeavors early on in my life and she still does, she's a strong beautiful woman and my guardian angel.

I also extend my thanks and appreciation to my son Glenn and daughter Gail and extended family and friends: Mike Flores and family, cousin Thomas Smith and son Thayer, Joe Taylor, Ron Smith, Janetta Mehl, Bro. Toliba, a great spiritual teacher, Henry and Marjie Fleming, Errol Hall, Dr. Lucille I joy a very knowledgeable lady of my life and love, Walter Nash, James Gordon my VA team leader and awareness counselor and all my fellow veterans in Trenton, Flor Navarro, Sonny (the blade) and Edie Hill, Dr. Reggie Bryant, the professor of WURD, Iyanla Vanzant, Oprah Winfrey, my aunt Mildred, Jim Duggins, Darren, Erika and Mack, Umesh and Archana Shah, John Edwards, Henry Hicks, Ron Dash, veteran's affairs advisor and major influence of my inner strength and character, Wiley Dubois fellow trooper 82nd Airborne Division, Bishop Henson, Bishop Wilcox's, Cynthia and Cliff Lewis, Judith Exterde, Ron and JoAnn Raccioppi, all of these wonderful people having played a major role in my life with their inspiration and well wishes during my challenge of my first book. They believed in me, Thanks for your support. Bob White, thanks for being there since the begining.

I also would like to dedicate this book to the men of the Fighting Deuce of which I served in Vietnam, 1966-1967. The patriotic men and women who have fought in every war of this nations existence and those who are commited on battle fields of today. I would also give my gratitude and thanks to the Black men and women who volunteered to fight in the Revolutionary and Civil Wars, giving their lives in winning the Independence of this nation and helping to unite it after the Civil War. I have a tremendous respect for those individuals, as much as they endured during slavery in horrific times. They still rose up to fight and win each of these wars, only to be continually disrespected as human beings and denied the rights by which the constitution was formulated. Yet they made a major difference, yet until this day people of this country do not understand or realize the role they played in this country's foundation and its freedom, wealth and economic growth. I feel the pain and sorrow as I read and researched the lives of these forgiving and courageous patriots, who not only fought the wars, but also had to fight the continued discrimination and racial injustice to gain respect, privilege, freedom and liberty enjoyed by all others for hundreds of years. One reason why I wrote this book. There's no greater cause to die for, then the liberty, justice and freedom they never recieved. May their story be told from this day forth.

Inspiring and supporting someone's dream and achievements are the true building of confidence to fulfill their purpose and I appreciate all the encouragement from some of the really great people I have known. My heart warming thanks and God bless.

The Common Foe

Since the Beginning

From Africa . . . . America
Slavery . . . . Free Labor
Superiority . . . . Indoctrination
Branding . . . . Lynching
Rape . . . . Castration
Discrimination . . . . Stolen Human Rights
3/5th of a Man . . . . Constitution
Denied Civil Rights . . . . Voting Rights
Holocaustic Killing . . . . Mass Killings of Black People,
Towns, and Churches
Stolen Inventions . . . . Hidden History of Contributions
to this Nation
Statue of Liberty . . . . Its History, Rejection, and
Acceptance
Stolen Legacy . . . . Legacy of African Civilization
Common Foe . . . . Inhuman and Racial
Discrimination
The Wars and Combat
Patriotism . . . . Revolutionary and Civil Wars
Outsourcing of Jobs . . . . Creation of Poverty in Our
Nations
The Stolen Votes . . . . Politicians Not Accountable for
Issues for Welfare of the People
Collapse of America
Financial System Allowing . . . . Misappropriations of Tax Payers
Funds

The Political Divide . . . . Bickering, Not Presenting Valid
Plans to Resolve Nation's Prob-
lems

The Tarnishing of Our
Nation's Image . . . . Influencing World Nation's to
Not Support America

Inciting the People with
Racial Hatred. . . . . Encouraging Racial Actions at
T-Party Rallies

The Total Disregard of
"We the People's" Welfare . . . . Missing Political Leadership
and Direction

It's All Here

Introduction

This is my story about my life in Philadelphia, Pennsylvania, my service career, my fight and confrontation with racism. In addition, I express my views and suggestions to address some divisive issues between black and white America by introducing African American contributions to modern civilization and other historical facts to some of our white racist brothers who I refer to as our Common Foe. Also, I would like to enlighten our African American brothers of the real struggle we as a race have endured and have yet to overcome here in this land called America. This is just a beginning to those interested in obtaining and following in the pursuit of the truth. It is a personal journey, a journey not only to find a hidden truth, but also to find the purpose of your existence. It is a committed journey where we encounter a spiritual and sacred enlightenment which resides within us all, the Divine. The deeper we venture into this journey, the more aware of our creativity forces. Furthermore we gain an understanding and wisdom and knowledge as we travel along the path to peace and joy and happiness as we share the beauty and oneness of all things.

I have shed the negative and embarked upon the positives and joy in my life. Along your journey we will share a common path because the power of enlightenment encompasses us all as one. We privileged few must reject the negative and work to eliminate those elements of our great society which promote divisiveness over unity, destruction over construction, chaos over order, hate over love.

Only the strong and courageous of heart will reap the rewards and treasures at the end. We as a nation can defeat the common foe. It is not about hate. Rather, it is all about love.

I hope you will enjoy this book. It is my first encounter with writing. Until we meet again, enjoy your journey and as I have stated we will be in touch for all good things come to those who have faith that the world will be the way it should be. So I will be in touch, if not in person then in spirit and soul and the wondrous channels of space and time.

Expand your mind to help God's plan contribute to the positives that reflect the change for the betterment of this system of things. Peace love and happiness be upon you.

I am James, a part of the Oneness that makes the Whole.

THE COMMON FOE
& RACIAL DIVIDE
OF AMERICA

chapter 1

My Step Father Benny Harrison

As a young boy, I grew up in the great historic City of Brotherly Love, Philadelphia, Pennsylvania. I was born at the General Hospital situated in the western section of the City. "Philly" was laid out in ethnic sections: Italians in the South; Irish, Polish and Germans in the Northeast; Jewish Center City; Blacks and Hispanics in the North; Amish, Center City, Mexicans in the Northeast. I used to think I was a "gypsy." It seemed like I've lived in every part of the City, we must have moved a thousand times.

I was the only child, born to Ruth Webb, a single young girl of eighteen. She later married my stepfather, Benny Harrison, in the early 1940's. I was born on March 12, 1939. Mom and Benny were together for approximately ten years before divorcing. My stepfather was an extraordinary man and I was very fond of him. He had great character. He was mentally strong, with high esteem and fortitude. He was an artist, an intellectual, physically imposing and very athletic. He played football, baseball and boxed. A very talented and accomplished artist, and painter., Benny was a First Sergeant in one of the Black Airborne Units that fought in Germany in World War II. I never saw any soldier who impressed me in a Military uniform, or in casual clothes the way he did. He simply was a sharp dresser, who dressed to impress. I also thought that when I grew up I wanted to join the Army and be as sharp as he was. He taught me Sports, especially boxing. He also taught me how to draw and paint. He painted a picture of a great Indian warrior Chief in full tribal attire, sitting so magnificently on a grayish white remarkable horse, which only a Chief could have mounted and rode. They were on the summit of a mountain overlooking the western plains, with wind blowing upon them, the Chief holding his splendid shield of armor, the feathers of his headdress tilted in the direction of the wind and the horse so gracefully poised in his stance. It was a great picture of beauty and character and the scenic earthy view of man, horse, and "mother nature". It created artistic harmony, and a beautiful balance was projected to all who realized that balance plays such a tremendous part in all things we admire and cherish.

One day I will draw and paint that picture. I vividly recall its impact on my being, while viewing it as a young boy. It sparked my creative mind set and inspired me to reach out for all that my stepfather was teaching me, of the wonderful world of art. I often ran into this classic in libraries, which periodically displays on covers of old western frontier magazines.

I excelled in creative art and had several paintings showcased around my country by Strawbridge's Art Shows in the mid 50's. Benny taught me well, being a strict disciplinarian who would accept only the best from you and required you to finish that which you started, accomplish more and excel in all your undertakings. "Be second to none!" and "Refuse to Lose!" were his demands.

I remember getting several low marks on my school report card once, that I actually begged my teachers to change them. I became petrified recalling Benny's warning. I know I had escaped punishment one time, but I wasn't sure I could ever do it again. So there I was! But the teachers had no mercy for me. Hence, no changes were made, so I began to cry. I cried all the way home knowing the grave outcome of the situation. I knew he had this old barber shop leather shop belt, about three feet long and four inches wide. He had cut splits at the bottom, eight of them to be exact, to ensure that when the belt made contact with my behind, it would sting in eight different places at the same time! Needless to say, after a few sessions with this very persuasive belt, there was no good "sit-down" time for several agonizing days. Drastically, my grades improved. I still feel the pain occasionally, and it's been damn near a hundred years ago.

Boxing is the Sport Benny taught me thoroughly early on; the jabs, hooks, right hand, footwork, speed, offense and the art of defense. He was really a tough guy. You had to be in those days. Especially in the Army. When you rise to rank of First Sergeant, you were most likely the toughest in the Unit. Toughness and discipline placed you there. I know, because I obtained such rank, during my service of twenty years as a Military Police Officer Law Enforcement Investigator. Later too, as First Sergeant. I indeed fulfilled my vision to emulate Benny when I grew up! I was so into Boxing that I would read about Jack Johnson, who was truly an amazing Black man! He became my first hero.

Benny had prepared me to fight and defend myself. "Dangerous streets lay out there". He used to say, "You never know what those people would do to you". To achieve that, he instilled strength, toughness, and the ability to accept and confront whatever challenges lay ahead. Almost as a warning and a premonition, I once saw him almost beat a man to death for disrespecting my mother in our house one night. The whole horrid situation kept me in a state of shock for a period of time. Such that when he taught me the tough game of Philadelphia fisticuffs, I learned quickly. One Saturday afternoon, I got into a fight with one of the bad kids on our block. He had a lot of audacity to confront me, thinking of his size – he was a little bigger than I was, and of his age – he was older than me. We must have fought for ten minutes! Man, I had my hands full with him. However, we wound up quitting. When I returned to our house and saw Benny there, he wasted no time in asking what was up. I told him I was outside fighting someone. He then told me he watched it through, and since I did not finish it up, I needed to go and complete what I had started! Saying that such a fight could have gone either way, and he thought I was sharp enough to beat my opponent. He convinced me, so I went out and fought again. This time a little harder to win, and I did. I went back to Benny and all was well.

I got into another fight a few days later. I was really kicking this kid's butt. I knocked him down, but there was a twist. He came up, took a bottle of coke from somewhere and hit me as I was moving away unaware, thinking it was done. The bottle sliced my face above the right eye. I turned back and caught him a few more times knocking him down again, until some neighbors broke us up, otherwise, I would have beaten him up real bad! Everything Benny taught me was working really great. Seemed like I was becoming the champion of the block. Even though I got cut, I still felt great not quitting and taking care of business. "Refuse to Lose!" was part of my character early on. Philly was a city of gang-infested streets. Every time we, as black kids, traveled around in some white neighborhood, we would have to fight with the white kids and sometimes even the adults as well. Yes, Benny's teachings proved beneficial for me, in the City of Brotherly Love.

Benny was someone who I admired and respected as my stepfather even until this very day. He was there for me, made a difference in my life. I give him lots of gratitude until this day. We had remained close until his death. He was my role model, despite the fact that was not my biological father. He was my hero and I called him "Dad". Many children inherit stepfather figures, and I applaud those men who stepped up, becoming the father for many kids who were left behind for various reasons by their so-called fathers. These men made tremendous impact in our lives. As I grew, eventually, I learned to forgive my father for what he failed to do. I remember an incident, when I came home from Airborne School, training at Ft. Benning, Georgia. I ran into him, I was then being noticed by everyone in the neighborhood, looking immaculate in my 82nd Airborne uniform. I had not seen him in years, yet, he wanted to show me off to all the people who knew him, trying to convey to them how sharp I was. He talked about all the things he had heard regarding my many accomplishments; of my boxing, and other endeavors excelled in. I recollected, that when I was on my way to Viet Nam, I wrote to him. Yet he never answered my letter. Now, in front of his friends, he played the perfect role, though in the real world, the only man who filled this void in my life was my stepfather. Other kids too reap the love and devotion of their stepfathers who were there for them. Posturing and grandstanding could never measure up to assuming and doing the father's responsibilities, the total commitment he never assisted or participated in the real father, in this rare situation, is the stepfather. They become our role models, our strength, teachers, providers, leaders, motivators, character builders. They inspire and instill faith, courage, pride, and all the essential qualities that create the positives conducive to establishing a winning tradition in our lives. These are the ones we cherish and love for all times. They are worthy to be praised, they balance the harmony, unity and family structure. It's never too late for fathers who just "disappeared" from their children to reach out to them. Forgiveness can be given in most cases and you might just play a role in your child's life. Pray to God if you are sincere. I am sure God and his love will make a connection for you, it just might be a very rewarding situation for all involved!

Benny was instrumental in creating the person I dreamed myself to become. He saw the dreamer in me and went ahead to prepare me to reach my destiny with faith, bravery, courage and heroism in my heart. Spiritually, physically, mentally, he sought and pursued discipline all the way through the utmost level of my childhood endurance, and succeeded in doing so.

I sum up such accomplishment knowing that today I exist as I am... and that is enough. I feel content.

chapter 2

My Mother

Ruth Harrison, my mother, who later became my life's angel, was the other major force of my living existence. A beautiful black lady, smart, of great character and very instrumental in influencing and creating the Jim Webb people have met and come to know over the years. The mother God blessed me with was the sole hand who stepped up to the awesome challenge to raise me as a single parent after her divorce from Benny. A mother's worse dilemma: she took charge of a very tough minded kid growing up in hard times on the streets of Philly. She, at times, worked two jobs in order to clothe, feed, nurture, house and keep me focused on school, and away from street gangs and peer pressure. Our relationship was fairly good at the beginning. However, it became very rocky after a period of time, especially when she had to work two jobs.

There were times I would be taken to my grandmother, other times, being left at some neighbor's house until my mom came to pick me up. These moves did not sit very well with me. I thought no mother worked all the time, never there when I needed her. I began to get a little bullish and hesitant at obeying her every demand of me. It was almost as if we were strangers. I ran the streets during her absence, met new friends, and accrued more bad habits from gang-related incidents. I learned early on there were three types of distinctive learning processes: Either you get it from mother and father, from school influences or from the slick and fast methods of the streets. The fact there was no Benny, the father image, no mother around, I was really left with much idle time to venture the streets after my boxing classes. Needless to say, the bullish kid now became "street-wise " and a major problem for the mother to raise and control. Grand-mom and the neighbors just could not deal with or control me.

One night, I was hanging on the corner with my boys, at around 9:30 pm or so when mom suddenly showed up and asked me if I knew what time it was. She stated that it was 9:30 pm and I was due at home at 9:00 pm. She then told me I better be home before she got there! At that point, here I was, thirteen years of age, just started boxing, blowing it off in front of the fellows I was hanging around with. She left as speedily as she came. Later I told the fellows I was going home after the grandstanding in front of them. I left. I arrived home about half an hour later, around 10:30 pm. The house was dark. I opened the front door, then walked about two steps in, when I suddenly felt the most excruciating pain, from a blow delivered by a 2x4 feet piece of wood, which my mother used! She hit me a second time. I fell against the wall. Almost immediately, the lights came on, and there was mom with the 2x4.

"Hold on, Mom, take it easy!" I yelled.

She hit me again, talking and hitting at the same time. I was in big trouble.

"Take it easy!" she said. "You had the audacity to embarrass me in front of your buddies! Why should I take it easy? When I tell you to be here at 9:00 pm it is actually what I mean!"

Man, I thought Benny was tough! I never knew mom had that kind of demeanor. She had stepped up and finally got my attention that one dark night, in the hallway of the apartment we lived in.

"You might be boxing and hanging the corners," she added, "but I am the champion in this house, and as soon as you acknowledge that, I'll let you get away. Do you understand?"

"Yes, Mom." I said.

She then told me to get up those stairs. I quickly got myself together, happy to be released from such agony, and darted up. On my way I still heard additional reminders. She said: "I am going to knock some sense in your head. And you better not be late for school in the morning!"

We laugh about this incident periodically today, mom and I. I get tickled and tell her, "Mom, you should have at least let me know you had a 2x4 in your hand!" She said: Why? So you could have been prepared? No way! I wanted to give you a surprise element!

And I think that helped you out in your boxing. Never let anyone slip up on you! Thought you had better footwork and defense" and I said to her: "Mom, I found out that you can't defend against what you can't see." She just amusingly smiled back at me. Mom had a major role in training me, getting me back on the right track and focusing myself.

After that day, I had let my ego out and began respecting my mother for the fighter she was, and listened to what she was trying to tell me, and show me then. It made a tremendous impact on our relationship. I give her credit for stepping up. Many mothers don't care enough whether their children were home by 10:00 pm or not. I have seen this Lady, my mom, work two jobs sometimes, in order to make ends meet.

However, the peer pressure got to me, and I wound up spending two years away from home. My mother came to visit me every visitation day. I excelled up there. I became captain of the Company B, played in the musical band for a period, and joined the Paint Shop because of its Art Program. I was tutored by Mr. Irving Lutz, a German Art Instructor who had lost a leg in World War II, an amazing man who showed me so much about the world of Art and Painting. He was a hard taskmaster, as hard as Benny, I believe. So I excelled under his tutelage.

I got into a fight inside the shop, one day with an inmate. I beat him up pretty bad. They had to get me off him. Mr. Lutz became furious and told me to get in the shop area immediately. He wielded his cane, threatening to hit me. "You better not hit me with that cane!" I said. However, as I went through the door, he did! The cane blow hit me across my back and shoulder blades. Another blow came, both unexpectedly to me, especially after he told me he was not going to do so. I realized I was in another Mom type incident. Someone slipped up on me. Mr. Lutz wrote me up later, and stated that Jim Webb would fight at the drop of the hat! That incident brought me to the Disciplinary Board. But my explanation of what had transpired resulted in my release, back to Mr. Lutz. Later on, he invested much time harassing my talents. I forgave him for his actions. I knew deep inside that my Philly attitude needed to be controlled if I ever wanted to be released. So I controlled myself as much as I could. Although I must say, it was indeed hard for me, especially after you become a powerful leader as I had become after a period of time there. Leadership came when I finally fought and almost beat the leader of the whole institution. A great fight it was! I got beaten, but three days later he went home, so I elevated my status into his level, so to speak.

Soon I got word that I would be released. I wrote home and told mom exactly what I wanted to wear. It was a thing to do, go out... big time! So I told her I needed a Peter Pan overcoat, a gray suit, an off-green shirt with matching tie and some black Stacey Adams, a very popular pair of shoes that all the "old heads" and sharp brothers wore on the block back home. She bought everything, but the black shoes. I was totally dissatisfied. So much so that I told her how upset I was! And that I was not leaving at that point. Mom looked at me stating: "Boy, do you know how hard I had to work, just to get these things together?" I tell you what, I don't care if you are not appreciative of what I have worked my butt off, to acquire for your coming home!" at that point I saw the tears in her eyes and a "bell" went off in my head, that my actions truly hurt her heart and feelings. I said to myself, "Jim, you better get on that train. You can always get a pair of shoes when you get home. Apologize to your mother. It's hard times out there." I knew she had to struggle to buy those clothes. So I apologized, got on the train, and headed home to the City of Brotherly Love.

It was a rough ride for me because I truly harmed my mother's heart. At that point in my life I began to respect mom more for the beautiful person she truly was and thanked her for all she had done for me.

I later went on to see this wonderful woman make a major transition in her life. She gave her life to the Creator of all things. She now calls me everyday and every call ends with a prayer to God. She is involved in her church today, visits the Nursing Home Residents daily to inspire them through their day, and she is in a Daily Call Program where she talks with Senior Citizens. She is very active with the young people in her community. I am very proud of this woman who has become my living Angel and I thank God for her daily. She is worthy to be praised!

When I grew up there were lots of unwed single mothers, as it is today, who are unprepared to raise children. However, I knew a few who were definitely in control of their children and were always there for their kids. I saw them there whenever I visited their homes. Some of these mothers lived with their family and were committed to staying home and raising their children as best as they could. I remember quite a few guys who excelled because their mothers got them into sports and other school programs. They were always there, supporting their children, ensuring they arrived on time for the activity they were involved in. Because of these students' sacrifice not to party nor run the streets, they became the exceptional ones, who we often would see: star athletes! Such that whenever the spotlight is upon them there's always the greeting: "Hey Mom!"

We, as Senior Citizens, family members and friends, teachers, Church Pastors and other associates of young ladies must make a concerted effort to ensure we constantly warn these young girls not to just lay down, give in and become sexual pleasures for some young or old guy, which could have devastating consequences that may ruin their growth and maturation process, as well as rob them of enjoying their early years. We need to advise them to look around, observe how young mothers suffer dealing with raising children, not being able to finish school because she is unable to hire babysitters, neither could she work because of the absence or lack of job skills and career knowledge. So, at such an early age she is already frustrated and demoralized. Without the presence of the child's father, who oftentimes was equally unprepared for his parental task, the mother becomes despondent.

We, as members of the village must help raise all young people to provide a balance in advocacy, to increase their level of awareness and provide a sense of dignity of their being. As responsible and concerned adults, we can help maintain the structure and welfare of our citizenry, our community. It's part of God's plan!

My mother addressed teen-age pregnancy, childbirth without child support, marriage to my step-father and then divorce with great strength and fortitude. Today, not many girls of her age then, with similar experiences are as strong as she was, hence they fall by the wayside, and never make it at all in life!

Indeed there could never be anything greater than the Mother of Men!

chapter 3

My Best Friend and Racism

My early years as a child was spent on 17ᵗʰ Street in North Philadelphia "Philly"1400 Block. I was about six years old when we located there, a mixed neighborhood. There were approximately six white families housed there, among twenty-five or thirty black families on the block. I recall my mother letting me out on our front porch one afternoon. I saw this white kid playing across the street by himself. We "caught each other's eyes" and waved at each other. Somehow I wound up across the street. We acknowledged each other and our friendship was started almost instantly.

His name was Terry. He, too, was an only child. We became inseparable as time went on. His mother was really nice, I hardly ever saw his dad. Our mothers would spend times together during the early part of the day. They, too, got along really well. Terry and I had the greatest of times together. He had a wagon, tricycle and scooter, which we rode all the time. We ran in the rain, made mud houses and played games in their house. His mother would make the biggest hamburgers, great delicious milkshakes and would buy us sugar daddy taffies that seemed to last forever. There was always cool aid and pies and cakes. I would spend nights there on some weekends. We shared birthday parties together. We were in our own paradise. We were truly blessed to have known and spent time with each other. Those were the greatest days of my childhood! We were innocent, happy children, bonding and sharing our childhood years. Our youth was exciting. Two children born into this system of things with love and respect for each other. It was an extraordinary time of our development. We were oblivious to the social structure and problems of the other world where our mind's thoughts had not yet allowed us to venture into.

We were just two children creating a wonderful and joyous time for each other, although the colors of our skin were black and white, it never made a difference to us. He had blond, reddish hair and blue eyes. I had short, curly black hair and brown eyes. It did not enter our minds that we were different. We just accepted, respected and loved each other. There were days when we both cried the biggest tears whenever our mothers called us to come inside for the day. What a beautiful thing it was when two kids, with different ethnic and cultural background understood the meaning of love and friendship at such an early age. It was truly a phenomenal period of my youth! However, a real bad incident happened and for some unforeseen reasons, found a way to disrupt our sociably treasured moments in time.

One day, Terry's father, who had a strong confrontation with a black family in the neighborhood, came home, enraged. This set the tone for what would change our childhood relationship forever, and expose us abruptly to a totally different kind of world from that which we were enjoying so much. I came out of my house that time and sought Terry. I saw him sitting on their doorstep, so I went over and spoke to him. He seemed withdrawn and barely responded to me. So I asked why he looked so sad. He finally looked at me and said that his father told his mother not to let him play with "those nappy head nigger children." Terry did not fully understand what he stated. Terry looked like he was about to cry, knowing he could not play with me from then on.

I felt really sad and went home to tell my mother that Terry and I could no longer play with each other anymore. My stepfather, "Dad" and my mother asked "Why?" I told them what Terry had stated to me, and that I did not comprehend it at all so it was all I could say. They understood my situation, so they lovingly told me to stay inside. Later on she and my dad, who was home from war at that time, sat beside me in the living room. They began telling me about that statement and enlightened me about the new world of Racism, Discrimination, Hate and other Black and White issues. They told me that we, as black people, were bought here from Africa and enslaved since the early 1600's. They spoke of the slave labor, the lynching, raping and how blacks were called "niggers", "savages", and "animals". Also, about how we were classified as properties and not human beings. That the white men considered us inferior and were to be slaves here in this country forever! They shared a lot of other horrific situations that were still happening in the Southern States, as well as in the Northern region of the country, most especially in Philadelphia, which they ironically called... the "City of Brotherly Love". My dad also told me of the racism he encountered in the segregated Army, and that as I would grow older, I would become more exposed to a similar experience. Hearing this, I became really afraid to grow up now. I was terrified! I was told, however, that although racism existed, there were some decent and respectful white people who were not racists. And that it was a bad situation Terry's father was involved, which probably caused him to say and act that way. Then my stepfather proceeded to remind me to take precaution going through white neighborhoods, to be always aware of racism in this city because they caused hatred! He also told me to read about the life of Jack Johnson.

That day, my parents prepared me for my journey into the real world, a world I was shoved into, although I was not ready for it, being just a harmless little kid. Learning of these sad atrocities, I really had no option but to step directly into the next dimension of my life, ready or not. I had to leave behind my cherished days, though almost instantly: my childhood reverie with my friend, who I loved as a brother. We had become one... until that final moment when I was introduced to our nation's Common Foe, Racism, with all its accompanying negatives that make it a real challenge! For us to confront and fight! I was ushered into the real world.

Parents, as adults must never involve their children with their hatred, racism, prejudice or any negative attitude. To do such to these innocent kids is the greatest sin any parent can do on earth, since this creates universal discord and chaos in life and violates the child's right to joy and happiness.

chapter 4

Philadelphia:
"The City of Brotherly Love and Racial Hatred"

Philadelphia, Pennsylvania is one of the largest historical cities on the East Coast, about a two-hour drive to New York, the largest and most populated. Philly has always had a large number of Blacks, the first brought there by the Isabella, a slave ship in the early 1600's. The numbers increased tremendously during their movement from the terrors and lynchings in the Southern States, especially after the Civil War. George Washington, our first President, owned many slaves, who were housed at the Nation's first Capital, located in the Center City.

Philadelphia is a very beautiful city, with a rich heritage of being the first capital of the United States of America before it was moved to Washington, D.C. our forefathers signed the Declaration of Independence there, the Constitution of the nation was signed there. There's the Betsy Ross house, the Planetarium, the Independence Hall, the Liberty Bell, beautifully constructed Art Museum renown for its wealth of prestigious collectibles, where portions of the "Rocky" boxing films were "shot" during the making of the series of the five movies. There's great night clubs and entertainment playhouses, theaters, fantastic shopping areas, phenomenal architectures, constructed cathedrals and churches throughout the city. There's a horse racing track in the Northeast, the Flyers, Phillies, Eagles and 76'ers sports facilities and boxing arenas in just about ever section of the city.

Boxing is one of the oldest sport traditions in Philly and is known worldwide for its history of the games and the many great fighters it has produced over the years. There's a wonderful zoo in the West section, also a really nice Black History Museum in Center City. Philly is also known for its Philly Cheese Steaks and the Old White Tower hamburger. I ate so many of these sandwiches at times, I could hardly button my coat. I was truly a "gofer".

There's the beautiful Fairmount Park, the Benjamin Franklin Bridge, the Spirit of Philadelphia Cruise Ship for night cruises, for dances, or utilized for day luncheons or mid-day cruises along the Delaware River. There's the Philadelphia boat shows and racing in the Schukill area during the summer months.

In 1960 I met my favorite entertainer, the "smooth" renowned Frank Sinatra while I was speaking with Frank Rizzo, then the City's Police Commissioner, outside of the Jewish synagogue. Frank was a good friend of Rizzo. Sinatra approached us, shook Rizzo's hand, then inquired about me. Rizzo introduced me as the next Heavyweight Champ. Sinatra acknowledged me with a "Hello!" and remarked that he was a great enthusiast of the game, and wished me well in my endeavor. I was truly impressed. He was my idol, I had a great collection of his recordings and had seen several of his movies. I was on top of the world. I had just turned 20 years of age. I later did a tribute about him. It was really awesome, I loved what he stood for. One of the beautiful qualities I liked about him was that he fought against racial discrimination. There was a situation in Indiana where black and white children had a racial confrontation about attending school together. Sinatra heard about it and flew there to address and resolve the problem. He spoke with them there at the school, reprimanded all of them, told them that his family were immigrants to this country, as most of them were, especially the blacks, and their struggles with slavery. He spoke of other ethnic cultures and problems they also endured. He told them to forget about their differences and how important it was that they get back to school, support one another, and become all they could become in life. Frank helped the great Joe Louis when the government ordered him to pay back taxes on two million dollars Championship checks he had donated to the families of those who died in the bombing of Pearl Harbor and to the United States Military Service Relief Fund. Frank gave him a job in Vegas and paid for his funeral services when he died. Frank was instrumental in helping another phenomenal Black entertainer's life during his early years, the extraordinary Sammy Davis. Davis died penniless. Frank gave Davis' wife money and also paid the house off which she was living in. Frank was one fantastic guy and I knew that for certain.

Philly was an awesome city, the old adage is that if you can make it in Philadelphia, you can make it anywhere. I am proud to be from Philly. Our legacy follows us around the world, there are some wonderful people in my city of all walks of life, but we need them all to step forward to resolve the problems that are deteriorating our city drastically, depriving us of the balance that will continually take us to depression and despair for our children, senior citizens, our communities, and nation as well. We must come together for a change, create that Brotherly Love attitude, and establish friendship and respect for each other, and stop this chaos of regression and hatred, and racial discrimination. Everyone must be held accountable starting from the politicians, the police, who are definitely out of control at times with assaults and questionable killings, and those bad ass drug dealers and young gangs utilizing our most feared weapon of today, the gun, to disrupt and terrorize the neighborhood. One of the most serious problems is that there are no jobs for our Black youth. There are constructions and other jobs not provided to them. They see their neighborhoods gutted of houses, whose empty lots now stand with weeds, growing and in filthy conditions, garbage and trash and not being picked up at scheduled times, creating a wilderness for our children and senior citizens to reside in. These areas should be paved over and utilized for playgrounds or sitting areas for people in those neighborhoods. They are presently used as havens for the muggers, rapists, and other villains who victimize our loved ones. No caring person should allow the City Officials to renege on promises made when they stole your votes to elect them to public offices. They sat by and allowed all the economic growth to be removed from neighborhoods; they saw the white business desert the black communities for the downtown areas, depriving these neighborhoods of any type of Grants to the Black people to open business, to replace those that made the mass "Exodus" to there locations. Movie houses for our children to attend, not there, corner stores, not there, clothing stores, not there, appliances, not there! Everything has to be bought downtown. No city funds are available for the black man, wishing to establish such assets to the communities. However, the illegal immigrants are finding grant money to open business and grants for housing. Our youth are not ignorant to the picture played out before them. Unity is the catalysis of my city. "Brotherly Love" motto, now more than ever, must be upheld.

A house gets torn upside down in the black neighborhood when someone was caught using drugs. However, down in South Philly years ago, a close relative to a white political figure was caught making drugs in a portion of a mansion they were living in. The drugs, large sums of money, and weapons were confiscated. The mansion was left standing. Why could it not be torn down, as in the black neighborhood? A Police Commander was involved in an accident, he was found to be drunk, he also reconstructed the accident scene and tampered with the evidence. The investigation revealed the truth. He was cited in the newspaper for his behavior, yet no charges were administered. He was just transferred to another job area, anyone else would have been jailed for a few years. A Police Commander who swore an Oath to represent and enforce all violations of the law, was totally in violation of never reporting the accident and when found to be at fault, falsified the accounts of the situation. He should have at least been removed from his Command and maybe a reduction in Rank.

There was an 11 year old kid who stole a hoagie sandwich from a neighborhood Korean store, and ran outside. The Korean store owner chased him for approximately two blocks down, caught up with him and shot him dead. The neighborhood residents protested, however, the store owner was not charged with that murder. Amazing how the balance of the law tilts regarding blacks. A child is killed running away from the store for a $1.98 hoagie and no charges. The scenario does not fit the action taken. These types of incidents should be challenged at the City Prosecutor's Office, the Police Commissioner's and the Mayor's, these types of situations need constant follow-ups for justice that never happened.

A Fire Chief refused to put out a fire that ignited on a home in the Move Incident. He swore to an Oath to protect and save lives and property as did the police commissioner whose officers got out of hand. No control over 10,000 rounds being fired. What were they responding to? No weapons were fired, no weapons were found in the house of the 13 men, women and children who died in that "Inferno" after the city mayor gave his okay to drop an explosive device on their home. The City Deputy Mayor was at the scene also, his presence there too, allowed some responsibility to be blamed for at his overall handling of that horrendous loss of life and property. What a terrible display of those Law Enforcement Officers and Fire Protection Department, no one had a plan. That's for damn sure, and the final results reflect that. What a disaster! Just another part of the holocaustic events in America against blacks for 400 years. Yes, Philly has had its tragic history of crimes and the Common Foe has kept a tight reign over these unforgettable crimes that will forever tarnish our great city and nation for years to come.

chapter 5

The Black Holocausts of America

The definition of Holocaust: Annihilation, Carnage, Destruction, Devastation, Extermination, Flames, Massacre, Slaughter, and Mass Murder. (Webster's New Dictionary) Black people brought here from Africa became the American Nigger who later became classified as cattle and property written into law by the countries' forefathers who later on referred to them as three fifths of a man or human being.

From history, we find out that Africans were captured or sold into bondage and slavery, and transported here to be sold and kept in servitude forever. They came here in ropes and chains, with shackled hands and feet. Once they were separated: men, women and children, they were dispensed to just about every part of the country, especially in the Southern portions. These slaves were a major factor for the economic wealth of this country, especially in the South, where they worked in mostly rice, cotton and tobacco fields for 12 to 16 hours a day, with no pay. "Free Labor" was one of the reasons the Civil War was fought. Most of your major banks and corporations benefited from this "Free Labor" to become empires in the corporate business world today. Some of these banks and businesses have apologized and contributed major funds for black scholarships and courses for black development programs. Millions of blacks have been killed in the 400 years in America.

After being shipped here to this country to endure some of the most heinous crimes imaginable against a black race of God's people, they were stripped of their human and civil rights, their heritage, culture and civilization, homeland, pride and dignity. Shipped in chains, crowded in living area, where urine and human waste, and the smell of the dead bodies were the most offensive odor ever endured by mankind. Tens of thousands died during these ocean voyages. Many jumped to their death, or were beaten to death whenever they rebelled. They were the walking dead in the new land, did not understand the new language. They were in a wilderness, governed by white terrorist supremacists.

These racists introduced them to the "**whip**" to beat them with, the **rope** taken from their hands, placed around their necks to hang them with, **chains** used to secure them with, as a dog or cattle to a tree or fence, or at times, chained to heavy objects to drown them with. The **branding iron** burned their bodies. **Billy clubs** were used to beat them with, **the gun**, yes, the almighty GUN which the white man developed and used to kill billions of human beings since its existence, one reason why they were able to win so many battle against the Native Americans, in their struggle with them, for a long period of time. Then they had the **ax**, used to chop individuals to death with, the **knife** to castrate black men and young boys, the **fire** where they burned them alive with, the **heavy shoes** they wore to kick and stomp until death, the **swamps**, **rivers** where they drowned them in and **dogs** were used to chase and maul them to death!

And then there was the **penis** used to rape women and young girls with, so when we see light-skinned blacks, it's because the forefathers screwed black women for their sexual pleasure and satisfaction. It's amazing how they could rape and sexually abuse a black slave woman, and hate the black male as they did. They would at times incite emotional trauma in black men and the children by raping women in front of them, taking away the role model image and strength of their fathers, to instill in them that there was no one there to protect them from this psychological, emotional, and physical pain, this horrific scene they were experiencing, and for them to know that no one was able to save them from this savagery, hideous torture, and abuse that their mothers were constantly subjected to. The fathers were defenseless, and those who tried to protect their spouses were whipped or killed. As a result, they would all have to live with these images, of this criminal and inhuman acts embedded in their minds and souls forever. One major thing in all of these incidents is that our Common Foe committed all of these atrocities against unarmed people. The Indians fought back courageously with the use of bow and arrows, they knew the terrain, had their horses, and fought gallantly for many years. They almost fought until the last man standing. It's one thing going to war with those who can defend themselves, and cowardly taking advantage of the unarmed and defenseless. That's why I admire Jack Johnson. He always stated that giving a black man an equal chance, he could achieve as well as any race of people. And he proved just that. Jack won the most prestigious sporting crown in America, the Heavyweight Crown, by defeating a white Champion so badly, they had to stop the fight. I give him credit for his efforts, his white racist brothers called him a coward, so these suppose-to-be superiors even hate their own kind. What a shame! The black man, who they called a savage, animal, weak, dumb, inferior and ignorant outsmarted, outfought and just totally embarrassed the Champion before there unbelievable eyes of America. The fight was stopped, the film never shown in America for years to come. The racist Americans, our Common Foe just refused to acknowledge that blacks were intelligent and able to accomplish any task given the proper equipment and knowledge. The black jockeys were the world's best before they were stopped from riding in America, as were baseball players before they were banned from playing with the whites.

One of the greatest airplane pilots was a black man from New York. He was refused a license in America, went to France, and obtained one. He was the first to do aerobatics. He was called the Blackbird, distinguished himself in Europe flying with the British in World War I. Betsy Coleman, was another refused a license. She went to France, obtained hers at the age of 19, came back to America and set all kinds of flying records, and even formed the Betsy Coleman Flying Club in America around 1918 or so. Just a few facts of achievements by blacks who were not given an opportunity to achieve on equal terms. What a tragedy!

However, blacks still remained the ignorant race, not able to achieve. And regardless of what they did achieve, they were also tarnished by the Common Foe, who continued to boost their superiority over them. The killing of blacks still continued. The Ku Klux Klan and white hate groups continued to lynch, burn churches, schools and murder black men; always a mob action. These mobs were really the cowards. It took 20 cops to beat and assault Rodney King in California. It took 3 cops to assault and beat a 67 year old black man in New Orleans, caught on National television. Two cops were fired, one suspended. What a cowardly and despicable character these hoodlums were, who invaded our Law Enforcement system to continue their atrocities against blacks. The Common Foe is everywhere, especially our Police Force, who can murder and corrupt with gun and shield, and still be found innocent, when it is obvious they are the villains of many acts, negating their sworn Oath to uphold the Law. The balance of justice has the scales tilted drastically against blacks. It has been, and always will be until we continue to monitor impostors who hate and discriminate against the blacks here in America.

No, Philadelphia is not alone in these holocaustic events. Just about every major city across this country has their share of them, and they contribute to the devastation of black people, and their communities. The American Negro or black man has been abused since their arrival here, and there seems to be no end to it all!

chapter 6

Race Problems in the Cities

New York

Blacks migrated to New York seeking a more liberal white society, however, they encountered atrocities far worse than they ever could have imagined. In the late 1800's the Irish rioted for approximately five days. They killed blacks on sight, all through the city, burning homes, property, killing children and adults. Then they set fire to an orphanage, where people sought protection. The marauding Irish mobs burned and lynched blacks, threw babies and children out of three-story buildings. They even tried to force their way into Police Stations where blacks had fled for refuge. The Irish did not want blacks in their neighborhoods, and applying for their jobs.

Another incident incited them even more, when two Catholic priests, protested blacks being allowed to move into a new empty housing development. So much for priests doing God's work. That and molesting all the children, and there's been thousands of cases over the years, and even ways to cover up their sexual assaults on their own white race of children. Not long ago, there was an article published in one of the local newspaper depicting approximately 50 priests who were accused by people who they had molested over the last 60 – 70 years. Most of the charges were ignored, stating the statue of limitations which I thought was absurd, because when they took advantage of these children, the kids were so traumatized, no one would believe their stories in most cases. Most only had the courage to come forward later in life, after suffering the shame and physical abuse, they harnessed in their minds for years. The Vatican replaced and reassigned many of the priests, only to have them commit the same abusive acts over and over again. So we see, that our Foe is powerful in all elements of life. During the riot, approximately 20 blacks were killed and hundreds injured. No one was charged for these murders and property damage.

Newark, New Jersey

Newark was a city with constant racial problems with housing, jobs, police brutality, and outright discrimination against blacks, over the years. In 1967, one of the bloodiest riots occurred in the city, killing 23 blacks, and injuring hundreds and costing millions of dollars in property damage. This tragic riot was the result of police assaulting a young black man. It lasted for about 5 days.

Rosewood, Florida

In 1923 Rosewood was burned to the ground by white mobs seeking a black man who allegedly raped and beat a white housewife named Fannie Taylor. The real story was later revealed. She lied, her white boyfriend had caused her injuries. A white mob, believing her original story stormed the black community causing a holocaustic catastrophe, killing men, women, and children, and completely destroying the whole town. The only structure left standing, belonged to two white brothers John and William Bryce, these two courageous men rounded up and hid women and children in their general store. The white housewife was not charged, nor any white people found guilty of these murders or destruction of property during this horrific, devastating criminal hostilities against these innocent people. We see that our Common Foe also takes advantage of, blame the black man, lies, it worked for hundreds of years. There was a case in Boston, Massachusetts, about 20 years ago, where a white man said a black man had killed his wife. The police proceeded to the black communities, raiding their homes, forcing and dragging black males outside with the police weapons aimed at them. They were harassed and interrogated. No lawful search warrants were ever produced in these home invasions, a total disregard of civil and human rights. A few days later, it was found out that the white man had killed his wife. These types of police responses were a normal reaction, especially in a very racist town, as was Boston. A white woman told investigators that a black man had killed her four kids. Later it was found out that she lied, and admitting killing them herself. About a year ago, she was seeking her release from prison on grounds of insanity for drowning her children. Just think how many black men have been lynched or murdered because of a little white lie.

Tulsa, Oklahoma

Tulsa, another black town burned to the ground, destroying a very prominent community of black business. Blacks built and owned all of the commerce: bus line, taxi company, restaurants, hotels, bakeries, banks, schools, housing, theaters, barbershops, etc. a very successful black town with unity and balance. Another little white lie caused its demise. I saw the movie and researched the history of events, all these towns were black, built and controlled, were destroyed totally by whites. Again, no whites were ever charged of murder or destruction. A grave injustice reflecting the abuse of the American justice system Tulsa's Greenwood area was extremely prosperous, exemplifying black fortitude to succeed in America, their creativity and accomplishment. All blacks in this country has asked for, is a fair and equal chance to excel and manage their own, as in building Greenwood, they established tremendous economic growth, development, and financial commerce, known as the Black Wall Street, of that area. Allegedly, after the destruction of the town, the State had offered funds to rebuild it, however, later reneged on the offer to do so. Blacks who remained and resided in a tent city, came together and resurrected the town on their own. Consequently, this incident deterred other blacks around the nation from trying to build and establish other towns that could possibly be the target of major white groups to evoke mob aggression to those who were certainly capable and intelligent enough to govern their own towns and business affairs. So much for the pursuit of economic growth, happiness and freedom of obtaining and sustaining your own destiny.

Investigation revealed 1115 houses and businesses were destroyed, looted, 300 blacks were killed. Approximately 6000 blacks were rounded up and jailed. There's been numerous riots across America in the late 1800's through the 1900's. Washington DC, Chicago, Illinois, Atlanta, Georgia, Wilmington, North Carolina, Rosewood, Florida, New Orleans, Louisiana, Elaine, Arkansas, Tulsa, Oklahoma, all because of our Common Foe's abusing and killing black people. Chicago Police shot and killed 15 blacks. No whites were shot and killed. Chicago Southside, 26 bombs exploded in black homes where they moved into white neighborhoods. Tulsa was constantly harassed by white racists, because of the wealth amassed by the blacks due to the oil industry in that town area. There had been numerous lynchings in the area of the town by major Ku Klux Klan mob groups, so it was just a matter of time before any type of incident would set the stage for the invasion which occurred. Unlike the other Tulsa disaster victims, the Katrina blacks were moved from the area, negating them to remain and rebuild their area of New Orleans or get the jobs that Halliburton Construction Company gave to the immigrants. These jobs would save taxpayers huge amounts of funds, which were paid out to relocate the displaced families around the country, most had to be housed in hotels and placed on welfare. These people should have been kept in the area to assist in the rebuilding of that city where they were born and raised.

Many of the immigrants were illegal in this country, had jobs that paid $16.00 an hour. The families relocated everywhere else, on welfare, had no way to return to work for those jobs to rebuild and resume their lives in a new city of which they should definitely have been part of. What an extremely outrageous situation to place these people in, after all they had suffered through.

chapter 7

Germany, Jewish Holocaust and the Black American Holocaust: We Must All Remember

Europeans had a tragic time in Germany where a holocaust took place, a horrible period lasting approximately 12 years, where millions of Jews were exterminated by the German forces, definitely a period of ruthless destruction of a race of people witnessed in that country. Each year the Jews hold a vigil in remembrance of those who were slaughtered and abused. As the Jews remember, let us here in America, never forget that Black Holocaust, that took place in America. The slaughter and extermination lasted here in this country for 400 years, even though the forefathers classified blacks as property, as 3/5 this of a human being, we as intelligent Americans know, no human is 3/5 ths of a man. The Creator of all things, miraculously birthed billions into this world, with different pigmentation, hair textures, sizes and structures. And I believe the world calls them all human beings, only the forefathers and one Common Foe took exception with God's work. Unbelievable how ignorant these fools look to the rest of the world. As the Jews pay respect to their own, so should blacks and those who realize the holocaustic significance of the burning alive of blacks, hanging, lynching, castrating, raping, murdering, and all the criminal and savage carnage inflicted upon these defenseless people brought here to be placed in slavery for their entire lives. These people or should I say, human beings, should be remembered with a special Memorial Day each year, blacks must set aside a day to pay homage to a race of people who suffered at the hands of white people, who, like the Germans tried to exterminate them all. Never must we forget these 400 years in the so-called "Land of the Free". There was no free-

dom, justice, liberty for all. It never pertained to the human beings classified by the whites as three fifths of a man, we must
never forget, because our Creator has not.

I must say that there are some wonderful white people in
America. I served in Vietnam with some, was raised up with some.
Many have made tremendous difference for me during my maturing years, some encouraged and inspired me to achieve my sacred
principles and values, of which I live and govern myself by. I thank
them wholeheartedly.

It's a necessity to make a concerted effort to come together as
relatives of our black ancestors, not only to those who paid the ultimate sacrifice dying and suffering for freedom, civil and inhuman justice, but to those who survived this period of inhuman
physical and mental abuse, and still were strong enough to overcome with faith, and mental fortitude to pave the way for those of
us here today. We say to those spiritual souls around and within,
"We too, shall overcome!" We thank you for your heritage and civilization that exists within us all. The holocaust shall remain embedded in us for all times. We remain strong in spirit, heart, and
soul, and blessed to continue your fight for equal justice, respect,
dignity, and for America to acknowledge your valor and courage
for this country's freedom.

Some lucky enough to survive the many wars, only returned
back to this country to be lynched and murdered, some still in uniform. What demented bigots our Common Foe is, most of them
never fought in any war. However, in cowardly mobs, these men
had enough courage to attack and kill these brave men who protected these ill-minded and retarded idiots as well as their families
and children. These are the devils that kept racism alive and well
in America to this day. Our hard-working people were deprived of
education. Adults and children worked and toiled for 12 to 18 hours
a day so that the white people and their children could attend
schools to get theirs. Blacks never entered a classroom to be taught
anything, until approximately 250 years of their bondage in America. The whites got their education, had nice jobs in public offices,
some went to colleges and excelled in the world of economic
growth. The black people paid for these whites to do this, with their

free labor from sun up to sun down. The white people never said "Thank You". The white bigots will always be indebted to black people. The black man fought to preserve the white man's freedom because the blacks did not receive any, neither did they get the opportunity to share in the economic growth whites received and share today.

There's reparation due for all those years of slavery, millions worked and died in those rice, cotton, tobacco fields all their lives, dying in those fields and never received a cent for their servitude. If America can pay the Japanese reparations for confining them for a two-year period in California during World War II, if this nation can spend billions in Iraq, they definitely can find the money to pay for all the criminal acts of bondage and enslavement for hundreds of years to black people. What happened during the Civil War, things were going so bad for the North. President Lincoln allowed blacks to join the Army which gave the North a tremendous advantage, to defeat the South. America is definitely indebted to these blacks. They made a difference. Read your history books.

We must ensure that this nation acknowledges the rights we fought and labored for, built, established, and accomplished, and we must set the tone for togetherness, clean up our images in dress character, bring back some pride to our neighborhoods and all elements we as blacks are involved in. Be first in all we do and second to none in all endeavors to excel. Keep the faith and be committed to be all you can be. Though the Common Foe does not acknowledge black accomplishments in America, no other race has given more for its freedom or wealth. We know of our struggles for this nation, and for this very reason we stand up for our ancestors, our children, for our race. Dignity and harmony for all people to share in the oneness of us all, when our Common Foe takes their blinders off, the truth will set them free. Again to the black ancestors I convey my utmost gratitude for the role you played in the building of our nation I thank you for the sacrifices you gave and for the love of this country that you volunteered to die to protect its freedom for all who live on its soil where your blood and guts are deeply embedded.

Peace be upon you. I love, respect and honor your contribu-

tions to us all, the freedom you fought and died for had no color.
You gave your life for the nation. We will strive to bring harmony
and unity for all people who are courageous enough to make the
balance of our country equal out. God bless your souls. The Holocaust will be acknowledged by us all. Thanks from a Vietnam
fighter who fought for the liberty and freedom of our country. I've
seen devastation of loved ones, I've been in the fire and I still smell
the stench of blood and waste. It lingers on in my mind, in my
dreams. Again I applaud your valor and for dying to keep us free
in a country. Until this day those ungodly bigots who have failed
to acknowledge what you stood for, let it be known that you stood
for and gave them the freedom they have, until this day. There's no
greater sacrifice than to die for what you believe in. You believed
in this country. You believed in its freedom for all. No you were not
just 3/5 ths of a man. You were a full-fledged American and a savior to our cause. We are proud of your ultimate contributions, they
stand uncontested and unblemished, God's treasure to this world,
yes, will forever stand, God bless your souls!

chapter 8

My Confrontation With Our Common Foe

Some years after moving from 17th Street, we located and apartment at 29th and Diamond Street, a neighborhood 3 blocks from Fairmount Park. We got settled in, I was enrolled in school, found new friends and enjoyed the street games we played. We played stick ball, marbles, football, baseball, and even some basketball, after an "old head" hung a metal rim up on a utility pole. The old heads really had some really sharp moves, and they taught the basic fundamentals of the game periodically, we had fun. We children always wanted to go to the park though, there were ball fields where every Saturday there were various teams competing against each other. One Saturday our parents gave us permission to go to the park on our own, only three blocks away, they told us to be careful, this was the first time we walked across 30th and 32nd Streets to the park. There were 5 kids and myself, all black 11 to 13 years of age. We started walking across 30th Street, and the three blocks we had to cross were all white residents. As we got halfway through 30th street all hell broke loose, the white people started screaming and hollering racial slurs, some even began to throw soda bottles and soda cans or whatever else they were throwing. Some began "siccing" their dogs on us. One of my friends almost got bitten by one of the dogs, one fell down cutting and bruising his leg and knee. We had no recourse but to continue our run for safety across those blocks. This was a terrifying siege of racial hatred. My heart was pounding uncontrollably, I never felt that kind of traumatic stress before and I was totally overwhelmed with fear and shock. Only thing I recall was telling myself: "Feet, please don't fail me now". I was mad, angry for the first time in my life, I learned to really hate white people. My stepfather had spoken of these white racists, he told me to read about Jack Johnson's Life.

I began reading about Jack Johnson, our great black Heavyweight Champion of the boxing world. I also read a little about slavery. That was from 1640 through the late 1800's. Johnson was confronted with it in the early 1900's. This was 1948 when I began reading about slavery, yet these things still existed. We pledged allegiance to the country and its flag each morning in school, it stated: justice, freedom and liberty for all, why was I being persuaded and indoctrinated about these truths that obviously did not pertain to me, because of the color of my skin and above all else, why were the white people not held legally and morally committed to the rules of the game they duped us into believing in. Early on, I found out that the game of life would not be an easy game to play, the rules put into play definitely did not apply to people who were my skin pigmentation. From that day on, I discovered who my enemies were in my own country. After falling to the ground in the park, I just laid there and cried. This was my first encounter and confrontation with my Common Foe and one I will never forget over the years. We found another way home, informed our parents, they said they would report the incident to the Police.

The following week-end, we began that same journey, again when we got halfway there, another siege, I think we ran faster than Jesse Owens who had won 4 gold medals in the 1936 Olympics in Berlin, Germany, Jesse was heralded as the fastest human, after being chased again across those three blocks, those racist whites had to think they were witnessing the challengers to his crown. We even amazed ourselves that we outran those vicious and aggressive dogs, I guess after those wolfhounds were trying to take a chunk out my black ass, I found a few more "gears" I did not know existed. We were told that the report was taken about the first incident, evidently the report was never turned in to the proper police, and no one had investigated on it. Maybe it was just totally disregarded, or that the people just didn't give a damn. It took some years before those streets were safe to walk through by black people who lived in that area.

There were community playgrounds in various neighborhoods that white people refused to allow black children to play on, reporting this to police officers never resolved anything. Most of the cops were whites and in most cases they would tell the black children to go home and stay out of trouble or would stand or sit in their patrol cars until fights would break out and blacks were chased off.

One day, we were playing on the street adjacent to one of the parks, and for the first time, I saw a black police officer who drove up and asked us why we were not playing on the park field, and told us it was not safe to play on the street area due to the heavy flow of traffic. We informed him of the harassments and fights we had gotten into, because they would come and chase us out of the area, not wanting us to use the park. After listening to what we had to say, he stated that it was nonsense, and for us to take the filed which was empty at that time, and play ball. As moved on to the field, some white adults and kids came up and told us to get out of the area. The black officer who was still sitting in his patrol car, a little way from where we were, got out of his car and approached us. He asked the white people what the problem was and some of them started screaming that we were not supposed to play on the field. The officer told them to shut up, saying that the field we were standing on belonged to the City of Philadelphia, for use of all people, for them to utilize, and not just for white people and since we were already there we could continue playing. He also told them to leave adding that if he ever saw another similar incident he would arrest those people and close the field to everyone. No cop ever confronted these people before; they would merely sit and stand around and watch the confrontations. We did notice the police officer speaking now with some white cops who were in their patrol cars at the opposite side of the street. From that day on, there were no more incidents at the playground, whoever showed up first took the fields; we later began competing against the whites.

We thanked the black officer whenever he came around on patrol. His name was Dave, he told us he was in the Army, same as my father. He made a tremendous difference, and was a man who made playing field even for all, as it should have been, he stood tall against our Common Foe and even started a friendship between us kids over the years. Because of his role, some of the racists seem to cast their hatred aside, had the white cops done their job correctly, maybe they could have established a different mind set and a unity among the people, especially the children. Dave was definitely a role model for us all. My cousin Jason, whom we fondly called Jake, came home on military leave from Fort Bragg, North Carolina, where he was stationed with the 82nd Airborne division, he was the sharpest looking soldier I've ever seen in uniform, boots were shined like glass, uniform pressed down, creases were razor sharp, his brass, buckle and insignias were blinding to look at. My stepfather was the first to impress me when I first saw him in uniform. He was definitely among the elite, he was a First Sergeant, but I think Jake was just a little more sharper. I think it was the bloused boots and the glider patch sewn on his cap, I told myself when I got old enough I would definitely be an 82nd Airborne Division master blaster, Second to None. Jake came and got me one day and we were walking down the street enroute to his sister's house, he was not in uniform that particular day, we were just strolling along when we heard someone hollering "Hey, you! Hey, you!" We looked around and only saw two white cops in a patrol car, pulling up abreast of us. They continued to shout and then one started whistling, motioning for us to come to the patrol car. I started to stop but Jake told me to keep on walking, all of a sudden the patrol car came to a fast stop in front of us, the cops came running up saying: "Didn't you hear us calling you to stop?" Jason at that point stated, "I heard Hey you and some whistling which I never thought was directed at us, I am no dog and Hey you could have been for anyone, I am a Sergeant in the United States Army, 82nd Airborne Division, Fort Bragg, North Carolina, and I don't respond to that sort of an approach. I could feel the tension in Jake and myself, and the cops as well, white cops were known for stopping and harassing blacks. I was so proud of my cousin, he was not intimidated. The cops asked where we were headed and Jake stated to his sister's house. The cop asked for his ID card which he showed them, one cop looked like he wanted to escalate the situation, however, the other cop checked his ID card and allowed us to proceed. Had Jake not been in the military, they might have tried to lock us up for some bogus charges. Again Jake showed me, you have to stand for what's right and refuse to allow anyone harass you, irregardless of who they are. I grew up, joined the Army, went to Jump School, graduated and was assigned to the 82nd Airborne Division, like my stepfather and Jake, I became part of the elite, sky trooper. I remained in the service for 21 years, great career, traveled worldwide, Japan, Korea, Spain, France, Germany, Africa, and Vietnam in 1965. I could go on and on, the same type of incidents are still with us, the nation is regressing in racial morality and justice.

chapter 9

The Major Killing Device of Thousands of Blacks in
America, The Noose

Reading back in history of this country we find the many ways
by which our Common Foe has killed, murdered, destroyed black
life, one stood out at the top of the list other than fire was the hanging NOOSE.

A major incident occurred in Jena, Louisiana not long ago,
where white high school students marked a tree on the school
grounds as the "White Tree Only." A black student went to the administrator and reported it, and asked of he could sit under that
tree, one of the school officials said yes. The next day the kid sat
under the tree. That evening a black kid was assaulted by three
white youths, he reported the incident, no one was arrested or
charged. The very next day there were two nooses hanging from
that same tree, that night a fight between whites and blacks broke
out, no one was hurt. Approximately a month later, a white youth
was assaulted by 6 black kids, 15 to 16 years of age. The white
boy went to the hospital, was treated and released, and attended a
school party later that evening. The six black kids were arrested,
released on bond, one held and placed in an adult prison to await
trial as an adult, even though he was only 16 years of age. These
facts about the incidents were only found out a year later when
the boy's parents protested judgment pertaining to the trial, also
requested to know why the three white kids who attacked the
black kid were not arrested and why those kids who marked and
hung the nooses from the tree were not apprehended and charged
with a hate crime and inciting racial tension and discrimination
on the school grounds. The three kids who hung the nooses were
suspended for 3 days and allowed to return to school. The han-

dling of this situation was a mockery of the school administration and the city's law prosecutor, the school officials should be charged for dereliction and negligence for not immediately having a school assembly meeting of all students regarding the marking of the tree after it was reported by the black youth who brought it to their attention and sat under it, also they are totally responsible for the hanging of the nooses the following day. Had the issue been addressed, the nooses would not have appeared. The nooses incited blacks to react, how could white children not know of the impact this would have on the black children at the school. Just about everybody living in that area knew that Louisiana is one of the most racist states in the south and was responsible for hanging of thousands of black boys and men. The Common Foe is constantly teaching their kids to be racists, hanging the nooses where whites sit signify if you sit under this tree again, hanging could be in retaliation for doing so.

The city's prosecutor should have reacted to those hate crimes perpetrated by those white kids, however, Reed Walters insensitive actions threatening the blacks at a student assembly, showed his racial motives by telling the blacks who were seated separately from the whites, looking directly at them and stating he could ruin their lives with the stroke of his pen, he also later stated he would try the black 16 year old as an adult and seek a sentence of 15 years for the attack and secondly he would charge assault with a deadly weapon, sneakers, the subject that Michael Bell was wearing. What a travesty of that type of mind set from a D.A. who's well aware of the significance of the racial hatred and double standards of the law. Walters had a chance to really contribute his wisdom and knowledge to suppress a very damning incident to the school, city, and above all the black and white students who from time to time need to learn of and discuss racial discrimination and hatred. He had a chance to teach togetherness to all of them for the betterment of their lifestyle, their unity and appreciation for the common cause of letting the world know they were willing to resolve their issues and become the role model for others who address racial hatred and discrimination to be aware of the racism blacks have faced in America, since 1640 until now.

Black History should be taught at all levels of our school system, especially where there are numerous races attending classes together. Maybe we need to address the administrators and City DA's so as to ensure that they are aware of their impact in education and law enforcement and the role they play to create a safe environment of love and respect for each other, especially our youth who have been taught racism in their homes. We all have that obligation to teach our youth. I coach boxing classes that are made up of just about all races and ages, the first 30 to 40 minutes we talk of racial problems, their school problems, the unity, togetherness and how to support each other. We speak of just about any community problems, world or personal issues, we have become like family, where there is concern for each other, and love and respect for God's balance of life. We have to make the right choices when dealing with our children, they are our future.

Since the Jena 6 incident, the NOOSE has become a device to reflect the racism in our country, it's still alive and well. On a campus of Gallaudet University in Washington, D.C., seven students, six white and one black assaulted a black student and scrawled KKK and swastikas all over him. There have been about a dozen occurrences in the past two months. A noose was found in a Long Island, N.Y. Police headquarters' locker room, at a Pittsburg bus maintenance garage and several high schools. For a dozen incidents to come to the public attention is a lot, stated the Director of Intelligence Project of the southern Poverty Law Center, Mr. Mark Potok. Scholars and civil rights advocates say the rash of episodes reflect the country's continued tensions over race. It's something in our culture that never goes away even though all the progress has been made. Dr. Phillip Dray, a New York writer on black history author: "At the Hands of Persons Unknown: The Lynching of Black America". Below the surface remains a hostility and distrust that can be easily awakened. He says nooses are unmistakable towards blacks, given the country's history of thousands of lynchings of black men in 19th and 20th centuries. In Winchester, K.Y., four teens were charged in August with terrorist threats for taunting a black classmate with a drawing of a noose, a confederate flag and someone being whipped and lynched. The mother of one says her 17 year old son wasn't doing it because of the Jena 6. She said: "I know he's not racist". She says he was only joking around. How many times have we heard mothers and fathers make those same statements only to find that their sons and daughters actually masterminded the same thing they say they were innocent of? The mother also said her son didn't know or understand the impact of the drawings and she thought he understands now how serious this thing is. At 17 years of age, believe me, he knew. Today's white kids are not naïve and know exactly what's going on, no excuses for them or school administrators or ignorant District Attorneys' the Secondary School for the Deaf where half of the 175 students were minorities, hired a Consultant to train the faculty and staff to deal with racists, all schools should follow suit. Hate crimes from 2000 through 2005 against blacks rose. No, it was not as stated by the school administrator the miscellaneous handling of the Jena 6. I read a book written by Daniel E. Johnson entitled "Come Home America: Is it God's Last Call?" One of the quotes is: "We are in the midst of a struggle over whose values will prevail in our nation". It's a very powerful book, it pertains to many issues of racial discrimination projected mostly at the black race. We as Americans have to be more vigilant with regards to resolving problems in our nation today. As parents we must ensure that we address the moral and racial issues. The City Mayor, Council and school administrators must be involved.

The noose signified racial hatred yet God gave us the power to transform such into co-existence, and the voicing of our silenced truth. Even though it lifted to kill, millions of dreams reached the stars while being pulled. The end of the rope brought us directly to our Creator who reached out to hold us. For neither the sun nor the stars have gone out of business, and neither has the black race. Nothing can dim our future, not even the choking of the noose. We shall overcome.

Despite the country's regression in racial morality and justice, we find comfort in the knowledge that no situation is ever without God's control and presence. Mediocrity of justice blindfolds the implementers' eyes, but empowers and strengthens the oppressed black race, and such will be the case until the end of time. We may never kill the roots of racism, yet as we claim the world's trust, destiny compels us to do it.

Where do these frantic attempts to kill blacks lead us? Why don't we sink in to the utmost level of peace and unity? Sublimity of life resounds in the universe, which upholds living without prejudice an antithesis to progress and development. Oh! What joy to live without discrimination, to be loved without racial apologies, and to dwell in perfect harmony and balance without falling off to some fiery holocaust, and coming from death to retaliate!

We shall uphold the fact that all men are created equal, coming from a mutual divine Creator, who allow good things to happen without foolish interference of bigotry and racism thereof, and that no truth may succumb to the deceiving forces of lies. One for all, all for one, creating love, jointly enjoying life's endless adventures in the spirit of camaraderie and love.

chapter 10

The Neighborhood That Stood Against Its Foe

I write this story to emphasize a point to those wanderers of the streets.

I was hanging on the corner with a few of the fellows, when one of our friends came up and stated that he had been jumped down in South Philly, so he asked us to go back there and rumble. We were all boxing at one of the neighborhood boxing gyms, in pretty good shape with that mind set-up and attitude that we could beat the world.

We agreed to accompany him, caught a bus and rode down to 5th and Oregon Avenue, got off the bus, walked two blocks to where he had his altercation. The people he sought were not there, someone told him where the fellows we were seeking lived, so we strolled up two blocks, found the street, turned down and was halfway down the block which was halfway deserted of any activity, when we finally located the house. We looked ahead of us, there were about 50 people at the end of the street, then we looked behind us, there were about twenty or thirty people there, then all of the people started pouring out from their homes, we were being set up. We realized what was happening and decided to fight in any event, actually we were in trouble. These people were ready to conquer all who showed up in their neighborhood, they were yelling and screaming for blood, we were blocked in, everyone was represented, the old and young, dogs, people wielding any type of weapon attainable, we were really in big trouble. There were at least two hundred people massed around us in this Black neighborhood. Suddenly we heard a man telling those up front to allow him to get through, pretty sharp-looking man, approximately 30 to 40 years of age, he stepped in front of us, and his words ran thus; "My brothers, what you see here is a group of people who refuse to allow any outside gangs to come here into our neighborhood and fight or harm anyone" and sensing a really bad incident to happen, he said "Let me tell you that we don't mind anyone coming here to socialize with anyone of your friends that happen to live here, however, we will not tolerate or condone anyone to come here to disrespect where we were born and raised, so hopefully you understand what I am telling you, again feel free to visit here anytime you wish, but without that attitude you brought here tonight, fortunately your partner told us he was coming back, which is why you are in this predicament. We are going to allow you to leave with dignity and respect, I trust that you get my drift" at which time he asked the people to open a passage way for us to leave, and we promptly did so. I did a little praying and soul searching as we departed. I reached a tremendous answer to my inner self analysis. Why did I not ask? If in fact my friend had indeed told anyone he was coming back, which is why we walked in such an ambush, another thing was very clear to me, numbers do make a tremendous difference. So the reason why your neighborhoods are being controlled by those killers and drug dealers is because those who live there were intimidated, manipulated, and lacked the courage to defend that of which they have lived, where there is no fight, there is concession and those who reside there become the hostages who are controlled by the few. When adults don't fight for what's theirs, they lose their self-respect, and most importantly the respect of their children who look to them for leadership and protection.

On the Street with the Running Feet

I heard a noise, then the running feet, then a yell: "Halt, or I'll shoot!" The feet continued, then a shot and a thud as the body hit the ground on the street of the running feet.

A car pulled on to the street, was slowly driven down the block, it reached a group of young men standing on the pavement, someone hollered out: "Run!" A shot rang out from the car, it missed its target, ricocheted off the wall and struck little Brenda in the head, then she fell dead on the street with the running feet.

The old senior couple sat in their darkened home, peering through their Venetian blinds, needing to go out to the store, but afraid to do so because of the drug wanderers making a transaction in front of their house on the street with the running feet. The children used to play hop scotch, jump rope, marbles, stick ball and have fun doing things children enjoy doing, however, the wanderers are taking over their street, sitting on people's steps, hanging on the street corners. The children are not on the streets these days afraid for their safety, on their street with the running feet.

I am bussed to school in a very nice neighborhood, really nice area, and then in the afternoon we are bussed back to home, where there's a drastic change of the environment, there's houses gutted out off my block and the weeds and trash accumulates in those areas, and I never feel safe, whenever I have to walk past these areas that creates an unsafe condition, I feel very embarrassed to come home to a street that seems part of a war combat zone, there's no safety there and I have no pride of my street with the running feet.

The Demise of the Wanderers

Again I reach out to the wanderers and violent people who are not conducive to our image and character of our race of black people, it's time for black unity, and acknowledge that there's enough crime committed against us to last forever, and now is the time for another serious look at where we are headed to. It's a new world, there's got to be a vast change, this is a huge corporate world today. Sharp, intelligent, and educated people are a must, so if you have any sense at all, you will put down the gun, there's no one out there who cares for you, you are just a pawn or puppet, utilized to hustle someone else's junk on the street, a fugitive constantly running from your pusher man, running from your inner self. Your family is praying for you out there in that land that robs you of your dignity and respect, you have none, you're in that dark cobweb corner with no way out, the cops are searching for you, you have no place to feel safe, nowhere to relax, constantly on the run, looking over your shoulder. Your partner got wasted for not having all the dust he hustled, the junkies are seeking you, saying you ripped them off selling some bad bricks to them, so where can you go, who can you turn to? It's plain and simple, fall on your knees and humble yourself to God who has created all those others whose lives have been taken by those low-ass pants wearing, narrow-minded aimless flunkies living in a world with one foot in jail and the other in your marked grave and rest assured, it's there waiting for you, it's your choice as I've stated before. There's no positive future for you in that dark world of deceit and deception, of death and despair, hopefully someone will reach out to you before the box is filled and prayed over with at your demise. If someone is telling you what is written on this page, and I know it's got to be recorded in that troubled mind of yours, if someone is telling you these things, I truly hope so, it only means God loves you and has put us in place to reach out for your life, make the choice, it states God helps those who help themselves. I was raised up in those days, seen a lot, learned a lot, the game is rough and murderous, it's an old game, but the rules remain the same. Look around you, who are you? Few like you ever get the time to find out, I've written all I could to you, make that change, it's your life. To the wanderer searching for his soul, it's a blind, horrific world, an endless, chaotic bottomless pit of no return. Your life is priceless; change your attitude, character and your heart. There's always hope, reach out and it will surely find you. Make the move. We are waiting on you.

chapter 11

A Nation's People are still in need of Change, We the People Must Step Up

There's got to be change where are we headed as a race of people in this country today. A racist hate crime was reported in Bear, Delaware a few days ago where whites defaced a black couple's home, wrote in plain large black letters: "KILL THE NIGGERS AND JEWS!" On the sidewalk of their home, case is being investigated by the community police. So we see again the Common Foe on each side of the coin, it's definitely alive and well. How about this one: Man, a 'little racist' guilty in daughter-in-law's death. A grocery store owner convicted of plotting to have his black daughter-in-law killed because she was not Indian. Chiman Rai, 68, was charged with masterminding the murder of 22 year old Michelle Rai. The native of India was upset that his son Ricky married and fathered a child; he paid out $10,000 to have her killed. How about this background? He taught Math at Alcorn State University, a historically black college in Mississippi, and later ran a Supermarket in a predominantly black area in Jackson. The baby was left unharmed, it seems to me this issue was with the son, not his wife, a statement by his son helped bring him to justice, stating his father was "a little racist" so at the age of 68 he decided to kill his son's wife and rot in jail. So as I related, the Common Foe is everywhere and could be anybody. In these troubled times, things I really learn to love are my God, life and freedom.

Again, I say our military personnel are employed around the world, engaged in combat, suffering from wounds, post traumatic syndrome, and are physically and mentally stressed. Only Love and Peace can save a nation that's full of hate, jealousy and racism. I attend a weekly Veterans Affairs meeting featuring mostly Vietnam vets and some Korean vets as well, and when I look around the room and see these brave men who are suffering from their physical injuries and mental stress, I ask myself, was it worth it all? And I grieve not only for these proud men who survived the dark battlefields of death, fighting to save America, but also for their buddies who unfortunately left their body and souls, imbedded in those fierce and consuming fields of no return. These veterans came home and still see our battlefields here where we live, yet some cannot even reclaim their peace of mind when they realize what they fought for is still actually engulfing and consuming their children and loved ones here. And believe me, a lot of them remain close to that bunker they inherited in Vietnam, Korea, because the inhumane killing grounds here are still taking away their family members and friends as well. Believe me, we are our brother's keeper, we support each other weekly, but our nation needs to be more concerned of those we live around, there's a lot of pressure, people are living with in these troubled times on our streets. So one of the things I always say is to be safe out there. There was a guy who had returned from Iraq a year ago, stayed isolated on the job, had a confrontation with his supervisor, left the job, got a gun, came back and killed the supervisor and four other co-workers before killing himself. So be truly aware of people you are dealing with, and we are finding that it's not just those returning home from combat where they learned to live by the gun, it's also those who have never fought anywhere, however, due to the stress of no jobs, high inflation, losing their homes and other added problems, they also resort to the weapons in times of mental stress. They're out there, pray for these individuals and whenever you sense a problem, reach out with caution to make a difference if you can. Again be aware and safe, we must be the ones who really care.

I was involved in an incident not long ago driving down through the center of a town, I noticed a large black man trying to wave down a bus, the bus driver avoided that stop, not wanting to pick him up, I continued to the store, upon returning down that same street at an intersection, the man was still out in the middle of the street shouting at another bus driver who refused to allow him on the bus. The guy was in disarray dress-wise and just looked like a dangerous guy. I pulled over, got his attention and asked what the problem was, he stated that the buses would not pick him up, and he was irate, I was trying to calm him down; someone had called a police unit. While I had his attention, I got him to tell me a little about himself, and where it was he wanted to go. He informed me that he had just been discharged from a mental institution, showed me his medication items and his discharge papers, we had been chatting for about ten minutes. He told me he was a former professional fighter and even mentioned some of the guys he had fought with, you could tell he had been in boxing form his facial damage, the flat nose, the scarred eye tissue and the cuts, plus as I stated he was a pretty big physical guy. Another bus showed up and refused to pick him up, the police unit came, checked him out, sensing he had a big problem, the bus drivers were actually afraid to allow this guy on their bus, so I told the officer that I would take him where he had to go. I had seized him up, I had heard of some of the fighters he had fought. At this time I became my brother's keeper, because if he had stayed out there trying to board a bus, he was just going to get himself in trouble, I was in pretty good shape, doing some boxing training at the time myself, thought I could handle anything that would arise, I was especially concerned that this guy was on medication, actually the institution that discharged him should have made arrangements for someone to pick him up. He had some military also, so I told the responding police unit I would get him to his destination, which was approximately 30 miles from where we were. I told him to get in after telling him of my boxing career as well. I drove him to his sister's house, he got out, knocked on the door, she let him in, and I drove on my way. Was I in harm's way? Could have been, but I think that that day I saved him from evidently harming someone else or himself, I think of one thing, that he respected me enough to trust me, especially after he found out I could rumble a bit myself. I recognized a potential problem and stepped up, someone needed to. Most people just gathered around watching, instead of acting, just like we hear of people getting beat or what have you, no one really cares or wants to step up and that's sad in many cases, and they do not have a right to do so, with all the guns and weapons out there today. In many cases if the villains and wanderers sense some people's involvement, they move on, but as stated be tactful at whatever action you take. It's a necessity to react, to see, identify, report whatever you have witnessed, these neighborhoods have to be taken back from these killers and thugs. You have a police commissioner and mayor who seem to want the best for the city and the people, with the proper law enforcement assistance, you can fight through this period of perilous times across the nation."

chapter 12

The Despicable Prejudice Discrimination and Racism of My Early Military Service

I was raised by a man who served his country in two conflicts and each time he experienced prejudice and discriminating attitudes from fellow-white enlisted as well as the white officers-in-charge. I enlisted in the service in 1961, was sent down south to complete Basic Training Ft. Jackson, South Carolina, and afterwards to St. Gordon, Georgia. I encountered lots of prior servicemen and recruits from the backwoods of the southern region. I encountered a white soldier who would later become my good friend, Pvt. Threadgill from Tennessee. He was definitely a racist, a young man who told me he had never experienced being around black people and another white fellow from upstate Pennsylvania, a Russian, whose name had damn near a thousand letters, both demonstrated their dislike for blacks, I was one of six assigned to my platoon. I was a strong-willed guy willing to have confrontations if need be. I had boxed in Philadelphia, where you refused to lose and be second to none. I knew Joe Frazier, Muhammad Ali and some damn good pros who came out of the gyms of that city. I was really sharp, had fast hands, good footwork and balance, sharp puncher with both hands, so I was pretty much equipped to deal with all comers.

I had my first confrontation with Threadgill who was spitting tobacco juice all in front of me in formation. I was really sharply dressed, booths highly shined, uniform pressed, creases were razor sharp, I told him if he spit any of that tobacco juice on my shoes, I was going to kick his ass right there in the formation, he rolled his eyes, but he never spit in that direction again. There was this Russian in my platoon, we had a little run-in at the "chow-line", in the mess hall, he was about 6'6 tall, around 260 lbs, he backed away from our little episode and that was just the first day, the rest of the week went fairly well, it seemed as if all of the white guys were watching me, especially after they made me company guide, after I out-drilled all of them. The first sergeant wanted all prior service guys to fall out, they did, he noticed I was still in ranks and said "Fall out! I know you are prior service as sharp as you are!" I said "No, I've never been in the army before!" I said that I had attended a military private school, he had us all drill and I outperformed the other 10 or 11 guys, so I became the company guide. I marched the company to the chapel that Sunday and was beginning to settle into my new profession. That first weekend we had free time, so I looked for a post gym, found it and started working with a few of the guys who went there with me. I located a heavy punching bag and started to work at it a bit, a crowd gathered, everyone wanted to know if I was a pro. I showed them a few things and we left. Next day everyone in the company heard about what transpired in the gym the night before.

The next Monday morning, the drill instructor asked me to report front and center, he said: "Webb, I heard about you, you and I are going to have a "hellava" exercise period this morning and I hope the rest of the company can keep up." Well, we did a hundred push-ups, the rest of the company was already laying flat on their faces, and we finished up with damn near 150 push ups. We went for a 15 minute run before breakfast. He brought us back to the company area, called the company to a halt, told everyone to fall out for "chow". I asked if I could continue running, he stated: "Webb, you are in damn good shape, continue on!" I left and ran for another 30 minutes before I returned, showered and fell out for formation. Already, I had a reputation around the battalion area. The following Saturday, I ran into Candy McFarland, a middleweight top contender from Philly, who was there giving a Boxing Clinic, small world. I boxed 3 guys at the gym, talked to him a little bit before he left, needless to say, the post knew that I was a Heavyweight fighter out of Philly, at that point I could not get Threadgill or the Russian away from me. We started to talk and learn of each other's background and began to know and respect each other.

The next week, the company was off Saturday, so they had some of the companies boxing against each other. I was in the barracks on a very humid day when the Platoon Sergeant asked me to come down and box because some guy named Hannah from A company was beating up everyone outside. I told him I didn't feel like coming down as hot as it was, so he tried to encourage me to do so and I refused. He left and approximately five minutes later I heard: "We want Webb! We want Webb!" He came back up saying that everybody was asking if I could come down and kick this guy's behind, so I went down, I saw Hannah who had just dropped this kid with a really nice right hand. He looked at me, I said, "Hey Hannah let's go a few rounds!" he stated: "Hell no, you've taught me all I know, no way!" Everybody began cheering and I went upstairs. I was taking these guys to the gym at night showing them about boxing, so now I was like a boxing celebrity around Ft. Jackson.

I am now there for about two weeks, and one of the platoons was having problems getting its people out to formation on time in the mornings, so being the company guide I went over and addressed that problem and informed them of how things would go the next morning to alleviate their problem. There was a kid from Florida, he was the champion wrestler from Florida State University, pretty big guy, evidently he had his platoon afraid of him, so I showed up the next morning. Everyone did as I had instructed the squad leader had them to do, except this big kid, in really good shape, so I told him to do as the others were, he got confrontational and totally ignored me, as he went to pass by I stopped him, he dropped his little bag containing his toilet articles and rushed at me, he swung at me, I side-stepped and hit this cat about 5 or 6 times in the face, knocked him backwards, blood everywhere, he got himself together and charged at me again. This time I landed about 3 or 4 more shots, didn't stop the charge though, he grabbed me, lifted me up with a bear hold around the chest, I put him in a headlock, only thing I could do, we fell to the floor over a couple of footlockers, he was working his way out of the headlock, and was on top of me. Someone pulled him up, I jumped up, here he came again, I connected again, knocking him down, and he got up. Blood all over this guy and again he came, I faked a jab, shot the right, two left hooks and finished him off with a short right hand, he was gone. I thought I killed this guy, blood all over, his nose was broken, two teeth were knocked out, and he had lumps all over his face and head. Finally he woke up and rolled over. I told him to get up and get his stuff and get in the latrine area before I really hurt him. He was crawling around finding his bag, got up, went into the latrine shower area. I felt really bad, he was messed up. The rest of the platoon got their things together and fell out for formation. I looked in the latrine area, checked him out and left him there. We marched out, I still had not seen him. We went and mounted vehicles to go to the rifle range. I was in the fox hole on the firing line when a jeep pulled up, the Captain and Sergeant Major, the Range Non-commissioned Officer called out over the public address system for me to recover from the fox hole and report to the Captain. He asked me whether I was in an altercation earlier in company are, I told him: "Yes, Sir!" He told me to get in the jeep. I had to report to the Battalion Commander. We drove back and I reported to the Colonel, as instructed. He told me that everyone was telling him, of the outstanding jobs I was doing as a company guide, however, he told me that the book he had in his desk was the United States Code of Military Justice and he had asked me about the incident I was involved in. He also asked me if I was a fighter, I told him yes I was, he stated he was investigating the incident that happened and if I was found guilty I could face up to five years confinement, forfeiture of all military pay and in a Court Martial. He stated: "It's amazing you haven't a mark on you, however, the other guy had major damage, had to be taken to the hospital". He asked me what happened and I explained to him what happened and that in fact the guy had tried to assault me and I was only defending myself as I had stated. He dismissed me and told me he would recall me after they brought the guy from the hospital. Approximately three hours later he recalled me, stated he had interviewed the witnesses and found I was in fact defending myself, he also told the clerk to go and get the guy and have him report to him. Approximately ten minutes later, the guy came in. He was in horrible shape, if only he had followed orders. One of the things revealed to the colonel, was that this individual was somewhat of a bully in the platoon, which is why the squad leaders could not get him to follow their instructions, he informed him of these things, dismissed him, only had some very serious words for me before he released me. My Company Commander and First Sergeant spoke with me and told me how lucky I was that those guys had witnessed him charging and swinging at me. Here was a case of a racist who didn't want a black guy ordering him to do anything. I was very fortunate to have all of those white guys of that platoon to tell the truth of what happened that morning. Reading about blacks in the service having to put up with racist people was a plus for me an on top of that I was used to fighting in white neighborhoods of Philly, racism was not only in Philly, it was everywhere; especially in the boxing world. Every time we fought in south Philly or the northeast against the Irish, we had to knock these guys out, because they were well-schooled and trained fighters and still today they have that reputation, so like I stated earlier being from Philly and growing up there had me prepared to handle whatever came my way.

Another important thing was that I had made new friends of other ethic groups in our unit, we learned to get along after a period of time and that was a great thing, we had to learn to live with each other, learn of our cultures, backgrounds and life's experiences. Threadgill was like my shadow and Avanisee is the Russian, as I called him, we became inseparable. I later started to call him Foots; he had the biggest feet I had ever seen. I told him one day, "Foots, you must have walked all the way from Russia, with feet like yours you could have walked on water to get to America". We became really good friends, matter of fact the whole company did great in working and drilling and accomplishing our unit missions, our company graduated with the highest standing of the cycle.

I was like their leader, especially after I beat the bully up and they saw how sharp of a fighter I was. I had the top honor as best dresser, received the highest marks in physical fitness and leadership abilities. I always recalled how at least 190 white guys held me in such high esteem, we had approximately 10 blacks in our training class. If they had not supported me with coming forward during my altercation with their statements, I could have easily been given Court Martial and put in the stockade.

I remember the Company Commander liked my attitude my soldiering and learning skills, he called me in his office after the assault case and told me how lucky I was that damn near every white trainee had spoken up for me, he told me he was impressed with my character and how unusual it was that they would rally behind my case. And also informed me that after the fight I would not be able to get into the Special Forces of which I had volunteered for, sighting the fight as the reason. He told me how he thought I could be a damn good soldier, maybe becoming a First Sergeant if I went to Infantry, but he was going to recommend me to go to Military Police School, where he thought I would excel greatly because of my leadership ability. He further stated that he reviewed my 201 File and found that I had some minor incidents in my hometown, which also negated my being accepted for the Special Forces group assignment, here was a white man looking out for me, he could have easily let me graduate and move on. Until this day I remember I have met a white guy who actually cared enough about this young black private to put me in such a selected branch of the service, I said: "Sir, how could I be accepted as candidate for Military Police School with my background at home and being involved in the fight here at camp!" He told me after observing me, getting things done in the company activities and the way I interrelated to unit personnel, he thought if they accept his request it would look good on my Service Record and would give me somewhat of a new beginning whenever I returned to civilian life, however, he was suggesting that I should make a career of the military and I thank God for putting that man in my life. Had it not been for that Captain, I would have been terminated from the service before I had finished Basic Training. I was a tough guy, that was the main reason he saw my character, I was a leader after only three days in the company. I wanted to excel in all endeavors, wanted to be second to none and I was. I had that Philadelphia swagger, I was like a Drill Sergeant in one week. I used to go to the gym and damn near all of those white guys would be there, I was having fun. The judge back home gave me three days to get into the military and I just made it on the third day around 2:00 pm. A Sergeant from the recruiting office called me and said: "You are in and need to be here at 4:30pm." I reported at 3:30pm, we were sworn in, taken to Philadelphia Airport, checked in and I was on my way to Ft. Jackson, South Carolina, the beginning of a 20 year career in Military Police and Investigation Branch.

I remember the Captain used to tell me, "Webb, I want you to get some of those fighters you are training and keep the peace around here over the week-end." I would laugh and say: "Yes, Sir!" One Saturday afternoon, I saw a lot of guys around the company area intoxicated and disgruntled, I asked what was going on, they told me a platoon Sergeant had sold them some alcohol and ripped them off in a gambling game over in the 3rd platoon barracks, I said: "Let's go over and check it out."

We arrived over to the barracks, I went in and in a platoon Sergeant's Office were two cases of 1/2 pint bottles of alcohol and approximately ten guys plus the Sergeant in there gambling. I went in and said to the Sergeant that there were a lot of intoxicated guys outside who stated that they had bought the alcohol from him and were ripped off in gambling. He looked up from shooting the dice and said: "Private, what the hell did you say?" And I repeated myself, you could hear a pin drop, then he yelled at me: "Private, you better get out of here!" I asked him who the hell he was hollering at, he looked at me, I told him, "If you don't stop selling the alcohol and gambling I am going to call the Company Commander!" I informed him that the captain told me to keep the peace here in the company over the week-end.

He shouted, "Get out!"

"Ok, I'm going to make the call to the CO" I said.

"What did you say?" He asked.

This time I told him, "If you don't give me a bottle of liquor and stop the gambling, I'm going to call the CO." He shouted for me to get out again. I said: "Ok, I am going to make the call." I turned to leave and he called me. I turned around and he said: "Go ahead and get a bottle." I reached in and got a bottle, looked at everyone, he started picking up his money, all the privates were shocked that I had terminated the gambling activities. I looked at him and again stated that the Company Commander told me to keep peace, and I take my orders seriously, he stared at me, I told: "You know damn well you are not supposed to be selling alcohol and gambling with recruits!" He looked at me and said: "Just leave." As I was leaving the recruits were in awe that I had stood up to Sgt. McDonald, they left and I closed the door on the way out. The Sergeant knew he was wrong, he had seen me boxing around and heard about the exhibition during the boxing clinic at the gym. I think he knew that getting into a confrontation with me physically he was a beat man, plus he was in violation of gambling and fraternizing with recruits. Had that information been revealed to the Company Commander, he would have been transferred and demoted. I later told the guys to never get caught up in that type of situation again and stay out of trouble and go back to their barracks. Two days later at the 1st morning formation of the week, I passed by him. He had that look of uncertainty on his face, looking as if to say: "Please don't tell the CO," I kind of smiled at him and kept walking. In the Army less than 2 weeks, I had established a reputation of my demeanor-character, and carrying out my orders, even though I knew that the CO was only kidding, however, I felt like he had given me an added responsibility, I was actually enjoying the Army.

I graduated and reported to go to Ft. Gordon, Georgia for Military Police School. Reported in at the reception station with my orders, was there approximately an hour, when I was called up with my records with a Major, he took my records and stated: "Who the hell sent you down here? You had a fight in Basic Training, the FBI found some incidents with the law in Philadelphia." I explained to him that the charges were dropped, as I verified on the back of the page by FBI Investigators, he took a look at the page, looked back at me, then read the letter from the Captain, told me to sit down because he had to confer with the Colonel. I was highly embarrassed and it seemed that I would be turned down from the attitude reflected to me. Approximately 20 minutes the Major called me back up, he said: "In lieu of my commanding officer's letter and along with the certificates for graduating number one in my company, I was being accepted to the Military Police and Investigation School, he also added: "Let those distinguishing qualities that earned you these certificates be the values and principles you uphold there, Pvt. Webb." The next day was a Saturday, so we had a briefing, got assigned our companies and unpacked and got ready for Monday, first day of class. As I was getting situated, I had to praise God for my blessings and also many thoughts and thanks to my Basic Training Captain. I was transforming from the tough guy into a law enforcement officer, what a contrast.

Again most of the class were white guys, there were approximately 100 in my class, about 12 to 15 blacks, and again I could feel the racial heat for a period of time, especially during the first week, this group had more educated and mature individuals. This was a lot of indoctrination to Military Police, Military Criminal Justice and investigators, mostly classroom and hands-on training in the field portion, opposed to the rifle training, filed maneuvers, combat readiness and war games and obstacles in Basic Training. The first 2 weeks was all classroom learning and Code of Military Justice, the various articles, prosecution procedures, basic investigation and apprehension guidelines, we covered everything from criminal military aspects and civilian laws and their commodities. Very interesting, we were tested every week, you only passed on predicated on passing those weekly tests, so we lost a few here and there, I was enjoying my stay there, and the law really opened up several avenues for me, the bad guy running from the Man, to becoming the Man, I was loving it. As the weeks went by we began to acknowledge each other, in our classroom discussions and during our break periods. I met a few white guys from Philadelphia, so we kind of hung out together. They both were from South Philly and we later found another guy from the center city area. In the first month I pretty much stayed in the quarters only going to the gym and to mess halls or restaurants along with the fellows from home. Matter of fact, there were two instructors from Philly also. The racial tension eased up and all was fine for the six weeks of an eight week course. Then it struck, the Common Foe raised its ugly head.

A week before graduation, a bunch of us decided to go to the service club where there were pool tables and various activities, we arrived, shot some pool and afterwards went upstairs to one of the lounge rooms to kickback, read and listen to some really nice music. We had just gone into one of the areas when we heard loud voices and running up the stairs leading to the three or four rooms. All of a sudden the door was kicked open, and two-angry looking white guys barged in the door and almost hit me if had not moved. We were standing there observing them, one of my classmates told the lead guy: "You almost hit my friend!" The guy looked at me and said: "Well he should have moved out of the way." I could not believe what he had just stated. He went on to say that he didn't want any shit out of no one, he just received a bad letter from his girlfriend and he was really pissed off, he continued to look at me. I felt offended by his comments, I told my classmate to hold my coat and told him: "Listen you never hit me with the door, however I think you owe me an apology for almost doing so, and for your attitude and verbiage, you seem to direct at me!" He said: "Look, I box and I don't want to hear any shit from you." I told him boxing was no big thing, he jumped back, his buddy uttered something, the guy threw a punch as he lunged forward. I hit him three times knocking him out before he even hit the floor, his buddy was shocked, it happened so quickly, he was actually frightened. I grabbed him by his collar and chest and yanked him face to face with me and asked him if he wanted any of what his buddy had just got, he was trembling so badly, there was no response, I shoved him back through the door, he stumbled and ran down the stairs. I looked down at his buddy, he was bleeding and instead of getting up he crawled over to the stairs and just fell all the way to the bottom. The guys I was with said: "Let's get out of here!" We left and went over to the bowling alley and went back to our barracks. We had heard about fights at the various clubs on post which is why we very seldom went to any of them, so again I was involved in a confrontation with another racist, I said to myself: "Man, if you get out of this one, you are a lucky guy!"

We had our graduation class that Saturday morning and a Sergeant in our class and three other white guys for Philly would make the trip home that day. We departed Ft. Gordon around 3:00 PM, we must have drove for about two hours when we pulled into a restaurant area, got gas and we decided to go inside for sandwiches and sodas to continue our home trip with. We all went inside, approached the counter at which time they started to order, a waitress came up to me and stated that they did not serve niggers there, that caught me by surprise, we were all in Class A uniforms, I was the only black, when I recovered, everyone said they didn't want anything and that we should just leave, I told them it was ok.

"Go ahead and order and I'll be over by the door," I said. Someone informed me that I could not wait inside and that I would have to wait outside, the guys again refused to order, but I insisted that they did, I told them that I heard about these racist bigots and should not have been caught off guard. I told them it's not like I came here to change that feeble mind set and would be out in the car. They brought the food and we continued on up to Philly pulling in around 1:00 AM Sunday morning. What an experience in my seven months of the south! After I got home I spent 30 days on leave.

After leaving Military Police Investigation and Law Enforcement School, I was sent to France. My first trip out of America was something I had really looked forward to while on leave in Philadelphia. I arrived up in New York City, at the debarkation pier approximately two hours prior, got out of the cab and was among thousands of servicemen being deployed, I was scheduled to sail over on the troop ship, called "The Rose." I found the pier and I could not believe my eyes, this was the largest troop ship in the fleet and believe me I was in awe. Never had I seen such a giant of a vessel, it surely lived up to its legend of being gigantic and powerful. It must have taken all day long to get boarded and processed in. I was up on deck and it was like I could reach out and touch that Lady who graced the harbor. We got underway late that evening, I was really excited, and somewhat amazed that I was still in the Army.

My first ship voyage, I went to bed shortly after leaving the city, woke up the next day, started meeting some of the other cruise members. There were a lot of privates like myself and many prior service guys as well. Later that day, a few guys from Detroit, Philly and Chicago found each other and became "homies" so to speak, the gambling, some guys had brought their alcohol with them, so it was interesting to see how everyone would spend their time. I was just trying to get acquainted to the flow of things, two of the guys I had befriended were fighters as I, and they had boxed around the states and had pretty good records. The third day out they wanted to have some boxing matches, however, the weather was really quite stormy, violent and raging winds all day, cloudy with rain, I thought to myself: "Man, if this ship is reeling and rocking, what were the smaller ones enduring, so I felt somewhat lucky."

I remember recalling what the blacks have endured during the Revolutionary War period, how they were hung and lynched and burned alive in military uniform, the same applied in the Civil War era. I read a case where a soldier returning to his hometown, stopped in a drugstore to purchase a few items, upon exciting the store, he was grabbed and dragged across the road to a wooded area, where he was lynched and castrated in full military uniform. There have been thousands of these incidents during that era, right up to World War I. Blacks have never been fully appreciated in this country, no matter what they have been through or accomplished. These brave and courageous defenders of the white wars paid the price of returning home with their lives. It was as if the white man never expected them to return, so what the enemy failed to destroy, the white tried to accomplish that task with the lynchings throughout the southern regions. The black man in America other than the Indians, are the most hated race of people in the country. You see what happened to the Native Americans, the white man tried to totally destroy them, except for those residing in various isolated areas. Since the days of their containment, the focus has been directed at black people who have fought in the millions to establish their fair share of what they have died for. Yet in 2007-2008 they are still finding ways to belittle blacks, hanging nooses, burning crosses, refusing them jobs, creating poverty across the nations, when will it end? And why is it allowed to continue, they have city councils, mayors, governors and other politicians voted to Congress or the Senate yet all remains the same. So when I got called a nigger in 1963 in South Carolina it was no surprise when Muhammad Ali was called a nigger and refused service in his hometown of Louisville, Kentucky a year later, I could see no change in the white man's attitude, my experience in the beginning of my career only exposed what I had read about in books, I never had or seen in my elementary or high schools, they did not teach of the black man's contributions to us blacks and damn sure did not teach it to the white children of their schools either, so we had whites thinking they were better.

Approximately seven days later, it happened, we must have hit a really bad area of the sea, winds were tremendous and relentless, the ship was under enormous stress, objects were falling all over the place, the Captain put everyone on alert, had everything tied down and secured, had everyone report to their bay areas and stay put. A few of us being adventuresome climbed up to another upper level, we peered out of one of the portal door windows and observed the chaotic scene, we went a little overboard and unsecured the door and stepped out onto the deck maintaining our hold on the railings attached adjacent to the door. All of a sudden as we gazed into the rage before our eyes, one of the highest waves was approaching starboard side, coming directly at us, it seemed as it was miles away, however the louder the noise the larger the wave had become, it was terrifying, we stood there unable to move, the waves were at phenomenal height. It looked as if there were no ending to the height of which we were witnessing. We were locked in time and space. We were paralyzed, locked in motionless, and then a great shock of an impact as it was already on us. "Ba-Bam!!!" It hit the tilt of our starboard side, as it tilted over, we observed something that I thought we would never survive; a deep mass of swirling water. It was like we were on a peak of water, as we observed the most frightful moment in our entire lives, all things seemed to flash in front of my eyes. I saw my whole life reflect as if my own eyes had turned inward to reflect all things. It was as if we had began to swirl, just like in the Bermuda Triangle, another wave struck knocking us back into the moment at which time I finally knew that the greatest force on earth is water. I also found out how insignificant I was in this system of things and how powerful my Creator, who created all things, was. We are each one of his treasures here on earth, of which we are all unique and HE knows everything about us. What a loving God we all truly have. On that night my Father allowed us to recover from one of the most unforgettable electrifying moment of my life. It was as if we were in God's hand and to this day, I truly realize how blessed I am to have taken that journey and sit here to reflect upon our divine purpose. We all have experiences we embark on as we go deeper into our heart to find the magnetic frequencies that instill the enlightenment of the wisdom and knowledge we inherit to become teachers and our brother's keeper. We are all of the One. We are to become teachers of the village. It takes the village to raise a child, it also takes the village to maintain all in the village as well. So if we are sincere, we search within to find our way. The world is there for us to obtain all we foresee, even though there seems to be so many barriers before us, but within our faith and hope and the courage to preserve the completion of our journey is right around the corner.

We got ourselves together, were able to secure the door and could not get back to the bay area fast enough. I jumped into my bunk, strapped myself in and closed my eyes and thought about what I had just witnessed and went through, it was definitely unbelievable, simply amazing.

Then next day, we got up, went up to the mess area, looked out of the porthole and all was well. It was one of the most beautiful days I've ever witnessed. We were just passing the snow white formations of the Azores, the sky was a crystal blue, there was the sun gracing those beautiful snow-covered ice structures, and as usual, I had no camera to catch such a phenomenal site. We were approximately a day from England where we had stopped to have a few guys taken off ship, one was in really bad shape; he had fallen in one of the shower areas and twisted his back. We dropped him off and proceeded on to our next stop which was Rota, Spain. We docked and were given liberty for that one night. There was a naval base there, however the guys saw no women around, so it was just us from the ship and the navy personnel stationed there. I stayed in one of the clubs with my partners, there were some do-wop singing, so we went up on the stage and sang "In the Still of the Night" and later went back to the ship.

It seemed like people always found a way to create problems.

The next morning we had just departed the shore area when there was an argument in the bay area. One of the prior service white guys had gotten picked up by the navy shore patrol and was released from the brig that morning and was threatening some of the guys he thought fingered him out to the patrol causing him to get locked up overnight. I had spoken to the guy a couple of times during our trip. I happened to come up abreast of the crowd to see what was happening, he was ranting and raving about being the baddest guy on the ship and asked if I thought he was. I told him I could not say that, he asked me why. I told him I didn't know who's the baddest guy on the ship is.

"Do you think you can whip my ass?" he asked.

"Damn right, I think I can whip your ass!" I responded.

"Come on out!" he said. I stepped out of the crowd and he reached in his pocket and pulled out a switch blade knife.

"I thought you wanted to prove how bad you were, why the damn knife? That shows me your confidence is not there at all" I said.

Meanwhile I had noticed one of those metal trash cans, I told him whatever he had in mind get to it, but if he wanted me to kick his ass, to put the knife down because I told him as far as I know, I am the baddest guy on the ship ready to kick his ass or anyone else's. He looked embarrassed and I told him to put the knife away. He looked around, put the knife in his pocket, smiled sheepishly, turned and walked away. I just knew we would wind up fighting, however I am glad it did not happen. He was a big guy just trying to intimidate everyone, another white racist. Before we reached France we became buddies, to the point where he even said how sorry he was for the incident to have taken place.

We arrived in France and processed off "The Rose." I was met by a few Military Policemen and took off in the sedan for a place called Periquex approximately 50 miles south of Paris. We pulled in the main gate at about 11:00 pm. As we pulled in, there was a bus parked in the gate area with about six MPs at its entrance door with its flashers on. The guys I was with went over as I, to see what was happening. The situation was there was a black soldier refusing to get off. I was the only black guy there. I saw the guy as I looked through the windows. The MPs there were just about ready to go on the bus and drag him any way they could. I saw an MP Sergeant standing there, I introduced myself and asked him if I could have a talk with him before things got ugly, he looked at me and said ok.

I boarded the bus, walked down the isle and approached him. I told him my name and asked what the problem was. He had had a few drinks, looked at me uttered a few incoherent words, and told me his name was Starks. I told him that I was Webb, a new MP assigned to the unit here. I also told him if he didn't get off the bus that I would have to be a part of kicking his butt and dragging him off the bus, and I really didn't want to be a part of that type of situation. And so from saving me from participating in that which was about to take place, he followed me off and the MPs let him go back to his barracks. After talking to my Detachment Sergeant I was taken to the MP barracks, checked in, showered and went to bed.

The next day, I was given the rest of the week to process into post personnel and get my things squared away. I also met two white guys that I went through the MP Academy with at Ft. Gordon, Private First Class, PFC Beldin and PFC Lewendowski. Both of these guys, before being drafted, were on the New York Yankee's farm team. Really sharp guys, they had told everyone about me, the boxing and being from Philly and all, so it seemed I fit right in. There were approximately 29 MPs with me being the only black assigned. I went over to Personnel check-in and one of the guys asked me where I was from. I told him I was from Philly and he informed me that were some other black guys on post from Philly. It was about lunch time, he asked me if I was ready for lunch I told him I was and he said: "Come on, I'll show you where the mess hall is." We got to mess hall and he introduced me to some of the blacks from Philly, I also saw Starks in the mess hall. I was greeted by most of the black guys, I stayed after lunch conversing and finally left to continue my way in processing. One guy had told me to come over to the club later that evening. I showed up at the club about 9pm that night. I walked in and it was pretty nice. The club had a nice layout and I had greeted the guys I had met that day. We were having some small conversations when Starks walked in. He gave me a look and came over to me and asked, "Are you the guy who was at the bus last night?" I told him I was. He stated to me that he did not like the MPs and that he did not think they could have taken him off that bus.

"We'll never know. The thing is you got off without any incident and I was only asking you to get off so I would not have been part of whipping you because that was definitely the plan" I said.

He looked at me and said, "I don't think you would have made a difference!"

"You never know!" I said again.

He got a little loud, like he was trying to intimidate me to a certain degree. I asked him what his problem was and he said he did not like MPs. Most of the guys were telling him to move on. I told them it was ok and whatever he wanted to get into was ok with me. I stood up. He was a pretty big guy. He played football on the post team and in college.

"Well if we have to bang, let's get it over with because I'll be around as an MP for two years or so" I said.

We squared off, he made a few weak moves, trying to set me up for a jab, however, I knew from the jump he was not what he thought he was. I changed my direction of movement, took the weak jab away. As he reached, as he was jabbing at me moving to his right, as he turned to throw the weak jab which brought back low, I shot a right hand over his shoulder hitting flush in the jaw. His face tilted downward. I shot an uppercut that caught him perfectly under the chin. His head was forced up from the impact and I turned the uppercut into a left hook and finished with a short straight right hand knocking backwards where he knocked over three or four bar stools as he landed on the floor; a Technical Knock Out (TKO). Some of his friends rushed over to get him together. The guys I was with said, "Hey, home, you are damn sharp!" we sat back down and finished our drinks and later left. Just like that, I had a reputation as the word got out that I had knocked out Starks at the club. It was like Saturday Night Live in the club.

Sunday I stayed in the barracks getting uniforms pressed and shining up my gear. Monday, Beldin, Lewendowski and a guy named Henry, all MPs, had to be taken to meet the Provost Marshall, a Col. Roby at his headquarters approximately 30 miles away. We arrived up there to see him, it was a mandatory meeting for all military policemen to attend his orientation. We walked in to him, he looked up and down, and stated, "Well we have a first here, a black MP, he looked at me, asked me where I was from and I told him from Philadelphia, Pennsylvania. He took my file records, checked them out and proceeded to question the others. He gave us his orientation about professionalism, Code of Conduct, and what he expected from us as military policemen in his command. We had been briefed about him on the way up. I knew he was a Colonel, Full Bird, been there for two years, was from Alabama and looked every bit of racist to me. That was my impression of him. After his briefing, he spoke directly to me: "Pvt. Webb, you are the first Black MP ever in this unit and because of that I expect you to be above and beyond expectation. I want you to excel in every way, there's a lot you will be faced with not only dealing with the other white MPs of this unit but the problems of apprehending and dealing with white soldiers as well. And let me further tell you, if you screw up, I am going to be the first to throw the book at you. Are we in agreement of what I just told you?"

"I fully understand what you are saying to me and I'll do my best to live up to your standard," I said.

He looked at me and then told us to stand up for a personal inspection. He inspected our haircuts, gear and uniforms, then he stepped back and told us he wanted to inspect our belt buckles. He looked at them, then he asked us to turn them over, he checked them, stepped back and stated, "Pvt. Webb, you are the only one who passed my inspection. You are the only one who has shined your belt buckle on both sides. I think we are going to get along just fine".

We were dismissed and driven back to our post where we had "chow" and were given the remainder of the day off. I said to myself I am glad the word never got out about the night before the club for some reason. I respected the colonel for his words to me. Now it was up to me to set the standards and I was prepared to do just that. Was he a racist, I could not tell but I knew I shocked him when he found out how much I paid attention to my personal dress character and military bearing. Some of those standards were instilled in me by my stepfather, my cousin Jason and the old heads that used to be in the neighborhood wearing those Stacey Adams high top comfort shoes. Their values were always pressed to the max, if one of those guys caught you disrespecting all they expected of you, you were in trouble. They taught us about being sharp and respectful in our neighborhoods. There's no such thing as those old heads today, a lost treasure in today's communities. Most old heads today are strung out on drugs and alcohol. They were a valuable asset back then. You respected your sisters, mothers and senior citizens all the time.

They taught you how to be tough, how to stroll that Philadelphia walk. A walk of confidence and swagger. I was in Vietnam when my Company Commander saw me walk by him. I had only been there two days and he called out to me: "Sergeant Webb!"

"Yes, Sir!" I stopped and answered.

"I knew you were from Philadelphia!" he stated.

"How's that, Sir?

"From the way you walk, pants a little up on the chest, are those Stacey Adams shoes?"

"Yes, Sir!"

"You're smooth! Carry on!" I laughed and continued on my way. They can never take the Philly out of me.

Getting back to my story, we got back to our post and had to report to our Section Sergeant, he was informed by the Colonel of his briefing and even how he was impressed with my military appearance and bearing. The Sergeant was there for two years of a three year tour. He had his family with him, really nice people. His name was Sexton, an old picking and grinding guitar player, like Johnny Cash. I even learned to like his western music, he was a pretty sharp old country boy. Sgt. Sexton assigned us to our shifts and squads. I was assigned to a gun-ho sergeant who had been there for about six months prior to my arrival. He was one of the Mps at the bus area that night with the Stark's incident. I sensed his aggressive attitude and that's why I asked Sgt. Sexton to allow me to talk him off the bus because this guy was one of those guys. Give him a badge, gun and a billy club, he thinks he rules the world, so already, I know somewhere we would clash heads together. Sgt. Sexton wanted me to be his driver for a week before going to the squad, which was perfect.

After working with Sgt. Sexton for days, I had learned the patrol routes, of the post area, also got acquainted with the town area which was about three miles form the post itself. I was introduced to some of the bar and restaurant owners, the local French Police Officers of whom we would be working with whenever patrolling the town areas. Sgt. Sexton was pretty sharp and very professional in his job performances and pretty much respected by the townspeople, it was a pleasure working with him there for that week. I was given off three days and would report to Sgt. Johnson, my squad leader.

During my three days off, I got with some of the black guys I had met and went downtown. For my first visit, they took me to a very nice club on the main street. It was a French holiday, the club was packed, most of the guys knew me by now and the word had got around the incident with Starks and I. The guys I was with knew a lot of girls of which they had introduced me to. Very fine ladies, I stood out like a sore thumb, as all newly assigned persons had to wear the uniform for the first thirty days. I was really enjoying myself dancing, after a period of time they had invited me up on the stage. We were dancing with members of the band. The band leader took my hat and gave me his, just having a tremendous time when I heard someone yell, "Hey, get the hell off that stage!"

I turned to look down to the dance floor, where I observed a burly red-haired, white sergeant wearing a Courtesy Patrol arm band on his uniform. He caught my eye and shouted at me again. At that point I yelled back at him: "Who the hell are you cursing at?" He screamed again, at which time I told him that I was coming down there to kick his ass. I backed up from the flood lights aligning the front of the stage, got a running jump to clear the first row of tables. When I landed on the dance floor, he was running to the entrance of the club. I chased him, got to the front door when his driver threw up his hands and backed away stating he did not want any trouble with me. I looked outside and the Sergeant was driving off in their courtesy jeep. I went back and approached the courtesy patrol jeep driver. I was surprised he knew my name when he said: "Webb, I don't want anything to do with this situation!"

Pretty sharp-looking Private First Class, I told him I was after that Sergeant he was supposedly driving for, and walked back into the club. Fifteen minutes later an MP unit came into the club, walked over to me and said that Sergeant Sexton wanted me to return to the post and return to him. I said to myself, here we go, in trouble already and started thinking what the colonel had to tell me. I got back to the post and those guys took me over to Sergeant Sexton. He asked what had happened at the club and that the Courtesy Patrol Sergeant had come and made a report against me and that I was restricted to the barracks. I told Sgt. Sexton that the Courtesy Patrol Sergeant had cursed and screamed at me and had he been more professional in handling and dealing with people, there would be no problem. Sexton said again to me I was restricted to the barracks and he would have to report the incident to the Provost Marshall and for me to report back to his office in the morning.

I reported to Sgt. Sexton the next morning. He had reported the incident to the colonel over the phone and called me in his office and said the colonel wanted to speak. The colonel asked me to explain what had happened regarding the incident. I explained that we were all enjoying a very good time in the club when this Staff Sergeant started screaming and using profanity towards me, of which I thought was not professional nor was it tactful. His actions as a Non-Commissioned Officer in the United States Army totally offended and disrespected me as a man and a soldier in the Army as well. I informed him that when I chased him, he jumped into his jeep and drove away leaving his driver standing there. I also informed him, as a soldier and a man, I would never condone anyone using that type of language or any intimidating attitude causing a spectacle of himself before all of those people and embarrassing me as well. He asked me if I thought my actions were appropriate, I told him I did, at which time he asked me to speak with Sgt. Sexton. Sgt. Sexton told me he had spoken with the Sergeant who was involved in the incident and a few other people and stated: "I also told the colonel that you were an exceptional and promising MP since you have been assigned here and there were some inappropriate procedures used by the Sergeant in handling the case and that the colonel had told him to resolve the matter."

Sgt. Sexton requested that I apologize to the Courtesy Patrol Sergeant, which I did not agree with. However, I thought it would be in my best interest to do so. He told me I was dismissed and I left to find that sergeant. As I was walking towards the mess hall, I saw him. Some of my fellow MPs who had been there a while had told me he was one of those hardcore Non-Commissioned Officers, NCOs, and that he had been involved in a few incidents since they had been there. One of those white guys who thought he had control over most of the enlisted men in his company. I called out to him, he stopped, I walked over to him and told him that my supervisor said to me I should apologize to you of which I am, however that I wanted him to know one damn thing. If he ever tried disrespecting me in any way in the future, I would be put in jail for kicking his ass. He got all red in the face and as we stood there I noticed he was actually shaking and trembling a bit. This was a total shock to this NCO to have a private speak to him like that. He could sense that if he had moved I would have killed him right there. I was on my real thin line and hoping he would do something foolish. I stared at him for a few more seconds and walked away. One thing I knew he could not be that bad guy they were telling me about because if he was, he would have never ran from the club that night before. I was getting a lot of attention because I had beat up Starks, who was supposedly one of the tough black guys on post. Plus Lewendowski and Beldin had told everyone that I was a fighter out of Philly and had quite a reputation. The post personnel used to see me jogging early in the morning and the guys I met from Philly were talking me up to damn near everyone they knew.

My time was up and I had to report to my new Squad Leader, I damn sure resented doing so, as I had mentioned earlier, he was gun-ho, very aggressive and a glory-seeker. He always had to have a quota of incident reports and traffic tickets each tour of duty. He had come to France from the Second Infantry Division, Korea. I just hoped all would work out ok. I reported to him, he gave me a briefing and assigned me to my rotating schedule. The post was really not that big. We had almost six or seven hundred personnel stationed there. It was a Supply and Signal Depot with military police and support personnel attached. We would run eight patrols, four on post and the other four in town. They were assisted by the French police officers to patrol the bars, clubs and the street areas. My squad leader, Sergeant Johnson, assigned me as his driver the first day we worked together. He told me of his duty assignment in Korea and some of the major problems they had over there. He also told me that some of the guys were telling him about me boxing and that he had taken some martial arts classes in Korea. He also told me how he was looking forward to returning there or another tour of duty. He informed me of the problems we as military policemen were experiencing with the various club hangouts by the troops there in town. He told me that the clubs were segregated, blacks and their areas of town, and the whites their sections.

We patrolled the town areas that day, the next day I was off and would report back to the following night for the swing shift, 3:00 to 11:00pm, again I was assigned to be his driver. I reported for duty that evening, checked our vehicle, picked up our emergency kits and attended guard mount. All went well for inspection. I picked him up at the MP station and we took off. We were on the road for an hour when he decided to pull over and check some soldiers' Pass and ID Cards. I didn't see the need to since they were only walking down the main street. They checked out ok and he had me pull over a couple of vehicles, all ok. It started getting dark and bars and clubs were beginning to fill up with American troops who were brought in by troop busses. The busses carried about forty people each trip. At 8:00, he told me he wanted me to check for Pass and IDs. We pulled up to a club and he told me to tell everyone to fall outside so he could check IDs, which I thought was unnecessary, as all seemed normal to me, however I did as I was instructed to. Most of the guys had known me or heard about me boxing so when I told them to fall outside they responded pretty well.

We left to another bar and did the same thing, pull troops and check IDs. After the second club, he wanted to check POVs, private owned vehicles. If you were a permanent party and an E0-4 or above, you could have or own a vehicle, so we started checking vehicles as well now, I am beginning to see how aggressive he actually was. He wrote two traffic violations, wrote up a couple of troops for minor uniform violations, after emptying two or three more clubs. I thought it was troop harassment, but continued to comply with his orders. We must have worked the 3-11 pm shifts together for the rest of the month. One problem I was having was him keeping me working with him after the shifts were over. There was a curfew where all military personnel had to be back on base before midnight, the last bus departed for post at 11:30 hours, anyone caught on the street was on Absence Without Leave (AWOL).

The 3-11 pm shift ended at about 11:30 pm unless you had an incident and needed to process individuals or finish up incident reports. As I stated, Sgt. Johnson had to get his quota before terminating his shift, so most of the time when the other shift had assumed the shift, he would hang around looking for people to apprehend, especially if he was not satisfied with his incidents for that night, meaning I would have to work along with him opposed to finishing up with the rest of our squad at 11:00 pm. There would be times when I would not get off until 1:00 am and believe me it was trying my patience playing his game. I told him one night that I was getting somewhat irritated hanging around after our shift was over, just to get involved in incidents the on-coming shift should be handling. He kind of laughed it off and stated how good I was looking being involved in these reports and that it made me look good to the Provost Marshall.

I informed him I was not about gaining a reputation and it seemed like he was using me to harass the troops. I also requested he find another driver other than me all the time. I had heard of numerous complaints being filed against him and I for forcing troops outside of clubs to check IDs. I was like the big bad black nigger using my authority to unjustly provoke the troops for no reason. I was beginning to be talked about because of his insidious glory-seeking. He finally selected another driver. I think I pissed him off to a certain degree because he would always have some off the wall remark to make to me whenever he was inspecting our shift at briefings and guard mounts. I just ignored him as much as I could. He often had Desk Sergeant duty and had to pull bed checks of our barracks. We all had to be present in the barracks by midnight curfew.

One night he came in the barracks, there were about twelve of us in bed and someone had brought some beer and gave us all one. We were lying on our beds when we heard the door of the building downstairs open and close so we hid the bottles. I had mine under the blanket between my legs. When he came in he looked at everyone. Some guys spoke but I just laid there wishing he would hurry up and leave because that beer bottle was ice cold. I must have had goose pimples all over my body and even shivering a bit. I was lying on my side, propped up under my right arm trying to keep my composure when he came over and asked, "How's Private Webb?"

"Pretty good" I said. He put his hand on my shoulder where there was a small hole in my T-shirt. He put his finger on it and started playing around with it. I said, "Sergeant, one thing I want you to know...I laugh sometimes but I damn sure don't play. I think you better get your hands off of me!" he laughed then I told him, "If I was not laying here in this bed, I would show you just how serious I am, you play with kids and I am a man who does not play games, however we can discuss it another time!" he gave us a sarcastic laugh and headed out of the bay area to leave the building, Man, I was so relieved. I damn near froze to death holding that bottle between my legs, I must have had chills for damn near an hour after he left. We were not authorized to have beer or liquor in the barracks.

On the second day me and some of the fellows got together and went downtown to a local club where we knew some of the ladies who worked there after being there dancing and just enjoying ourselves. I had been dancing with one of the ladies. We got back to the table where she was sitting and as I turned to leave, a French guy asked her to dance and she refused. This guy just went off on her venting in French verbiage, I knew from the jump must have been very demeaning to her, this individual was sitting with a few guys watching us for a period of time, evidently, he asked her to dance and she refused and he started his vocal outburst, I went over and asked what was going on, she informed me that he got upset because she would not dance with him and he had called her a slut and a whore, I intervened, he shouted something at me and I punched him in the mouth, he fell backwards, fell up against some tables and chairs and ran out. I went over to her and asked her to join us of which she did.

The moment arrives. After seeing that she was okay, I went up to the bar to get a couple of cokes, while standing there, staring in the big plate glass mirror that gave a view of the entrance door, I saw, the one and only come running in the door, someone must have called or maybe the guy had flagged down the MP Patrol, there he was Sgt. Johnson, he came running up behind me, in the mirror, he made the wrong move, he grabbed me up around the shoulder. I said, "This is it!" I raised up my arm on the shoulder he had grabbed me on, and spun around breaking his hold and hit him, he went one way and his white MP had went the other, he was laying out on the floor, his driver a white boy named Nance froze in his tracks, the Sergeant got his senses together, somewhat got to one knee, he stated, "Webb, you are going to jail!" I reached down and punched him two or three more times and told him, "If I was going to jail that I might as well finish him off!"

Pfc. Nance was still in shock, all of a sudden the guys I was with had grabbed me, trying to get me under control, I did not know who it was at the time as I threw one guy up against the wall, threw a right hand, he must have been one of the sharpest duckers I've ever seen, I missed his head and damn near broke my hand as it made impact with the wall. They finally got me outside and under control and the Sergeant had gotten himself together, he was all banged up, Nance had called for back-up MP Patrol, when they arrived they said, "Man, you are in trouble, we have to take you in." I said, "Okay!", got into the jeep and was escorted back to the post. Sgt. Sexton met the patrol at the gate and told me I was under apprehension, was restricted to the barracks and was to pack my belongings, that I would be under armed guard and escorted to see

Colonel Ruby in the morning and that I would more than likely be confined to the stockade.

That night I packed up all of my gear and belongings and showered and laid down for a few hours until the escort arrived about 8:00 a.m. I was placed in the rear of a 3/4 ton vehicle and there was another armed patrol behind the vehicle I was in. I said, "God-bye!' to all of my squad and the rest of the MPs that were there and was on my way to see the Colonel who had initially warned me if I ever got in trouble I was going to jail, so I was prepared to do just that. I had my satisfaction whipping Sgt. Johnson's ass for utilizing me as some sort of bully to harass and disrespect the troops and depriving me of my free time working for him to achieve his quotas. On the way to see the Colonel, I could hear the post personnel cheering after hearing Johnson got his ass kicked.

Champion Joe Louis

Fought for Our Nation, It's People and Our Democracy And Symbols By Which We Stand Against MAX SCHMELING, Representing ADOLF HITLER Proclaimed Superior Aryan Race of Germany, Victorious JOE was hailed as One of Greatest Champions Ever.

Joe Louis Barrow (the Brown Bomber) was one of the most devastating punchers to ever hold the Heavyweight Championship, and was one of my childhood hero's. Joe was born on 13 May 1914, Chambers City, Alabama, he died 12 April 1981 in Las Vegas, Nevada. Joe held the Championship for 11 years and defended it 25 times, an extraordinary and phenomenal man, who became America's second black heavyweight champion. His reign as Champion began on 22 June 1937 when he knocked out James J. Braddock in the 8th round. America was still in racial disarray as far as blacks were concerned. Blacks could not vote. There were too few jobs, poor housing and education systems, and little or no welfare. Jim Crow and discrimination were prevalent everywhere, especially in the southern states.

Blacks were not allowed to ride public transportation, had to utilize back doors, had separate water and toilet areas, and were not permitted in theaters or movie houses. One of the most insulting, humiliating, and degrading situations was that during the 2nd World War, some of the southern states held German prisoners in various facilities, these prisoners were allowed in all these places where blacks could not patronize. What a slap in the face, especially to all the military black veterans who fought and served in World War 1 and those fighting for their freedom, citizenship, human and civil rights in a war in Europe, against Germany from where these prisoners came.

Yes, Joe as did Jack Johnson would inherit and play a substantial role in America against a white racist society, Jim Crow and mass killings, lynching, raping and beating of black people. Joe often stated that "his major fight was not in the ring, but against Jim Crow and the white supremacy and superiority mind set of white America". America became threatened by the white Aryan racists of Germany, who's leader, Adolph Hitler, was telling the world that they in fact were the supreme superior master race. As they began defeating and conquering some of the main countries in Europe, starting World War II. The United States was threatened so much so, that when word of a rematch between Louis and Schmeling was made public, Joe, who was now the World Heavyweight Champion was summoned to the White House in Washington meet with President Roosevelt. Schmeling a former heavyweight champion had ended what was becoming such a brilliant career, Louis had won 20 fights without a loss. He knocked out former heavyweight champion Primo *Carnero* and Max Bear in 1935 and seemed unbeatable, until he was defeated by Schmeling in their first fight in 1936. Their first fight depicted Schmeling a force of authoritarianism and Joe a fighter of America's democracy of the free. After Schmeling's stunning victory over Louis, Hitler again begun promoting and boosting the fact that Schmeling's major defeat of seemingly invincible Louis and America's freedom and democracy further established the superiority and the dominance of the Aryan race over the rest of the world.

Joe arrived at the White House and met with the President a

few days prior to the fight, which was scheduled to be fought in New York's, Madison Square Garden. The President told Joe how important this fight was to America and world at large, that he was representing his race and all America, told him to win this fight for our nation and for freedom world wide.

23 June 1938, the eyes of the world were all focused on New York's Madison Square Garden, on that night the brown bomber entered the ring where the building was scratched to its capacity of wall to wall people, the champion disrobed revealing a sweat glistening superbly chiseled powerful and muscular brown body, a body that all who looked upon it knew, Schmeling was in serious trouble, the strength and power dominated. Joe acknowledged the crowd, spoke a few words to Jack Blackburn, the bell rang, the light beamed into Joe's face, the face was intent, eyes focused on his prey, he moved in position, this handsome fiercely man poised to release all his thoughts and will power to defeat the foe. On that night Louis fought for his pride, dignity, respect and for America, he represented a black race, he fought against racial discrimination, for black economic progress, he fought his heart out for white oppression to be lifted from the blacks of this country. He fought for blacks to be recognized and respected for their contributions they have made to this country. Joe fought for equal chances and opportunities for the unity of all races to come together, he carried a tremendous burden in the fight and gave such a fierce display of his God given talent, physical strength and total dominance, an aggression never before witnessed in such a short period of time. Schemling was totally crushed within seconds of the very first minute of round one. Joe reached deep into his heart and soul to make a difference in America and for that one treasured night, that will be remembered for all times. America embraced each other, blacks and whites, their voices became as one, as they shed their tears, opened their hearts and for a brief time extended their love and tore down the racial divide, as they let out one thunderous cheer that was heard world wide as they dance jubilantly in city neighborhoods and country towns within our nation. Joe lifted America's character, reestablished her image, he laid the foundation for unity, for trust and respect Joe delivered, could America

arise to the task of her new challenge? Joe earned his crown of life, could America earn hers? Joe Louis became a symbol of hope a black man was America's greatest hero pound for pound and he placed his crown in the nation's hearts forever.

In 1926, at the age of 12, his family relocated to Detroit, in 1932 Joe lost his first amateur fight and was totally devastated. Joe who had been deceiving his mother for years was secretly learning to be a boxer. His mother who had been paying for him to take piano lessons, became very distraught, when it was revealed to her he was learning to fight, however, she persuaded him to continue after she lectured him about lying to her and instilled in him the principles and value of life, especially truth and honesty. Joe went on to win 50 of his 54 fights, 43 by knockout. After such a superb amateur career, he drew the attention of two wealthy black men, John Roxborough and Mike Jacobs, who introduced him one of the best black trainers of that era, Jack (Chappie) Blackburn who became his sole trainer until he died. Chappie taught Joe the fundamentals of boxing, the balance, jabs, right hand, left hooks, combinations, hand speed, feinting and ringsmanship. Under Blackburn's tutoring, Joe became one of the most feared fighters ever to grace the boxing ring. His execution was a thing of beauty, his short powerful accurate punches to body and head was something to behold in such a violent sport.

After Joe became Champion, winning the hearts of this Country and others world wide in defeating Max Schmeling and lying to rest Hitler's claim of the Aryan superiority, he had a few more title defenses, became a very popular figure in America. Joe had opened a club, had a Joe Louis soda company, also had a very great tasting candy bar, tried his hand at acting, portraying himself in the Joe Louis story. Joe loved the ladies, was a very dap dresser and carried himself with class, dignity, and respect; and continued to speak out for racial discrimination and equal rights. The War in Europe continued to escalate and America began preparing. Jobs in ammunition plants opened up, allowing blacks to gain some employment. After Pearl Harbor, America joined the War against Germany and Japan. Joe joined the Army as to support his patriotism, which opened the door for many blacks to step up following Joe's lead. During his service tenure he boxed exhibitions in the States as well as in Europe. Joe was very displeased when asked to box in a segregated show, he refused to take part in that situation. Joe had established a relationship with some politicians in Washington and in the military. Joe made some phone calls to these persons and vehemently expressed his dissatisfaction with the segregated facilities on military bases. Joe protest resulted in desegregation mess halls, barracks transportation of troop buses, theaters, movie houses and enlisted and NCO clubs. During these many exhibition Joe always stress unity and respect for each other regardless of race, creed and color. Joe made a statement regarding the war, he stated "with God on our side how can we lose."

During the war, shortly after Pearl Harbor bombing, Joe fought two professional fights, which generated a million dollars for each fight. Joe donated the full purse from each fight to 1, The Army Relief Fund, 2, The Navy Relief Fund. This money was to support the families of the service persons killed in the bombing of Pearl Harbor. A few years later after leaving the military, Joe was charged by the US treasury department for not paying the taxes on the 2 purses he had donated in full to the Army and Navy Relief Funds. This put a tremendous burden on Joe financially from the very beginning, causing a huge problem for him to pay. Consequently Joe's business assets were confiscated. After seeing no relief from the Government, Joe who had retired undefeated had to come out of retirement to earn some money to pay his debt, however, there was no way he could catch up as the debt was turned over to tax collection department, IRS. The major problem was that the IRS allowed 3 years of interest on the tax debt before applying the debt against him. Joe was broke, Frank Sinatra one of Joe's biggest fans arranged a job for him at the Sands, in Las Vegas where worked until he died.

Joe, an American Hero, symbol, patriot, fighter against America most deplorable and despicable racial segregation, Jim Crow, discrimination, human, and civil rights violations, was hounded to his grave by a country whose President had to call this black champion and make such a tremendous request for him to represent this nation when America had no image or character other than allowing the Klan, and other supremacy groups to terrorize, lynch, murder, rape and violate black people, who have fought in every war since the beginning of its existence. This story should never have ended this way. The same President who called him in or who ever was voted in, should have exonerated this champion of that debt. He never took a cent from either of those million dollar purses, someone could have made the adjustments when the checks were transferred to those government agencies. I had posed the question earlier, could America or the political persons who ran this country handle the challenges of making things better for all? No, because the injustices allowed to happen in Jack Johnson era was still rampant during one of the greatest champions reign. Heroes are those who accept the challenge irregardless of the outcome. There's some beautiful people in this country who have made many efforts for change, whites, Hispanics, Native Americans, Orientals, blacks, we have to make change of our attitudes for better harmony and unity in America. It's ironic that Max Schmeling an Aryan white man, who after being defeated by Louis, returned to Germany where Hitler called him a coward and a discredit to his race, and Frank Sinatra, a man I refer to as the Master of his game, became the heroes in Joe's dying days. Schmeling financially supported and visited him regularly from Germany. America never showed up, it allowed Joe's humiliation. Just think what would have happened if Joe had lost that fight of which the President and all America put their hope and faith in. I would hate to have to write about the racial hatred of blacks and the killing and the name calling in the after math of that scene. Praise God for a great person, a wonderful champion and a man worthy to be applauded for what he contributed to this nation. Max Schmeling called him the greatest heavyweight he ever saw. Thanks Joe, we remember.

chapter 13

The Ultimate Decision

Back to my story... We arrived at Colonel Roby's office about 9:00 PM, I was escorted to a room adjacent to his office, when I walked in, I was surprised to see Sgt. Johnson sitting there, he looked like someone had stuffed a granny green apple in his mouth, I later found out that his nose and jaw were broken, I went in and sat in the far corner of the room. About ten minutes later a clerk told me to report to Col. Roby, I walked in, needless to say I was sharp as a tack, that morning, creases in my uniform were razor sharp, boots like a piece of glass and my brass uniform accoutrements were blinding to look at, I strolled in, stopped approximately five feet from his desk, snapped to attention and rendered one of the sharpest salutes ever recorded in military history, Gen. Patton would have sat up in his grave on that one. Col, Roby gave me at ease, I fell into a parade rest in front of him looking straight ahead. He said: "Webb, you know you are going to jail." I said: "Yes, Sir." He leaned back into his chair, and said: "I understand you have been doing an outstanding job at Periquex from Sgt. Sexton, as well as the Post Commander who has called me earlier today, now I want you to tell me what the hell happened?"

My answer was: "Sir, I took your orientation very seriously and committed myself as always, long before I ever came here, to be the best I could possibly be, at all of my endeavors. After hearing of the high expectations you wanted me to achieve, not only for myself as the first Black military policeman ever assigned here, but also for other blacks to see that I could excel and make a difference in the law enforcement branch of the service. I told him my progress had unfortunately been interfered with by a very over-aggressive, arrogant, overzealous Sergeant using bad law enforcement tactics to extort and harass the troops of their rights to enjoyment and privacy, and utilizing me as an enforcer to meet his set quotas of incidents during shift tours. I also related to him of me hitting Sgt. Johnson, I was responding to someone grabbing me from the rear, I thought it was the French man I had been fighting with earlier, it happened so quickly and that Sgt. Johnson never said a thing before grabbing me, which I thought was poor police procedure, 1 also told him I stood before him responsible for my actions. Col. Roby looked at me, told me to tell Sgt. Johnson to come in and for me to wait there till he called me back. I informed Sgt. Johnson to report to the Colonel. He went in and closed the door, at which time I heard the Colonel begin shouting at Johnson. It must have gone on for about five minutes or so, when I heard the Colonel tell him to get out of his office, he came out looking like a bomb had been dropped on him. Several minutes later the colonel asked me in.

"Pvt. Webb, I am going to try and help you out of this situation, predicated on what you have stated and also because the Post Commander at Periquex informed me of the ongoing belligerent and unprofessional conduct of Johnson, there's been numerous reports of his confrontations with enlisted and officers as well. I am sending you back to Periguex, you will be on restriction to the barracks and will report every hour on the hour to Post headquarters everyday until I can notify Sgt. Sexton of my decision, is that understood?" I said "Yes, Sir!" "Right now you are looking at a general Court Martial, however, I'll see if I can help you out, you are dismissed." I snapped to, saluted him, did an about face and left his office. I had tears welling in my eyes as I came out of the building, and a different opinion of the man that I thought was racist from the very beginning he had set his eyes on me. God definitely had me in his hands. My squad personnel who had brought me up there was waiting, and gave me all smiles when I told them what the Colonel had told me. One of them told me: "Man, you are one lucky guy, however Johnson needed his butt kicked for all the things he's been pulling since he arrived there from Korea." We got back, Sgt. Sexton told the Desk Sergeant to have me report to him when I got back. Sexton told me he was glad to have me back and also the Colonel told him he would try to help me, the case is damn near over, he also informed me he would utilize me as a clerk on the midnight shifts until he heard form the Colonel. So I pulled Radio Operator and Desk Clerk for about five shifts. I got off on the morning of the fifth night shift, went to breakfast at the mess hall, left there and went to the barracks, was laying around after doing some exercises and punching on a heavy bag. I had put together to keep in shape, when I got a call to be at Sgt. Sexton's office, I met him at the designated time, he told me I had to report to a Major at personnel to go over the court martial proceedings. l reported over to the Adjutant Office, he called me in and told me to have a seat. I sat down and he read the charges of which I was being charged with, he also read to me the provisions of what the United States Code of Military[7] Justice stated and was informed that I was getting a summary court martial for the disorderly conduct on Sgt. Johnson and I would be fined $75.00 for two months and would remain on restriction for thirty days and would continue to work on the midnight shift duties as assigned by Sgt. Sexton. The Colonel had in fact helped me out, I could have received a jail sentence in the stockade had I received a Special or General Court Martial of up to five years and forfeiture of all pay. I thought to myself there are some really good white people here on earth after all. My Basic Training Company Commander and now, Colonel Roby. l knew I had truly been blessed. I praised God for all things along my journey of life.

Working the midnight shift was really nice for me, I learned the Desk Sergeant's job, Radio Dispatcher job and Clerk, I really got my typing together as well, I was one of those hen peckers. One of the functions we were responsible for was calling all status reports to Barconne's main head quarters, all the calls had to be patched in by the post operator every two hours from 12:00 to 6:00 AM. One particular morning I could not make contact with the civilian phone operator which was operating out of the post phone dispatch office, it was like a hotline set up. After failing to make contact I had to dispatch a patrol to see what was happening regarding the negative responses. They made contact and had the civilian female operator call in, I told her I was concerned about her not answering phone, I also informed her how vital the calls were, she got upset,

I told her let's have no more problems, if so I would make an incident report and hung up, I called the French interpreter to call and confirm what I had told her earlier, I think she got upset, however she answered every time I called after that. At about 6:00 AM the interpreter came in and informed me that the operator wanted to speak with me, I told him to let her in, she came in with two guys, her husband and brother who was the Heavyweight Champion of France. Evidently she had gotten upset because I gave specific instructions about her answering the phone and about the report I told her I would submit if I could not reach her, whenever I had to forward the status reports and other essential report information to Barconne, she came in and told me she was upset, I asked who the two men were that were with her, she informed me one was her husband and the other her brother who was the Heavyweight Champion of France. I told her this was not about her husband or her brother, it was about her, not answering the phone which she was required to do, that's what she was being paid to do, if there's no answer, there could only be one of three things, the line is down, she was away from the line, perhaps in the bathroom or she was sleeping and if there's a problem it's up to me to initiate a patrol to check on you or whatever the problem may have been, and also told her she was getting paid to do a job, all this I had the interpreter to tell her, her husband and brother I was glad to meet them, and to her brother that I boxed myself, his eye got really big, and he asked the interpreter that he would like to box with me, at which I replied: "That would be great." I shook his hand, she still looked a bit upset as they left. The next day I was off, I got a call about 11:00 AM from the interpreter stating there were two cars of French men, one of whom was the French Boxing Champion there to see me. I walked down and met them, the Champ was asking for me to go downtown to the gym to box with him. I called Sgt. Sexton who was in his office and told him the Champ of France was there to see if I could go downtown to box with him, he stated you know I cannot allow you to do that, I said then call the Colonel since it's the Heavyweight Champion of France, it might make a difference. I then related to Sexton of what had happened with the telephone operator. I said the guy probably wants to kick my butt.

Sexton called the Colonel, and told him what was happening. Sgt. Sexton handed me the phone, the Colonel asked me one question: "Webb, do you think you can beat him?" I answered: "Yes, Sir." He told me to tell Sgt. Sexton to give me a pass and that I should call him as soon as I got back of which I thanked him and would call as soon as we returned.

We arrived at the gym, were met by a few boxing trainers one who understood English and we communicated very well. I told him I needed about twenty minutes to get prepared for our boxing main even, we laughed. Also I told him I needed some gear to wear, while he was finding the equipment I noticed that the Champ's sister had entered, I knew she did not want to miss this show, I nodded at her as she was sitting at ring side.

I geared up, jumped three rounds of rope, went three rounds on the heavy bag shadow boxed for about five minutes, had a nice sweat going and felt that rhythm beginning to flow, my body was moving very well, my hand speed and combinations were sharp and I was really feeling great, the Champ had finished his light workout, got in the ring and was having his head gear put on, jumped in the ring, got geared up, we both agreed that we were ready, the bell was rang, the Champ came straight out at me, instead of me meeting him head on, I danced to his right causing him to turn in that direction, as he did so, I fired three jabs, connecting with two of them, shot a right hand that missed, came back with a left hook that bounced off his head and danced out of reach. I noticed he had no footwork, most European fighters were the stand up, straight type of guys, however, a lot of them had good reflexes and head movement, we got in a few pretty good exchanges, I missed a lot of shots early on but after settling down, I was on target pretty much for the first round. The next round, I mostly just doubled, tripled, jabbed and moved getting out of the way of his power punches, whenever we had exchanges, I was hitting three to one, moved back then on the attack, sometimes five or six punches and when he thought I was going to retreat I would pivot and right back with the flurries again, I got caught with a few good head shots, however, I controlled most of the action, he was damn good and we were even going toe to toe at times, I was having fun, it had been a long time since I had boxed other than in Basic Training, it had to be about nine or ten months, so it really felt great dealing with him, the last round I pretty much controlled all exchanges, we had a big ring, so my footwork and movement was making him to set and reset as I would jab, set, jab, move, set him up to come in when he hid at times, I would step inside also get the combinations off and finish up with some deadly power punches at the end. I walked over to my corner, had the head gear removed, looked at the Champ's sister, her eyes were really wide open, she was impressed, the Champ came over and told me great work, all the trainers were all over telling me how fast I was, great hands and movement, they told me I must be Champ of America, and laughing and talking up the three rounds we put in, they all wanted me to come back, one guy wanted to be my trainer, they were really great people and I enjoyed myself tremendously. The Champ's sister and her husband came over and told me how they enjoyed the match, they told me to get washed up so they could take me out to lunch, we went to the Champ's father's restaurant in the middle of the town, had a nice meal, they told me, no beer or wine, you are in training and laughed, I did get a glass of wine, they drank more wine than them water in France. We must have stayed there for about an hour, I met his father and his wife, great food, then I told them I needed to get back to post. The Champ's name was Jan-new, he got everyone together and they all stated we want you here next Saturday, to do it again, I said fine, and we left for post. I arrived back, told Sgt. Sexton the Colonel wanted me to call him when I returned. The first words I was asked was how did you do, you think you beat him, I said, we had a very good boxing match, I gave him a lot of movement and fast combination, if I had been a little sharper, maybe so, it's been a long time since I actually fought in the ring, I think he was a little sharper than I was at times, but it was a great workout. The Colonel said, they told me you are really good, I asked the Colonel do you think I can go down there next Saturday, he answered we shall see, have Sgt. Sexton call me Friday, I said Yes Sir and thanks for the opportunity to box the French Heavyweight Champ, and hung up. I thought the Colonel must have been a boxing fan, during our conversation, he said he knew Sonny Liston, our Heavyweight Champion was from Philadelphia, I said Yes, Sir, he is from Philadelphia and I have met him once and that he was one of my favorite fighters. I told myself if he likes boxing he will grant me a pass for boxing Saturday. I also took the opportunity to thank him for helping me with my Court Martial.

I also found out that Sgt. Johnson had been relieved of his duties and was transferred to another duty assignment per order form the post commander, very good news I must say. The following Saturday I was granted a pass to revisit the gym, I was totally shocked when I got there, it seemed as if the whole town showed up, there were people all over the gym. I also had the opportunity to meet a few more fighters, we put on some exhibition, I was being treated as the main star, the French loved their boxing, I had the opportunity to visit Paris where they had a statue of the great Marcel Cedan, the smooth middleweight who had died in a plane crash in route to America to fight Sugar Ray Robinson for the crown. The following week my restriction was up and I started training in town periodically. I received a call from Sgt. Sexton, he asked me if I was interested in the inter-service boxing in Europe, I said I would love to, he told me to call the Colonel, I called, the Colonel said: "Webb, I am going to send you up for that boxing team because I can't have you boxing around beating up my MPs." He laughed, he said what do you think? I told him I would appreciate the opportunity to fight for the team, he informed me someone had enquired about me, he stated he would set up patrols to get me, up there that night we were like 300 miles from where I was stationed, he called for rendezvous points for each MP unit to set up, he told me, he knew I would be interested, for me to get packed and to be ready at 6:00 PM to make my trip to Ingrands, a town just above Paris. I was in the southern part of France, he told me I expect to hear some good things from you up there, good luck and I'll see you when you come down to get paid. We made it up to Ingrands, at about 11:30 hours, I met the Boxing Coach a SFC Holmes who checked me into the gym area, where all the fighters were, he informed me we would have trials tomorrow to see who makes the team, so get squared away and prepared for tomorrow, he also stated he was looking for a damn good heavyweight.

Sgt. Holmes got everyone up at 5:30 AM, we were on the scales, weighed in, dressed and on the road for a three mile run, got back, did some light exercises, showered and to the mess hall for breakfast, it's about 8:30 when we all returned to the gym. We were told to check the blackboard adjacent to the ring to see who we would be banging with for eliminations. There were six heavy-weights and about four to six at each other weight class. My first fight was against a guy named Edmonds, about 6' 6" 240 pounds, I weigh in at 218, 6' 2 1/2" Edmonds was one of the oldest there, about 30, I was 22 everyone else was in my age bracket, Edmond was pretty sharp out on the floor, the bag and his movement did not look that bad. We were first up. Pretty good three rounds of which I won with jabs attacks, movement and uppercuts and over-hand rights, he never moved his head, big target. I used lots of an-gles, I moved on to my next opponent who was Gene Strahand, a former sparring partner for one of the world's top heavyweight contender's big Cleveland Williams out of Texas, Sonny Liston had stopped him twice and Ali took him out in seven rounds. Stra-hand was all inter-service Champion for a few years, however Holmes wanted him to fight light heavy. Strahand was about 6' 2" 210 pounds, I was impressed with his foot work, prior to our fight we were scheduled to bang, first after lunch break. Strahand was inter-service Champion for a few years, he was about 27-28, re-ally a sharp banger with both hands. We got geared up, entered the ring, bell rang, we came out, got a few jabs, I shot a right hand out of position, he countered with two punches, left and a right that made me see stars the next punch I partially blocked, however, it caught high on the forehead, my vision cleared up as I fell back into the rope, he made two full sharp jabs, I spun around off the rope, shot and connected with a right over the shoulder, shot a hook to the head, missed my follow-up hook to the head and moved out of range, this cat was really good the three rounds were explosive and lots of aggression and strategies the cat could punch pretty good, he was a damn good banger and got my respect early on, good thing I had been working with the French men, he was really good reminded me of banging at home in Philly, each sparring ses-sion was like the main event, no one gave you any breaks, that's why Heglar stated if I can win in Philly, I can win anywhere. Heglar won the middleweight crown but refused to be called "champion" until he came back to and beat Willie "The Worm" Monroe and Boo-aloo Watts, both had beat him in Philly. He was almost beat a third time by Benny Briscoe, Heglar earned that title, those were some really dangerous fights, but he got the job done. When you went to the gym in Philly it was like World War III. We called Philadelphia the City of Brotherly Love and in the gyms that meant if your buddy was down you kick the shit out of him and every fight was Refuse to Lose and Be Second to None. I teach that old school mind set to all I train around Jersey today, everyone calls me Refuse to Lose, and if that works for me, it damn sure applies to all who work with me. No one can ever tell me he's better than me, he has to prove it. I made the team, the other two got eliminated. I was really having fun, in the service now, doing something I loved to do.

The Colonel was elated that I had made the team, we had various tournaments all over Europe, we fought just about every two weeks. I fought up in Berlin, Germany at the historic Olympic field where the great Jessie Owens wont he four gold medals in 1936. I fought a really tough guy by the name of Frank Mulligan who was the reigning All-Service heavyweight. I was the Com-Z Heavyweight Champion of the southern regions of France. We fought there in 1962 an awesome fight.

I lost by one point decision, it could have went either way, it was one of those knock down drag-out fights, I really wanted that one, that would have capped it all off, I beat myself up for a few days but got over it. There were some beautiful fighters in the military were really talented, most of them were pro caliber, all they did was fight, in special services. I later ran into Mulligan some years later, at Ft. Dix, he had retired there with a girl he married in Germany. I was stationed there in 1971, I was walking down the street, heard someone call my name, turned around, saw Frank standing there, he said: "I knew that was you, how could I forget that walk!" He turned to his wife and said: "Baby, this is the guy who I showed you the picture of in that Championship fight in Berlin." He stated: "Man, you almost took the title that night, that fight was really a thriller!" We laughed, he had retired and had opened a pawnshop in Wrightstown, adjacent to Ft. Dix, New Jersey. We went in to get his photo album and I flipped the pages to where the pictures of our slugfest were, that was 10 years earlier, he told his wife as hard as this cat was hitting, how could I ever forget, we talked briefly and I left the shop, finished my business there in town an reported back to Fort Dix where I had returned to after leaving Vietnam.

chapter 14

My Airborne Wings

Upon my return to America, I was getting assigned to Ft. Monmouth, New Jersey. I was there for approximately sixteen months when I got the opportunity to sign up for Airborne School, I was given a physical test, passed it, and was on my way to Fort Benning, Georgia. As my stepfather and cousin Jason I would finally get the chance to earn my jump wings. Fort Benning was a huge military base at the time of my assignment there, they were forming the Cav Air Assault Division, CAV, to ship out to Viet Nam in 1965. I was an E-4 in rank, training was going pretty good for the first week, mostly physical conditioning then advanced to landing tactics, then to jump tower, then it happened my encounter with a racist white Sergeant. We had a class of about fifty, there must have been ten or fifteen blacks there. All of our instructors for tower week were white, very gun-ho. We had just reported to the field for our first day of instruction on jump procedures out of the 34-foot towers. Airborne training is a lot of harassment and intimidating tactics, a lot of screaming and hollering almost like in your face type of situations, it was ok. I could deal with that part of the training.

This particular day this Sergeant was telling some off the wall jokes and using some of the class members involvement, told the class he was the toughest guy out there, then pointed to me, saying: "See that E-4? He's not tough!" He also asked a class member if he thought I was ugly, they guy was reluctant to answer, he told him: "If I tell you to say he is ugly, go ahead and say it, he's not going to mess with you!" He asked him again: "Ain't he ugly?" The boy never said anything, at this point I did not like being the butt of anyone's jokes, so I jumped up from my sitting on the ground and stated: "Look here Sergeant, I did not come down here to get messed with, I came down here to get this damn training, and get the hell out of here, and I don't think I want anyone fucking with me!" He looked shocked, as did his assistant, you could hear a pin drop at that point, he got a red flush in his face, he responded with: "Oh, you are that tough guy from Philly!" I said: "I am not that tough guy from Philly. I just don't want to be played with." Our class leader stood up, everyone else was still seated on the ground, before he could say anything, the Sergeant said: "Ok tough guy give me 20 push-ups, at this point he was trying to laugh himself out of a bad situation, they usually dropped you for 20 push-ups every time you made a mistake of their instructions. I told him I would give him a hundred I just did not want to be messed with, the Captain sensing things were easing up sat back down next to the Chaplain, said something to him, meanwhile I dropped down, I was really upset. I began doing pushups, I must have done about sixty when he told me to stay down in the leaning rest, I told him I could stay in the leaning rest all day, it did not make a difference to me. I must have stayed in that position for about five minutes before he told me to recover and take my seat on the ground. He was still laughing a bit, he said we try to brighten the training mood every now and then but specialist Webb won't allow us to have any fun, so we will get on with our training procedures. The class lasted about 45 minutes, we got a break and shortly afterwards we were formed up to run our three miles back to our barracks. We got back and was released for the day. A lot of the trainees came over and asked if I was ok including the Captain, I told him I really didn't enjoy that type of joking, he told me to hang in there if you want to get those jump wings pinned on my chest, he also informed me that those instructors could phase me out of the program with marking my progress report with bad marks, he told me to Lighten up a bit and let nothing stop me from getting those wings. I felt a little better after our talk. The next morning I was the third man in the right door or stick as they call it, I ran up the tower steps to meet that same Sergeant I had the encounter with the day before, his first words to me were: "Ah, here's that cat from Philly," I told him "No, I am not that bad guy from Philly, I just don't play games. He checked my harness and began attaching my backpack cables, swung me around, checked all attachments and told me to take my jump stance in the door, he told me to make a good exit on the count of three and to ensure I pull up at the end of the cable run, he smiled gave me a nod, he also ensured my feet were together and "Go?" hit me on the ass and I was out of there, had a good tight body and proceeded to the 250 feet parachute drop, we broke up into six teams for motivational purposes, we had some who were phased out because they did not have confidence enough to jump out of that 34 foot tower, it was as if you would hit the ground too quickly, so it was a mental thing, a lot of guys could not get themselves together, the 250 foot first jump was only completed whenever the individual dropped the yellow flag, which was the signal for the tower operator to release your drop chute, all of my team members made their drops, we had several guys phased out of our training company. The last week we made the required jumps, had the wings pinned on our chest, a very special moment, I finally accomplished my goal.

chapter 15

My Vietnam Assignment

I initially was assigned to the MP Company of the 82nd Airborne Division, Ft. Bragg, then reassigned to the 272nd MP Investigation and Security Combat Group, First Field Forces Camp Dermont, Viet-Nam, the most highly decorated Military Police unit in the Nam war. We were everywhere providing gun jeep coverage for convoys, village sweeps for POW's, operated POW Camps of captured prisoners, we assisted the White Horse Korean Division, supported the 101st Airborne Units as well as the 82nd, Conducted missions with the 25th Infantry, provided highway-security patrols along Route I, the main central region's main supply lines, up through the mountain areas, provided security for the First Field Forces Combat operational Mission Control headquarters. We were engaged in a major combat missions attached to the various combat infantry units throughout the operational area of the first Field forces Mission Control Areas. We were known as the Fighting Deuce, we had a unit who fought and supported each other regarding color or ethnicity, there were no black or white issues, we were all one under one damn good Commander Captain Stephen R. Taylor, a black man who took interest in all members of the Deuce, we never left on any assigned mission or patrol without a personal briefing and inspection of all gears and equipment as well as your explanation of what your responsibilities were and what role you played in the operation. He was a leader and molder of men, we respected him and would follow him all over Viet-Nam. He emphasized doing the best you could at whatever the endeavor or commitment was, never divided, fight for all, never leave the all and die for all, if need be and "we should always remember we, as soldiers are walking in the legacy of those men of valor who fought for pride, freedom, world peace and harmony. I had the following thoughts, their bodies lay dead and battered, their spiritual existence entered immortality, they never died, their souls just rose up and faded away in the universal galaxies of time itself, to regain part of the "ALL" from whence they came.

Viet-Nam seemed to be the war that cast racism aside, I saw white and black working together side by side, protecting each other, crying over their wounded and dead brothers, I saw unity in that madness, I saw the mental depressions and breakdowns, I saw a man shoot himself, the dead bodies, guts and body parts blown all over the place, I watched the body bags piled up to be shipped out, I saw those who lost their arms and legs, no there was no time for racism from these very courageous soldiers, there was not time for it, always on the move, always in some type of ambush or firefight and this madness lasted for eleven year, what business the most powerful country in the world was doing fighting eleven years in a country the size of Viet-Nam? Had we not learned from Pearl Harbor? President Truman used two of the most powerful bombs to end that conflict with Japan. In Viet-Nam it was as if we were fighting with our hands tied, as Frederick Douglass told President Lincoln: "Use your assets!" that case it was the slave, manpower, in Viet-Nam the bomb could have been used as early as 1967 at the Tet Offense in Saigon, it never happened. We fought in places were areas were "OFF LIMITS!" The Shell Oil and rubber plantations, Mobil, Shell all considered private properties, we got attacked from one of them and could not respond instantaneously. I was like Marvin Gay, I wanted to know "What the hell was going on?" There was the training of the Vietnamese soldiers to handle some of the battles areas we have secured, gain ground, turn it over to them, moved on, "guess what?" on the way back, Charlie was in control again! When it got tough, those Vietnamese soldiers were throwing their weapons down and fleeing the area. Same thing they are trying to establish in Iraq, it's been cases of it not working there. These vital lessons learned form the past yet America keeps deploying only to cause high death rates of our men and women there. Soldiers are refusing to return there for additional tours, some have committed suicide, some have personally injured themselves opposed to returning there, seems no end to this tragic period of time for America. The cost of living is outrageous, gas prices, oil prices, no jobs, poverty all over, people losing their homes, food prices high, jobs still being outsourced overseas leaving the very people who helped build those businesses on welfare. That was one of the most crushing blows to this country, outsourcing jobs, a slap in the face to the American workers, don't we make anything anymore here at home? One thing this Government is to maintain is jobs for its people, things happen when people do not get involved in their country's welfare, those things are actually what you see, the government of the people and for the people is not working in the best interest of the homeland at this point.

We continue to deploy to fight wars, all great civilizations or powerful countries crumbled, because of the abuse of the people they call upon to fight for their cause, however, it does not pertain to the little people, in wars small people suffer the most, read and check your history. So we continue to fight and downgrade ourselves and country, it seem as though we are seeking to build an embassy there, reason? At the moment there's no timetable for it to end. Viet-Nam, same situation, economy collapsed, no jobs and poverty and problems across the nation, now it's more of the same. WAKE UP PEOPLE! At this point you are your own worst enemy. We are reliving the Viet-Nam era all over again, I hope the end result is not the same. We could not even make a dignified retreat from that country, we left thousands of tanks, hundreds of planes and helicopters on the ground there, we had people fighting for spaces on planes hanging on the runners of helicopters when they were taking off from the embassy, one of the most chaotic military situations I've ever seen, and we, the soldiers took the blame for not handling and winning the war, we had our hands tied, yet we were held responsible for the outcome! We were trashed when we returned, we were called losers, killers, cowards, they spit and threw at us and until this day, I've only had two people thank me for being there. But we did make some changes, after a period of years, the Veterans Affairs established clinics and health centers to help Viet-Nam veterans deal with Post Traumatic Syndrome, PTS, which most of the troops are experiencing from their tours in Iraq.

I am still stressed from what we suffered in Viet-Nam, as I stated before, no nation really wins a war, their major casualties on all sides, in death, marriages crumbled, the mental depression, many will join the street people of today and there are thousands out there still yes, there's a need for change and I know that for certain.

The Viet-Nam era did unite the white and black divide to a certain degree, however, in 1997 we see racism and discrimination of the Common Foe in full force once again, I've seen no voted politician elected to our governing body of the country stand up to denounce this major cause of black people suffering in their struggle, to compete for jobs and all other equal entitlements offered to all others, including the illegal twelve million aliens still here in this country. The politicians who still have their blinders on when it comes to "racism" that cannot be allowed to continue, so watch who you vote for!

chapter 16

The Shameful Betrayal of Black Soldiers by
Gen. Pershing

France, Germany and Spain were really some beautiful
countries to have been to see and travel in. One of the best things
was that I experienced no racism form the people of those countries. Their outlook on life was totally different from the United
States and in every part of those countries. I traveled in they treated
me with respect and diplomacy in their restaurants, bars and clubs,
etc. Only time I, as a black man, ran into negatively was when
around U.S. military post or bars, where the white soldiers had
tried to encourage the owners of their establishments. To not allow
blacks in their clubs or restaurants, there were often racial fights between the whites and blacks, so the same old Common Foe had
tried to influence these good people to discriminate against black
soldiers however, in most cases they never succeeded in their ignorant endeavor. The same thing they did in the Revolutionary
War, Civil War, World War I, World War II, Korea and Viet Nam,
they thought they could take that racial attitude and implant it in
those places. They could not pull that off in France, there's a gigantic memorial erected there in Verdun, in honor of the most decorated unit to fight on that soil, the soldiers of the *369th* Infantry,
the all-black unit from New York. America never gave that distinction for that accomplishment, however, the French thought so
highly of the valor and courage those black troops exhibited, they
built one for them there, as I viewed that awesome memorial, how
proud it made me feel that these people who did not look at the
color of these black men who the American white soldiers refused
to fight alongside of. And what made this almost rebellious situation so asinine was that they convinced a General in the United

States Army, a Field Commander of all the United States Army troops assigned and sent there to fight against the German soldiers, that they were superior and too proud to fight with them. A field Commander is the ultimate decision-maker, he's the Commander, he had a chance to make change and he made one of the most idiotic decision ever recorded in that war, he was influenced by those white soldiers personal racial hatred, made a decision to separate the American black forces from the American whites. He assigned the whole black regiment to fight with the French, told the French to take the black troops and use them as they saw fit, the French put them in their uniforms, gave them weapons and trained and briefed them of the battlefield areas, assigned them a sector of terrain to deploy and defend, and until this day, they are still remembered and recognized as the highest decorated unit that defended their soil with their bravery and valor, the monument speaks for itself. Gen. Pershing was like Washington and all the others who were more concerned about their self-image, than making change for the better of our nations races. He was a racist, what a waste of stars they pinned on him, they called him the Supreme Commander of the American Expeditionary Forces there in France, Pershing totally embarrassed the President who is the Commander in Chief of the Armed Forces when he made a decision to give the black troops to the French when they arrived into their country, stating he had no use for the blacks because the white soldiers have been constantly complaining about fighting with or alongside of the blacks. Pershing let his prejudice and racism show, when he gave in to the white troops complaints, when did the voices of the white troops dictate such actions from the person appointed Supreme Commander, he was later ridiculed in a newspaper mocking his decision, it stated Pershing put the black troops in a hand basket, took them to France and gave them to the French. He was definitely not a MacArthur or Patton and I might add and also Gen. Emerson of whom I had the pleasure of being under his command in Korea, they called him, the Gunslinger, if anyone caused problems for his troops, white, black or otherwise, they were in big trouble, he made his soldiers fight as a division, and they learned to overcome most of their differences, as McArthur and Patton, they would have been committed to the war instead of some white soldier's inferior egos, that what commanders do. They went to France to fight a war not to bring their racist bigotry and ignorant discriminating white racist problems. I thought Pershing was one of the most irresponsible military commanders to ever wear the rank of General. They sent the *761st* Tank Battalion to Patton's Third Army in Germany, World War II, an all black battalion, he addressed them upon their arrival, welcomed them to his Third Army, told them of their mission, told them it was not their color, death has no preferences, he only wanted them to fight in his unit and be the best black tank troopers to excel above and beyond his expectations of them, it was not a white or black Third Army, it was the Third Army of "One for All" and "All for One." At the end of the war, Patton made a major contribution in awarding that unit for playing such a significant role in the amazing accomplishments the overall unit had made, and if you ever read the history of the Third Army under Patton, you will know why he held these Black tankers in such high esteem, he was a leader and molder of men and I commended him for handling his newly-assigned black troops the way he did, he made them welcomed, he made them feel needed, he showed them love and respect as he did all of the troops of which he commanded. He stated that heart, execution and valiant men win wars, not racist. NOTE: Pershing was also disrespected by the French Commander as well, at war's end he wanted to pull the black troops back from the French who would not relinquish control of them until they had a special ceremony, awarding them their country's highest awards by their government after they released these proud black men back to their racist counterparts to return to a still divided country. The monument was a very tearing time for me, it was erected at the base of a large burial ground with rows and rows of memorials built there. In America, the white officers in charge of the unit endorsed a recommendation for six or seven years, it never got done. There's an annual parade held in New York honoring those warriors, they were good enough for the French, but not in America. It's amazing that happens when people love and respect you, the blacks never got that love and respect from the whites here at any time, after fighting and dying in all wars ever fought on this soil.

Matter of fact after each war, blacks who survived were subject to lynchings upon their return home, many in uniform, this is the "Thanks!" blacks received for defending America's white man, his property, his families, his economic wealth he accumulated off their free labor, after World War I was over 252 black men were lynched.

I had a tremendous time in Europe, I traveled, met some very fine people, enjoyed boxing for the Inter-service Boxing Tournament, returned to my military police unit where I finished my tour of duty patrolling Braconne after being reassigned to the larger post facility, I found that many officers and regular soldiers were just as prejudiced as in state side assignments in Germany, France and Spain, there was certainly that mind set of the whites to influence bar and club owners not to patronize blacks, and I often found that whites would cause a divide, so the same conditions were established as in America, the hatred was full-blown, I saw it firsthand as a military policeman assigned to patrol town areas, other than that I enjoyed the people, cultures and the beautiful countries. I was in Europe for three years.

chapter 17

My Hero Who Set the Standards of Being a Black Man in a Racist Nation: Jack Johnson, The Destroyer of the Barriers

Jack Johnson was America's first black heavyweight boxing Champion, born in Galveston, Texas, 31 March 1878; he died in Raleigh, NC on 10 June 1945 in an automobile accident. In the late 1945 a poll was conducted, it named Johnson the greatest champion of all times. He won the Championship in Sydney, Australia on December 26, 1908 by dethroning the reigning champion, Tommy Burns. In 113 fights over his career, he only lost 8. The leading white heavyweights John L. Sullivan and Jim Jeffries refused to fight him, claiming that to do so, would sully the sports reputation, Johnson continued to fight superbly and gained international recognition which forced a deal to be made for him to fight Burns in Australia. He beat him so decisively that they refused the film to be viewed here in America; so much for the superior white myth. Johnson shattered that racist self centered idiotic belief that they were better than blacks. He took their hearts, tarnished their pride and self-esteem. No, they could not handle the truth, Jack had only just begun, destroying those very fragile barriers put in place in America. No, America was not ready for Johnson. The film could not be shown here in America, those whites had told their children and their women that blacks were beasts, not human, but animals, a Black man beating and manhandling a white man, even though the film could not be seen, some pictures were published. They told their children they were superior, now their children and women were seeing a black man whipping a white man as the black children saw their siblings, mothers and fathers whipped and lynched. This was not supposed to happen in America, whites had no answers for their women and children. What a feeble minded idiot to make such a statement. The pictures they displayed in many newspapers will live deeply embedded in their hearts and minds forever. Johnson standing over Burns, proudly displaying his superbly conditioned black masculinity, smiling, that picture spoke volumes for blacks who were constantly beaten by whites.

Johnson became a major black hero during that era. Johnson was not America's champion; he was champion of the world. Some stated, "he was one bad nigger." Johnson was a free black man, proud, flamboyant, educated, world traveler, respected in all other nations except in America, he raced cars, acted in several Hollywood motion pictures, was a matador in a few bull fights in Spain, writer owned a night club in Chicago, was a business man, dressed immaculate, was a charmer of women of all races, was married to two black ladies and three white women. Johnson loved flashy and expensive automobiles and loved speed, he just had fun and lived life to its fullest. Jack was a powerful man who would not lower his standards or be denied his human rights to appease the white racists and bigots, here in America. Johnson was well respected around the world where he developed strong bonds with many influential people in Spain, Russia, France, Mexico and Australia. How ignorant whites were to think they could break this prominent and powerful world champion who was loved and accepted worldwide. It would never happen. Johnson withstood major obstacles in his years as champion, an outspoken and defiant man who was against racial injustices bestowed on black people in this country.

It was a time when whites still forced their supremacy on blacks, when slavery was fading out and total discrimination and abuse of a race was setting in. Blacks were being lynched at random, children beaten, women raped all over the south and in the north as well. There were no jobs; blacks were housed in isolated areas of the cities and certain parts of the country, living in substandard houses, no education programs in many areas. Blacks were kept in servitude, like cattle on farms with no government aid to provide adequately for themselves. The government and politicians were so busy trying to ruin Johnson, that they lost their focus regarding aiding of the blacks, if they ever intended to do so. When Johnson was afforded the opportunity to fight and defeat Tommy Burns, a cry went up for the "Great White Hope." America just about forced Jim Jeffries, a former champion out of retirement to take up their cause. The fight took place on July 4th, 1910; it was called the Fight of the Century. It was held in Reno, Nevada. Johnson again shocked America, he totally destroyed Jeffries; he never had a chance. Johnson was a fine tuned champion, who displayed awesome punching combinations, masterful defense, aggressive offense and punching power, flooring the much larger Jeffries several times before they mercifully stopped the onslaught. The champion again showed the racist and so called superior bigots, as well as sending a message to blacks; if ever given an equal chance they could themselves succeed as well as anyone else, regardless of race, creed or color. Johnson was truly a pioneer for black people to look up to, he gave them hope, strength, pride and above all else, he showed them how to stand tall among your enemies and fight courageously for your principles, values and convictions. Jeffries was called a coward to the white race; how many making those statements would have had enough heart to even get in the ring, let alone fight that Bad Nigger, as he was referred to. Again I must salute Johnson for his accomplishments and what he achieved. During his fights, there were only a few black corner people in the crowds of over 100,000 people, most of them shouting threats to kill or shoot him, he still showed amazing confidence and maintained his focus and fought so magnificently, he was truly the master of his game. In these crowds were the racists and bigots who took part in inciting other feeble minded white, to lynch and kill and abuse black people in the many cities and towns after seeing Jack humiliate and soundly outclass their great white hope. No way was America ready for Jack Johnson.

America was infuriated with Jack, the black people had a hero, and whites felt threatened that they would rise up against them. Whites burned black towns and killed hundreds of people. No whites were convicted for any of these horrific crimes. Shortly after, it was released that Jack had married a white lady, the whites were up in arms this was the most important media news, it traveled coast to coast. The woman's mother apparently against the marriage, made a false report to law authorities that Jack had abducted her daughter. The lady, Jack's wife Lucille Cameron, came forth the next day and stated that she had not been abducted and had married Jack of her own free will and accord. This news really shook up the social esteem and moral for the racist whites across the nation. Cole Blease, governor of South Carolina was so mentally outraged that he made the most powerful statement regarding it. He stated that "conviction and severe punishment will be the consequences of any black man who puts his hand upon a white women," and he vowed such a marriage that had happened between a black man and white woman, was a total disgrace and embarrassment and would never happen in his state. It was also stated that laws were in place to have them imprisoned for the violation. It was stated that in the south "we love our white women, hold them higher than all things, and whenever anything comes between a white man and protection of the purity of the women of the nation and his state, he would destroy it in her defense, regardless of the final outcome." Another politician was so adamantly distraught in his vicious hatred of blacks that he stated "he would rather his daughter, be mauled and killed by bear or lion as to her telling him she lost her maidenhood to a black man." Where were Governor Blease and the other political figures concern for the protection of young black girls and women from being raped and from the sexual advances of white men? Not a single white rapist in South Carolina had ever been tried or convicted for his crimes through orderly process of courts during Gov. Blease's time in office. There were laws put in place in most states across America against interracial marriages. Most have penalties of being fined and incarcerated of both women and men. Many white women paid price along with the man they chose to love regardless of his race or skin color. There's been interracial marriage since the beginning of civilizations and dynasties in this system of things. There's nothing greater or more powerful enough to keep sexual and physical attractions apart. Love will always find a way in most cases, that's the way of life. How did feeble-minded racist bigots think they could control their white women? Another fragile barrier Jack Johnson knocked flat on its back.

Jack not only married one white woman, he married three. One lady was a rich to do woman married to a wealthy banker. She divorced him and married Johnson, stating that "Jack was the best man she had ever been with and that she would love and cherish him all of her life". No, America could not deal with Jack Johnson; he was one bad dude. The American government began a witch hunt on Jack, he was under heavy scrutiny, some state figures wanted Johnson killed, lynched, jailed or stripped of his Heavyweight title; however, the rest of the world was happy with their champion and would not respond to such inappropriate measures with America. They wanted him defeated in the ring. In Chicago, approximately 200 whites even hung a dummy of the champion in effigy. Pinned to the figure was a note which read, "This is the end of Jack Johnson." They were wrong. Again Johnson proved that the white supremacy and superior thinking white racist and bigots were only human after all, they were weak minded, arrogant, naïve, vindictive, irresponsible, extremely dangerous and hostile. What troubled times for Jack, the radio, newspapers and media made millions featuring him. Johnson never buckled under the social pressures and harassment, maintained his charming and flamboyant character and continued to enjoy life.

Finally, a well orchestrated trap was sprung. Someone contacted one of Johnson's white female traveling buddies, who had stated she had been spawned by Jack, to testify that she had been transported across state lines to work for Jack in a pleasure house. Jack was arrested for a violation of the Mann Act and was sentenced to one year in jail, while awaiting sentence Johnson left America, lived in Russia, Spain and Cuba. A title fight was arranged for Jack to defend his championship against Jess Willard in Havana, Cuba, April 5th, 1915. Allegedly Jack was to lose the title to Willard and be allowed to reenter America to see his dying mother and spend the one year in jail. Johnson lost to Willard by a 26 round knockout. There was a large controversy behind the knockout because pictures and film showed Jack lying on the canvas with both arms extended over his face blocking the sun, however, Willard was declared the Champion. Johnson later claimed he threw the fight in keeping with the agreed deal.

Johnson proved that white America could not accept a white man being beaten fairly in the ring, yet they could beat and lynch black men as they saw fit, they could not handle a mutual love affair, a black man with one of their women, yet they could rape and abuse black women, regardless of race, creed or color; blacks had a right to choose. Johnson's actions traumatized America so badly, that states north and south voted in Bills banning interracial marriages.

Fredrick Douglass, one of the most treasured Black America's spokesman, abolitionist, author, orator and defender of the "Right of Man," fought against and became one of the most powerful speakers for justice and human equality. He spoke out against white supremacy and the government for having left the black man deserted, defrauded, swindled and an outcast man in law, free, in fact a slave. Douglass, as Johnson, had caught hell from America from America for marrying a white woman and had to deal with the terrorist threats as Johnson wrote in 1884, "I could never have been at peace with my own soul or held my head up among men, had I allowed fears of white peoples popular glamour to deter me from following my convictions as to this marriage. I should have gone to my grave as a self-accused and self convicted moral coward." So as Douglass, Johnson lived by his own self morals and self convictions, and governed himself accordingly, like the old song I hold so dearly in my heart, "I did it my way." I read my history, I follow my boxing and also I followed the many tragic situations in America's racism and double standard, which still confronts us all. Douglass also stated, "We as Americans claim to be highly civilized and a Christian country. I fearlessly affirm that there is nothing in the history of savages to surpass the blood-chilling horrors and fiendish excess perpetrated against the black people of this country by the so called enlighten white people of the south." The charge of assault upon white women "he pointed out were only a new excuse to degrade the black man, and to pave the way for his entire disenfranchisement as an American citizen". He not only blamed the ignorant lower-class whites who composed the ranking file of mobs, but the men of wealth and respectability were the real cause of the mobs and its deeds. Douglass painted the picture very well, Johnson's parents who were highly spiritual people, took his blinders off early in his life, so he could see and prepare himself for his journey, adventures, obstacles and challenges along the way. Johnson returned to the United States after the fight, to see his ailing mother and serve his year in jail.

Johnson during the course of his life, refused to be dictated to or be denied his freedom of choice, regardless of the threats of tarnishing of his crown and his reputation. The champion won out in the end. Johnson, as I stated earlier, was voted the Greatest Heavyweight Champion of all times. Johnson received thousands and thousands of well wishers upon his return home during the train rides through major cities and parades in New York and Chicago. Johnson was a treasured gem in the boxing world as well as in his game of life. He destroyed the white supremacy and superior myths, that they were the chosen people and this country belong to them. He fought through adversity to achieve his goal in life. Johnson will remain far and above those whites who could not accept and respect him as a human being and champion of not only America but of the world. Jack was a hero not only to blacks, but to many whites as well. He proved to all if given a fair chance on the playing field and all other life dreams and endeavors, that you must be truly and duly prepared as in most cases you only get that one chance and then the door never seems to present that opening again. Only those who seize the moment and demonstrate all the God given talent they posses will excel to become Champions; enjoying all those tremendous rewards for accepting challenge and winning it all. Jack was a true champion for all the people, he left us with the above. There have been many Heavyweight Champions along the way, but none who deserve to wear it so proudly, then the colorful and flamboyant John Arthur Johnson. He was simple fabulous.

Amaze an Grace, how sweet it sound.
Jack Johnson knocked Jim Jeffries down
Jim Jeffries jumped up an hit Jack on the chin
An then Jack knocked him down again.
Yankee's hold the play
The white man say pull the trigger

But it makes no difference what the white man say
The world champion's still a nigger

Jack Johnson, one of the Greatest Black Heavyweight Champions of all times, was inducted into the International Boxing Hall of Fame in 1990. Jack continued to give boxing exhibitions well into his 60's and was involved in several businesses and other ventures before his death. Yes, the white supremacists, bigots, ignorant and weak minded Americans were challenged and defeated by one strong Black man, who shattered all their racial barriers. They could not harness his dreams. Jack showed the black race how to persevere in spite of the obstacles put in place for their demise. One of the greatest God given talents to us all, is to reflect back and remember the beauty of those who have given us strength and the fortitude to accept life's challenges and fulfill our dreams. We saw the film, Jack, you were one great and courageous man or as they stated "one bad nigger."

chapter 18

Educate Yourself and Your Children

People who continue to hate the Black race, have created a very tragic mind set in their children, they have taught them that blacks are inferior and should be sent back to Africa, and have no right to be here in this country. How wrong could these dumb idiots be! 99 % of this nation's populace who call themselves Americans come from other countries of the world, so that statement holds true for all, I am a black man and can say: "Go back to France, Germany, England, Korea, China, Russia, Iran, Iraq, or wherever!" These type of people are the uneducated and ignorant who have been indoctrinated into frivolous mind set, who do not know their history and are just racists, unaware of the major contributions blacks have made in this country. Believe it or not, blacks are the reason they still have a country that they think they own. I encourage them as well as all others to read their history especially black history that's been excluded from most of our educational institution's curriculum, read about slavery, the wars blacks have fought in, economic growth of the wealthy because of blacks free labor, the discrimination, the racism, the lynching, the injustices in court cases, the job and welfare programs, the inventions that blacks never got credit for because they were not white.

The first heart surgery at John Hopkins Hospital was performed by a white doctor and a black doctor directing the procedure. This black doctor later trained 200 other white surgeons to do this delicate surgery; their portrait now hangs at the main entrance of the lobby area of the hospital today. The Tuskegee Airmen, an elite Black World War II Air Force Combat Troop was phenomenal for what they accomplished in military combat aviation history. As pilots flying on escort duty for bombers, they never lost one, during their two years of duty assignment. This record was an outstanding achievement that has never been surpassed by any white escort group providing a similar duty. These skillful and great black pilots received 280 "flying medals" for such period of time in combat aviation history. I could go on and on of black accomplishments, your libraries are full of black documented history. Before you start judging people by their color, know who they are and what they have brought to the table and accomplished here, and you will learn not to utter those meaningless words so quickly. Those people who profess to be religious have failed to adhere to the scriptures which speak of controlling your tongue especially if you are not aware of the resulting embarrassment or harm it could bring to you and the others.

The truth of the matter is that this earth which we occupy for such a short period of time is God's, we are only here to maintain it, to teach and adhere to his wishes of love, unity and balance, however, the white Common Foe have been in a racist and hateful relationship with blacks ever since, who were forced here into slavery in 1640. Who can tell why? American life is now being a concerned for all, and that includes the blacks as well, to improve the whole universe. If your religion is not addressing that then you better seek your salvation elsewhere, because your soul is definitely lost and remains with those malcontents set to destroy this world we all have to live in, it's not too late for change, the door is still open, seek within yourself and you shall surely find that divine wisdom, and knowledge that can manifest the new you, where you can open your eyes to see where you can make a difference for the betterment, here and now.

Children are part of a phenomenal miracle, conceived in birth with God's love instilled within, that love is bonded with both parents, especially the mothers because they are the first teachers we inherit. Parents are responsible for nurturing their characters and structured egos, children are largely who their parents have programmed their conscious mind to establish distinguishing qualities of their personality early on. Parents' negative teaching to their children impede their psychological responses to life, love and hate, predicated on what they are taught to believe. As we see the whole world is in chaos largely because of love, hate, jealousy or wealth since the beginning of time. It's been that way. Cain killed Abel because of hate and jealousy. America is no different from any other major world power that existed in hate, jealousy or wealth, they were troubled and disrupted because they could not control these major factors of life. Countries fight among themselves because of different fractions, or ethnic groups that hate their fellow countrymen.

Hate consists of intimidation, jealousy, greed, selfishness, fear, superiority or inferiority complexes, and failure of the governing forces to address the concerns of all its people's problems which causes a divide among the people nationwide. The world exhibits these components, the world is all at war everywhere and is suffering in general with senseless vicious irresolvable disputes. Great civilizations have crumbled because of the hatred we are projecting to each other here in America.

This is not 1640 where black people were harmless and accepted physical abuse, one white man shouted: "We are proud to be white!" Well blacks feel the same way, they told America that in the 60's and 70's that they were black and proud. The Common Foe can hate as much as they wish, but they must not put their hands on or assault anyone. A white person wrote an article to a Trenton newspaper stating that the state should not apologize for the role it played in slavery, that the people responsible for it are dead. They may be dead, however they played a major role in teaching their children how to be racists, and that mind set lives on as we can see. I think someone ought to apologize to black people for the deeds done by racist whites of the past. We see the looks we get, we feel the hate, we know the past. We were in Alabama where whites bombed a church killing four innocent young girls, we saw 4 city blocks burned down killing 14 people, women and children forced to burn alive in the 80's, we heard of the police officers who rammed a broomstick up a black man's rectum. The world saw the 16 cops beating Rodney King on national television. Who was watching the banks, businesses and the community while these unauthorized patrols were partaking in whipping one black man's behind? We saw the Government turn back a boat of black refugees from our shores, not allowing them to land and seek refuge in this country, they were from Haiti, while there was a mass of refugees allowed from Cuba, we saw the Nooses hung from the trees and other places across America, we saw an 11 year old black boy chased down 3 city blocks and killed by a Korean merchant for stealing a two dollar sandwich and no one was charged, we read about the young man hung in front of his grandmother's house, the incident called a suicide, and case closed. So all these things happening today are madness and outright racism, this type of attitude had to be taught by the old of the past, to be continued on through this period of time, even when our nation is sending our youth off to Iraq and Afghanistan to protect and save the people, when there's no progress being made to correct this 340 year epidemic here. An apology would mean someone cares enough to step up and do it, no other race of people have endured that type of hate for those many years, it would definitely be a start to heal old wounds that lay, past and present. Respect for the black race has long been overdue for his contributions made up until this point in America.

God has blessed all mankind with **love,** yet man has found a way to tarnish that love with racial discrimination of others in this nation and world. A parent is the key to our hatred personality when they teach innocent children these despicable traits that have been destroying billions of mankind over the period of our existence. We in America find that the Common Foe has embedded hatred in white people from the very beginning of enslavement here, they taught their children that blacks were inferior, ignorant, were such subservient people, were 3/5th of a man, etc., these embedded teachings became a dynamic influence on their psyche, whites made blacks address their young children as Mr. or Miss, blacks were kept from reading or writing and not to make eye contact with any whites; a list of do's and don'ts were in place throughout their 250 years of enslavement. Blacks did not have to be taught to hate after years of terror, deprived of their manhood and dignity, it shattered psyche and emotions, resulting in gross resentment towards his captors, while they had to learn to suppress that hatred and even found themselves forgiving the white man in most cases; they forgive so strongly that when the country was losing the revolutionary and civil wars, blacks volunteered to fight with them, hoping to influence the white man to respect and free them, this never happened, most things still exist today as far as racism and discrimination are concerned.

Black people, despite all the hostilities and racial hatred endured, still believed in Martin Luther King's Dream, as a nation we can get to the Promise Land, as a nation we can accomplish our unity and harmony to reflect that change/that's so badly needed, especially from those who want to govern this country part of the Promise *Land* King spoke of is the land of which our nation's white house sits upon, where the politicians promised during their election speeches, they would honor the words they spoke out to us all, so we as a people united must hold these promises to be true, of their obligation committed to all the people and ensure jobs for all, affordable health plans for all, that our complete history is taught to all, to ensure all young and old know not to judge people for the color of their skin, but truly by the color of their character, we have been blessed to forgive of the past for the lynching, the murder and violence they afflicted upon us, we still represent this country with pride and courage. All you need is to forget your ignorance, see that it's a new day, a day in our lives that we have made change and the change is for the betterment of prosperity and the advancement of this nation, in spite of the forces that try to maintain the hate barriers at every avenue of progress, as the old Black spiritual song, My Country Tis of Thee, Sweet Land of Liberty, of thee I sing, land where my father, mother, brother and sisters have died, of thee I sing, let freedom ring for all the people of race, creed, or color. Let's defeat the discrimination, the racism, and overcome to do God's will, we are not responsible for our skin pigmentation or the color of our eyes or the texture of our hair, what you see in people of the world is what our Creator has given us, how great that is to be blessed with, it would be a sad day if we all had to look white in a land of billions, one thing I truly know is the beauty of the blend of people where they come together they are harmoniously grand to enjoy what they represent to the world, a total reflection of the ALL which we all are a part of, God is all things for all humanity. There's some really wonderful people of all walks of life who have been instrumental in seeking and supporting this effort and I appreciate their every effort. These men, white people, in my life whom I am very fond of played a major role in my young social life, in my military career they were there; our parents are the teachers, however, along the way we encounter social teachers, spiritual teachers to enhance our growth from an outsider's support, perspective, they taught me well, I've also learned from many other cultural people around the world in my military period, 21 years, the people of the world have much to offer and I appreciate all lessons taught and time they all have spent with me. As we progress to look forward at a totally different picture and perspective let's establish a more powerful movement to obtain all that is needed from our inner selves for the wisdom and knowledge to understand who we are, what our purpose of life is, and where we fit into God's most sacred plan of Peace and Love for the land upon which we live, and for all creations that we see and enjoy and to cast aside the trivial differences to love and respect all our brothers and sisters, our seniors, protect our youth, and save the babies as we embrace and share the love of our Creator and all mankind. We must always remember we are his greatest treasures on this earth and we must respond to that question I continue to propose to you: Are you strong enough and courageous enough to say...

I AM

The Time Is NOW.

chapter 19

The Ultimate Sacrifice that Earned Blacks their Rights to America's Civil and Human Entitlements

Blacks have fought and died in every war in American history, yet they are continually denied fair and equal rights, the nation is still plagued with discrimination, hatred and double standards.

War is the worse catastrophe man could ever embark upon, all feasible and rational safeguards, preventive measures should be pursued to their fullest extent to avoid this horrible devastation, where there's never a clear winner. All who evolve to participate in such disasters will forever endure a lifetime of injuries, loss of limbs with sustained emotional and physical trauma throughout their lives. They will remember the dead bodies of friends and foe, the bloody and smelly battlefields, the hollering and screaming of the wounded asking anyone to put them out of their excruciating pain and how they almost pulled the trigger to end their suffering, they still visualize the young and old people running all over the field screaming from wounds and burning skin peeling from their bodies in flaming fire and dark clouds of smoke,, running all over and yet never escaping the image of hell they were engulfed in.

The combat veteran retains the pain, the suffering and as hard as he tries to conceal the images, when asked, the tears would fall from his eyes that are the horrid mirrors of reflection of all he has seen and endured, he tries to remain in the moment of his sanity because he knows once he leaves that focus, the eyes reflect back to that bloody battlefield from whence he came, where he lost the love and enjoyment of his youthful years to become a listless individual who remains bottled up with inner pain and fear. The men you see wandering the streets, they become the thousands of homeless people we see sleeping in wooded area of our cities, sleeping under the overpass of our highways, the others are in our hospitals nationwide for their rehabilitation to learn to use their artificial body parts or being treated for the visions that their minds will not release them from. Thousands return home to their families only to be isolated from them because of their behavior, they are feared and no longer the husband or father their young children used to love, he becomes a villain in his own home, until a separation and divorce is awarded in civil court. These are the brave, patriotic young people of the nation who won or was defeated in a hellish and evil war. Many of my comrades in era of the Viet-Nam war never ever got a "Thank you!" for the role they played in a war of which we fought for 11 years and came home without a victory, no parade, no welcome home band or waiting arms, we came back and allowed to go directly home to families, only to cause a fear for our loved ones, we were called murderers, cowards, spite upon and verbally assaulted. I have continually asked myself: "Why?" Why were we fighting a war for 11 years, we had the resources to have ended it from the very beginning. I later understood that we fought a war with our hands tied. What a price we paid for that everlasting period of my life.

So as I stated earlier there never is a winner in any war that brought only sorrow and despair. The veteran support clinics were largely a result of Post Traumatic Syndrome suffered by returning combat troops from Viet-Nam.

The dead brave and valiant heroes lay in millions of grave sites in millions of places here at home and around the world, the known and unknown and there are those yet to be found who gave their lives to defend their nation's honor. These souls have paid the ultimate price for all entitlements promised under the country's democracy and obligations to all returning veterans medical and compensation welfare. These men and women fought for someone else's religious views, someone else's power struggle for fame and fortune, someone else's want for whatever the country's assets and resources, many fought and died from someone else's want of expanding their land, ideals and principles, they fought for those who wanted to rule the world and all things and we all know that will never happen, yet it's been that way since the beginning of time, the good book says: "There will be wars and rumors of war and it's been on point until this day.

These liberators in some cases were just naive young youth, thrust in defending or aggressively fighting for a cause they could never truly comprehend in their short span of life, yet millions died, many died, engaged in heroic valor, and there were those who demonstrated these patriotic elements who were submitted for these prestigious awards but never received that recognition. I knew a black hero, Medal of Honor recipient, earned it in 1943 and 1944, he was called in 1992 and received it at the hands of President Clinton, his name was Vernon Baker, 92nd Infantry Division. Discrimination in war and peace, will it ever end? There's thousands of cases such as these, however, blacks were never recognized or just did not receive them, incidentally the ceremony for Baker, also honored 6 other black recipients at the White House, I was so proud of him receiving that medal, it took almost 50 years, totally amazing, he wrote a great book entitled "The Price of Valor" where he credited a white Major who had pursued that award for him, just goes to tell us all that all things happen in God's time. Another reason for these acts of valor not being addressed was because the news reporters never covered the actions of the black units.

Those men of valor who died perhaps are the lucky ones, they never had to experience what the surviving veterans had to face and deal with, upon their return to America. Those returning home from the Revolutionary War, murdered, lynched and forced back into slavery. In the Civil War the same thing applied, even though Lincoln had signed the freedom emancipation, thousands of blacks who were let go from the military forces were either killed or recaptured, and forced back into slavery after the Union Army troops pulled out of the south. The old plantation owners regained control of those properties, as there were no jobs given to blacks, the owners would track them down and claim them from law enforcement confinement facilities, where blacks were housed in most cases for loitering in town areas, and many went back of their own accord in order to have a livelihood; they were left out and stranded, no jobs, no food nor housing. So for those brave men who returned, there were more of the same situation, after the Revolutionary War and Civil War eras. That Common Foe was still in command.

Let's take a brief look at our war years. I go back to the Revolutionary War: Here we see a war regarding land and resources much needed by the British, of which America refused to give up. Thirteen English colonies in this country belonged to Great Britain for about 170 years. For approximately 30 years before such span of time ended, there was a constant friction between the British Monarchy "Crown" appointed governors and the English colonists. In 1763 the British defeated France, who controlled a vast number of colonies in North America. At that point the British claimed all the land east of the Mississippi at which time the English colonists' rebelled and revolted against the English Monarchy. This war became the struggle for independence in order to free themselves from England's control, establish a self-government in colonial America. The British wanted more economic control of the 13 colonies where they maintained 75% of the export industry, tobacco, rice, indigo and cotton. Also included in their revenue was a sizeable profit from the slave trade. On April 18, 1775, after numerous rebel conflicts with American patriots in Lexington, Massachusetts, the war for American Independence began.

At the time of the war, the Black slave was considered the most valuable commodity of the nation, a war fought for slave profits, land, resources and control of commerce, these encompasses all we mentioned above and I add freedom, however, not for the blacks. Yet they fought and died for the white man's freedom from England, and to save this country for it to become the America it is today.

As we review our history we find that the black man played a major role in winning the white man's independence. Blacks have fought in other conflicts in America, however, the Revolutionary War was one of the most crucial one, which by right should have earned blacks their freedom from bondage, as well.

We all know how valuable the black slaves were here in America, the economy, the work force was the most important than anything else in this land, yet the black slaves were released from this labor force to fight and defend. So the slaves not only worked for nothing, they fought and died for nothing as well. Here we have a white race who claimed to be the superior race, calling on black slaves to fight and defend this country, many of white men sent their slaves instead of taking up the cause themselves, the black man designated to be the equalizer to accomplish the freedom from England.

We find that after 3 years of fighting, George Washington's forces suffered thousands of hardships and death on the battlefields, so much so that his field commanders were desperately pleading to him for more manpower, some of these commanders was General Varnum, Lieutenant Colonel John Laurens, Marquis de Lafayette, a General who fought for the American forces. Most of Washington's forces were grossly in need of bodies, Colonel Laurens wrote in 1778 that the war has become a dangerous situation because they were unable to raise the quota of troops for the expected on-going campaigns. His ultimate remedy to this situation was that the blacks reinforce the manpower, he was convinced that he could raise 3 to 4 battalions of negroes, that it was the most expedient in the present state of affairs and that the slaves were the most rational idea to resolve such situation. He went on to say: "I have not the least doubt that the negroes will make very excellent soldiers. Approximately 50,000 slaves fought gallantly above and beyond expectations to help secure the nation's independence.

They fought in the continental army and various militias, these slaves were promised to be free after the war, there would be certain stipulations which were: that the slaves would be classed in four general groups:

Slaves who had run away from their masters to enlist Slaves who had be sent to serve in place of their masters

Slaves who had been purchased by the government from their owners

Slaves who had enlisted with the promise of being freed at the end of the war.

However, when the war ended, there was a rush of masters who claimed back their slaves as properties in spite of the fact that these negroes had endangered their lives for American liberty, and for their freedom from slavery.

The war ended on October 19, 1781, the British surrendered at Yorktown. Washington determined that the slaves who served their country so faithfully should not be handed back indiscriminately to their masters. Accordingly, when petitions of their owners came to his attention, he ordered a court of inquiry for that justification. He reneged on the promise that they had believed in and fought for, only to set them up to pursue their case in a racist's court, hence, very few were set free, and all others were reclaimed and placed back in bondage once again. Washington who was later elected as President, refused to address the slavery problem in the "Land of the free," although he knew the blacks deserved to be freed.

So that check that Dr. Martin Luther King Jr. spoke of in his "I Have a Dream" speech, which he aptly called a check with "insufficient funds" was long overdue., Blacks have been duped with political false promises for hundreds of years, irregardless of how long they labored and died, fought and died. Yet we are still here struggling with lies and deceptions. Only unity, determination and holding our elected officials accountable to such promise will blacks in this country gain the respect and recognition they truly deserve to materialize. We must unite with all ethnic groups working for that goal of **equality** and **justice.**

Let's Keep the Faith! The Forgiving Black Souls Who Made Great Sacrifice for Freedom and Justice in America, Only to Be Denied of it

The humble abused slaves who were classified as less than a human being and laws were put in place to declare that they and their children would be slaves by the English colonists forever, responded to the call, to save a nation destined to be defeated by the great armies of the Motherland who had overwhelmed them. A great and ingenious field commander made one of the most important request of his Commander-in-Chief, George Washington, that would turn the tide of this nation's defeat into one of the most brilliant strategies, resulting in a major victory that changed the balance of a world power, to establish the beginning of a colonized country into an independent nation the United States.

They were brought here in bondage, empowered as slaves, branded, whipped, raped and inhumanely thrusted into a new world of terror and horrific physiological trauma, that would last for over 400 years. The place we know as America was established by refugees and immigrants sent here to build working colonies to reap the resources to benefit the growth of an empire, England.

Setting up in this new land were immigrants of various nations: France, Spain, Portugal, Netherlands, and England to gain profits from gold, silver, copper, iron, coal, cotton, rice, tobacco and other resources. These Europeans as in the African destruction of black civilization used the same tactics here. They came, befriended the country's indigenous people, the Indians, who were the original settlers of this new land, the Indians assisted Europeans when they introduced them to corn, potatoes, peanuts, tobacco, cotton, rice and other products and their ways of life and culture. Upon gaining their trust the Europeans then became their enemies who conquered and destroyed much of their culture and history. The same scenario played out in Africa. The European was a ruthless invader who enforced his savagery upon them around the year 1500, the great advantage over the Indians was the same as in Africa, the use of gunpowder, their writing, communication system and ability to fuse or melt iron, they also infested the Indians with numerous diseases, colds, measles, smallpox, syphilis, they were also introduced to the great joy juice, the whiskey which helped to weaken their thought process and demoralized them as well. As with the Africans the biggest downfall, was that their tribal unity, they became a divided nation, something America is going through with its black race, the Europeans indoctrinated the black slaves in bondage, causing blacks to mistrust and disrespect each other even to this day, here in America and other black nations as well.

The Common Foe has done his job superbly throughout the black world of which he has dominated for thousands of years. When they controlled African nations they hired or formed blacks to control and kill other blacks, which exist today in most of those countries, they called them mercenaries, hired soldiers, one thing we tried to do in Viet-Nam, in Afghanistan and Iraq, there's thousands of Iraqis trained soldiers who work for the United States, turning their weapon in, according to national media coverage, it did not work in Viet-Nam, a lesson we should have learned from that experience, at times they could not be trusted to fight against their own kind, if we didn't learn from the past, what does the future hold? The same scenario holds true here in America today, when jobs were outsourced placing poor blacks into poverty, the removal of the law enforcement in black and white poor neighborhoods which allowed the poor to vent against them who have to survive, allowing drugs to run rampant in neighborhoods without law enforcement, created the problems America faces today. With drug infested and unemployed people, there's a divide, some genius came up with such idiotic plan to remove law enforcement, how could that actually happen? I grew up in Philadelphia, where these gangs lived damn near in every neighborhood, unbelievable, no city with a reputation like Philly should be unmanned by police presence. I blame the city elected officials for creating the unsafe streets, the killings and crime that's happening there today, also the responsibility falls into the hands of the citizens who sat by and allowed it to happen. What we have is poorly trained cops and poor drug infested people, causing problems on both sides, WAKE UP PEOPLE, you need jobs and better police and law enforcement relationships in communities. There should be floods of people in those council meetings each time they have one, the Mayor's Office should be inundated with concerned complaints to correct those issues. I just had to write a little of what I see, as a major crisis in our city today. There's a challenge for every adult in those neighborhoods to get involved with the youth as well, as the police or what you will have is hired mercenaries who will be the judge and jury, as with those three blacks abused on national TV, what a negative reflection for a city to live with.

Back to the chapter matter:

We know how the Indians and blacks were dominated and divided, the Common Foe has dominated for thousands of years, as did the blacks when they reigned for a great period of time. No one rules, especially when there's a divide.

England became the dominant power in the new land and after the divide a lot of Indian tribes sided with England opposed to the immigrant colonies. The white man was enslaving the Indians who chose to fight and die than to become slaves. The first black slaves were brought to this country in 1619, the bulk of the slaves escalated up to millions by 1640. Slaves here in bondage were called upon to secure the independence from the British, how did that actually happen? An abused and oppressed people chose to respond to the call of battle for the same barbaric people who worked them 12 to 18 hours a day, called them animals, savages, not human and yet when the British were overwhelming and defeating them, they called upon these blacks who were deprived of their dignity, human rights, maltreated, terrorized, children as well. Only an act of God could this scenario play itself out. As God forgave us, these slaves must have forgiven these fanatics. The slaves changed the face of the nation. On March 29,1779 a committee in Congress did fully approve Col. Lauren's request to incorporate the blacks into the army to fight for the colonies. Over 50,000 blacks fought in that conflict, hundreds were killed by the same white racists when they returned home to their slave status, racism still alive and well. Approximately 100 years later, this country is divided over free black labor and control of its rich resources. A Civil war ensued, with the Union army suffering high degree of casualties against the Confederates whites, once again asked the blacks to help save the Union and unify the country. In return for their volunteer service they would gain the freedom, 350,000 slaves stepped up, to once again make a major contribution in saving the Union in one of the worse massacres of humanity on this nation's soil. Again, afterwards no freedom, no honor, only continued racism, discrimination and lynchings continue. As we see today, 2008, nooses are still being hung, the black and white issues still remain, in our Democratic campaign between Hillary Clinton and her black opponent Barack Obama, she stated that whites would not vote for him, what a racist and blatant statement to make, did she see the millions who had, blacks voted for her, why did race have anything to do with it, the Governor of Pennsylvania made the same comment in front of Philadelphia's Mayor, that whites would not vote for him, what do they see that I don't know of other than the color of his skin, it seems that will always be a serious issue here in this land of freedom and justice, there's millions of blacks and whites that refuse to accept the prejudice that keeps this nation, on these few pages reflect that in the case of the millions of blacks who stepped up regardless of the skin color of those who continued to harm them, they still fought and died with them in the many wars fought for the cause of defusing injustice and prejudice, we see them fighting and dying in Afghanistan and Iraq, white and black and all ethnic groups pitted together for survival, just take your blinders off, read your newspapers, the comments of racists, you see the injustice and racism everywhere.

If the white man really knew history and the contributions blacks made for them to enjoy this freedom they have today, maybe things would change, the past history, gives us so much to repent and acknowledge of our black race.

Forgiveness has been the staples of the blacks suffering here in all of these years, it was not religion, which has been the greatest cause of worldly conflicts, spirituality has been the major factor of overcoming and prevailing all injustice. Black free labor made all these wealthy dynasties throughout America, yet they refuse to resolve the question of reparations, they can never pay blacks enough for that free labor, they can never make up the job market which refused to hire blacks, or for the killing of innocent blacks who were exercising their voting rights or the education they were never allowed for over 250 years and it goes on and on, the lynchings of blacks without any court system ever convicting anyone.

Blacks lived in chaos and still do in this era, jails are full of innocent young black men, many are being released only because of DNA being tested upon the request of those true lawyers in search of the truth, there's truly some worthy white people who have assisted in revealing the truth for justice, equality and human rights, regardless of the color of skin.

I spoke of forgiveness, as our Divine Creator who has forgiven us, so should we forgive those who have harmed us in every way.

Only when a person who's in tune with him or herself have that power, compassion and wisdom to forgive, this is not religion, this comes from the spirituality of heart and soul which this nation's large family of racist does not possess. It seems that white people of Europe and other nations have a different perception of black people. I understand that millions of whites pray and worship a Black Madonna, Poland, France and many other countries, there's even word that the Pope does also, if that would happen here in America it would create a vicious racial outbreak of these religious white Americans, who do not want to know the real hidden truth. I have never heard of a black man being lynched in Europe, yet they hung thousands here for looking at white women. In other countries it's no problem, I was in Africa, white servicemen were shacking up with black women, never saw a white man hung with his genitals stuffed in his mouth, it's amazing how well blacks are received in many other white nations, France still respect the black man for fighting and defending their country, yet of all the fighting and dying for America, our place of birth all we see in most places is hostile reactions and prejudice, let it go, people, you will live and feel better for it, believe me. Today's world is not about wars, it's a spiritual era now, it's a totally different mind set for just about all knowledgeable people, if we are to succeed we must step up to a higher dimension and embrace the beauty and balance in our attitudes and character, they say "what the world needs now is love, sweet love" that's the only thing we should be thinking of, it brings harmony, the tolerance for understanding why we are actually here and that our purpose is to reflect through love, unity of one people, one nation.

Man has the power to manifest **all** things that he's capable of thinking, that's the power of Universal Laws, how far have we come in our individual love, **know thyself** and the windows of the mind and universe shall receive that Spiritual Love of which we seek, it all happens from within our hearts and souls, the love of the world is a negative one, one filled with hatred and despair that keeps the chaotic racism alive killing us softly, not allowing us to obtain that infinite wealth of wisdom and knowledge to embrace all the positives to achieve and possess the beauty of all things.

There's no substitute for our individual journey, it's mandatory for all life to embark upon, all hearts and souls have to be reborn, find that life's purpose, fulfill it and move on to another dimension, giving way for other new hearts and souls to reap the balance and harmony of all we have put in place for them to keep the Peace, Joy and Love, that are the spiritual elements of our enlightenment that are sacred requirements to traverse this system of things back from whence we came. One of the most crucial part of our journey is learning to humble ourselves and forgiveness, as those black souls who were forgiving, fought for their oppressors, the lesson is for all who came before us or will follow, we must be humble and forgiving to project our souls through the eye of the needle to see the Glory the Kingdom of God our Father.

The ultimate truth has been written and will reveal itself in its time, is it too late to influence people to correct this sinister attitude of racism today? Whites today have been taught they are a superior race of people and still look down on all black people as their ancestors did. There's no superior race of people in this world. The Germans thought and maintained that theory until Hitler's world was destroyed, the Africans ruled, yet they met their demise and many other countries could not hold on to their control of things either, all things must change, nothing remains the same. Superior people, smarter than all others, there are none, we see that blacks after being denied an education for over 250 years yet today blacks have intellectual people in all phases of knowledge, capable of competing with any race of people of this era. The white Common Foe closed down major schools rather than allowing 14 black children in them, what a travesty, refusing thousands of white children to attend their classes, seems to me if they thought they were that much smarter than all others, there would have been no problem maintaining that intellectual status. We see blacks as philosophers, astronauts, astrologers, astrophysicists, Nobel Prize winners, doctors, lawyers, corporate business men, professors, scholars, inventors, writers, journalists, TV commentators, millionaires, owners of newspapers and top selling magazines, Army Generals, Marine Generals, Air Force Generals, Navy Admirals, scientists of all fields of development, great singers, ac-

tors and sports idols of their games, blacks have been teachers of
the universe since the beginning of time, the antiquity of the great
Pharaohs during the Ethiopia and Egypt civilizations speaks of
their rule, their wisdom and knowledge, the powerful history has
been all but erased, however, no man hides God's creations and
knowledge forever, it's now therefore all to pursue, many of the
world's great philosophers were taught in the great Universities of
ancient Africa. I've seen and heard wise and knowledgeable people of all walks of life, Africa, Egypt, China, Middle East, Europe
and other nations of this planet, there's always something new to
discover from others, no one people own all the knowledge of this
universe or controls all levels of intellectual growth or concept.
There's only one source who sees all and knows all and that universal knowledge and wisdom resides in us all and as we journey
within our hearts and souls, we find the true meaning of our purpose here, at which time the Creator allows us to see and reveal
the intellect of which we need to accomplish our task of life. We
all have the capacity to receive that of which we need to succeed
at whatever our endeavor may be, we are God's greatest creation,
given the best learning system ever made however, we all bring
something to the table in various fields of intellectual knowledge,
there's always room to learn from something or someone, somewhere, somehow, so unto those Common Foe who think they are
superior, keep searching and some of that hidden knowledge people have been trying to hide for thousands of years is going to kick
you dead in the behind, you have been kept in the dark too long,
but it's all about to be revealed, so get ready for there's a change
a coming, it's going to do one or two things, make you hate black
people even more or give those forgiving black souls who made
the ultimate sacrifice to help save the nation upon which we stand,
that in itself will make you tremendously enlightened of your new
role of negating the racist discrimination and embrace the love
and respect for your black brothers, who are still forgiving for the
unity, harmony and balance of the land of which we love and cherish. Again, I say all men are created equal under GOD and for one
to set himself on a pinnacle is absolutely absurd, we are all His
children in this world.

KNOWLEDGE and WISDOM are the ONENESS of ALL where FREEDOM, JUSTICE, FORGIVENESS and LOVE is shared by THE WHOLE.

The Contributions of the Valiant and Courageous Black American Servicemen, "Second to None

As a combat veteran who has experienced the heat and chaotic casualties of the battlefield, I know the painful trauma and psychological effects of it, the mirror of horror never seem to fade away, it's a constant reflection that the courageous, valiant and heroic brothers, of thousands who have fallen to their death or wounded who have left their blood, guts and tears on the soil of America and around the world, at large. American warriors have the distinction of engaging in far more wars around the globe than any other nation that exists today. Dominican Republic, Nicaragua, Canada, Haiti, Japan, Korea, Kuwait, Viet-Nam, Europe, Cambodia, Afghanistan, Iraq, for such a young country, America became very powerful in a short span of time also became land hungry for expansion of its territories. The worst conflict involvement in America has been Haiti who won their sovereignty from the French and U.S. in a rebellion in the 1600s and Viet-Nam where they won their conflict with the United States and the sovereignty of their country. The U.S. has open marketing with Viet-Nam, however, refused entry into the United States of Haitian refugees, turning them back to raging sea waters on numerous occasions, but allowed Cubans to come ashore and establish their citizenship within one year. The Haitians are still refused entry into America and sanctions by the United States still remain in place since the President Clinton era, why the racist double standards, a nation trying to influence its leadership around the world, continues to step in its own muck, continuing to hold onto its ego idiocy from their involvement with them in the 1600-1800 era, this small little country is being deprived of food, while America sends it elsewhere to various other countries in distressful situations regarding food aid. World leaders lead by example, If America can forget Viet-Nam,, why not Haiti where no American lives have been lost since the 1600-1800 era? Rwanda, Dufar, black countries in Africa, people killed by the millions, yet no help from President Clinton or by the administration presently in house at this time. If we are to be leaders less not show any discrimination in obvious racism. We as black soldiers and military servicemen have fought for all other ethnic groups, yet have failed to support black nations as well.

A very important fact is, that black people here in America, still look for equal justice of which it provides for all others. I can imagine how black slaves felt after being asked to volunteer to fight, after being enslaved for over 150 years under extremely murderous and horrible conditions. Being asked or forced to volunteer, because in so many cases the owner sent slaves in place of their children or themselves, to help defend the very fanatics who were being defeated by the British. The same effects I still possess after 45 years, had to project those travesties to the forefront of their minds, manifesting these horrid images of insanity of their fragile mind, causing their grieving souls to reach the torrid emotional point they had learned to submit to over the years to retain their composure. Or else they would be battered or lynched for the very thoughts of what has tormented their very souls, while being held captive over the years. Some, they found a way to deal with their inner spiritual forces that seem to make them understand the role of a forgiving man, who continually listened, as the voices told him all things will in due time, change.

The slaves had developed the power of Now, their spirituality connected with the Divine laws of life allowed them to endure, persevere and overcome the tragic past of which they had suffered through. Living in the moment which existed at that very instant, enabling them to close out the yesterdays and deal with the immediate power of the moment, that in itself was courageous and powerful, it enabled them to accept the challenge of Now, for the vision of change.

Between fifty to sixty thousand black responded and made a major contribution in defeating British for change. When we read history in its truth, factual form we see that these black men of valor made a difference between victory or defeat in two major battles: Bunker Hill and Breeder Hill where they fought, which was the deciding cause of the British surrendering. Peter Salem, a Black man became one of the first heroes for killing one of the British leaders, Major John Pitcairn, causing the British to retreat in their quest to conquer Breeder Hill. Crispus Attucks, another black who played a major role in the Revolution, when he rallied along with approximately 50 whites protesting the British troops guarding the Custom Commissioners, his actions was hailed by the American patriots as heroic and the main reason that sparked the Americans to revolt, a monument was erected honoring him and four other white martyrs in Boston Common in 1888.

As American fighting men we took our sworn Oath of Allegiance to this country to defend and protect it, its people and government of which we serve, for freedom and justice for all. This has not been the truth, only part, that was. I fought and defended, however, returning I found no equal justice as of yet for efforts we provided to secure these very important entitlements of which all other ethnic groups enjoy, why not the black man? History shows these black slaves fought and made a tremendous difference in all conflicts, yet foreign people migrate here and are classified as citizens, reaping the rewards of freedom, equality and justice - we saw not. Our cemeteries are full of blacks who earned the rights to enjoy this country as whites do, no other race has fielded more combat soldiers defending America than the black and white on the battlefields, other ethnic races began fighting in large numbers in World War I, so when you speak of who made this country, it's the black and whites, they were the major role players in the Revolutionary War. Blacks are still referred to as 3/5th of a man, and our voting rights have to be renewed every 20 years, that's ridiculous! The 12 million Mexicans who violated our immigration laws and borders will be full-fledged citizens and have complete voting rights before blacks, born here, fought for, died for the country, get their just dues! Until the Constitution is ratified or amended, it will remain soiled with the blood and guts of every black man who has died or fought for its unity and freedom!

Slaves were brought here to provide free labor, building and working 18 hours, 7 days and only to be abused and unappreciated for doing so, then when the white man's colonial and civil wars were unwinnable, they came to seize the blacks to take up their cause, if, as they say, this is their country, they should have won those wars on their own. Once they allowed the black man to share in their struggle for their freedom, then the Black man has an invested interest in that which they fought and died, not only on the battlefields, but those who returned, got lynched or murdered paid a price as well. This country owes a debt of gratitude of which they have never paid, when those issues are resolved, maybe we can be respected as a world power, where the rest of the world can see that we, as a nation have righted the wrong against a black race, who we thrust into battles they should not have fought or died for, if in fact they could not claim America as their own, as whites do!

There have been many wars and conflicts of which blacks have been a key part of. I write about a few contributions which encompasses thousands of told and untold stories of the glory of thousands who tried to make a difference in the mind set of the racist people, in a new and developing nation that had faith to change their lives from the turmoil of such a powerful and negative discriminating system, they gave their love to this country, fought and died for it, hoping to change the evil white man's concept of them, they in their efforts became the blessed, because in spite of the circumstances, they showed and demonstrated their humility in the eyes of our Creator with the hope that one day this hateful white man would truly see that Love will, in time, conquer the evil that exists. At this point we have seen no change from the 1619 to the 2008, however, things does not take place in a time period of which we live, for all change manifest themselves in the Creator's time, these valiant men and women who have suffered on this continent will someday be remembered for their deeds and accomplishments, in time, it will reflect what they endured and gave for the change they paved the way for, however, will never see through human eyes for they will be blessed to see it from afar, I thank these mortal souls both black and white because, there's been faithful white people who have given their lives in assisting blacks to overcome their dilemma and still sang "My Country 'Tis of Thee, Sweet Land of Liberty, Of Thee I Sing."

Black contributed to the Declaration of Independence, the Spanish-American War, the War of 1812, then years later became part of another gruesome war of conflict between two white factions of men who tried in their ignorance, greed and hatred of one another, fought one of the most telling factors about their barbaric savagery that damn near destroyed each other, and we thought they only hated Indians and black people, they didn't 't even like each other, so what did they do to further kill their own kind, they came to the black man to assist in killing of their own white brothers. The white man not only tried to kill all of the Indians, he killed and damn near worked the black man to death, yet he had the audacity to seek out the black man to assist in his ruthlessness killing and butchering off his white brothers in a Civil War.

The white man, since the time of enslaving blacks here has showed the world of his evil savagery, his murderous inhumane, violent, ignorant, merciless and cruel and offensive bastardly ways, came and asked the black man to assist him in his killing fields all over this country. As we see in the history of the country, the white man has always been the villain, he came here killing Indians, enslaving blacks as well as murdering and lynching, raping and abusing and yet he came to seek their help in killing his brothers, the Cain and Abel of this garden of evil. The blacks and Indians learned a bit from this individual, he taught them the savagery of crime and hateful elements of wars, that embrace our nation's streets and communities today. We saw them beat and damn near killed a Rodney King, 21 cops in play, here recently beat and abused three unarmed suspects in the Philadelphia streets under the guise of law enforcement, all of these, mentality stems back to the Indians and slaves who were killed and tortured for decades in this country and they call the same people they taught to kill and destroy, animals, they taught that mind set in their quest to rule this country, even if it was to kill their own kind to do so, they made killers of innocent slaves and created that murderous mind set we see that exists today, amazing how they fail to take some of the blame for the past and present, I only see racism contributing to the elements that keep us separate instead of uniting to resolve ethnic problems and improve our harmony here and now.

Two hundred thousand blacks fought in the Civil War, boosting the much-needed manpower to help defeat the Confederates who were overwhelming the Union armies because of troop strength these black soldiers served above and beyond expectations in all battlefields, 16 American black men were awarded the Nations' Medal of Honor.

- The Indian War: 18 black soldiers were recipients of the Medal of Honor serving with the 9th Cavalry, 24th Infantry and 10th Cavalry of the Buffalo Soldiers.

- Spanish-American War: 5 black soldiers were awarded the Medal of Honor serving with the 10th Cavalry.

- World War I: Medal of Honor awarded to a member of the 371st Infantry.

- World War II: 7 Medals of Honor awarded to members of the 370th Infantry Regimen, 56 Arm infantry Bn, 366 Infantry Regimen, 413 Infantry, 761st Tank Bn, 29th Quartermaster Regimen, 614 TD Infantry.

- Korean War: 76 Medals of Honor awarded, 24th Infantry Division.

- Viet-Nam War: 2 Medals of Honor awarded, 501st Infantry, 22nd Infantry 3rd Marine Recon. 69th Armor, 17th Cavalry, 27th Infantry, 16th Infantry, 4th Cavalry, 5th Artillery, 60th Infantry. 16 Medals of Honor awarded to United States Naval Personnel.

There were thousands of blacks who earned Silver Stars and Bronze Stars for their heroic efforts in all branches of services during the Viet-Nam era, there were also many who never received these prestigious awards from all wars fought because of Company Commanders and other racists in the Chain of Command who denied these brave soldiers of their just due.

1966 Viet-Nam, I was the Platoon Sergeant of 3 Bronze Star Honorees, one of whom I stay continually in touch with, I first met him upon his arrival to my Military Police Company, a 17 year old white kid from New Jersey, the fire and adventurous look in his eyes, who went on to serve valiantly, defending against the enemy with valor and courageous tenacity. I saw him grow from his "infancy" as a young warrior to an seasoned combat veteran, his name, Ronald J. Raccioppi, a man of whom I appreciate and hold in high esteem, I've since met him again after 41 years, a family man with a wonderful wife JoAnn, two great sons and a dog, Nitro, that's in his shadow every step of the way, a business man and great asset to his community and the world at large, a person I love and respect, and will always share and be a part of the Fighting Duece, 272nd Military Police Company, the highest decorated MP Co. of the Viet- Nam War era. I salute them as well, especially Col Stephen R. Taylor who was a Captain in Nam, our courageous leader and role model, he exemplified the "Be Prepared and Be Second to None," Thanks for your support, Ron!

Up until the First World War era there were not many motivational black figures to look up to, there were lots of lynching of servicemen returning home, there were several riots in various cities where whites did not want blacks moving into their neighborhoods and competing for jobs. The military had very few blacks serving, yet along with the white soldiers blacks were engaged in the Dominican Republic, Haiti, and Nicaragua conflicts, after these wars were over most of the black soldiers were released. Many fell on hard times in areas where poverty, racism and discrimination existed, Jack Johnson was a role model and inspiration for millions of blacks, he had continuously questioned racism and not allowing blacks to be hired, Jack told the white racist, that if they gave blacks jobs, they could accomplish any task given to them, he also told them to make the playing field even for all, he would also tell blacks to pursue their dreams and when the door opens, be prepared to take care of business. Most whites hated Jack for trying to inspire blacks, never to give up inspire of the racial barriers, Jack used his life as a role model, he pursued his dream for eight years, before given that opportunity and winning the Heavyweight Championship of the world. The journey was tough, however, he kept himself in shape by fighting as often as he could to be totally prepared when the opportunity presented itself. An image of strength and character coupled with courage, pride and dignity who possessed a powerful personality and Refuse to Lose winning attitude, a man who told America whites who thought they were superior to blacks, that blacks could accomplish any and all things if given the opportunity. Jack was the hope and pride of the blacks during that era.

Jack beat up so many white contenders, that the whole nation was seeking a great white hope to defeat him, it was embarrassing to the white Common Foe who told their children and all others that the white was superior to blacks, then all of a sudden this black man showed up and beat every white man's behind for ten years, the whites had to be asking: "What the hell was going on?" Jack would be smiling, joking, dancing and prancing and totally outsmarting, outclassing and just proving he was the baddest nigger on the planet. A search was underway to find that superior great white hope to save face of the white supremacy, their children now began to see that they were lied to, and discover what they were told just was not so. We further see as did they, what a powerful force he was. Jack damn near killed their great hope, the police had to save that poor individual from being totally destroyed. The police jumped in and stopped the massacre. The white people was so frustrated they resorted to lynching innocent black people that very day.

Nobody rules this country or world forever, however, if you have a good system in place that provides for all of the people you can stay around longer, people only want to be respected and treated fairly that's the key to harmony within a nation, bad leadership and decisions are responsible for our nation's shortcomings from the top down, it needs to change, old systems and people who make policy need to move on, for someone to remain in one position for 5,10,15 years holds up new ideas and procedures, nothing is meant to be around forever, even the cells of our total being need to move on so new cells can replenish our system, the same holds true to the nation and universe. The white man continues to show different forms of racism, but it's just as deadly, when people don't

speak up against the charade being pulled over your eyes, then the
results is jobs being outsourced to other countries, neighborhoods
being torn apart, filthy streets and policed schoolhouses, no law
enforcement in your neighborhoods that allowed drugs and crime
to manifest themselves Millions of people here against our border
policies bringing in drugs, all of our family members being sent
off to wars around the world, jails full of people that's being
snatched off the street, hospitals closing up, no new jobs to replace
the outsourced ones, nooses being hung, blacks and Hispanics and
poor whites fighting each other while the old elected officials continue to sit and allow things to happen not in the best interest of this
nation. We must open our eyes to change for better leadership now.
We must have leaders who are willing to lead. Al Sharpton should
not have to come to Philadelphia to protest a beating of a black
man in the streets, leaders should contact their city officials as well
as their congressmen to address issues in a timely period of time,
thing is adults have lost respect from their children who see them
sit there and do nothing when major issues need to be addressed,
the church pastors need to respond as well, we are only the way we
are because of our own divide, Jack Johnson spoke out for 10 years
in spite of threats, he responded, this nation owes you a source of
income, not to take your jobs away, the wealthiest country allows
an overcrowded populace with no jobs, welfare is not the answer,
believe that, you see the conditions all around, all over, it just is not
to be so, where is your Jack Johnson? All history happens for a
reason, it reflects the problems of the past that should not exist
today, Wake up, people! You're sleepwalking!

On September 1915 a call for a draft of blacks into the armed
services was made in preparation for a possible conflict with the Al-
lied forces against Germany, in 1917 America entered the war and
again blacks played a major role in Europe, 367,000 blacks served
in mostly combat roles and again proved their patriotism and love
for a country they had learned to love and honor. As my stepfather
had instructed, I read about Johnson, he was God-sent, to take black
people to another level of their spirituality and black awareness, no
one could have been more positive for blacks, who were still in a
wilderness, seeking to find their way, to make positive transition in

a white nation of hate and despair. No man could have been more influential, a world Champion, that was loved and respected around the world, he was the catalyst for change of a black race, who excelled in all avenues of endeavor of that era, a pillar of strength for a people, who though free were deprived of their voting and equal opportunities and freedom as whites in this country.

The country had come out of a very tragic Civil War dilemma, where whites tried to annihilate their own race of people, where their ignorance and jealousy of each other had to once again call upon and incorporate the services of blacks who were still abused and socially deprived of the free entitlements to help fight in Europe for the freedom of oppression, another white man's war.

World War I found a different type of black man, who was ready to accept the challenges to make change, they no longer held their heads down, they exhibited a new mind set to pursue their rightful place in this nation. Great contributions Second to none.

369th Infantry
"The Hell Fighters"

The 369th Infantry Regiment out of New York was the first major black combat unit sent, they were called the "Hell Fighters," they distinguished themselves by being the top performing combat unit of the war. World War I was the largest combat conflict that was fought in the history of mankind up to that time, the result was enormous mass destruction of property and lives, to a large degree the fighting took place in long stretches of dug-in trenches for miles across the front line battlefield zones. They became muddy, cold and filthy, rat infested hell holes, where men were exposed to poisonous chlorine, which was used extensively for the first time in any war, incidentally the gas mask credited for saving thousands of lives, was invented by a black man. The soldiers of the 369th spent more time in trench line warfare than any other unit and performed historically under inhumane condition setting their goal of excellence under such horrid conditions. These men were determined to show their mental and physical strength and fortitude, these elements were the deciding factors in their battle of not only fighting in the war, but also to the idiotic irresponsible military commanders who chose to assign them to the French and to those unappreciative white Americans who continue to believe they were better than other human beings.

The men of the 369th never could understand why a General Officer would make such a decision, in doing so, he allowed the white enlisted soldiers to carry their racism onto the battlefield. On the battlefield all things were made even and they proved to Gen. Pershing and racist so called elitists that the very words Jack Johnson, had told the nation: "Make all things equal, and the black man could accomplish anything a white man could! They proved that they were 'Second to None.'" The unit returned from France and marched down 42nd Street after receiving recognition from America's Commander-in-Chief Their march was very unique in that they were the first Army unit ever to march in a 16-man front, a French ceremonial formation, a very proud occasion, they gave black people something to be proud of, they marched so magnificently, strutting in harmonious cadence to the musical rhythm being played by the band, the highly precise movement by one man reflected by all simultaneously, they marched erect, shoulders back, chins tucked in, arms swing 6 to the front 9 to the rear as they approached the reviewing stand where the command was given: "Eyes right!" with the snack of the neck and a twist of the head all in unison, as the bearer lowered the colors a review stand, the black as well as white people just went wild screaming and hollering for these gallant men who were the new heroes of the day for all to see, they gave their all to receive the very best. The very scenario of which the senators tried to prevent, materialized on that day in New York City, the Black soldiers arrogantly strutted and performed like no other unit in that parade, they were the chosen few who earned their just dues, and received their deserved and rightful appreciation from black and whites, especially to the black children who call them their heroes, the 369th were prepared and was "SECOND TO NONE" on the Battlefields of France.

Unfortunately things were not that great for thousands of veterans returning back home, they faced hostile and often violent receptions, hundreds were lynched, the Ku Klux Klan killed many across the nation, riots broke out in major cities, one of the deadliest was in Chicago, 23 blacks died, 15 whites and a total of 520 wounded on both sides. This wave of violence effectively crushed black hopes for social advancement. A city official in New Orleans told a group of returning veterans: "You niggers were wondering how you are going to be treated after the war, well, I'll tell you, you are going to be treated exactly like you were before the war; this is a white man's country and we are expected to rule it!" Many veterans were lynched in uniform. The reflection of those days exist today, whites who think they rule have resorted to hanging nooses, as our brave military personnel are being killed and wounded in Afghanistan and Iraq, it's totally ridiculous, racism is the reason this country will never rise to its ultimate influence as a world leader in this new era, of a totally different intellectual and spiritual mind set Our Black soldiers of World War I in spite of their treatment, have added volumes to an American Black legacy to our archives in history, that will reflect what they have accomplished and achieved, the standards they established for our young children to cherish and always remember to be proud of the progress they have made inspire of the turbulent journey of racial discrimination, murder and abuse, they overcame by their strength and fortitude this history is very vital for our young children to cherish and always remember to be proud and realize they are very special in God's world.

chapter 20

World War II and the Tuskegee Airmen; "They Flew Above and Beyond the Call of Duty."

A large majority of blacks were selected to once again answer the call to military combat in Europe, Pacific areas, Asia, Japan and North Africa. Again blacks assisting in the freedom and oppression of other ethnic people of the world, when right here in America the racism, lynching and murders against black Americans was still going strong, segregation, Jim Crow and no justice. Black servicemen were refused service in white restaurants, 16 black officers were refused service in Fairfax, South Carolina, at which they shouted:" Go to hell and Hi, Hitler!" in a California restaurant a fight broke out after four black servicemen were refused service, Frank Peterson, a Three Star General and a pilot was arrested for impersonating an officer trying to enter a Base Air force Club, charges were dropped the next day. There were racial conflicts against blacks in uniform by whites in 47 American cities, including Mobile, Alabama and Harlem, the worst being the riot of the war took place in Detroit 25 blacks and 9 whites killed. I was denied service in a white restaurant in South Carolina in uniform in 1961, Muhammad Ali was refused service in Louisville, Kentucky, Black poet Langston Hughes posed trenchant questions for American society"

Look here, America What you have done Let things drift until the riots come Yet you say we're fighting for democracy. Include me? 1 ask you this question cause I want to know how long I got to fight Both Hitler and Jim Crow.

Yes blacks stepped up again and racism stepped up as well, the great Joe Louis was the World Heavyweight Champion who coined the statement: "God is on our side, you can run but you cannot hide." when asked about the war, Joe was instrumental in getting the military to disintegrating military bases, their bus system, mess halls and living quarters of barracks, as Johnson, Joe was a black role model for blacks across the nation, joined the Army and helped increase the black volunteers enlistment program.

Another important volunteer draft was put in place, a program for blacks to sign up for Tuskegee Aviation program to see if blacks could actually learn to fly airplanes in combat situations. The program, however was not totally backed by elected officials of Congress, where the Common Foe also reigned and stayed in the seats of that Cabinet to keep racism alive in this country. Many of these elected officials were of the old school of thought, that blacks were still stupid and not qualified to step forward to exhibit their ability before being judged, however, the old prejudiced minded Foe was outvoted by the sound minded whites, who, I salute wholeheartedly to allow this program to go forward.

This is another lesson of how white people never getting the information about black people's contribution to this country, they never allowed black history to be taught in their schools, even those senators who voted did not follow black history and advancement The call for this program was set forth on the 25th of August 1941 to teach and train blacks to fly, it was set up at Tuskegee Institute in Alabama. Since a lot of the civilians and military did not want the program to happen, it gained enough votes, however, to establish the school, it was the same old rhetoric, blacks in all past wars were good enough to fight and die on battlefields, but were still ignorant and unappreciated people after the battles were over, was right back to being discriminated by the racist bigots who had no problems calling upon them to die in these wars, but were not looked upon as citizens who had earned their rights to the independence, freedom and justice of which they died or fought for after accomplishing their mission.

In spite of the treatment the black men always responded to their challenges and pursued their dreams as the great Champion had instilled in them early on, the biggest part of that of which Johnson related to them, was: "Be Prepared," when the playing field was made even and in this case of these airmen, it was just that opportunity to show and let the world see that they were more than 3/5th of a man and could stand with the best, if given that chance to prove it. The door was opened and they responded to accomplish their dream, what a journey they embarked upon!

They came from all neck of the woods, cities of America, they were dark-skinned, light and in between complexions, a true mix of black men. They were tested at the evaluation center to qualify, each and everyone passed with high scores, received their results and sent to Alabama to begin their training at Tuskegee. Along the way on the train ride through the south, the train stopped and picked up more passengers, the conductor moved them from their section seats and told them they had to relocate themselves to the rear of the train, upon making that transition they noticed their seats were being given to detained German prisoners, they questioned the move, but were told to comply and move on, they could hardly believe their eyes, they were actually experiencing racial discrimination, it was a devastating awakening, after all blacks had fought and died for, they were only second class citizens, looked upon as less than these prisoners who were killing Americans on battlefields all across Europe, who were also killing millions of Jews in gas and chemical facilities, yet these young black men were treated with disdain in their place of birth, so from 1619 until 1941 the white society of the country continued to show the double standards for black people, even embarrassing them in front of their enemies.

The white people have never been taught the real truth of black men, women and children brought here to be slaves, the contributions they have made in building the wealth of major banks and corporations of this country and the major role they played in our wars for freedom and they never taught white people or their schoolchildren that black people had been flying planes way before 1941 in America. The first black pilot was Charles Wesley Peters, 1911, and Eugene S. Bullard, both had been refused license in America, they went to France to obtain them, Bullard was the only black fighter pilot in World War I, flew for the French, he was also called the Black Bird and was the first to do the stunt designed creative flying which we see by various military flying groups today. The first black female pilot to be licensed was Betsy Coleman who learned to fly and obtained her license in France as well, a U.S. Postal stamp honoring her was issued in 2000. Blacks had been flying since 1908 in training flights, they had their own flying clubs around America in the 20's. Blacks made the first Trans Atlantic historical flight across America in 1932, this valuable information was not privy to the general white populace, what a travesty, these type of conspiracies to hide the truth is absurd, it gave the impression that blacks were just stupid, half human beings here to be used, abused, and disrespected. All are born equal under God's hand, unlike the white scientist who keep saying whites are smarter than blacks, that's not true and has never been proven, any white man who states that is naive and a total idiotic. History shows you that, we had black scholars and qualified teachers, some who even taught white people in many fields of intellectual curricula around the nation and world.

Show me a white man who states that they are smarter or more intellectual, we can find a black man to match his wits in any field.

The black students showed up at Tuskegee, checked in, handed in their test papers, their scores were met with some doubt of their validity, the non-believers made them retest, the outcome was mind boggling for them, this time the scores were even higher than the original ones. Who, now became the dummies of the scenario? That operational training officer who was the nonbeliever. It's like Lt. Flipper, the first black graduate of West Point in the late 1800's, only black in the class of 100, no one of the white cadets socialized with him during his tenure there, no one wanted him to graduate, reason, no white cadet could not justify how a black man who is supposed to be inferior and ignorant could graduate ahead of any one of them, so the pressure was on them. How could they let a black men graduate ahead of them, so isolating him hoping he would get discouraged and drop out of the class, was the only reason and maybe they were told to employ their action by the academy, who did not want to see a Black man graduate from that military institution. Flipper was smart and determined, he was strong of mind and soul and continued on with his journey to success in his dream, all intelligence is granted to all of us by God at our birth into this system, we only fail when not properly nurtured and taught from our very beginning, we are blessed into this life with God's Love, human rights and the capabilities to comprehend all that is taught to us as well. These students were in pursuit of their dreams and after obviously seeing the racism and double standards against them, bonded together to erase these injustice and misuse of the black man's intelligence, fortitude and courage to be the best they could ever be. The bond became the greatest the military aviation stories ever recorded in history.

Shortly into the program the obsession of the Common Foe became deplorable as they continued to fight the program, inspire of all the astounding progress being made. The black General Benjamin o Davis Jr. fought those senators tooth and nail to give those young men the chance to finish the program to reap the rewards. The pressure was so adamant from its senators to terminate, that it became the concern of the First Lady Eleanor Roosevelt so much so that she flew there to see firsthand how the program was progressing. Upon her arrival and a briefing of the program, she inspected the training class and requested to fly and be taken on a flight. The school-commandant selected one of the instructors to take her up on that "gorgeous day for flying." Upon seeing the white instructor designated to take her up, she turned to the commandant and stated: "I don't want to go up with him, I want one of the black trainees to take me up," at which time one of the class trainees was selected and took her up on a solo. Amazing how God gets involved in things. All things are done for a reason, this courageous woman put her life in an unproven student's hands opposed to going up with a qualified white pilot, that was God providing his presence at that moment. Everyone of the commandant's white instructors were shocked that she would trust her life with that trainee, however she was putting her life in the Creator's hands, because of that tremendous flight on that day Her hands leveled the playing field and allowed those Black men to pursue their dreams, which up until that day was in danger of perishing from even happening for them. Again I commend those gallant men and this great white First Lady who fought against racism in this country, to step forward and make a tremendous change in these young men's lives and the other major changes of awakening a racist country. Mrs. Roosevelt was very instrumental in getting major social and employment open to black men and women. She also told the commandant to get those black pilots involved in the combat flights in Germany upon their graduation. Armed with the First Ladies' endorsement these men must have made an agreement to finish the program and excel to be the greatest fliers of that war. They were dispatched to Germany where they ran second class missions until Gen. Davis, this black Unit Commander again fought with those senators to get his men involved in combat fighter missions, the request was granted and we know the final outcome of black courage and valor that set records and achievements that still stand today for all to see. White bomber pilots who have followed those black pilots flying skills and their superb escort missions safety rate - began to request them to be assigned to their bombing mission under the white escort fighters there were too many men and planes lost. The bombers got their wish, the Tuskegee airmen of the 332nd flew over 500 combat missions for a period of over 2 years, never lost a bomber to enemy fire or fighter pilot attack these courageous able bodied intelligent and aggressive fighter pilots who vowed to be the best there was for themselves, their families, race, air corps and nation, an amazing feat for these Black airmen, who many thought were incapable of flying. The only school instructors that ever fought in aerial combat were not the white instructors, but Black men who flew with the Canadian Air Corps and had more combat flight time against enemies than any white pilot there. These black pilots were efficient in teaching tactical and maneuvering procedures and their students exemplified all of what was taught them. I am really proud of these pioneers who paved the journey for thousands of fighter pilots to fly and defend our skies today. The heralded Daniel "Chappie" James , the first black four star general in the air corps was a product of the Tuskegee experiment. Jack Johnson's words were loud and clear: "Be Prepared" and "Be twice as good as all others." A word of gratitude to those who flew above the clouds to protect their bombers and to defend the skies in such powerful and complex aircraft with precise skills, where every split second was a life-or-death situation. You have accomplished your dreams, recorded your legacy in our hearts and etched it in the skies, of which you soared forever. Thanks for a job "Well Done!"

chapter 21

761st Tank Battalion

Gen. Patton's 3rd Army was on the move in blitzing across the German battlefield defeating the enemy and destroying everything in sight, his tank units were getting bogged down periodically, he called back to Command Operations and requested the best tank unit available dispatched to provide support for his final push against the German Panzers, the 761st Tank Battalion was dispatched. Patton quickly showed up to welcome them, the 761st was an all black unit, upon his arrival to welcome and inspect them, he saw that they were an all Black Battalion, he stated: "I asked for the best and they send you Black guys!" He inspected the group and then told them again: "I asked for the best to join the best fighting force assembled, the 3rd Army. I will know if in fact you are the best, you will have to show me that you are, not only show me but show all of these men of which you are joining if you are the best, then prove to me that you are, but not just for the 3rd Army, the enemy, yourselves and your race as well, and they did just that.

The 761st set a phenomenal record, they covered more ground, captured and destroyed more enemy tanks, killed and captured more enemy troops than any other Tank Battalion during the war in Germany. At one point there were doubts that African Americans could learn to be tankers, they not only learned, they excelled in their performance in them. After the 3rd Army Division accomplished its amazing feat in such a devastating and overwhelming defeat ever recorded in Europe, Gen. Patton made a special awarding ceremony to acknowledge the black troops of the 761st, he announced to them that they had indeed impressed him with their professional skills and performance and had distinguished themselves above and beyond his expectation which was a tribute to the

Tank Corps of which he loved, but also to tell the military and the
Black race as well, he stated: "You are the best and should be proud
of your accomplishment, I am very proud of you and I salute you
all." Again, there was the doubt, there have always been doubts,
and the doubters always become true believers of the black soldier, regardless of what his job was, hell, they ought to know they
always excelled, they were even the best cotton pickers as well!

Their white commanders Col. John Bates and Phillip Latimore
stated: "These men only wanted to prove they were the best and
wanted the world to know that they were."

The Proud Achievements of the Other Major Half of the
American Black Man, the American Black Service
Woman, and her Contribution to the Military

Black American women, as our men, have a long history in
the military since the Spanish American War, 1898. They distinguished themselves in many branches of the military, they served
as nurses, supplies and hospital medics in medical confinement facilities, quartermaster units, personnel record sections, as lab technicians, in operations and logistics, as battlefield surgeon assistants,
military postal clerks, mail handlers and signal corps. And later on
in years were active as unit commanders, combat infantry women,
test plane fliers, military scientists, lab development technicians,
surgeon general of the army and branch units, and have served hon-
orably in all areas of endeavor. A rich history not taught in any of
our schools around the nation. They have so much to be proud of,
a legacy that's a must to be recognized and appreciated. They have
served in Europe, Viet-Nam, Korea, Afghanistan, Iraq, World Wars
I, II. During overseas' assignment, these women became social
companions to our black troops who were isolated in segregated
service areas from the white soldiers.

The American black women have made tremendous strides in
the racist country, no other female ethnic group has suffered the
degrading humiliation, rapes, lynchings, burnings and being used
as human torches and burned alive by the white bigots of the land
of the free. From 1891 to 1921 forty five black women died, sev-

eral were young girls fourteen to sixteen years old, one woman was hung next to her fourteen year old son, who had worked all day for a white man, when finished he asked to be paid, the man hung him. His mother looking for him, saw what was being done, ran down to save the boy. The white man and a few others took both of them and hung them under a railroad overpass. Another woman who was pregnant, was hung from her ankles, gas poured on her clothes and set on fire, her stomach was cut open, the unborn child fell to the ground. A member of the mob crushed its head with his feet. So our women have been traumatized for nearly four hundred years, but in spite of these atrocities against them, they still remained strong of character to overcome. They are the fine women of today and I applaud them for all they have done and accomplished in these crucial times of this nation's history. I write these next lines especially to all the Black women and all others included:

"A Tribute to the Women of the World"

One of the Creator's most precious gifts to the world and mankind after his love is woman. Women have always been a major force in the history of the world. Women should be thankful on a daily basis to the ladies who came before them. They were single mothers and congress-women. They hail from the sports arena to soaring into outer space. They preach the word of God and whisper to a frightened child in the night. They are in the board room and classroom. You will find them in the courtroom and operating room. In the world of art and entertainment they have done it all and the results have been breathtaking. I would not pretend all of these accomplishments were without major struggles.

As women you would not be winners you see in everyday life without conflict. Some of the ladies who made changes are known around the world, others are just in your neighborhood. Neither is more important than the other. Some that I admired may not be your heroines, but you all have different reasons and needs. You have been mothers, sisters, aunts, nieces and grandmothers. You have been wives, lovers, motivators, nurturers and life givers. In all these roles you have made the world a more desirable place. You have given the world numerous gifts. Among them love, kindness, friendship, loyalty, elegance, charm and humor. For a variety of reasons, some of you have had to raise your family alone. In spite of the challenges you have raised remarkable adults. Our schools need to teach your children the amazing history of womanhood. There are still areas in which you need to improve yourselves and the world. You need to come together as females regardless of race, ethnic background or religion. Differences should be celebrated. There have been dark times in your history. You need to be there for each other and learn from the mistakes. To achieve a complete life you must start with a spiritual foundation that lies within. A faith that will nourish you in times of crisis and to praise in times of joy. You are all daughters and a mother is a gift to be cherished, love her, learn from her and when she is gone respect her memory. Another amazing gift from our Creator is the ability to reflect of our past and enjoy the wonderful time spent with them.

Remember, the lessons you teach the women of today will be carried into the next century. Today is a gift that is why we call it the present. You as proud women need to search your hearts and souls for dreams. With your faith and love they will become your reality and your timeless gift to all people regardless of race, creed or color of skin.

JAMES L. WEBB, 2000

There's lots to be done, especially with our young black girls and I look to you the teachers of the Now to reach out to reestablish that pride of our young girls who have yet to find their way and in many cases it's because of teaching and nurturing them have not been consistent with today's society and system of things, being allowed to exist that's not conducive to establishing standards, and other elements for the betterment of their growth. You cannot afford to be the mother who allows your children to become part of the wanderers of the neighborhood, affiliated with gangs and negative ones who have lost their way, this is the time of Change, have no doubt, believe what you see happening before you.

We as a people have been disrespected too long, and I write this to enlighten our race of people and others who choose to change the leadership of elected city officials who at times never show up for personal involvement of the issues at hand, they solicit your vote and support, you must hold them accountable for change, that's called people power, where's Philadelphia's Al Sharpton? Speaking out at council meetings, seeking a period to address issues with the mayor and police commissioner, this should be the time of change, the old agenda is not feasible anymore. There needs to be new standards of business that are related to all by the mayor, this is a new set of elected officials, one thing is real, we all have eyes to see and must have the fortitude to insist upon new standards for the betterment of our people, the city, and all major issues that need to be addressed. There's going to be the "stop and frisk" tactics used, ensure your community is aware of techniques that will be utilized, if it's done tactfully, no problems, however, if it's an intimidating approach many problems for your children, being jailed for their reaction to some overzealous police officers grabbing or pushing them around, instead of tactfully explaining why they are doing what they are doing to them. Listen to your children, some have meaningful issues to discuss. I've talked to various youth and it seems many have lost respect for their parents especially when they don't see them fighting for change in their communities, trash not being collected causing filthy streets, potholes not being filled, old vacant lots, where houses used to stand are rat-infested, areas that could be hiding places for addicts and other suspicious persons to hang out in. There's the thousand-man walking patrols, maybe they will allow some to ride along in their patrol cars to monitor street activities, that way they can get to know the cops who will be patrolling their neighborhood, and that way they will get to know some of the guys on the streets as well.

I respect you for all you have been through and have accomplished thus far, we as parents can never stop enlightening our children in their journey of life, again I thank those ladies who spent time in the military, I spent 21 years in the Army, and to all of you, you are worthy to be praised.

Black Women of the World, I Love You!

Note: Safeguard your children, they are the extension of our past and future, these kids are housed in doom and gloom, dirty sneakers, pants down on their asses, cuffs dragging on the ground, wrinkled hooded jackets over their heads. A dress code is needed, pressed pants and shirts, shined shoes, we have got to restore the pride and image of ourselves and our children.

Neighborhood's standards of appearance need upgrading, the mayor should not have to organize a day to clean up the city, the neighbors on your streets are somewhat responsible for its appearance, however, do hold the mayor and sanitation department responsible for removing whatever needs to be collected and carted out of it It's a pride standard, it needs to be maintained all the time, neighborhood unity a must, Saturday, neighborhood clean-up day. Again, pride is the case in point. I come over the bridge into Philly, those new homes rebuilt along Rt. 76th looks nice, however, there's trash bags and other objects that give the area a filthy view, if the city is responsible for that garbage, then coordinate with your city officials or the mayor's office to have that mess cleaned up, also see if there can be some type of plants or trees that can be planted along that strip, like up around the housing complex office authority building. It looks like night and day between the two areas, however, it's not just there, its all over the city. When the city tore down houses because they caught people doing drugs there years ago, it left a void there, weeds and trash were noted everywhere. Those empty spaces should be cleaned up and made into sitting areas or small play areas for little children, these city blocks in some areas look worse than some third world ghetto areas, so it goes on and on, however, now is the time to move in this new administration to correct the images they created in those neighborhoods years ago. If the city can acknowledge a cop killed in line of duty, which is the hazard of that profession, then they should also play a part in any innocent person killed by them, as in the New Year's Eve killing, where a man was killed and a small child wounded after one of two officers fired into a crowded house where people were celebrating the coming of the New Year. I hear many cases, wherein they thought someone had a gun, only to reveal there was none. Those killed individuals are someone's family member, just as important as any police officer, so people grieve on both sides of the bullet. The mayor and/or police commissioner should address that issue, someone needs to be held accountable for the action that took an innocent life from its family members.

chapter 22

The Police Must Establish Better Community Relations

There's all kinds of hate posters and letters being posted around the city, let's look at the Move incident again where 14 innocent men, women and children were fired upon with over 10,000 rounds, forced to stay in a burning house, no weapons were fired at the police officers. The city deputy mayor, police chief and fire chief all over the scene had allowed some tactical force person to drop an incinerate device or bomb that caused two city blocks to burn down, these officials should have been removed from their positions and brought on charges of negligence, never happened, and no one from the city ever issued an apology. These people belong to, not only their family but to the human family as well. The first sign of fire, the blaze should have been put out, as a fire chief, as same as police commissioner who both swore an oath to save lives and property, save, they did not - it was one of the most perilous times in Philadelphia, forcing those people back through a door in the back of the house to be burned alive. So do you have reason to fear for your life when you see three men get assaulted by 19 white police officers? You bet you better be, just remember the holocaust that happened there! The city never mourned those people, so when you read of cops with Ku Klux Klan posters in their wall lockers and see the outrage of the police, it's threatening and cause for concern. These two scenarios reflect unprofessional police procedures and standards, the world saw the Move incident as well as the beating of these men. Nowhere in any law enforcement manual or training procedures taught at the Academy, tells officers to be the judge and jury upon arrest of anyone, so when officers take it upon themselves to assault and brutalize people, it's a chargeable offense, should be addressed swiftly and a statement made by the mayor who's responsible for all things that happen in law enforcement. He's the Commander-in-Chief, the Police Commissioner and all law enforcement are in his hands, their training, their department, their reactions and above all else their standards, and in this case with the "out of control" police at the Move incident, should be the constant reminder of how "out of control" cops can cause grief, cause disrespect for them, the embarrassment of the city which projects Brotherly Love. Where is it? The city, a racially divided one, always has been and will remain so, unless the new mayor and commissioner continually tries to keep their police in order and establish a new relationship between police and communities. One of the answers is to have community briefing with representatives from the neighborhoods and police commander in charge of the area. Another is to establish walking patrols again, and also while there's 1000 men who want to volunteer for street patrols, allow some of them to ride along with or walk along with the police officers. I've seen all three situations work for the betterment of relationships and the solution of crime.

So ladies, I've put a lot in your chapter, one thing about woman, they can initiate change at home, with their husbands or other halves to motivate action needed to correct basically things of the home and children and at times to keep your other half involved in these efforts for change. I've just touched on a few things I think needs a family's awareness. I do applaud the mayor and police commissioner responding to the last incident of improper enforcement procedures, it could have been done a little earlier. I've seen people riot the same night as incidents occurred, so it's important to make an immediate announcement to these incidents. One of the worse riots in the 70's was when police officers beat a black young man in the streets of Newark, people rioted for three days, twenty people killed, blacks and whites. The city of Philadelphia was very lucky that people did not react to the Move incident. Another case was when the police officers rammed a broomstick up a black man's rectum in New York, it took damn near a year for someone to cross the thin blue line to identify those racist and inhumane individuals. We have a long way to go to defeat and to correct things that cause a bad image so I encourage all to see the vision before us, the universal laws allow us to see and react for whatever is for the betterment and balance of our people.

One reason I write about issues is because there's a need to keep everyone abreast of these concerns. I was watching Cops, the TV show the other night, they were featuring the Philadelphia police, the scenario, a white senior officer riding with a rookie cop, (Black), they rode by a black youth standing on the sidewalk, the senior cop told him to move on, the kid said: "I'm not doing anything, I am just standing here!" The senior cop told him again to move on, the kid asked again why he could not stand there. The cop pulled over and jumped out of the patrol car and stated: "Oh, you are one of those tough guys!" grabbed him, pushed him up against the wall, frisked him, put the cuffs on him, again telling him: "You are one of those tough guys!" then put him in the car and rode off, no doubt they locked him up. Now the other side of that incident could have been: "What are you doing standing there, move on!" When he asks: "How come I have to move, I am not doing anything?" Listen to the pitch of his voice then say: "Well, if you don't live in that house we need you to move on because there are so many incidents around and we need you to move on, if you don't live there, you can't loiter in front of other people's house." This gives him an explanation which, if he refused, then he becomes the tough guy and you can lock him up. You must give a cornered dog a way out or he will try to bite you, in most cases the youth would have moved on. Just something to pass on to your children: when approached by police, it's best to just move, rather than ask a question why, because some officers get offensive as soon as you ask them a question. I did a little law enforcement for a period of time before transferring to another career. I did some highway patrol, would pull over a speeder, ask for all necessary documents and would proceed to inform them why I stopped them. I would say: "Sir" or "Ma'am, I pulled you over for exceeding the posted speed limit in accordance with title such and such of the states' operation drivers manual, number, paragraph, which specifically stated so and so, of which you are in violation." Then I await for his comments, some would give excuses valid in some regards, others would get attitudes, etc. but either case I would explain to them the recourse for their violation and the results it could have if in fact they were involved in an accident. In many cases after even issuing a summons, they would thank me for taking the time to make them understand the consequences of driving fast or driving recklessly, or whatever the case may be which could cause an accident, resulting in death or injury for someone or for themselves. And that's the main reason they have to comply with the regulations stated in their driver's manual, is so that I could issue a warning predicated on traffic situations. Some, just a verbal warning in a very tactful and professional manner, and in many situations, people getting the tickets would thank me for the time I took to refocus them on their responsibilities to themselves and loved ones, of their vehicle or to the other vehicle, if in fact there was any vehicular accident, so tact and professionalism is a must, especially when dealing with these immature youth. When you handle them properly, maybe you are just getting a little respect from them to relate to others about the situation in a good and positive way. Those youths have seen so much on both sides of the line, so locking that kid up was not justified when I watch the scenario unfold. These are just my thoughts to safeguard your children, they have to expect to be locked up if they give any indication of resistance or becoming belligerent, all it takes for trouble to come, sometimes is just to look at a cop in the wrong way. They will put you in cuffs stating you looked at them with threatening gestures. Talk to your children and save them from the jail.

chapter 23

The Other Side of the Common Foe

All through this book I have written about the violent and racist white man and his inhumane treatment of black people, well now I speak the other side of him, what we learned from him over the 400 years until today was to be expected. This other side is a murderous lifeless murderer, who has seen the trails and tribulations of a black race of people in their period of existence in this country. The history of black suffering is everywhere to be heard about, read about or even experienced first hand, these ignorant and murderous villains armed with guns and drugs are the number one criminal element today. These infested minded souls are responsible for some of the most tragic crime ever recorded in America today, especially in the city of Philadelphia, these corrupt feeble-minded wanderers have killed your mothers, fathers, sisters, brothers, grandparents and precious children and babies, on the streets and in your homes. The wanderers of doom and gloom of whence they live are leeches that sell drugs in communities, rape and hustle the young girls intimidating and physically abusing our senior citizens, so we have traversed over 400 years of the white Common foe, only to inherit the fate of these inhumane savages as their white counterpart do. **These are the black terrorists of our city today,** these violent young black men are everywhere inflicting these tragic incidents upon our neighborhoods, he's that wanderer the Bible spoke of, when God branded him, Cain for killing his brother. The Bible scriptures has lessons to be learned from the very beginning the wanderer killed his brother, instead of loving him and being his keeper, as our Creator intended it to be.

We inherit two worlds when born, the physical one and the one's inner self spirituality and there's a drastic difference between the two, in the physical world, man has been fighting and killing

each other in the name of their religious convictions, the world of
which we see is going on. The spiritual world of self universal spirituality finds the love of all of God's creations. This, I've never
been taught in any church that life is a journey of which we all
must embark upon, which tells that he who finds himself from
within finds God. The journey is one of the toughest to pursue, it
takes courage, faith and fortitude, and many lose their way, as the
journey is very demanding. It's like going into the eye of a chaotic
windstorm where the obstacles challenges our tenacity to fight
through for deeper in the storm is the knowledge of enlightenment,
where once you gain a foothold you begin to shed your worldly
intrusive thoughts of the physical to find the spiritual where love
has never killed anyone, where in our spiritual state we humble
ourselves for the ultimate, the wisdom and knowledge that connects us with our true selves, and the purpose of life is revealed.
And we all have that love, and the main thing is to share that love
and understanding of which you received in the name of our Creator, with those that are still seeking to find that balance and harmony of all things, which we do in God's name, not ours. As the
scripture says that of which I do, I do in God's name, not mine.
The Bible also tells us to pray for our leaders and politicians because only when they have made their personal journey will they
have the eyes to lead and handle the enormous burden of which
they inherit, they more than any other should know that to lead is
to lead in partnership with the Creator of all things, that their
strength and judgment comes from that inner spiritual force which
enables them to handle all things, which is guided by the power
within the universal laws of this system of which we exist. The
journey allows us to see that love, wisdom and knowledge is the
power of ruling mankind in this spiritual Universe where we are
only here for a short period of time.

So these wanderers and all others failing to seek the truth are
in for a rude awakening, most of them already are experiencing at
this very moment, there's no way to escape the writings are all over
this world. There's a price you pay for your ignorance sooner or
later, what goes around comes around, it's only a matter of time,
and time does not wait for any of us to get it right. The wanderers

are the very harassed and lonely, living in the dark shadows of a sealed box with no way out. The wanderer is lonely, friendless, always looking over his shoulder, no real place to stay, never knowing when the bullet comes for them, it's never too late though to give up your gun, find a new life, shed your horrific life, seek help in another area, seek your forgiveness, seek that inner love and partialness. God is a forgiving God and I've seen the worse of the worse become a changed individual, this can only be done by you, it's all good but the very beginning starts in your hearts, so false attempts are not accepted, for the God who has created all this, yes, the God that created you knows your heart. So blacks have forgiven millions of the Common Foe for their ignorance, they even fought their wars for them, yet they still tried underhandedly to continue the racism and discrimination. Although these bad killings and tactics are only learned behavior from our white ancestors which still remains with us until this day, in most cases, no jobs and no way out for these wanderers from the wilderness they live in for many depressing years have caused these behaviors to remain. However, it's not too late to rid yourself of the gun and drugs. God loves you if no one else does. Give God your life!

chapter 24

Muhammad Ali; The Greatest

Ali was born Cassius Marcellus Clay in Louisville, KY on 17 January 1942. Louisville was a segregated town, well known for its long history of racial violence, discrimination, Jim Crow, police abuse, civil and human rights policy and its affiliation with the Ku Klux Klan who terrorized and lynched black people. There were segregated churches, restaurants and other facilities up until the 60's.

Cassius began boxing at the age of 12, after someone had stolen his bicycle, he was trained by a white police officer, named Joe Martin, later in his career he was trained by Sugar Ray Robinson and Angelo Dundee. Cassius had a tremendous amateur career, went on to win a gold medal at the Olympics held in Rome, 1960. He was fantastic, he displayed his amazing accomplished boxing skills to the world, gave them the fast hands, excellent and accurate execution of punch combinations, great balance, beautiful footwork, coupled with graceful body movement, ringmanship and physical toughness, proclaiming himself even then as "The Greatest."

Cassius growing up in Louisville, seeing and experiencing racism and discrimination was totally shocked and humiliated after returning from the Olympics and refused service in one of the city's restaurants, even after informing them of who he was and what he had just accomplished at the Olympics for America, he even displayed the gold medal he wore so proudly around his neck. They still refused his service and asked him to leave. This action deeply devastated him and crushed his ego, he got extremely distraught and threw the medal in the Ohio river. Years earlier as a young intelligent and proud boy of 13, he could not understand seeing the racial turmoil in Louisville and America, he was growing up in a period when blacks were struggling for their human and civil rights. His parents talked to him about various racial situations, he was told of the tragic murder of Emmit Till in Mississippi and the arrest of Rosa Parks in Alabama for not giving up her bus seat to a white man and moving to the back sections designated for blacks. The racial hatred was escalating with the double standards and abusive treatment of blacks. He saw blacks being beaten by whites and police officers as well, saw children and women being bitten by police dogs, kicks and stomped, sprayed with high-powered water hoses. Cassius was seeing the vast injustices of this nation, a nation governed by black robes and white justice; police officers who swore an oath to protect and defend against lawlessness turn their backs and even took part in these vicious attacks, as innocent blacks were mauled in the streets for the whole world to see, one damning display of America's justice. These racial problems began to stimulate his demeanor, the restaurant incident was really appalling in 1960, it showed him that he was now a game player and that from the time he was 13 until almost 19 years of age, there had been very little progress in dealing with corrupt, prejudice and horrific racist people and elements in the country at large. He had to find a way to cope, find some positives, opposed to the white negative racial chaos being focused before his eyes.

Cassius was an advocate student of boxing history, especially reading and viewing tapes of Jack Johnson, who he would refer to as his hero, was an extraordinary great Champion who had a tremendous impact on his life. Johnson early on in his life identified his biggest enemies in America, the white supremacist, racial bigots, injustice of law, double standards, discrimination, poor whites who were led to believe they were better than blacks and America belong to them. These same incidents exposed to him in the Johnson films were still actually happening before his eyes some 50 years later in this country, During his traveling to Rome, stopping in various other countries, seeing and meeting people of all walks of life and nationalities, making new friends was a great experience for him. He noted how people respected and related to each other, he saw no prejudice or attitudes against blacks, no segregated restaurants or any other facilities that practiced racism, a tremendous mind set was inherited, developed and absorbed within.

This new demeanor established within was never accepting being second to none, never be intimidated, accept all life's challenges, regardless of what the outcome, stand and fight for your beliefs, principles and values. He also reflected upon the deplorable experiences and traditions of racism at home, he was 18 years of age. He came home with these convictions, an Olympic gold medalist champion, only to be insulted and embarrassed. A young man who was so proud of his achievement with such positive aspirations, realized that his dream was not just to be the future heavyweight champion of the world, but he also realized he would have to be a fighter against racial injustices here in America. White hatred had forced his plight for human rights and laid the foundation for his inter convictions of picking up the torch for blacks, human rights and to seek and have some input at creating love and unity among all people.

Cassius begun the process, he looked for answers to what was happening in his country and finally found some support for his enlightenment and life's purpose. He found that light in the person of Malcolm X who befriended him and began to tutor him in the sacred and spiritual principles of the Nation of Islam. He found peace of mind as he studied, he discovered a different world of pride, togetherness, independence, respect, economic growth, great education and teaching system, youth development programs and a undying love and worship for the Creator of all things. They carried themselves with pride and dignity, yes, America had laid the challenge for Cassius to become one of the greatest and influential people in this country. He studied and learned well and was later anointed the name of Muhammad Ali which means "Worthy To Be Praised, Most High" by Elijah Muhammad who was his mentor and spiritual leader of the Nation of Islam. After Cassius Clay's incredible and shocking victory over Sonny Liston in February of 1964, he revealed to the world that, he was a member of the Nation of Islam and would no longer be known as Cassius Clay, and that his new Islamic name of which he would now be known by, was Muhammad Ali.

America was involved in a war with Viet-Nam, before Ali won the Championship he was classified as 4F, not acceptable, after it was learned that he had joined the Nation of Islam it was changed to 1A acceptable for military deferment. A lot of people were furious that the Champion had joined Islam, some even called him anti American, not patriotic, especially after refusing to step forward at a draft board induction center. Ali stated at one point "he had no quarrel with those Viet-Con," when he made that statement, America as well as the rest of the world was in chaos, denouncing and demonstrating against the war, which has taken more than thirty five thousand American lives and a very high number of casualties. Americans were burning draft cards, demonstrating and rioting in every major city in the country, and running to Canada, rather than being inducted. It was evident that America's plans for winning the war were not working from the daily television and media news reports. Ali stood fast in his convictions, he also explained his reasons for refusing the draft, he stated that "I have searched my conscience and I find I can not be true to the beliefs of my religion by accepting such a call, I will not put on an American uniform to go around the world killing innocent poor brown people to appease the white racist supremacy and dominance over black people here in America."

Ali was stripped of his title and not permitted to fight here in America, nor was he granted permission to fight in other countries, he was convicted in 1967, given 5 years prison term, which he appealed. America tried to strip Johnson of his title in 1910 and the World Boxing Council stated, as the title was won in the ring the holder of the title must lose it in the ring as well so America was in violation of the World Boxing Council's rules and in doing that they deprived him of the rights to make a living and support his family.

During his exile from the ring, Ali addressed the double standards as to who would be drafted and those who would not; he spoke of certain wealthy Hollywood actors who were eligible, not being selected to serve. There was issue of ministers being exempt, he was a minister of his religious faith, why the double standards, if it applied to him, it should apply to all others, those answers were never given. Most people in America and other countries just got behind him and supported his cause. At this point blacks, whites and others were united by this man's actions against a war, he called unjust. America was exposed for numerous other problems with the war. Ali took this time to travel around to the major colleges to address his issues against black racism and discrimination; he became a major influence to people not only here, but around the world as well. It was mind battling how this young black man could generate that kind of response worldwide. He became the biggest idol in the world. Ali proved to the world that, great people who become Champions, heroes and leaders have the same courageous heart, determination, tough mental fortitude and the moral strength to step up and accept the challenge and stand with undying convictions for whatever is right, that in the end faith, truth and the light will expose and conquer all.

No, America was not ready for Such A Man, they molded him with racist hatred, white supremacy, deceit and deception, terrorism, physical and mental abuse by whites and their law enforcement, practices of discrimination and the many injustices of Jim Crow barriers, these barriers were not strong enough to break this man who was totally committed to this worthy cause, "even if it meant dying or going to jail" so he stated. Ali knew there was no greater power than that inner spiritual force that he knew controls all things. God created this man for this battle he faced. He was a fierce individual force for this country to deal with. In the ring there were none greater, he was gallant, forceful and relentless at defeating his opponents, outside the ring he was a tenacious gracious and knowledgeable warrior, attacking the racist adversaries infringements on human and civil rights. He exposed the judicial system being utilized in the so called democracy of America, and the blatant physical abuse of law enforcement against peaceful march demonstrators, allowing Klan members to board buses in southern transportation terminals to beat and maim freedom riders, he spoke of black and white issues that kept poor whites and blacks fighting and hating each other to prevent harmony. No, this country was not ready or prepared to deal with such a man, who's will power and focus for the betterment of this country's social and racial reform was a major commitment at this point in his life.

Ali was a force behind a race of people who needed a hero, a symbol of strength and pride, they saw a handsome young black and gifted young man and Champion, who made them look deep within where they found that Black was beautiful, he made them feel special, he gave them something that could not be tarnished, a new identity, he was the beacon of light for this nation and the world. A people's Champion for all times, the people began to echo his early believe, that he was indeed "The Greatest."

chapter 25

War is Not the Answer

I spent my tour of twenty one years in the military, Viet-Nam 1966-67 never in my wildest dreams did I think I would see the nation, I live in, known to be the most powerful in the world, struggle in Viet-Nam for 11 years, where we not only never defeated the enemy, but totally embarrassed our nation in the eyes of the world. A country of enormous power and wealth trying to force its ideals, values and principles of a democracy upon the world at large. Our country manufacturers more munitions and weaponry than any other, allowed a war to continue for 11 years. I think if I am being sent to fight in any combat situation, that all available weapons and means would be utilized to our advantage to minimize the death, injuries, time spent in traumatic mental stress and time away from family would be implemented. This was not the case in Korea or Viet-Nam and it's even worse in Iraq. The result of not adequately preparing the strategies for employment and deployment caused tremendous turmoil and chaotic demonstrations across our nation and in a lot of other countries as well calling for the ouster of our troops from Nam, the same scenario is present today regarding Iraq.

Pulling out of Viet-Nam was the most pitiful military disaster ever witnessed of our nation's combat involvement around the world. It was, our Commander-in-Chief and the military, Commanders had no clue how to stabilize Iraq or the operational recovery of our troops. Now there's no timetable to pull out, the most powerful words I had ever heard was from one of our military's most highly combat decorated generals of our era, General Colin Powell, a man of enormous experience of combat planning, was a major evaluator of troops needed to sufficiently engage and stabilize enemy forces as well as civilian populace, the words Powell, the National Security Advisory to President Bush uttered to the President and the world on National TV and still ring in my ears today was: "If it's not broke, don't mess with because if you break it you will have to fix it and we have not yet found a way to fix what we have broken. No one listened, especially the Commander-in-Chief, it was also noted that there was a split between Powell and the President on his recommendation recorded in Newsweek magazine, however he did make a very crucial presentation before the World Council regarding vials of a nuclear building substance which provided a cause for the attack on Iraq. Even though vials were found, no weapons of mass destruction were reported by our weapons inspection team, what was the urgency for such action? Another lesson we failed to acknowledge from Viet-Nam was that war proved to America that nations will fight to the last man standing when invaded by any superpower choosing to enforce a change in their country's culture, heritage, sovereignty and religious and spiritual beliefs. Those people had fought and defeated their Common enemy, the French, there was no need for us to respond to that situation, the French had control and occupied Viet-Nam for damn near a hundred years. Before we went to Viet-Nam a person wearing the uniform of an American soldier was respected worldwide, however, after being run out of there, the image of the American man in uniform was never looked upon as the savior or policeman of the world again, now that image of us struggling to enforce peace between three different warring ethnic groups fighting against each other and us, brings the world's eyes upon us again, of invading, destroying and killing innocent people, if they would have only listened to Colin Powell, the world would not be in its present predicament today. The people who decided to invade never fought a war, yet put us in harm's way, where will it lead, only God knows. As a combat veteran in numerous conflicts, at times I would have to reign in young Officers coming out of Officers Graduate classes shipped to Nam, trying to fight a war there, using "classroom tactics" and various "exercises" conducted in our wooded "training fields" here at home. It was just not the way it was done in the actual fight, at times many of them would get offended when admonished, however the ones who listened to the seasoned combat Sergeants quickly learned to make adjustments to the "live or die" situations presented to them, they became very good young officers who were respected, who earned the respect of their men, because the bottom line was to operate as ONE in the unit and that's what we now need to come together in this nation where all people are appreciated or tolerated for the betterment of our nation. I was "Medivacced" to a field hospital in Japan from Nam, housed with the wounded, missing arms, legs, mentally distorted. I saw these brave young warriors crying out at night, pleading for someone to end it all for them, the blacks, whites, Hispanics, and other ethnic groups, and at no time did I ever think any of them as 3/5th of a man as the Constitution still reflects of black men after more than 400 years, that needs to be changed, now this cannot be allowed to remain in this document, again I say we have fought in many wars with the white man, more so than any other American group of people and whenever I read of the contributions on all battlefields, when I see the white burial crosses around the world and here at home, I only see the proud, the valiant, the courageous and brave housed in those graves, and after all they have fought and died for, the Common Foe still allows racism to tarnish our country, the French erected a monument for that black unit that Gen. Pershing gave to them because the white soldiers refused to fight with them, it's amazing the French would think that highly of them, you cannot find one monument in New York erected to immortalize those brave unappreciated 3/5th of a man, but the Divine Father allowed them to be recognized in spite of the racist mind set of this nation.

So back to what we were told, there were no weapons of mass destruction, the people had to be liberated, then there were the reports that the people would welcome us with open arms, that never happened. It was as if we just had to go there. After Kuwait, all tanks and equipment were left in place there, a factor I figured one day we would be going back there. After Hussein heard of our intent to invade, he tried to purchase parts for the F-105's that America allowed him to utilize against Iran, he could not purchase parts from Japan or any other source, then I knew it was just a matter of time before we would be going back to that region. Some old man many years ago told me the worse war we would ever be involved in, is right where we are today. America got duped into believing this would be a cake walk, when we went back to Kuwait, mounted the tanks and drove across the desert to capture Baghdad in 14 days, it sounded impressive, but I knew these people would pull back to the cities and towns to make their fight, main reason they could not put up the F-105's to cover any action in the open desert, same tactics used in Viet-Nam in many of the vital towns and cities in the upper region in the first field forces area, these battles went on for months of "give and take."

One thing about America, what we did not anticipate was a powerful resistance in Viet-Nam, however, we were there for 11 years we called it a police action, who the hell came up with that? those people had been fighting for 20 years against the French before they defeated them, Iraq, these people have been waging war against each other for thousands of years as well. I go back to Viet-Nam era shortly after World War II ended, Ho Chi Minh came to the United Nations and spoke about assisting him to get the French out of his country. Ho Chi Minh was an ally who fought with our American troops all through the Japanese islands along with Gen. Mac Arthur so after the war, he asked America to return the favor, in asking the French to leave his country. America refused to help. He stated after hearing the United States refusing to assist, that he would go back and drive the French out of his land. Shortly after waging tough battles with the French, the Vietnamese army trapped the last large forces of the French in the high regions near Kaysan, the French requested help from America, we sent advisers there for a police action, but he found out that the Americans were supplying the French weapons, and so he went public to the United Nations, saying he was surprised that the Americans were actually helping the French, and that since they were involved, Viet-Nam would not only kick the French out but would defeat the Americans as well. Why did we turn our backs on the Vietnamese people who helped us fight against Japan, a nation who had bombed and destroyed Pearl Harbor, we should have remained "neutral" as both were allies with us in fighting World War

II. Things began to reveal themselves in Nam after a period of time, it became a political war, which we fought with our hands tied, it was like all the Mobil, Exxon, Shell and other rubber plantations were "off limits," like private property, we had to seek permission to retaliate against any hostile opposition coming from within them, we only started heavy bombing of the Hanoi area during the end of the war effort, in 1967 when the enemy lunged the TET offensive on Saigon should have been the time to do so, it was like we could not bomb above the 38th parallel that heavy bombing came approximately two years later. America must remember we are no longer feared by those nations as far as foot, plane and tanks go, it was 11 years in Nam and now five years thus far in Iraq. We as a nation must learn to respect other nation's culture, ideals, religious views and their commitments to their way of life. We are the youngest nation in the world, just like a new baby finding its way in the universal system of things, we have been very fortunate to have acquired wealth and technology that we process today, but we must not think all people want to be like us or want us to invade and change their way of living whenever, they have internal problems of their own, it will not work. This last move has cost us dearly in terms of billions of dollars and the lives of our military committed to this disastrous war, we have killed thousands of the people we said we wanted to liberate, their country is in turmoil and we have not gained that which we set out to achieve, we are scheduled to move into a U.S. Embassy that has cost us millions of dollars to build there, when our citizens here are dealing with poverty, high gas prices, mortgage problems, hospitals, schools being closed, security problems with the 12 million Mexicans who violated our security policies, people hanging nooses, racism still being a problem to be dealt with, jobs still being outsourced, police officers causing problems in cities around the nation with their affiliation with the Ku Klux Klan especially in Sandusky, Ohio and in Philadelphia where two detectives who have been on the force for 7 and 11 years were suspended and transferred, however, they should also investigate all of their 7 and 11 years cases of which they were involved in for those periods of times, because of the thousands of innocent peo-

ple incarcerated by racists police officers. They had police officers that have falsified police reports, assaulted and have cost the
tax payers millions of dollars for their police atrocities on people,
there's so much we need to correct here before we can be the policemen of the world. Our elected politicians must work to restore
the means of improving and solving our problems here in our own
country, we have placed our welfare in their hands, only to find a
lot of them violating and abusing their position in offices they
have been elected to. We have a long way to recoup what we
should be standing for as a nation, unity is the key, the nation as
a whole needs uplifting and better leadership as a whole, there
must be change where all eyes of the nation are on the same page
to achieve these goals, now. When we can learn to solve our nation's problems, we will be able to become a major influence on
other nations, as of now, our actions against Iraq has been a dis-
mal abomination of our nation's power, our troops economics and
standards of which we stand. An unnecessary involvement in Iraq
has caused a recession, social devastation and total disarray of our
government and people at this point we not only have to find a
way to fix what we broke in Iraq but also need to find a fix for
what we have allowed to happen here at home. Especially the
black white racism.

No, war is not the answer, as mentioned earlier, all great nations of the past have collapsed from power because of abuse and
total disregard for the backbone of their nations, the small working
people who are called upon and forced to defend. We stand as a nation and prosper as one. Giving our nation's jobs to other countries
was the most cruel, devastating and disrespectful act thrust upon
these people who fought and worked to embrace the wealth of the
corporate business world of America, what a disgraceful ploy by
the rich and the government for allowing it to happen.

As a nation we must generate our spirituality from our creator
to seek a resolve for problems of which we are confronted with
today, they say it's a time for all things, and I truly believe it's a
time to humble ourselves before God and ask for unity and harmony to find a way to overcome, something that Martin Luther
King Jr. was seeking at his demise. There is such a thing as nations

falling out of God's grace, when it resorts to terrorizing, killing and destroying innocent people for the sake of power, revenge, greed and to rule over others, this is not part of the Universal Divine order of things, we can definitely see War is not the Answer, if we as a nation of one people can humble ourselves in prayer to overcome and to create the balance needed for all, that blessing I am sure will be granted. It takes all to ask and seek Change now. If we allow ourselves to be divided by a Common foe, then we will continue to self-destruct, things happen for a reason, the abuse of our people, the misuse of their welfare and resources is the downfall of what we are suffering through today. A nation divided not understanding their rights under the nation's historical documents, leads to being manipulated by the few, there's only change when there's one plan, one voice. The wholeness of anything, is to ensure we have all the pieces, as a nation we are part of the whole, everyone has a role in seeking Change. Seeking change is in the journey we all have to make, a journey within ourselves to truly understand the purpose of our individual existence, the journey is not easy, you must have the courage to persevere on its course, at which time you will understand, because you will shed those blinders to remove that darkness, to see and understand the reason you are unique, one of a kind you will discover who you actually are and the purpose you play in this system of God's Plan, stay the course, the longer the journey the more enlightened you will become of the hidden secrets of the soul, a new dimension of magnetic frequencies where you find that peacefulness of the moment in the universal harmony of all things. Whites and Blacks must resolve their hostile differences.

No, war is not the answer, when will it end? This is the beginning of the 5th year, as stated the nation is at its lowest financial and economic drain, a recession deeply embedded with no solutions to regain balance. This war is affecting our military personnel returning home as well as their families, the suicide rate is up, then there's still Afghanistan taking more of our troop strength, the Russians were involved there for 20 years without a victory, we can be employed there for years, searching caves, mountains and terrain regions in search for Bin Loden.

A lot of our elected officials still refuse to address the recession, it's okay if you are financially secure and have resources to live among the rich and famous, however, for those of little or no income, it's mental and devastating, trying to maintain a simple lifestyle on welfare, no jobs, no help or hope in sight as prices continue to soar, making it very difficult to provide food and necessities for the children clinging to them. I read where the French were awarded a government project from the U.S. why not allow that project be done here by American workers who are struggling to survive during this crises, not to grant the bid to United States workers is totally disrespecting and depriving them of that income. I also read the United States has built a U.S. Embassy for the sum of 74 million in Iraq, when we need medical aid and other essentials are needed, schools, hospitals are not being funded and they have spent 74 million on an Embassy, how long are we intending to remain in Iraq, what a travesty it's like misappropriation of Government funds that should have been spent here at home, spending that kind of money in another country when we have thousands of people living, starving and streets. That money could nave created jobs to build housing facilities for the homeless or funded into the welfare checks to help with the steady increase of prices on needed commodities.

There's 12 million Mexicans here illegally, that will be competing for any available jobs that should be given to American citizens first. Our national security was violated and on top of that, it's a known fact that most of the drugs coming into the country are from Mexico, how many are infiltrated terrorists, we have no way of knowing, it's just amazing that they are still allowed to remain here. If they have violated our borders security policies, they should be rounded up and returned and forced to utilize the immigration system, like all others who wish to gain citizenship. Years ago approximately 100 Haitians were refused entry into the country and forced back into the raging sea on a vessel that barely made it to our shores, where's the justice and balance of equality for all? We are searching people for hours before they can board a plane, train stations patrolled by K-9 patrols, people stopped and searched at random, yet we allowed 12 million people to walk across our boarders, unchecked, jeopardizing protection of our country, so much for national security, how vulnerable we are, if we allow that to go unchecked, we are subject to any and all threats to our country, to allow that to happen in such crucial circumstances is a gross negligence and waste of taxpayers' money to enforce security measures to negate another catastrophe, It's amazing that 12 million people would go undetected and in such a short period of time, almost as if it was orchestrated. 100 Haitians were denied entry, but 12 million Mexicans walked right through the back door of our nation unchallenged, racism is still very much alive and one of the major causes of the nation's downfall and divide. No, war is not the answer, it's the black white issue that is, there's a war going on and yet white people find time to hang nooses and show hatred towards black people since 1640, there's our young service personnel dying in Afghanistan and Iraq for freedom and safety, and yet they have to worry about their relatives being threatened and harassed and abused here in this country, it's totally absurd that the Common Foe and his white racist will not respect blacks and believe me the nations of the world know this racism exist and they also know that we have not yet grown to be leaders of the world at large, it has to be resolved if we are to succeed in doing that, for all blacks have done, he's still reflected in the country's constitution as 3/5th of a man, unbelievable.

The white man brought blacks here, killing millions along the way got here he began killing the Indians and blacks as well. This country has been fighting wars here and abroad since 1640. There was the war against the British, the Civil War, where they almost killed each other off in a divided country. When will wars become the last resort? World War I we marched in victory, World War II we marched in victory, these victories were only achieved by world involvement in fighting them, Korea was called a police action, no victory and American troops are still stationed there after 50 years or more. Viet-Nam, no victory, Afghanistan still ongoing engagement there. We are in our 6th year in Iraq with no end in sight and I doubt if we will march home victorious down any street in America, I only hope veterans will be welcomed here with open arms, with dignity and respect, something we as Viet-Nam returnees were unable to do.

It's hard for me to believe that the Iraq situation happened the way it did, that we did not reflect on Viet-Nam experience to ensure the lessons learned would be adhered to in planning our strategies of employment. One of the biggest factors in Nam, was manpower, we did not have enough troop strength to take and control areas of engagement, so right from the beginning more troops were needed, the command were instructed to train the Vietnamese to assist in controlling areas we had fought and secured, problem with that was it never worked, if we were there they would fight, however, the moment we moved into another combat mission, we knew damn well they would give that area up, causing us to fight for that same area upon our return, this has happened on numerous occasions in Iraq already. Another problem was that we just about went alone, the French, Germans and Russians refused to commit their troops, stating they did not think it was right to go in Iraq to kill innocent people and destroy their country when it was found out there were no weapons of mass destruction, another major problem was that they could not get a bid to reconstruct the country, those bids were given to the Becktol and Haliburton Construction Companies, based in South Africa and owned and operated by Americans, there's major money to be made by construction companies during and after destruction of defeated countries. With their support it would have been much easier to deploy in the four sections, each ally securing and controlling their designated operational combat areas. Other than the 130 thousand to control all areas, there would have been a substantial increase in troop strength of about 810,000 if the British would have sent the same amount, totally a different face on the whole picture and it would have been over within two years period. Another very important factor, is never underestimate the enemy, we found that the Koreans were fierce fighters in defending their country, Vietnamese same thing applied, we fought them for 11 years, Iraq's same thing we forget these people have been fighting in their countries against enemy forces for thousands of years, I found the Vietnamese fighters to be very well-disciplined and courageous fighters as were the Koreans and now we find another determined foe in the Iraqis, they have not the big tanks, airpower, but they as the Japanese, Koreans,

Vietnamese, would live only to make that great sacrifice for martyrdom, these people have been invading, killing and destroying each other since the beginning of time, we as Americans only began to play the game of war for approximately a thousand years if that long, we have only just began as a nation, made vast technology in weapons science, etc., some of that advance knowledge was gotten from other countries resources, a great German scientist played a major role in us getting our space program in orbit. So it's not always the most powerful who win at the end of things. Weapons are not the most powerful force in the world, it's wisdom, knowledge of manpower and how and when to use them. General Patton stated that men win wars not machines, most of the combat generals knew that, however, were not granted the manpower from the very beginning. People who have never fought a war cannot direct the manpower or logistics to win one. In Viet-Nam the allies commanders pleaded with President Johnson for more troop strength, however, when it came it was too late to make a difference. So we have in Iraq a determined foe who will have to be dealt with not with weapons, but wisdom. The longer we hang around over there under strength, just adds to our being there much longer, it's like a prize fight, the longer you let the enemy hang around the more vulnerable you become. The British fought the Zulu African nation utilizing artillery and rifles, got beat by a proud African nation using bow and arrow and spears and battlefield strategy, in Iraq they have established pockets of defense and offense, it's got so bad we are constructing a wall through some of the hostile town areas, the new Commander-in-Chief will definitely have his or her work cut out to alleviate this. When will it end, how many lives, how much more funding , how much more suffering here at home, only God knows. This has to be handled with a great deal of diplomacy and tact, if not this could escalate attacks upon our personnel to even include the Iraq's that we already armed and trained playing a major part in these attacks on our personnel, a lot of people there still hold us responsible for the loss of loved ones and destroying their country, a lot of these people are right in the army we trained and armed. Orchestrating plans for bringing our troops home will be a very touchy and important evaluation of all the factions in place, the eyes of the world will be watching and praying, you can believe that.

No, war is not the answer.

In the future we must ensure the world body of nations (UN) plays a major role in any problems of Global Conflicts, that's the purpose of it, establishing such a World Embodiment of Representatives from all worldly nations to resolve our conflicts that may arise worldwide.

chapter 26

The Peace Pipe

I used to read about the Indian civilization, one thing was very interesting to me and that was the peace pipe, whenever there was a confrontation among the nations, they would designate a tribal area to have all the chiefs to congregate to talk and resolve problems before the two warring tribes went to war against each other. One of the major factors was the peace pipe, they would formulate the traditional sitting circle, each would sit and meditate to raise up their spiritual consciousness, after reaching that level of awareness, they would all let that spiritual frequency embrace them with their individual chantings in their various different sacred volumes to the Universe where the forces would generate a certain calm as those vibrations and frequencies seemed to flow into one distinctive sound of worship to the Creator of all universal things, at which time all these wisdoms and knowledge would blend into one, in harmony with the ALL, their prayers being heard and answered, the Creator's spiritual forces engulf and brought them all to the moment of being connected to all things with love and peace of mind, enhanced with this moment where all worldly and intrusive thoughts did not exist, the chanting would stop, the spiritual elder would light the peace pipe and smoke on it until it seemed as if the smoke rose into the universal flow of things, the pipe was passed to all present. As the last chief finished, the pipe was handed to the senior elder who stood up, the pipe was held high to give homage to the spiritual forces and to God for allowing them to seek his input to that which they had prayed and chanted for. The senior elder would stand and announce, by the universal order of laws and all things: "We are all in agreement with the ultimate decision of our Spiritual Father, that peace among our brothers has been restored and all will be in unity with Love and Happiness throughout the great land of the Buffalo," the rest of the tribal council stood, embraced and all was at peace.

The whole scenario is predicated on the higher source that controls all things and times, should be prayed to for the spiritual Oneness of universal and divine laws to become part of that which we of all creeds, color, ethnicity humble ourselves before his grace to seek a resolve through his presence of our conscious awareness that we of many, are his creation, a human race, reconciling to calm and restore the Peace, Love and Happiness in our Garden of Life. We come as a world embodiment of people to seek a blessing to embrace and resolve a righteous solution for those holding the hostile and aggressive anger, and to further realize it is our sacred responsibility and commitment to acknowledge that we are our brother's keeper and utilize all of our resources granted, as one family of many nations under him of which we exist and stand, to find that harmony, that unity, that Brotherly love to restore that peace throughout the boundaries of Mother Earth. When we as a people learn to pursue our journey of spiritual oneness with our Father, we learn to drop the negatives and pick up the burdens of all of life positives, we were blessed here into this system of things by Love which will transcend the essence of all time, back from whence we came to the Love of Oneness the **God of us all. No, war is not the answer, Peace, Love and Happiness for all *is* the answer.**

Our purpose here was to till and cultivate Mother Earth and take charge of all resources handed to us and above all else to keep the peace, love and happiness throughout this world for all mankind regardless of race or color, we are all God's treasures and after knowing this we further see that no one Nation or People were ever made to rule this world, all you have to do is look in past history that eventually reveal all things to those who seek and find their spiritual enlightenment and those who have tried throughout the beginning of time have failed, because nothing remains the same. The African Black man who formulated and established the first dynasties, civilizations upon earth, ruled for thousands of years. They built phenomenal structures that's mind boggling, even until this day, they were the original scholars, teachers of sciences, liberal arts, medicine, law, astrology, theology, vast technology, those great philosophers were teachers of the European white men who came and befriended the black man, and his teachings, cultures in those ancient temples and universities in the great cities of Moroe, Napata and Timbuktu after acquiring the secrets of these advanced technologies, he deceived them and later invaded their country, killing and depleting it of its major resources of that era, gold, ivory, rubber and after conquering, he enslaved them, destroying the writings, books and retained buildings structures and land designs which we see in some of our major cities around the world today.

So, as stated, he who conquers discovers the treasures and hides the truth from the rest of the world, giving the impression to millions that the black man never had a heritage, civilization or any purpose in the development of the world. Truth has come forward to those who search for it, they say: "Seek and you shall find!" Never limit yourself to any one source of anything, especially when that indoctrinated form of literature is that of those who enslaved, massacred and isolated you from the rest of the world. I encourage all to read and open your eyes to the stolen legacies of a once powerful Black African culture and the significant role in world knowledge and development. There's plenty of Ancient Black history available by really great studies written and translated by some historians who combine Africa and Egypt as one, two books I find enlightening are: "The African Origin of Civilization" by Mercer Cook. "The Destruction of Black Civilization" written by Chancellor Williams and many more especially written by German and French historians. It's a beautiful read, however, I am mostly concerned with the culture, heritage and legacies of those who have endured much and achieved much in spite of our wondering existence here in this country where we have given so much and received nothing in return.

If this nation fails to adhere to universal laws and the laws of which it stand for, it will only continue to meet its demise by those racist and discriminating powerful people who have failed to right the wrongs over hundreds of years, what we and the world are seeing is the beginning of this nation's fall-out of God's grace and that of the world at large. At this point there's hope we need Change, we must adjust to the needs of our poor people, our children, our economy and social wellness, and that's done with strong, powerful people who recognize our problems and initiate the appropriate formula to stabilize our nation's policies, select a wise and knowledgeable council who will sit and listen and plan the appropriate plans for the betterment of the nation and its people, no matter how long it takes, good ideas and thought input are discussed to put forth our best programs that will benefit the nation and people as well. Like the Indians, we must seek the spiritual presence of God for His blessing on all we set forth in play. A meeting where all issues are discussed, where all resources are reviewed and established, where that Council is united to that Presidential leader, there must be a bond between all at the table, sometimes it may take hours or days, there's no time limit, there's only the hard thought-out plans to be put forth at the end of the day. The American people has been poorly led over the years, especially with allowing their only source of income, depriving them of making an honest living to support their families and the racial discrimination that allows double standards and poverty.

Again I reemphasize, War is not the answer, looking at Korea and Viet-Nam and now Iraq shows us that. War of the futures should not be the final answer without the input of the people, the people want to feel secure and in the hands of competent elected officials before fighting wars that will place them in harm's way, loss of jobs, high economic prices and loss of loved ones, what the world needs now is Peace and Unity. There's a multitude of people on our nation's soil there has to be a concerted effort to build a relationship of all the masses, there's no such thing to label a race of people as 3/5th of a human being as the constitution still reflects, to establish the equality for all, it must be changed as we as a nation move in for the betterment of all of our citizens.

War, what is it good for? Absolutely nothing! It's not the answer, Love of spiritual self, understanding and God is!

To all, one Love, Peace!!!!!

chapter 27

America's Most Shameful and Horrid Tragedy,
The Civil War

From April 1861, to April 1865 the North and South fought one of the bloodiest wars in this nation's history where we again see it was primarily fought over free slave labor and control of economic growth in the south. Blacks as free men and slaves had fought the war of 1812, Mexican war and played a major role in them, however, the Civil War was where they became the sole source of manpower to change the outcome of this violent and hostile conflict between two factions of white men, who were unwilling to agree or accept change. So it came down to pride and honor that cost approximately 364,511 deaths for the north and about 280,000 estimated deaths in the southern ranks.

Once again, as was in the Revolutionary War, the black slave, already working for no pay, being abused and corrupted, was again taken out of his slave status in order to fight and die for the white man's cause, of which they were never compensated. This fierce power struggle was a very critical period of the war for the north. President Lincoln was overwhelmed with requests for more manpower, and at that point a call for every able-bodied white man to step up to take his patriotic place in this raging catastrophe. No one in his wildest dreams thought that this war would last for 4 years, however, when the white man was fighting for his pride, dignity, honor and power there was no truce to stop the bloody massacre they were inflicting on each side, there was only either defeat or victory.

As in the Revolutionary War where trusted field Generals persuaded Washington to utilize the slaves' manpower to defeat the British, now we see Fredrick Douglass who was a man of color with whom Lincoln confided with periodically. Lincoln was told by Douglass that he was fighting a war with one hand tied behind his back. Douglass proceeded to tell Lincoln that it would be an ideal way for the blacks to fight for their freedom. Douglass at first was adamant in his getting Lincoln to sign the Emancipation Document. Lincoln never signed it until 1863, however, he did authorize the use of slaves to augment the much-needed manpower to defeat the south. At the war's end, there were approximately 200,000 black men fighting in the Union army.

We see that the slaves were victimized in every way possible, stepping up again to fight for their equal rights, their dignity, honor, pride and freedom. They showed the world their courage, valor, patriotism, high self-esteem as they fought and died for the liberty we all are enjoying here today. This was a very tough role for the blacks to play. The white man thought he could win such war without the slaves, and yet thousands of whites actually refused to go to the battlefields alongside black men. The old Common Foe was alive and well, even on the bloody battlefield. In many history reports you find the black Units showing up to save the white's behinds. When I was in Viet-Nam we fought as a Unit and learned to depend on and respect each other as our brother, despite his color. Eventually, the white soldiers saw how proficient and courageous the blacks were, such that their views were altered. The white Union troop commander was stunned by the bravery and valor the blacks displayed, under combat situations. Although there had been the notion that blacks were not smart enough to do this and that, however, in every war fought the black man has left an indelible legacy distinguishing himself in everything. Given the same training and guidance as all others, the black man would rise to the topmost, the elite in all endeavors and challenges in life. Blacks gained honor fighting in the Revolutionary War, the War of 1812, and the Mexican War as well.

In 1862, the Union regiments of slaves began appearing on the battlefields, some even fought against their southern masters, a Colonel Thomas Wentworth Hegginson, sent streams of letters to the daily press detailing the solid conduct of his soldiers, who faced a rebel infantry unit, a cavalry unit, and an artillery position, and in each battle they came off "not only with unblemished honor, but with undisputed triumph." As stated above, the Common Foe were there swearing to "shoot any negro that would shoot a white man, even if he was a rebel." Blacks not only had to face the enemy, but watch his white comrades as well who could not accept blacks as their military comrades, threatening to shoot them instead. Blacks were forced to return to their slave-masters, the white men where they came from. There were hundreds of slaves who returned home, only to be lynched, shot, or burned alive, some even in their military uniform. That's how strong whites hated black men, on both sides of the "battlefield," abroad and at home as well. All children should be taught this hidden truth of racism at all levels of our school systems. It's part of this country's make up.

Black soldiers knew they faced the enemy from all sides; any lesser man would never have volunteered to fight and die if only one of his feet had shoes. They understood that if captured, they would either be killed or enslaved. Executions took place wherever blacks fell into rebel hands, the infamous massacre at Ft. Pillow may have been the most egregious of official rebel policy, but it typified what black soldiers could expect from their enemies. As a black soldier declared, we will ask no quarter, and rest satisfied that we will give none. Blacks willing endured all these dangers and hardships for the sake for freedom and liberty. But the racial hatred and prejudices they suffered from the white Senior Officers of Lincoln's administration proved more galling than anything they might have expected from rebel troops. They fought for less pay, inadequate medical care, spent more time on combat lines and had to endure some of the worst racist' officers in the Union Army. At war's end a question was asked: "What would the white's position and treatment of blacks be?" The Massachusetts' Charlestown Advertiser cut through the debris of war and racist' propaganda to clearly identify the issue facing the country once the fighting came to a holt: The nation, meaning the individuals who comprise America must learn to treat the blacks on the simplest principles, of even justice. They are' treated neither with harshness nor with softness, nor as servile class, not as natural inferiors, not as a degraded race - but simply as men.

I was assigned to provide security for a Special Forces' group in Europe. A holding area prior to their departure for the east, I had the opportunity to converse with several of the team members, and one thing they had told me which remained with me today, was their motto: "Never give up, never get captured and always find a way to win or die trying to do so." The Fort. Pillow incident was one of the worst massacres of blacks in this country, the deadliest of wars. Whenever I read about it, I feel the spirit of those gallant men who laid down their lives with such "Refuse to Lose nor give up" spirit. They fought and died for what they had committed themselves into, that they were worthy to be free, and be respected by a nation who had abused them since their arrival on this soil, they showed all who were there what the ultimate badge of courage was. They knew that it was better to die fighting than to suffer in the hands of any southern white man, they knew the terror and horror, such had been inflicted on them from day one, the branding of their bodies, the lynchings, the whippings. They saw their people burned alive, hung on trees, or crucified on buildings, heads hacked off, genitals castrated, brains blown out. So as one soldier stated: "We ask for no quarter." Neither shall we give any. The blacks made up their minds to die, rather than to beg for mercy for their lives, choosing the only avenue to pursue, death. I only have one life to give and I give it dying for the freedom of my people, and to be acknowledged for all I stood for, that I was a loyal and courageous warrior who died for change of the nation, for liberty of all people, one nation under God, for which it stands. All great warriors never give up, they just die and fade away in their mortal dignity and grace, to be remembered for what they stood for, in giving the world their greatest gift, their lives.

In World War II some American soldiers refused to give up, were overwhelmed by the Japanese, as they continued to fight despite being outnumbered, some were even captured. The Japanese gave these men the country's highest honors for their courage and bravery. These soldiers were awarded the titles of "Martyrs" in a Ceremony where they got beheaded. The only thing that counts in combat is that brave men die for what they hold dear to their hearts and that's for "CHANGE," and for the betterment of mankind. Soldiers are always fighting for someone else's cause, we can only hope that here in America, the dream of Martin Luther King will become a reality, for which blacks have fought and died for, and although we know not when, we shall endeavor to pursue it, to fight and die for its cause, and seek respect and equality, and justice for all! Those who demonstrated their bravery and courage deserve to be called "Martyrs," they deserve it.

The black man was imprisoned here to be slaves and build the wealthiest economic system ever established on free labor, and yet, the white man found every way to utilize him to fight his war. In many readings of the hostile contempt and abuse they inflicted on those defenseless people, I often wondered why those slaves fought for the hand where they suffered so greatly from. Revolutionary War, little pay, thrust into combat situations as front lines, defensive where they should have been in support of the white troops. And yet they fought, after the war was over, they again suffered at the hands of their slave masters, who, instead were opposed to setting them free. Another 100 years later, still no freedom, they were asked to fight in the worst war conflict ever, however, after the Civil War was over, some progress were made. They were freed, albeit for a short period of time. During this phase of about 2 years, Blacks got elected to political offices, the Senate, the Congressional Office in many southern states. Blacks bought homes, started businesses, bought and operated farmlands, and things seemingly looked prosperous, a new foundation began to take place for thousands of blacks who had survived the war years and the racist' whites they lived among.

Suddenly the Union army pulled its troops out of the south, the new President signed a bill allowing old land owners to reclaim their plantations, at which time those government officials were removed from their positions and worse of all the Ku Klux Klan began their massive operations of destroying black schools, raiding farms, killing the black owners and their livestock, burning homes and murdering and lynching at random, one month after the Union had pulled out, those slave masters reclaimed thousands of slaves, of which they had documents to show ownership, and forced many blacks back into slave bondage. Thousands of blacks escaped to the north seeking for jobs, housing and places to live, while others even made it to Canada, a safe haven for blacks during such period. Yes, the Common Foe totally terrorized the south again. If Lincoln had not been assassinated, perhaps things would have been set in place to provide safety, and other major policies regarding placement housing and jobs for blacks during this reconstructed period would have been done. This racist' activity was an ongoing chaotic period of which blacks were totally controlled and again destitute in this racist' world. Approximately 240 years of slavery, 4 wars with black involvement for a white man's cause, still in bondage. What a psychological dilemma to endure, these white psychopaths show us that again blacks are only human property, pawns, used to suffer free labor and keep money in the white man's pocket, and to fight and die for his freedom, his liberty, his justice and his country, and this proved to be only the second part of his control to keep blacks totally insignificant in this country. From 1640 to 1866, back to square one, and it only gets worse for the Lady in the New York harbor, who would crumble if the blinders she wears would suddenly be taken off to reveal what the rest of the world has been witnessing for hundreds of years, the racist has been deceiving all that she stands for, and represent, she's been upset and disgraced and seemingly has no purpose to continue beckoning those of other nations to come here. She will only see the symbols for which she stands tarnished and in disarray, yet we still live in faith and hope that one day, she can stop shedding her tears and again, stand proudly when we, as a nation become as one.

We the People Must Accept the Challenge and Commitment of Reestablishing a Proud Character and Image of Our Nation, What are Wars Good for and Why the Need for Military Bases and Embassy there in Iraq?

Our past has revealed the relentless struggles for the equal justice for all people of this nation, regardless of race, creed, or color, the price paid as a people has been astronomical, in terms of death, tax, dollars, jobs, poverty, social unity and much more. It seems after every war the rich get richer and for others it's the on-going social racial discrimination, hostile violence, especially against black Americans. Today after few years of fighting in Iraq of which all races have played a major part, one way or the other, there's still the racist and hostile confrontational issues affecting our cities, there's drugs, the ongoing killing of our youth with these uncontrolled hand guns, or major problem, simply outrageous and there seems to be no end to it at this point. As I asked what are long drawn-out wars good for, there's absolutely nothing for our nation or the little people who fight them to feel proud of, especially when we bring back no victory, case in point, Viet-Nam, that war was only terminated after eleven years, because of the voice of We The People who demonstrated in damn near every street in every city of the country. The people initiated the change, as their public actions and voices influenced their opinion, after the huge death rate and financial hardship of the people and the government of maintaining it.

Now, we see Iraq conflict has the nation in its worse depression of our times and only seems to get worse, gas prices, no jobs to replace the outsourced, loss of homes and businesses, a and yet they are talking about building at the cost of millions an embassy and a number of military bases there, when infrastructure, medical facilities, social programs and much more to attend to here at home, setting up these bases does not assure national security for the country, I believe if anything's going to happen to this country it will be from an in-country source. If in fact these bases and embassy are required, then ensure that your elected politicians and officials address the need for these facilities and why should we still be required to maintain a force there? We The People should have a voice regarding our troops being in that region for who knows how long, we still have troops stationed and employed in South Korea for the last 60 years, why is there a need to maintain troops in that country? Let it be known to us, it's your right to know and have it explained by our Commander-in-Chief It seems that after this combat mission is over and their government reestablished there's no need to maintain forces there to ruin their country. It's their right to do so. Again we should not have to police that country, that their right, exactly when will the Mission

Be Accomplished? The same scenario happened in Viet-Nam and got us involved for 11 years and what did we prove? Only that they ran the French out and kept our forces we sent there to defeat and run their country, which caused our country and military world total embarrassment. We should learn from our past as I have stated before.

It was totally unacceptable for our leaders to allow 12 million Mexicans to enter this country in what seemed like overnight, and they are still here illegally with extended entitlements, what a gross travesty to allow such a magnitude of people of unknown identities, people not accounted for and still remain at large. The Mexicans demonstrated in city streets to speak, we the people did nothing to protest, wait until jobs become available and see who is first to be hired, jobs should be given to all citizens first and foremost, one of the biggest riots of New York was when the Irish burned and killed blacks because they were competing for jobs of which the Irish thought they were entitled to, 18 blacks were killed including several children, and 180 injured, so there will be problems over job whenever they become available with these millions of excess people here competing. So if in fact your congressmen and elected officials do not sign bills to return them, then look for trouble. As I've stated they should be rounded up and transported back and allow them to utilize the immigration system allowing in about a million a year. If not there will be a lot of blacks unemployed, as is the situation today. We The People must ensure your elected officials do the right thing, if not black people will remain unemployed as usual for a long period of time.

The people of this nation are utilizing all of their financial resources to maintain and survive this war. However, we hear Halliburton and Becktel corporations are making billions on reconstruction contracts. One of the reasons we never got any troop support from France or Germany is that they could not get a piece of the construction bids that went to the two American companies. Had they been able to receive any of the bids, they would have sent at lease another 200,000 troops, which in turn would allow the containment of controlled sectors from the very beginning. What are wars good for other than killing lots of the enemy, lots of innocent people and total destruction and making money, the American government and people were really upset because the French stated it would not send its troops to kill innocent people without a construction bid, the newspapers, radio and television ran statements regarding not buying any French wines or any other imported materials sold here. With those much needed forces available, this whole situation could have possibly been over with a few years ago. As in Viet-Nam and Korea we failed tremendously by underestimating the total situation by giving in initially without enough forces to begin with, and by the time we send for a backup force, the enemy has already their fields of battle and have damned near overwhelmed the small force sent in there from the beginning. In Iraq the situation got chaotic when we allowed the people to riot for three days after we took Bagdad at which we never were able to secure any portion of the city streets, that period of time allowed the enemy to make an assessment of our troop strength and time to prepare his counter-contingency measures for deploying their reactionary force, we never got to that control and still have not done so. What is the outcome? Who knows? It was thought that we would be welcomed with open arms, however, it did not happen, lesson learned is that invading and taking or trying to change ones country is the hardest task ever to complete by any power if the people are not in accordance of what you have done, especially after killing children, senior citizens and causing deployment and breaking up of families and destroying where they live, if that resentment is there from the beginning, they become the most formidable, willing to die for their land, culture and family as we saw in Korea and Viet-Nam and now Iraq. The old wisdom and knowledge applied to all three of these wars and that is: "Only fools rush in." I stated earlier that the only time we became the winning force was when we were part of a coalition of world forces, World War I, World War II, we marched so proudly and had the respect of the world, however ever since then, we as a military force invading and fighting alone have never returned victoriously to march anywhere. So what are wars good for? Look around you and it all reflects into your eyes.

What's in place definitely should not be the norm, as we see it we voted for the betterment of people and nation, first and foremost, Americans and others around the world are paying a tremendous sacrifice at this point fighting wars all over the world as we continue to do, is not the answer, we must not try to be the policemen of the world, what the United Nations job is, or should be, predicated on whatever a country's internal problems are or whether the crisis involved the country. Their leaders should be brought before the embodiment of the world council, the UN to address and resolve whatever problems they are having with all the powerful minds I see sitting in that huge chamber where I am quite sure some type of resolution can be initiated and implemented, knowledge and wisdom before weapons, bombs, death or destruction. I do believe the council voted and asked the President not to invade Iraq and Colin Powell had at that time also suggested not to go stating: Don't break it because if we did we would have to fix it. If the UN is to remain body of world leaders then they should have a vote into any world war actions. One other important thing our voice should have been heard, the voice of We The People, first there was - there were no weapons of mass destruction, then the picture changed, to go in and save the people - two different stories or causes given at that point. We The People should have asked for clarification, because the people are the ones to fight any war of a nation and I think that would have been justified asking for clarity from our leader. We spent eleven years in Viet-Nam who would have thought the most powerful force in the world would be engaged there for eleven years, if I am not put in harms way, I would expect that all the major resources would be used to end the conflict and return back here, eleven years like going around in a maze. No, wars are just not the answer in this age, nor is it a period to resolve any other nation's civil war conflicts. Remember we had one, however, no outside forces ever showed up. Iraq's civil war between its factions, Korean civil war between north and south, Viet-Nam civil war after the Viet-Cong had defeated and ran the French out. If in fact after this war would be over I think we should never employ in one unless it is another world war, just my opinion. It's a necessity to empower the UN to govern world issues and country conflicts where all will vote to determine the action to take and if there's a need then each country must be required to assemble a UN joint force to deploy to keep the peace between the two countries, that way countries would not have to totally disrupt that country to enforce a peace truce. We The People of the Constitution was put in place to in fact allow the people some input in cases where leaders were not leading for the betterment and welfare of the people or nation. It gives the people certain rights and a voice input to the governing of the nation. It states "of the people and for the people."

There was an election of which votes were not accounted for, states not following proper voting procedures, voting poll machines found to have glitches in them, however despite all those problems and discrepancies, the government allowed a President to be elected, there should have been another voting date and the incumbent President extended for a period of two months to ensure a new and fair election was conducted, that did not happen because You the People never voiced your dissatisfaction of the outcome, however, I heard all kinds of complaints from disgruntled persons, if you don't speak up, you just fall in place and comply to whatever is thrown your way. Read the Constitution, the Bill of Rights, your Declaration of Independence, know your powers. The Mexicans only here for about two weeks marched in every major city across America to make the national officials hear their voices and evidently it worked, because they are still here. You don't have to be a rocket scientist to know when something is not right, we have level of courts to make judgments on whatever is legal and what is unjust in the law. Utilize them, and then in some cases some issues might just be overturned, we owe any legal injustice of our people or our nation to he challenged fairly. The outsourcing of jobs should never have been allowed to happen, it was like slapping all the hard working people employed in those businesses in the face. One of the most necessary elements the government needs is to ensure its people have jobs. The number one requirement for you and your family is to have means of livelihood and a place to live, and to have security. The Americans showed just how much the little people meant to the country. They sold you out, We The People must ensure you hold those elected officials accountable for their actions, you can hardly find a steel plant in America today. Some years ago the government closed your shipyards and industrial plants and made a deal with the Japanese to repair all ships. It outsourced the country's steel industry for Japan approximately 25 years ago. Not only must you keep track with bills passed by the Senate and Congress, we miss out on lots of things because whites and blacks are steadily hating each other while the rug is being pulled right out from under your feet. We The People must be abreast of things happening to and around. If you don't look out for your children's future, then who will? You have worked all your life to be able to afford to buy a home, send your children to colleges or universities, however, your most important need has been outsourced, how can that happen and with the 12 million Mexicans here, no telling when you will be getting a job in the future, especially if you are black, there's two major construction jobs in this area, guess what? No blacks employed on either one, where's the mayor to make all things fair. Why not all races" There's double parking on Broad Street in south Philly, they have been doing it for over 50 years, if they allow it there, why not north Philly as well? Why the double standards, then that creates an unfair system? If in fact we stick to our standard, then that should be addressed. We The People must have the mayor to resolve that as soon as possible, that's why people get upset, they see different sides being played unjustly.

chapter 28

The Amazing Jumpmasters: Triple Nickle 555th Airborne Regiment & The 82nd Airborne

Early in the book I wrote of my cousin Jason and my stepfather wearing their military uniforms, my dad was really sharp and I was so proud of him whenever he came home wearing his, however, later in my years I saw that my cousin, who had come home having been on leave from the 82nd Airborne Division of which he had enlisted in, was sharp too. I was sitting on my doorstep, 17 years old at the time, on a summer day, when I happened to see this man from a distance, in uniform. Even from afar I was impressed with the upright rhythm of his walk, the way the uniform was fitting. All the brass emblems glittering, the military uniform creases pressed in the pants and shirt, the jump boots sparkling from the shining glass-like finish on the leather, the shoulder lanyard of medium blue, the cap with the distinctive Airborne insignia of which he wore tilted to the right side of his head with the glider patch in line with his right eyebrow, with the double A's (AA) insignia patch on his left shoulder. The soldier was like a one-man walking parade, people were stopping whatever they were doing to admire this amazing walking mannequin. As he drew nearer, I liked to have jumped out of my shoes, it was my cousin, Jake! This was the first time I had ever seen anyone dressed sharper than my Dad, he was truly the most immaculately dressed soldier I had ever laid my eyes upon, including my dad. I ran down the street to greet him, I went to give him an embrace, at which time he like came to a halt at the position of attention and extended his hand, not wanting me to grab and disrupt the placement of all he was wearing and displaying so proudly. I grasped his hand and told him: "Jake, I'm going to join the 82nd

Airborne Division Unit, so I can wear that uniform!" He laughed and I said: "Trust me, I will join up and become part of the 82nd Airborne Division, you have given me a dream!"

I wrote how I had that confrontation with one of my jump instructors and how the class leader, the Marine Captain told me to settle down and not let my temper be the cause of not getting my jump wings. I am so happy that he was there for me, I calmed down and went to complete the course, earning and accomplishing the goal I had dreamt of, since the day Jason came home and gave me a role model to compare myself to. One of my proudest days was the day they called my name out at the Graduation formation which went: "Specialist Webb, assigned to 82nd Airborne division, Ft. Bragg, North Carolina." Whenever I look at my 201 File with Awards and Medals, I always dwell on the Jump Wing Parachute Badge Award and whenever I see myself in uniform, I see Jason within the mirrors of my eyes, because I, too, wore that uniform in the same manner, to impress all that would look upon my presence. As I progressed into my career, my main Motto to all I ever trained or supervised or who became a part of my squad, platoon or operation section or as a Company First Sergeant was: "STAY SHARP!" and "BE SECOND TO NONE!" and I ensured that all knew exactly what these words meant, to be sharp in your dress, job performance, your attitude to achieve excellence in all endeavors of your life, to ensure you are Second to None at whatever game of life you choose to play! In Viet-Nam, the word in my platoon was:" STAY SHARP" because it could be the difference between life and death. In Korea I was instrumental in putting together a Tact Squad of 50 military policemen to control the villages along the southern portion of the DMZ, I had special belt buckles made which had engraved on them "SECOND TO NONE" and "STAYSHARP." I even gave the Korean soldiers assigned to my unit the same buckles, they were overwhelmed that I thought that much of them.

I was sitting in my office one day when the First Sergeant told me to be present at a 3:00 formation to receive an award, I wondered what I did to receive an award. At five minutes to three I showed up, there were several vehicles from the Korean army parked adjacent to the portion of the field where the troops were formed in formation. The Company Commander called for me, the First Sergeant called the unit to attention. I came up front and center, reported to him, he returned my salute. As I stood there a Korean Commanding Officer approached with his staff person, he stepped in front of me, I saluted him, his staff officer started to read the award, entitled "Achievement of Merit in Korean Service." It read:

"Sergeant First Class James L. Webb has made a major contribution to the Combat Readiness and Mission Accomplishment of the Second Infantry Division. During his tenure as Platoon and Tact Squad Leader, Second Infantry Division, he showed the highest degree of Initiative, Distinguished Leadership, and Excellent Exceptional Enthusiasm in accomplishing all the tasks assigned to him. His keen understanding of human nature and unswerving desire for excellence, permeated each and every subordinate, resulted in a level of achievement above and beyond that which even they thought themselves capable. Furthermore, he exerted himself to promote the common bond of friendship between the United States and Katusa soldiers of the Second Infantry Division, his performance while serving in the Republic of Korea reflects great credit upon himself and the United States Army."

I saluted the Korean commander, he departed, formation was released, I later learned that the Korean soldiers that were assigned to my Tact Squad had been totally surprised at me awarding them in a special squad ceremony, the same buckles I had given the American soldiers. I would promote them to supervise American soldiers at various times and I would tell them, we are one unit, we work together, we excel together, we are the best and have to remain "SECOND TO NONE." This is what Gen. Pershing should have done, instead of the action he took with those black soldiers, who became the highest decorated of World War I, I took these assigned Korean soldiers and made them proud of themselves, they learned well, at times there was miscommunication, but that was expected, when two different cultures come together and make a concerted effort on both sides to understand and respect each other. These Koreans were proud of me and until this day I still reflect back on that day, because the little gift of a unit buckle made such a difference and created a feeling that they belonged and were looked upon as equals. This made them cry in many cases, they were so overwhelmed of that tiny little gift from me, it was really huge in their eyes, such that they got the "word" to the top commander of the Korean military, who in return honored me for my small token of understanding, love and appreciation for these Korean soldiers who in fact made me feel very proud to have them serve with us, I made them feel "SECOND TO NONE!" This same scenario could be established here in this divided country if the Common Foe would only acknowledge and respect black people for all they gave in the development and structuring and freedom of this country, they could feel proud of these small gestures for peace and harmony of these two races.

The Rainbow Covenant
God's Love for Mankind

As we read the scriptures, we find where God destroyed his first creation of mankind, for their chaotic behavior, ignorance and calamitous ways. Not adhering to and being totally obedient to his commands of them. In time the people became evil doers, because of the lack of spiritual leadership, causing God to wipe them off the face of the earth. How wonderful our God is, who by way of his Rainbow Convenant, gave a promise never again to destroy his people. He told us that the Rainbow would come in the cloud of the sky as a constant memory that He granted his people. Yes God has blessed this earthly race of people, He has shed his grace on our country and world, yet we find ways to not appreciate his blessings and continue to tarnish that love of which He has bestowed upon us. This time, he promised never to destroy the people again, however, there are repercussions for our disobedience and evil ways, that is, we all have choices this time and will be held responsible for our deeds, as we encounter the journey of life. Which will be full of trials and tribulations, wars and disasters allowing us to see just how sacred life is and how we should be constantly aware of our purpose and that is, being our brother's keeper and insuring we are in keeping with God's demands of Peace, Love and Happiness for all mankind throughout our nation and the world. One God, one people, one world. Those who have eyes let them see, who have ears, let them hear and speak out against injustices that are blatantly before your eyes in a racially divided country, that speaks of Liberty, Justice, and Freedom for all. Our country is in total chaos and void of leadership for our governing political system, who has not been accountable for the welfare of its people, and has jeopardized the image of our democracy's principles and values.

How significant God's Rainbow Covenant is to the world, it is also spoke of by Jesus, reflecting around God as he sat upon his throne in heaven, it's a constant reminder of His love for us, can we say the same of our love for each other, I think not. We must ensure the people leading our country do so by unifying its people under God's grace. We should also have a testimony to our love and praise for our Creator, for all He has blessed us with in our life time. Seize the moment to do so. Extend your head to help the plan of Love and Peace for mankind, it's been long overdue and it begins here at home in our nation, where the multiple ethnicity of our races of people form the various colors that blend the brilliance together creating the beauty of that wonder that engulfs our world.

Peace and Love

James L. Webb

Ft. Dix Patrol Supervisor - 1975

Basic training in Fort Jackson, SC - 1961

Stacey (One sharp MP) and me in France - 1962

Guard mount in France - 1963

Carrying Army colors - 1964

Gendarm patrol members in Angoline, France - 1963

1st platoon shift personnel prior to my inspection - Camp Casey - 1974

Airborne training at Ft. Benning, Georgia - 1964

Sexton and I patroling the town area - Angoline, France - 1963

Beldine and Lewendowski - 1964

Ron on the firing line

Members of the Fighting Duece completing mission Vietnam - 1966

Standby and personnel check - Natrang,
Vietnam - 1966

Combat missions of the Fighting Duece
1st Field Forces, Vietnam - 1966

One of the finest officers receiving an award for the Fighting
Duece for valor and heroism in Vietnam - 1966 - '67

Homeboy Sgt. Mack and me - North Philly - 1975

Members of the MP Investingating Team - Camp Casey - 1973

Korea - 1976

Brother Lindsay presenting the pork to retiring 1st sargent - 1978

Young Mr. Webb Boxing

Boxing team preparing for exhibition - Camp Casey - 1976

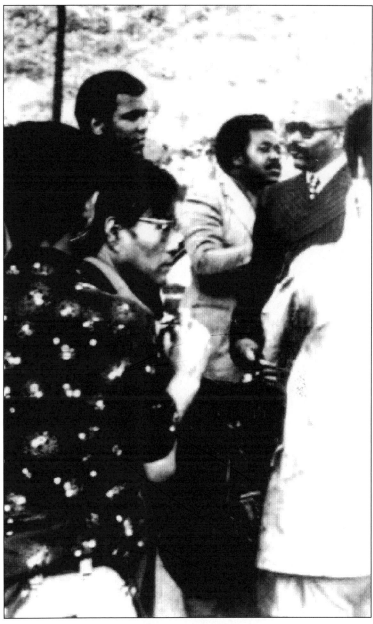

Guarding and escorting the champ

Ali flexing his muscles before sparring with Sgt. Nobles - Korea - 1976

Muhammad Ali sparring in the Philippines - Camp Clark - 1976

SHOW TIME! For those who Refused to Lose and were Second to None at playing their game

Victorious Army boxing team - Philippines - 1976

Ft. Dix - 1976

Office party with my investigators - 1978

At a picnic party, Ft. Dix, NJ - 1974

My aunt Mildred and mom - 1979

Walking the dog - Fairmount Park, Phila. PA - 1981

One of the best Veteran support groups very meaningful focusing on
unity and the moment - Trenton, NJ

Training boxer Marcus Smith of Riverside at Basic Fitness in
Lindenwold, NJ

Sonny, me, mom, and Mike

US.AB (Boxing) Conference meeting - Phila. - 2001

chapter 29

Follow-Me Airborne, Second to None

Just about the time of the Tuskegee experiment, there was a call to establish a paratrooper evaluation class of volunteers to see if the Black American soldier had heart enough to jump out of airplanes and fight in Airborne units. As usual the old negative attitude came up from the white racist and doubters, that blacks could not do it. Seventeen black soldiers volunteered and were sent to Ft. Benning, Georgia to participate in this program in 1943. After reporting in, they were assigned quarters and scheduled for physical training and packing jump chutes, all paratroopers learn to pack their own jump packs. After training on the rigging and mock training stations for several weeks, it was jump time. The word was out that no one thought these black troops would make it through the course. These soldiers had made up their minds that all would prove all doubters wrong. The jumps lasted for four days, all became qualified, they set a record as the first class where no one phased out, they opened the door for other blacks wanting to be Airborne troopers. It must be said that no one wanted them to accomplish the course, other enlists joined up to be assigned to the 82nd Airborne Unit, problem was they were not assigned to any airborne unit. They were kept in minimal jobs of riggers and packing and shipping supplies to other white airborne units. The unit had been increased to about 400 men, all completed the training and were informed they would be assigned to combat units in Europe to fight, it never happened, still packing and shipping supplies to combat units. After the second promise to be shipped overseas, which never happened, they were alerted to form a fire fighting force to combat the raging forest fires ravaging the western coastal areas. After being held out of the war, they welcomed that opportunity just to do something meaningful. They were equipped with special firefighting jumpsuits and equipment, and were then thrusted into the eye of a very dangerous environment of fire and smoke. This type of jump could be very hazardous, jumping into fire, smoke and the wind, at times there would be no accurate visibility of any landing area, and another great vulnerability was landing on treetops where, if your feet are not at the right position, and strong enough to break the branches, you could possibly be impaled by the sharp pointed branches on the way down through the tree. These men fought some of the fiercest forest fires recorded in those areas, for months suffering some casualties for that period of time. They played a major role in fighting and controlling fires in those areas. They received letters of meritorious service for their acts of bravery and efficient fire-fighting skills, enabling others to set up and get control of the violent raging disaster, saving lives and properties. They only wanted to be shipped to Europe to be involved in combat, only to be sent to fight fires and save lives.

Finally, the war ended, our troops were returning from Europe. Upon their return from Germany to Ft. Bragg, North Carolina, Gen. James M. Gavins, Commanding General of the 82nd Airborne Division, wanted an account of all airborne units and personnel. A report had been turned in, minus the names of the Triple Nickels 555th Regiment, however, Gen. Gavins had heard about the unit and the tremendous job they had done out there in California. So General Gavins made an inquiry and found they were returned to Ft. Banning, Georgia. He stated that all Airborne troopers would march down 42nd Street in that parade for those returning from Europe and said that: "Those men of the Triple Nickel would take their rightful place and be assigned, as intended, to the 82nd Airborne Division, regardless of being all black, they are Airborne and belong to my Division."

The parade was held in New York, wall-to-wall people, when the 82nd Division approached the reviewing stand led by Gen. Gavins, the proudest division marched in their magnificent elegance as only the 82nd could, in their impressive spectacular combat gear, and for the first time in history the people of America saw the first Black Airborne troopers of the 82nd Airborne Division. They were displaying their Regiment Colors of the Triple Nickels and believe me, they were the proudest of all, they had accomplished their dream and were finally recognized by one of the greatest Commanders who knew no skin color, like the well renown Gen. Patton. He only knew warriors who wanted to fight and defend their country's honor. There were many assigned at that point, they all gave thanks and gratitude to their fearless leader, to the man who placed them in their rightful place among the elite. At one time, the Triple Nickels had 1200 men in the unit, which was later assigned to Germany during the reconstruction of Berlin.

A special report was presented to the world featuring the tremendous job the fire fighters had done controlling that tragic catastrophe, saving lives and properties in that region. No mention was made of the efforts of the black men of the Triple Nickels. It was already known that the First Black Airborne soldiers were discriminated against by the military, as was the case with the Tuskegee Airmen. They were kept out of the war doing meaningless job assignments, until Gen. Davis fought with the Senators with the help of Mrs. Eleanor Roosevelt. An inquiry was initiated as to why the troopers were never given news coverage of their efforts in those fire regions, the reporters stated that it was not intentional, it was just an oversight, and apologized for the news story. The clamor for answers was requested again by Gen. Gavins, so an updated coverage was done giving the black troopers their just due. Simply amazing how truth always shows up one way or the other. We see that the Common Foe is everywhere, he even reports false news stories and write things that are just not the total "TRUTH." I cannot remember the name of our white Marine Airborne Training leader, however, wherever he is, he also instilled that "SECOND TO NONE" and "BE SECOND TO NONE" attitude. During his last jump, he made it with a fractured and bandaged ankle to inspire all who followed him, which was the motto of our class: "FOLLOW ME!" To him I say: "Thank You for your words of wisdom. At that point you played such a major role in my life! And I still have those wings that were awarded to me, to you I say 'SIMPER-FI!' those courage - traditional words of the Marine Corp of which you represented proudly, during our journey to having those wings pinned in our chest distinguishing 'America's

Best.' I was glad to follow you and the Pioneers of the 555th Triple Nickels for paving the way for the thousands, you set the standards of being SECOND TO NONE, AIRBORNE ALL THE WAY, ALL THE TIME!"

They Were the 9th and 10th U.S. Calvary known as the Buffalo Soldiers

The wagons were circled with fire, burning, dead and wounded soldiers strewn everywhere hurdled behind them, with little or no means to fight off another assault by their Indian attackers, they again felt the ground tremble and thunder from the hoofs of the horses' feet. The sound and the rumbling noise became more intense as the riders came nearer, these terrified settlers desperately clutched their loved ones, crying, praying and screaming, as they awaited the inevitable, the sound of hoofs, ".. .de thump, de thump, de thump." Hurdled there in the middle of the fire and smoke billowing skyward, the dust and smoke gagging their throats, burning their faces and eyes "...de thump...de thump," some of the younger boys broke loose from their frantic mothers arms, running aimlessly, the sound of the coming death unbearable, the end was near, one boy ran between the burning wagons to behold a large cloud of dust, he fell and stumbled to his feet, crying and hollering for someone or something to save them. Suddenly his eyes became clear, he could not believe what he was seeing, out of that visible mass of dust he saw riders, one holding a banner high above them, then he heard the sound of a bugle and the sound of a cavalry charge being played, it was unbelievable what he was seeing, he began to scream to the others, that the soldiers were coming. As they got closer he read the banner, the 10th Cavalry which was being held high by this magnificent rider on the powerful and beautiful horse, their rhythm was like poetry in motion, they all came running to see these soldiers who had to be God-sent, to save them, as the boy watched their approach the Guideron bearer dipped and lowered the colors as he made eye contact with the boy who now knew all was okay, and he snapped to attention and gave a really near perfect salute, as the soldiers continued to pursue the Indians, the little boy joined by his mother and others heard his mother say: "Thank You and God bless!" The boy hugged his mom, they were crying, he looked up and said: "Mom, I never knew they had black cavalry soldiers." His mom said: "Neither did I, neither did I!"

These soldiers were black soldiers made up from the two all-black regiments, that made up the 9th and 10th U.S. Cavalry. They were formed at the very end of the Civil War to combat the Indians across the western plains. These black cavalry units endured constant wars with the Indians for many years. The name "Buffalo Solders" was a name given them by the Indians, because of the Blacks curly hair, which often had dust layers clinging to their hair, mustaches and beards they wore, and also for being the fierce soldiers, whenever they engaged in the many battles over the years.

These Buffalo soldiers played a very significant role securing the land from the Indians, they also protected wagon trains with settlers seeking land, fought off cattle rustlers and other bad men roaming the plains. Most of the soldiers were slaves who served and fought in the Civil War and opposed to returning to that predicament volunteered for the new established regiments to clear the plains for the white man. The units suffered the same as before the racial problems were mostly from the other white units, in several confrontation many were killed by white soldiers who never were charged with outright murder.

General Custer refused to acknowledge these Black soldiers, however, these Buffalo Soldiers had to secure Custer's famed Seventh Cavalry on several occasions before the racist general and all of his men were massacred.

These soldiers as in every war fought exemplified themselves above and beyond expectations of courage and valor. They were the main force who fought the final campaign that forced victories, one of the greatest of all the great chiefs, including Geronimo, Crazy Horse and Sitting Bull - into Mexico where he was finally killed. The Buffalo soldiers earned many Congressional Medal of Honor.

A book written by William H. Leckie reflecting their accomplishments, sums it up as follows:

"The experiment with Negro troopers... proved a success by any standard other than... racial prejudice. By 1891 the combat record spoke for itself. They had fought on plains of Kansas and in Indian Territory, in the vast expanse of West Texas and along hundreds of miles of the Rio Grande and Mexico, in the deserts and mountains of New Mexico and Arizona, in Colorado, and finally in rugged grandeur of the Dakotas. Few regiments could match the length and sweep of these activities - the 9th and one other Cavalry were first rate regiments and major forces in promoting peace and advancing civilization along America's frontier. The thriving cities and towns, the fertile fields, and the natural beauty of that once wild land are monuments enough for any Buffalo Soldier."

Nevertheless, in 1992 an official monument to the heroism of these men was erected in Bronze statue of a trooper astride his horse at Fort Leavenworth, Kansas, where the story had begun 126 years earlier. Colin Powell, the Chairman of the Joint Chief of Staff, made the dedication as the 302nd Fighter Squadron, a unit of the Tuskegee Airmen, flew over head, the monument was the creation of black sculptor Eddie Dixon.

I was stationed at West Point Military Academy and upon my arrival there in 1977 I first encountered the Buffalo Soldier Field adjacent to the cadet parade grounds. Also the first black man to graduate from West Point and was assigned to the Buffalo Soldier was Lieutenant Henry O. Flipper, 10th Cavalry. Flipper was harassed, isolated and discriminated against during his 4 year tenure there, no one ever spoke to him other than his instructors, yet he graduated in the 10th place of his class. Let it be known that the top cadet graduate of each Class receives a Henry O. Flipper Certificate of Honor achievement and standards of which he stood for in spite of the tremendous racist pressure to endure, that in itself is a credit of his tenacity, courage and commitment to excel and accomplish his goal regardless of the barriers in place. He refused to give up, as did the Buffalo Soldiers of which he was a very important role model. The Buffalo Soldiers Banner displays the image of the Buffalo of which the Indians hold as one of their highest religious sacred symbols "Worthy of Praise."

The beginning is a little scenario I called envision happening in many of their missions. There was a very historic part I read r garding them refusing to kill when ordered to do so by their white officers who ordered, to fire on a group of homesteaders, point blank, they were unarmed, the soldiers looked at the white men and women and children, took pity on them, disobeying the officers, thus saving a lot of civilian lives. They made a difference...
"SO MUST WE."

chapter 30

Experience of War: Post Combat Suggestions

I would suggest that anyone returning home from an overseas war zone area should seek, immediate traumatic stress disorder evaluations and counseling from certified doctors to insure that he or she understands the meaning of such conditions. Each and every individual screened and monitored who is asked about having any physical, or emotional stress, mental depression, aggressive behavior, sleeping problems or any type of psychological related incidents should he noted and acted upon.

No one was there for me upon my return and this allowed me to take these traumatic and stressful conditions home to my family and into my society of which I had been called upon to give up, to fight for my country. Someone should have been there to insure I was not emotionally abused by my experiences from Vietnam. Very few have come back with a sound mind. The effects were instilled in most of us from day one.

A major factor in these debriefing evaluations and counseling sessions should include wives and husbands of these service members, group sessions or better yet, family members only.

"Experiences in the past and present defiantly find that soldiers returning without help have committed suicide as well as killed wives and children. Going home to my family, wife, and children without counseling found me examining my new identity. "While once loyal, loving and caring husband and father, now I was a new individual in their lives. I was waking up all hours of the night sweating, could not sleep, suffering from insomnia, became aggressive to any noise by my children, screaming at them occasionally and frightening them to distance themselves from me. I was on guard mentally and I felt the isolation being built up against me in my own home. My wife became afraid and could not feel the trust and love she once had for me. "We became separated because she felt she and the children were not safe around me. My ISG got involved and requested that I move into the barracks after I had only been home for approximately a month. I was relieved of my duties for assaulting three prisoners in the stockade where I worked. I was up for a court martial and reduced and assigned a much more isolated job.

I truly believed that had I and my wife received this type of counseling, I could have saved my marriage and could have readjusted maybe with my wife's understanding of what I was dealing with. "Until this day she has never forgiven me for the rage and attitude I thrusted upon them. So, I strongly suggest everyone returning home receive mandatory counseling, so at least the loved one will know what to expect and if the love is there, she or he can assist that soldier in some type of recovery.

That was 1966 - 1968. Today I am still plagued with these disorders. No one was there for many of us. While in the hospital in Japan, I chased a doctor off the ward early one morning, only because he knew me; I did not get any disciplinary action against me; no one seemed to notice these strange behaviors at this point. I should have had major counseling even before leaving the hospital. At that point, I began not even trusting myself I was out of total control. However, I was allowed to come home to my family when I was not sure of whom I really was.

No way should anybody be allowed back home to their wife and children without letting them know that it will take a lot of faith and willpower to work at a readjustment especially from the wife, who will have to be willing to learn of this traumatic mental abuse, that she must be strong and supportive in order for it to work.

I was a true victim of the military, a total lack of commitment to a vast problem that was allowed to engulf thousands of service personnel 'This was a gross mistake not having programs in place to deal with these illnesses affecting us upon our return home, These types of mental disorders have been understudy by mental science studying psychological symptoms and patterns affecting our military since late World War 1, Not to recognize that this was a major problem and not to set forth means to counteract it was really negligence on the military commanders and those appointed to prevent these types of disorders that took so many of our patriotic young men and women. This is truly appalling, I weep whenever I see doctors and medical interns in various cases not identifying or treating vets with respect in many of the VA hospitals I have been to. I've seen vets rescheduled for 4 to 6 months, when they would need to be seen sooner. I have seen vets waiting 6 to 7 hours just to see a doctor. I have had an incident with a care provider who did not seem to be interested in my medical history when I was assigned to her and even refused to allow me to see a doctor. I wrote the hospitals administrative branch supervisor explaining and requesting a new provider, which was taken care of.

Never have I ever been in a hospital or seen a doctor who took an oath to help and assist patients in their need of medical assistance and to treat vets with an honest interest in their welfare, instead they refuse them medical services. I would encourage vets returning home to write letters to VA offices, administration officers, or even congressmen, whenever encountering these types of doctors or these student doctor who sometimes seem not to have a clue when working one on one with the patient. I think, we have earned the right to be treated fairly, professionally and tactfully when seeking medical aid and assistance.

I would tell returning personnel, especially those retiring or those whose enlistment is up, to seek, out a VA branch where they can attend weekly sessions to keep themselves abreast of ongoing programs and policy changes, where they could also relate with fellow military combat persons as themselves. The sessions have been very helpful for me in dealing with my personal problems. They give me an outlet of expression and above all else, the support of the group and the knowledge of a team leader, his input, his assistance with various issues, filing claims, connecting and setting up appointments and any other issues they may have to he inquired about. This has been a tremendous asset.

Again I have been highly motivated since attending the Vet Centers group sessions and it's nice to feel the love and concern we have for each other as well as the respect we share for one another, lastly, I would relate the importance of staying connected to the oneness of all things. God is there always and is the source of correcting our balance of self.

chapter 31

Just Not White Enough They Said

In this nation we, as Americans were taught as children in our innocent world of venture and wonderment, that competing for the prize is the ultimate goal of our growth. We developed that concept as young children, in schools around our nation, where we see and feel the urgency to be better, stronger, faster than the other kids. Our fathers taught us to be tough, smart, and like them or our big brothers who we see playing sports in school or in the park recreation center. We see them achieve their goal with pride and dignity, they accept their trophies and receive the recognition from other children who begin to look up to them as their role models. They see their big brothers, or their fathers, running, exercising, practicing, and through our eyes we see the total preparation of their determination to get totally fit for the challenge of fame and fortune. We marvel at their efforts and we decide early on, I want to be like my big brother or my Dad, the red blooded American pride and joy of our school, neighborhoods and communities, where we receive the accolades of being special. Yet for many of thousands they had these ideas and dreams, only to find we were not allowed to chase our dreams, that it was only an illusion, that never would they materialize. We would never compete for the prize, or be accepted as the victor or champion. All the years we played our dream games we ran the bases, we hit the balls, we fielded the hits, we tagged them out, made that crucial throw to get them out at the plate, we stole that extra base to score that run that won the game, or we received the kick off and ran it through all opposition to score, or we blocked that ball carrier negating any yardage on that play, or I threw that pass, caught by the receiver for the winning touchdown or I ran a consistent race just off the pace setter's left, stride for stride, I was in good position and when we turned for the final stretch, I excelled, came abreast of him and then passed for the lead just before the winner's line, winning the

race in spectacular form. And I would set up the ball on the puck
and swing at it like my father did everyday when he took me with
him to practice. I was amazed at the sound of the golf club, as it was
swing at the ball, the sound of the impact and my eyes would follow
the flight of it until it landed far away. I recorded his form, the swinging motion, and I did it just like him, because all of these things were
part of my dream, to be like him. Or I sat on the side line watching
the green ball hit the other person who would scramble around to
get in position, to hit it back to my big sister. I watched her reaction,
at times she would miss, but not too many, and at times there would
be volleys back and forth between the two of them. It was just fantastic and I was caught up wanting to play that game, my father took
me to my brother's high school where I saw him be introduced after
he ran onto the court. I saw him in jump ball action to start the game,
saw my brother receive a pass from another teammate, watched him
catch the ball, stop, raise up and shoot for the basket. And I heard the
sound, "Swish!!!" as the ball drained through the net, what perfect
form! After the game, my brother's team won, I was telling about
that shot all the way home!

I was proud of my brother, and even prouder when he and his
team won the championship, and received their jackets, or I was with
my Dad who took me to the gym. I saw him change into his training gear, wrap his hands, the bell sounded, he would shadow box
for three minutes, another bell, he rested, another bell, resumed the
shadow boxing. It seemed everything worked from the sound of the
bell. Even when he moved on, to jump rope. What fun! And rhythm
he had! He was really smooth in his body motions, he was jumping
to the tune of "ain't no stopping us now, we are on the move," next
thing I saw him climb into the ring, where there was another guy
dressed in gear just like him, then there was the bell, and they began
moving, punching and swinging at each other, then I noticed just
how much faster my father's hands were, he was hitting the other
guy almost at will, and exchanging punches. He was hitting the guy
at least six or seven to his one or two, what a tough guy my Dad
was! I really admired and respected him. He was my Dad, tough,
strong, courageous, with big muscles, strength and power, he even
knocked the other guy down two times in one round. I knew one

thing, if my Dad told me to jump, I would say: "How high?" When it came time to bring my report card home, I would check it for all good marks, and if there were any bad or low marks, I would begin to cry, people asked me why I started crying, and I would think if they only knew how tough my Dad was, and I just could not upset him with bad marks, he was just that tough not to let me get away with anything less than the best, I always had the picture of him punching and knocking that other guy down, so many times, so why would little old me want to upset him at home, no way! My grades excelled tremendously! And I called that saving my behind! I had a few bad marks on one of my report cards, I got home, my tears had soaked my shirt I was wearing, it looked like someone had thrown a bucket of water on me. I showed my report card to Mom who in turn took it and showed it to Dad. I heard a roar as he called my name. I was trembling so much, I damn near fell to the floor, he said: "Come here." I found the courage to go to him, expecting the worse, my behind was already feeling the pain. I stood there, ready to collapse, could not stop the tears. Mom had already told me I was in trouble, then it happened. With the most gentle voice, he said: "Son, you know I always stress good marks from school, now sit down here and let's see just what caused these bad marks." He actually talked me into feeling so embarrassed. I was lost for words to express myself. Anyway, he told me how important my grades were and how he was proud of me, and if there was anything I could think of that caused my grades to reflect those marks, he wanted to know. He went on to tell me how important education was for my future, and how it was a necessity to be the best of the class and in any other endeavor in life. After our conversation, he told me to never let him or my mother, and most importantly myself down, ever again. And I never did! So you see, there's pride we carry housed inside. We, as children, grow up wanting to be "Somebody" wanting to exhibit our skills before the world. All that we have seen or experienced at a young age to compete and excel to be all what we can be, this never happened in many of our young lives. We were the outcast, we were the ones the people said we're dumb and ignorant, not smart enough to play the game and above all else, we were just not *WHITE ENOUGH THEY SAID!*

chapter 32

Basketball

I can never imagine thinking of writing about Basketball, it has an extraordinary history revolving around and within it so I am only highlighting a few interesting historical facts and some of the pioneers and magnificent black players of the thousands who have graced the playing fields and made the game what it really has become in America and around the world at large. I should call for back up on this one from my main source of knowledge of this cherished game of America's past time of enjoyment, my source would have to be Sonny Hill, the great Sonny Hill who covered the sport, played it and is a walking legend of its history. Sonny is also renown for playing baseball as well, you mention Johnny Sample, Wilt Chamberlain, "Doctor" Julius Ervin, Oscar Robertson, Elgin Baylor, Kareem Abdul Jabbar, Earl "The Pearl" Monroe, Wes Unseld, Moses Malone, Andrew Toney, Maurice Cheeks, Ervin "Magic" Johnson, Isaiah Thomas, Dominique Wilkins, Robert Parish, Marques Johnson, Sidney Moncrief Lloyd "World B." Free, Akeem Alajuwon, Michael Jordan, Ralph Samson, Dan Roundfield, George Iceman Gervin, William "Pop" Gates, Bill Russell, Walt "Clyde" Frazier, Willis Reed, Albert King, Buck Williams, and a special mention of the Harlem Globe Trotters, who have magnetized people worldwide with their classical ball handling and orchestrating player skills, just phenomenal, and their tradition is still apart of the Basketball today.

Each of these players named here are among the best players of this game, bar none, they were smooth, graceful, superb ball handlers, play makers and could hit that basket from any position on the court, they were certainly created to be SECOND TO NONE at playing the game. Each and everyone had the total game, that the fans of the world could bear witness to. They possessed it all, the jump shots, the fade away, the sky hook, the finger roll, the slam dunk, the dribbling and beautiful ball handling that could shatter the back boards. Again, these guys could dribble down Broad street, across the Ben Franklin Bridge and down the aisle of a 747, they would fake out the opponent, stop, raise up and hit that jump shot from any three points and, how sweet the sound, all net "SWISH!" one of the greatest sounds ever heard on the Ball Court! The black players brought their A game, each and every time, it was just a marvelous time to behold for the basketball fans of the world, these guys were absolutely fabulous, some of the games and fantastic shots and finishes will be forever etched in our lives, the greatest among the selected few.

The game has a very rich heritage, its history is really a good read, about the discrimination, the threats, and various situations black players were involved in, and still keep themselves focused to put it all together at game time. The Harlem Globe Trotters which team was originated by a white man, Abe Saperstein in 1926 after watching black youth playing in the north side ghetto areas, he saw skill, talent, and then organized their potentials, talked five players into formulating a team. He called them Savoy Big Five in honor of their home court, the Savoy Ballroom in Chicago. The team was playing so well, he decided to take them on the road and renamed them the Harlem Globe Trotters, doing so to give the impression all his team was widely traveled, although most of his players had never been to Harlem much less outside the United States. The team later had traveled five million miles, to almost one hundred countries and have played before over sixty million spectators. Saperstein proved to be an excellent promoter and the Globe Trotters became international favorites. They played before a white-tie audience in London's Wimbledon Stadium, in the cow pastures of Morocco, and before Pope Pious XII.

Basketball is one of the biggest sports game in America, if not the biggest, incidentally three of the Globe Trotters went on to be very successful in pro basketball, they were Nat "Sweetwater" Clifton, Will "The Stilt" Chamberlain and Connie Hawkins. The WNBA has been very successful as well featuring some great female ever to play the game. As I have stated, check out the history of the game, and these amazing young players in the game today, establishing themselves among the chosen few. Sample and Sonny were my favorites, I used to watch them play at the recreation center at 25th and Diamonds on many a Saturdays, it was great to see Sonny and Wilt go at it, Chamberlain was sharp, but Sonny had that finesse and the jump shot to make it interesting. Most of us who knew Sonny Hill called him "The Blade." Blade, STAY SHARP, you guys have given me many unforgettable memories!

The black basketball players are "SECOND TO NONE" and have exemplified themselves to the world from the very beginning, in the early 1900's until today. They have truly earned the white man's respect, as well as all others and the sound of their names etches sweet memories for all time in The Hall of fame. Thanks for a job well done, we excel at whatever there is, so that 3/5th of a man just continues to prove someone made a drastic error in their ignorant categorization of another race of human beings in that Document we know so well. I quote a Master at his game, he states: It's not what people know that gets them in trouble, it's what they know that just is not so." Dr. Reggie Bryant, that's a classic, if it were not I would not have shared it with you all!" Truer words have never been spoken, what they wrote, we see as blacks, seeking fairness for what we have given since day one, here in this country. They do know, we know, that those words just isn't so!

HORSE RACING: THE DENIED WHO BECAME THE GREATEST AMONG THE SELECTED FEW.

As I wrote in "How Sweet The Sound," Blacks have been entertaining the white man since his early days in slavery, especially in sports, there was boxing, horse racing and rodeo. Let's talk about horse racing, one of the biggest sports of today in America and around the world.

When the Moors conquered and drove the Groths from Spain, they brought with them the Arabian horse of the Middle East and started breeding this very special horse that originated in Egypt, after several years breeding was successful, creating a much larger horse, height about 65-70 inches and weight increased from the

500-600 to 1,050 pounds. The horses that came out of Libya into Egypt were the ancestors of today's thoroughbreds.

King Henry I of England heard about the value of these special bred Arabian horses and purchased a stallion in Spain in AD 1110. He bred the stallion with strong powerful mares, the results were astonishing, he then brought many more of the stallions from Morocco. The owners of these purebreds took great pride in them and would make wagers as to who had the fastest and greatest horse riders. At first horse racing was the sport of kings, but later it became the sport that attracted audiences throughout England and the Middle East.

In 1644 Colonel Richard Nichols invaded and conquered the Dutch territory called New Amsterdam, he became the first English Royal Governor of New York. He was a horseman and enthusiast, in 1665 he built a two-mile course near Hempstead, Long Island, called it New Market, honoring a place in England. This course was just a few miles from the present Belmont Park Street.

The imported English Thoroughbreds were bred here in the Colonial south, eager to emulate the British the plantation owners of Virginia, Maryland and Kentucky imported and started breeding these prized Thoroughbreds.

The job of grooming, feeding, breaking, exercising and training these horses was turned over to the slaves. And when it came time to race these magnificent horses, it was the black slave who rode them to victory or defeat. Although official records were kept, the names of these black slave jockeys and trainers never appeared in any of the racing programs.

So you see, the 3/5th of a man, the piece of property or chattel, as recorded in our Constitution, the dumb and ignorant were actually instructed to groom, train, break, feed, exercise and jockey them in the races, are you kidding me? Mr. Charlie trusted these black inferior at all things with one of his most valuable racing stallion, did I miss something along the way? These historical findings and writings must be mistaking, what is amazing is what you can find out when you follow the Universal Law of seek and you shall find. Slaves did it all, picked cotton and took care of all other resources, worked for nothing, fought and died in fighting in white people's wars, saving them from being defeated by the British to save their quest for this Country's Independence, also saved the Union from their defeat by the Confederates, that allow this land to become the United States. These slaves did it all, without them where could this country have been, now we find that they made many more millions racing and taking care of these money makers and lending their names to these Empires in terms of these Racing and Breeding farms in Maryland, Virginia and especially Kentucky. The white man would have been in a world of trouble had it not been for our Black ancestors, who in fact were intelligent, hard workers, possessed faith and courage, were loyal to the slave owners, until their death, who only wanted to be recognized and treated fairly with dignity and respect from those who constantly inflicted so much pain and suffering even today. The whites did not acknowledge these patriotic souls who saved this country from whatever fate we will never know, but we do know that our black ancestors built this country from the very beginning. And especially during the war conflicts. As President Madison, his wife and staff were deserted and abandoned by 4,000 American Colonist troops guarding the White House in Washington D.C., the Presidential family and staff had gone out to watch the battle, only having to flee the White House as those cowards refused to stand and defend, one reason the slaves fought to the end, if they refused to fight, they would have been lynched, hung, burned, or nailed to trees and buildings, and murdered. So for that alone blacks fought with fierce determination and valor which is recorded in most history books that reflect a thorough research on their fighting records. Like everything else, it is hidden knowledge, not shared to the people of this country. So now we see even these slaves made millions for their owners by taking care of these precious animals and becoming great at all phases of the racing game only never to be mentioned in it at all, from very beginning. Sounds like we have heard this all before, we have and it all comes to light sooner or later, the laws of the Universe, how sweet it is, nothing remains hidden forever, search and you will find, so I am just shedding some light on a treasured history that should be known. Fact of the matter the slaves were good enough to be recognized or mentioned in records and programs. I love horses and racing, that's why I write about them. It's been thirty years since there's been a triple crown winner, the horse is one of the purest athletes, it will run its heart out for you. Believe it or not, the elements done by the slaves caring for these animals were the most important of all, the horse develops its confidence and character by the firm voices and the gentle hands that guides it. Jockeys who ride wildly whipping and pushing has not a connection with that horse, it's all communication, rhythm and body action, the whip is only a tool to focus the horse on. Most great riders in close races, only have to talk and show him the whip to get him to respond. "Man A War" one of the greatest ever, had a black groom whom he loved and it was mutual, you could not get him out of the barn unless that groom was there, he was a fighter until he died, in Kentucky. The groom had raised him, talked to him, rode him periodically, slept in the barn with him, went everywhere with him. "Man A War" was retired from racing, the owner still kept the groom. People would come from all over the world to seek him, however, if the groom was not there to show him, it was a "no show." The horse died, and approximately a year later, the groom died too, he was almost 80 years old, the only groomer the horse ever knew and would listen to, the horse was totally dedicated to him and loved the man, so when you see a jockey whipping, ranting and raving, it's all show. I have a collection of all the triple crown winners' movies, and there really are some amazing stories behind many of them.

In 1866 the first Jerome Handicap at Belmont Park was won by a black jockey named Abe who rode a horse called Watson, Abe went on to win the third Trovers States at Saratoga Springs in 1866, riding a horse called Merrill. 1875 the first Kentucky Derby at Churchill Downs, Louisville was won by a black jockey named Oliver Lewis, riding Arisitides in 2.37th of a mile and a halftrack. Black jockeys won 15 of the first 28 runnings of the Derby.

The best winning average in Kentucky Derby history, two victories, one second and one third in four starts in Jimmy Winkfield, Isaac Murphy was considered one of the greatest jockeys in American history, he was the first man to ride three Derby winners, according to his records, he rode in 1,412 races from 1875 to 1895, winning 628, no other rider has yet approached that mark. By the 1880's he was so well renown that horse owners would put up big money just to be first in line for his services. Murphy rode Buchanan to victory, 1884 Derby, Riley in 1890 and Kingman in 1891. His record of 3 Kentucky Derby wins was not equaled until 1930 when Earle Sande came home in Gallant Fox and was not passed until 1948, when Eddie Arcaro won his five on Citation.

Murphy had style, flair land was a pleasure to watch, he was a great judger of pace and instance, a superb jockey known for his come from behind finishes. Murphy also won five Satonia Derbys and four of the five American Derbies at Washington Park. He won the Swift, the Trovers and the Saratoga Cup. He also rode a horse called Salvator to three victories over a horse called Tammy, ridden by the great white jockey, Ed "Snapper" Garrison, the last of the three being the classic of the times where Murphy coming from behind to catch the Garrison with his neck hugging and wild-whipping, got the attention, but Murphy got the win in a most thrilling finish.

Some often noted black jockeys: Williams Simms, won Kentucky Derby 1870 and in 1894 also won it in 1898. Jimmy Winkfield, he won the Derby on His Eminence 1902, that was the last Derby played by a black jockey. Alonzo Lonnie Clayton, great jockey who rode in the 1885 era. James Soup Perkins 1897 to 1900 era, George B. "Spider" Anderson 1871 to 1890 era, John H. Jackson 1879 to 1894, Jimmy Fox claim those fame in racing, he rode 6 winners in one day at the Latona in 1909 and riding five winners in one week. Robert "Tiny" Williams 1865-1879. Anthony Hamilton, 1886-1895, Henry J. Harris 1891-1900, William Porter 1891-1901.

There were many outstanding black jockeys, and the dominated the game for a long period of time up until the Kentucky Derby in 1911, Jesse Conley was the last, and rode in that Derby, they just were discriminated against. After Jack Johnson won the Heavyweight Championship beating the legendary Jim Jeffries, the great white hope in 1910, there was violence everywhere, race riots all throughout America, racial discrimination affected just about all black people, especially the black athletes. Johnson's beating Jeffries showed just how fragile and insecure white people were.

Jack demoralized Jim, as well as a nation of sore losers. Jack did only what Champions do, beat him, it was the white people's fault taking a man out of retirement. As their great white hope Jeffries was brutally beaten by a superb conditioned Champion who held that title for 8 years after beating and embarrassing him. The very whites who sought him out to fight Johnson called him a coward and traitor to the white race, so much for loving your brother, let alone a black man who was loved and respected worldwide.

I have to end about horses with this. I had an uncle down in Maryland, my first visit to his farm I was about 11 years of age. We got down there from my home in Philadelphia, my first time on a long trip. We arrived, I met him, my aunt and their children, later some of the children were showing me around when I noticed this really beautiful beige color horse standing out in the field, I fell in love with that horse right from the very beginning, I asked if we could ride it, they told me to ask Uncle Norman. I just dropped all else and ran back to find him. I asked if I could ride the horse, he told me if I caught her I could possibly ride her. I ran back and told my cousin what he had said. Growing up my stepfather had started me to drawing and showed me a picture depicting a great warrior with his headdress, shield and spear, sitting on this magnificent beige and white horse that was so powerful and graceful looking. I drew many pictures of horses, but never painted that particular one, I always say I'll do it, and after this book I will paint that scene - of that warrior and horse at the mountain top at the edge overlooking the western plain below. I have it implanted in my vision. My cousin and I took off to catch the horse, her name was Mable, matter of fact my uncle told me if I could catch and ride her I could have her, but he had to keep her on the farm. My cousin and I finally caught her with many apples and carrots, of course, I think we only caught her because my cousin knew how to get her attention, it was fun. We put the rope over her head and I found a box and climbed on it and managed to get on her back, then helped my cousin up. Man, I was elated with my first horse and she was mine. We rode Mable for 2 to 3 hours I just did not want to get off Eventually she got upset, we were on her for so long, she reared up and guess what, you know the deal, I slid right off her back and damn near broke my neck, hurt my back. I could not even move I laid there, she never moved away, after 5 minutes of laying there trying to get myself together, I saw something sliver in the grass. Thinking it was a snake, I found some unfound strength, pulled myself up, I never let go of the rope we had put around her neck. I got up then let go of the rope, Mable galloped away deep in the wooded area, my cousin was okay and we finally hobbled to the house, never told my uncle we fell though, I told him I had fun, he said "You mean to tell me you two have been riding Mable all the time?" We said: "Yes, Sir!" We left early the next day. I waved to Mable really wanted to ride one more time, but figured I would be back in a week. As we left I asked: "Is Mable still my horse?" He said: "Yes!" I thanked him and told him I would be glad to come next week and how I really enjoyed our stay.

Well next week came and we went back down there, I could not wait to see Mable and ride her again, well upon our arrival I was the first one out of the car, I saw Mable, I went running towards her, someone looking would think I was Jesse Owens, hollering and screaming her name, I was saying: "Mable, I am back!" I was waving, trying to get her attention, finally she looked my way, her ears perked up, she took a good long look, as if to say: "Oh no, not this crazy kid again, ain't no way he's going to ride me all day." I was still running towards her, all of a sudden she fluffed her tail a few times, reared up a little, turned and started running away form me towards the woods. Suddenly it dawned on me that Mable was not going to let me come near her ever again, I stopped, out of breath and finally got the message, she disappeared into the woods. I never rode Mable again, I was the only kid that had a horse who I could never ever catch to ride after the first day. I went walking back up to where everyone was standing, my uncle looked at me, with a small grin on his face. "You could not catch Mable?" He asked. I said "No Sir. It's as if she was running away. He stated: "You rode her damn near to death the first time." He said that horses were like elephants, they never forget, he laughed and walked away saying: "She's still yours if you can catch her." Then everyone began to laugh. I never ever caught or rode her again, I said how smart she was, when I left I waved at her, as soon as she saw me... back in the woods she went. Later I found how intelligent horses were, I used to work for a produce vendor from a horse and wagon and I always wanted to drive the horse. He would go down in south Philly to get the horse and wagon early Saturday like five in the morning, at seven we would load the wagon and travel around the neighborhoods selling vegetables and fruits, and terminate the day around six, get back and unload. And I would always ask to take the horse and wagon back. One evening Mr. Payton said: "Okay." And asked if I knew the route. I answered I did. Well about 9:00 pm I started out from 23rd and Columbia Avenue to get to 4th and Bainbridge, it was dark and I took off going down Ridge Avenue Broad Street, where there was Father Devine Hotel, and a water trough in the middle of the intersection. That was the last thing I knew, I had fallen to sleep. I was awakened by someone saying: "Hey kid, don't you think you should be going home?" I looked around, I was in the wagon, the horse was in its stall. The horse had taken me all the way from Broad Street in north Philly to 4th and Bainbridge that was in south Philly. That was phenomenal, how smart horses are, he knew the route better than I did, even without my assistance. Horses are truly treasures to mankind, they have played major roles in every war man has fought, up until Iraq, even in Viet-Nam. The Viet-Cong utilized horses to transport weapons and supplies from the north to the south mostly at night, through the jungle trails. I am still waiting for that Triple Crown winner. I was so disheartened when barbary went down and Big Brown's being pulled up fiasco, bad ride by the jockey. It takes a superb conditioned horse and the great awareness of the jockeys to put all three together, maybe between now and never worry it will happen once again. Horses will always have a spot in my heart and I thank our Creator for this special animal in our world.

chapter 33

Track and Field

The ultimate goal of track enthusiasts is to compete in the Olympic Games and Olympic stars gain worldwide recognition for their abilities. The first modern Olympic Games took place in Athens in 1896. At that time there was no Olympic Committee in the United States, and no funds to send anyone to the games. However, Robert S. Garrett, captain of Princeton University track and field team and three fellow students decided to participate. Paying his own expenses James B. Connally, a Harvard freshman, joined the group and the Boston Athletic Association raised funds for the others. With little time to prepare, they arrived in Athens and proceeded to win nine out of the ten events they entered, a remarkable record was set. No blacks participated there, however, in 1904, George Poage, an outstanding hurdler and quarter miler, who had exceptional college records for the 440 yard dash while attending the University of Wisconsin became the first black American runner in the Olympic, finishing third in the 440 meter hurdles in the third Olympiad, held in St. Louis.

After 1904 blacks began to participate in national track and field competition to a greater extent. Howard P. Drew , a great black runner won three nationals title, 1912, 1913. Sol Butler of Dubuque, Iowa, won the AAV title in the broad jump in 1920. Blacks broad jumpers began to dominate the event, winning twenty-six nationals championships in a span of thirty six years. Olympiad held in Los Angeles, Eddie Tolan of Michigan and Ralph Metcalfe of Marquette both won gold and silver medals for America in the sprints, both over the other for gold and silver medals. Tolan went on to compile a remarkable streak of triumphs in amateur racing. In more than three hundred races, he was beaten only seven times. Metcalfe went on to win 100-meter dash. He and

Owens also ran on the 400 meter relay team, taking home a gold and setting a new world record in the process.

The first broad jumper to surpass 26 feet was Sylvio P. Cator, a Haitian. On May 25, 1935 at Ann Arbor, Michigan, the amazing Jesse Owens jumped 26 feet, 8 inches, setting a world record that would stand for nearly thirty years.

The 1936 Berlin Olympics commenced, the world was beginning to respond to the tyranny of Adolf Hitler. Rumors of inhumane treatment of the German Jewish population was spreading far and wide. Hitler was spreading his doctrine of Aryan supremacy - the concept of "pure" German people who, in Hitler's terms, comprised "The Master Race." This scenario set the scene for one of the most supercharged Olympic games of all, it had all the elements of politics, and an undercurrent of racism. Hitler was confident that his Aryan supermen would totally and completely destroy the Americans due to the fact that the American team had blacks on it. One of Hitler's spokesman, Dr. Julius Streicher considered blacks to be "little more than trained baboons." Guess what? Hitler's dreams were demolished by one person, who was he? The great legendary man, Jesse Owens, a black man representing America, where blacks could not play baseball, football, tennis, basketball or be recognized as the Heavyweight Champion. Blacks were refused to be allowed in restaurants, hotels, theaters, had to ride the back of buses, were being denied jobs, housing, still being lynched and murdered, as were the Jews in Germany. Yet this one courageous black man defaced and embarrassed his racist Common Foe's morbid mind. It's amazing how we black men happen to be utilized in so many of white American conflicts, couldn't 't even vote in America. And do remember, the Tuskegee Airmen enroute to Alabama to see if they could fly airplanes had to get off the train they were riding on, leave their seats and give them to German prisoners of war, who were part of an army killing Americans and innocent men, women and children in Europe, as the Americans did to blacks here. Somehow it seems we always find ourselves defending and fighting for America, who did the same thing Hitler was doing in Germany. So once again the black American who the Common Foe said "was not white enough" to play his games - even though we were actually red-blooded Americans, was just not white enough, they said.

So the scene is set, Hitler is being frustrated in the Berlin Coliseum, because of one black man, the grandson of an American slave. We see, history is only repeating itself. Whites here called blacks 3/5th of a man, ignorant, savages, not intelligent, can't do this, can't do that, that the white man was superior to blacks, and on and on, and like I've stated, that 1619 mind set ruined this nation. There's no race of people on this planet that can claim that status...despite the fact that blacks were deprived education for over two hundred years, they have achieved and excelled in all intellectual, economic, social and business endeavor in every key element. The Common Foe has to let that idiotic mind set go and give credit where it's due. And in many cases blacks have performed above and beyond expectation, to the point that whites are afraid to give us a fair chance for jobs, housing, etc. It's time for Change, it did not work in Hitler's time, neither has it worked here in this country. Soon white people and their children will read and acknowledge blacks' contributions to making America a great nation. The weakest link that needs to be shored up is racism. This Book is also geared to enlighten blacks of our rich heritage and history which was never taught in our public schools. So here's a beginning, know where we originated from and what happened here in slavery, and all we have accomplished for this country, only to be disrespected. And it's only the American black man that rose form the ashes off to stand among the best on battlefields, or wherever we have made major strides and impact on this nation. This land is ours just as much as theirs, only the pure of heart and soul will understand this. The ignorant Common Foe still holding on to their false concepts of life are being reached out to, also. It may open their eyes to see a little more clearly, as Ali stated: "Years ago all angel cakes were white, the angels were white, God and Jesus were white, however I find lots of black angel cakes now, black angels and Christ Jesus pictures, God, unknown." There's even a black Santa Claus now, you hear and see white people pray to a black Madonna all over Europe. Why is that so? And I know the European people know more about history than American whites will ever know. So I am just trying to inform you of some of the other side of their story. Their story of world history is one thing, I am only concerned of black heritage and accomplishments here for starters, if we all learn what happen here from 1619 until now, that will give us all a new beginning.

Owens's story is not the first such story. President Roosevelt summoned Heavyweight Champion, Joe Louis, to the White House and informed him that America needed to keep the title here in the States. He was fighting Max Schemeling, the great Heavyweight from Germany in Madison Square Garden. At that point the President told Joe he was representing the country, defending democracy, and fighting against the Germans who Hitler was claiming to be the pure Aryan - superior race. A black man being asked by the President to fight for the country's democracy, the people and his own race. However, Owens was the major focus of Hitler in Berlin, in 1936. It seems that black Americans always played a major role in these events and one thing they have consistently done is bring home the "Prize."

This Olympic of 1936 was one of the greatest ever, as the whole world watched, it came down to Jesse Owens, the kid I write of that had these dreams embedded in his childhood images, the American black, red bloodied kid who was just not white enough in America, the grandson of a slave who endured the hostilities, racism, separate justice system, lived under the Jim Crows and racial barriers, the hatred, the 3/5th of a man syndrome, lived in poverty. Born in Danville, Alabama in 1913, James Cleveland "Jesse" Owens was the seventh child of a sharecropper. At the age of six he was already working in the cotton fields. They later moved to Cleveland, Ohio for better livelihood. Jesse's dad was employed as a laborer. Jesse's older brothers who could read and write were able to find steady menial jobs. His mother and sister were conscientious domestics. When Jesse went to school, he met Charles Riley, coach of the high school track team. Jesse had been watching the team train, whenever he was on his way home from school, passing by the high school field, where they practiced. He was in the fifth grade. Coach Riley would observe him standing at the edge of the track watching the team practice their training drills and running exercises. The coach noticed him and one day encouraged the scrawny little kid to prepare himself for the high school track team when he graduated. Jesse did his running exercises every morning before school, under the tutelage of Riley for a whole year before he went to high school. When Jesse entered high school, he had developed one of the most picturesque running style ever witnessed by the world of track and field competition. He was all grace with an upright fluid motion, he seemed effortless, with tremendous leg kicks, with tight body that gave him poetry in motion rhythm, like the sounds of the wind, he was the runner that God gave to the world.

In high school Jesse was entered into his first formal competition and lost, but soon he became the school star, setting his world scholastic record at East technical High School. He had a year of unbroken string of victories and record breaking performances. And was a natural for all the scholarships offered him. After conferring with Coach Riley, he decided to pay his own expenses. He enrolled at the Ohio State University, with no scholarship. He was in the class from 8:00 am to 3:00 pm, worked out on the track for two hours, worked as a night elevator operator earning $150 a month, was home by 1:30 am, got a few hours of sleep before his deadly routine started again. Larry Snyder, an outstanding coach at Ohio State University worked with Owens, honing his starts and forms to augment his natural talent. Jesse had a back injury, but overcame it and was able to enter the big Ten Memorial track and Field Meet on May 25,1935 at Ann Arbor, Michigan. He made track history: From 3:15 to 4 pm he jumped 26 ft, 8 1/4 inches, a world record; he sprinted 100 yards in 9.4 seconds, tying his own record; he ran the 200 yard dash in 20.3 seconds, another world record. No one has matched that magnificent record in one day - or to be more specific - in less than an hour. He was born to compete in the 1936 Olympic, the event that would crush those superiors to inferiors before the world.

Germany was awarded the honors of holding the Olympic Games of 1936. Amidst rumors and press reports of book burning and open concentration camps, Germany sought to symbolize the cultural superiority of the Third Reich. The symbolic German eagle appeared everywhere on the Olympic grounds. The United States protested, stating that to attend the Olympics would suggest approval of Hitler's policies. Avery Brundidge, President of the US. Olympic Committee, insisted the games were international, not national, and was sports, not politics in question. And he refused to discuss Semitism, religion or racial problems. However, Brundidge did react to the Olympic pamphlets reading: "Among inferior races, Jews have done nothing in the athletic sphere. They are surpassed even by the lowest Negro Tribes." Brundidge was able to secure a promise that the Germans would not discriminate against Jewish athletes however, never did address the comments made against the Blacks referring to them to be "lowest Negro tribes," but that was life as usual for the American black men referred to as black tribes as United States never protested that. Before the games started, anti-Semitic signs were removed, a relay of three thousand men brought the Olympic Flame across seven countries to Berlin. Despite Hitler's anti-Black propaganda, Jesse Owens was a heavy favorite of the German people, the Nazis conceded this point when they featured his picture on the official flyers.

It was a great day, perfect weather, people from all over the world came to witness this event where the superior Aryan Supermen would completely smash the American team, largely because the American blacks was on it, as mentioned they considered blacks to be "little more than trained baboons." So Jesse Owens became the one man, the world was watching, the other to be focused upon was the Aryan's pure race leader Adolf Hitler, the torch was lit and the ceremonies completed, the games began, this was one of the most monumental Olympic of all times. On this glorious day in history a race would be acknowledged, as their leader had predicted, or one Black man would emerge victorious - shatter and demoralize a ruler who despised Jews and Blacks. More people watched this event than ever recorded: it all came down to two persons, the man in the stands - whose self-proclaimed thoughts of superiority of his Master Race expected his athletes to win, and the Black man on the field - labeled part of the lowest class of a Negro tribe and highly trained baboon. What tension and anticipation! Every conceivable emotion surfaced, tears flowed, and roars of the rich and poor echoed in the jammed coliseum, with radio announcers updating spectators and listeners of all events, people worldwide glued to their short-wave radios. It was indeed a beautiful ceremony, as the flags were carried, the crowd sang "Deutschland Uber Alles." The athletes stood tall, proud and determined, Jesse as all others had totally prepared for this once-in-a-lifetime spectacular event that would remain in the hearts of the world forever, for on this day that little kid "Jesse" who watched the older boys practice their runs and field drills, had seen in his dreams that he would at one point in his life realize his dream "TO BE SOMEBODY." And truly on this memorable day the two hearts, two souls clashed, one who already proclaimed himself to be the greatest and the other to prove that a false claim was made, that it just wasn't so. The game began.

One of the most exciting event starts the action, the 100 meter dash, and who's in that first race? Jesse Owens, he hit's the finish line in front of Metcalfe and tied the world record at 10.2 seconds. Hitler thought his superior runner should have won that one, right from the jump his pure race of superiors were one behind the black American. Hitler was not happy, you could see his body language and facial expressions. The next day Owens was up again on the broad jump, another prestigious event of the game. He fouled on his first try, you could hear the roar of the spectators, second attempt he fouled again. One more try, can he make it all? All those years of training, practicing, dreaming of this day, two failures and now for one more attempt. Then one of the strangest things happened. Seeing Jesse a little upset with himself, Lutz Long, the German champion went over and introduced himself to Jesse, Long was also competing for the long jump record, put his hands on Jesse's shoulder and told him: "You are 100% when you jump. I am the same. You cannot do halfway, but you are afraid you will foul again."

Long calmed Owens and encouraged him to recount his measurements. Owens took off, you could hear a pin drop. He soared through the air, came down, setting a world's Olympic record that day: 26 ft, 5 1/4 inches. Long jumped 26 ft himself, came over to Jesse and warmly congratulated him. The two men from different worlds became close friends for many years, as did Joe Louis and Max Schemeling after their fight in New York. That scenario would never have happened in America - whites were busy telling blacks they were not white enough, let alone competing against them. Lutz Long in my mind, was to share part of the win by Owens, he was a man's man who only wanted to compete against the best, he demonstrated that - when he approached one of his competitors who he wanted to beat at his best, he's definitely one of my heroes of that game, and I was not even on the planet yet, but have recalled that story for years after reading of Jesse Owens. Long is the kind of individual the world could use today, as we seek friendship here in our nation, for unity and peace.

The 200 meter dash was Owens's third even, he set another Olympic record by clocking 20.7 seconds, Hitler jumped out of his seat enraged and truly out of control, this must be a dream he's telling himself at this point of the games... this cannot be! What the hell is wrong? Did they send the A Team? Who were those out there not living up to that image he created in his morbid mind? So we see the white Americans did not want to compete against the blacks and lose, same scenario, their parents told them they were superior to black people. And when Lt. Flipper out of West Point finished in the top five and Jack Johnson beating the great white hope, whites were so embarrassed that they did not allow the film to be viewed in America. So be careful of what labels you place on yourself because you might find out "it just isn't so." Jesse then ran the first leg on the American 400 meter relay with Metcalfe, Foy Draper and Frank Wykoff. Owens received a record, setting four gold medals, and the relay team set a world record. Hitler went berserk in the stands, ranting and raving in one major Olympic event, his pure Aryan race was reduced to being mere people as all others were. The "Black Auxiliaries" as they were called by a German newspaper carried their share in that Olympics.

These blacks went on to win in this competition. Ralph Metcalfe won a silver and gold medals. John Woodruff became the first Black American in twenty four years to win the 800 meter race. Fritz Pollard, Jr. finished third in the 100 meter high hurdles. David Albritton won a silver medal in the high jump, Archie Williams and James LaValle came in first and third in the 400 meter run, Mack Robinson, brother of Jackie Robinson, placed second to Owens in the 200 meter dash, Cornelius Johnson, set a new Olympic record when he soared 6 ft. 7 5/16 inches.

While Johnson, the first black champion of the 36 games was receiving his medal, he looked up into the stands and saw Hitler leaving the stadium. Johnson just smiled. Several German winners had be led to Hitler's box and were personally congratulated by Herr Hitler, he refused to acknowledge Jesse Owens, the most decorated, medalist, of the games. Then on top of that, upon returning to America there was a ticker tape parade for him, and reception at the Waldorf Astoria in his honor. However, in keeping with racial policies of the hotel at that time, Jesse had to take the freight elevator to the reception room, again from World hero representing his country, won all the honors and came back home where once again it was revealed that blacks were just not accepted and recognized, but were rejected in this nation. After all the preparations, his dreams, his accomplishments before the world at large. Owens was belittled here in the place he represented and fought for in Europe to exhibit his God-given talents, to crush a world symbol of Jewish and Black racism and hatred, only to return here to be disappointed and psychologically abused in his land of birth where, in fact it exhibited those same racial philosophies as those of which he crushed in Berlin. There could have been an exception to the rule to let him use the main stairway, that was 1936, today 2007 hanging nooses caused more racial divide.

Muhammed Ali returned home after capturing one of the most prestigious honors of the 1960 Olympics, walked in a restaurant and was refused service. How proud these men were to have accomplish these noble deeds representing a nation that continues to refuse to accept and acknowledge their effort, the dignity and pride of which you carried their banners on your shoulders, only to be totally rejected by these racists. Joe Louis fought and defeated his opponent in one of the most needed wins to boost this country out of an economic depression, out of moral mind set it was suffering through. So much needed was this victory that Roosevelt called him to the White House to ensure Joe knows that the nation was depending on him to defend American democracy over German superiority. He did what he was asked to do, the country never lived up to its expectations, so we see Johnson, Owens and Louis - all loved worldwide, had their dreams crushed and tarnished in the very country of which they were born in, were racially abused, and disrespected. It seems to never change for us as highly trained baboons. These are interesting reflections of a country who just cannot readjust to change that's needed here for it to thrive upon what it allegedly stands for. One thing about that period of time with Hitler, was that he was able to accomplish so much with his people in a short period of time and that's because in the long run he had them believing in themselves as one race of people and normally, people are followers of leaders that know the psychology of the mind. We have not reached that point as of yet to unite all the people for the common goal of all, being one nation. That's the one, the whole, and the balance of all three is the harmony of it all. Owens died on March 31st 1980 but he has not been forgotten, his granddaughter Gina Hemphill carried the Olympic torch into the Los Angeles Coliseum during the opening ceremony of the 1984 Olympics.

Track and field has a very long list of Black Americans "winning Traditions" all over the world, from 1946 onward, they responded to all challenges achieving their inner goals and winning medals and setting hundreds of personal and team records after the world war era. The games resumed in 1948 in England, some six thousand athletes form fifty-nine nations participated, excluding the Germans and Japanese, despite a heat wave, continuing rains and muddy fields the Olympics went on as scheduled. Time demanded dramatic heroes and American Harrison Dillard, whom they called "Bones," was like Jesse Owens and his goal was to accomplish all that Owens had. In 1947, 1948 he won 82 consecutive races, competed in the 1948 Olympics and tied Owens' Olympic record of 10.3 seconds for the race. Dillard said: "When I stood there listening to "The Star-Spangled banner," seeing the American flag fluttering and watching my name hoisted on the score board, I felt that this was the end, the absolute climax to everything for me." Helsinki in the 1952 Olympic games, Dillard was another gold medalist in the 110 meter high hurdles.

Blacks at one time did not excel in distance running until Frank Dixon won the distance race at the Millrose Games. There was Ralph Boston who broke Jesse Owens' record in the broad jump with a 26 ft., erasing Jesse's record set in 1936 of 26 ft. 5 1/4 inches. That phenomenal jump was recorded in 1960 Olympic games in Rome. In 1961 Boston jumped 27 ft. 1/2 inches breaking his own record in Moscow, in 1964 Olympics in Tokyo he finished second, and in a Modesto, California game, he set a new record of 27 ft. 4 1/4 inches which was broken by Bob Beamon's unbelievable jump of 29 ft. 2 1/2 inches at the "Rare Air Olympics" Mexico City in 1968.

The fabulous Wilma Rudolf, truly one of the most courageous athletes of her era, born on June 23, 1940 in St. Bethlehem, Tennessee was the 17th of 19 children. She weighed barely more than 4 pounds and seemed unlikely a candidate for any Olympic. She contacted double pneumonia, scarlet fever, and later polio which paralyzed her legs. Her entire family was trained to massage her legs, after years of medical treatment she was able to walk with the help of a corrective shoes and leg brace. At the age of eight she began running in the elementary school and in high school. Wilma won every race she entered in. Her recovery was more than complete. Competing within the state of Tennessee. She won every dash from 50 - 220 yards for five consecutive years. Not only that but she became an outstanding basketball player and was named to the All-State squad. When she was only sixteen, Wilma scored 803 points in 250 games for her school. She entered Tennessee State College, was tutored by the famous track team coach Ed Temple, showing great deal of confidence. She said she intended to become the most outstanding American woman runner. In the 1960 Olympics things started off really bad, however there was a lot of attention given to this pretty long-legged twenty year old black woman who was called "la Gazelle" by the French, and the Italians called her "The Black Pearl." Her practice runs was drawing enormous crowds, then it was time for the first 100 meter dash. As the gun sounded Rudolf was gone, with every stride she lengthened her lead, she outdistanced the whole pack by at least three yards, setting a record of 100 meters in 11 seconds flat for her first gold medal. Wilma became the first American woman to win three gold medals in Olympics track and field competition. She was voted "Female Athlete of the Year" by the Associated Press. In 1961 Wilma won the James E. Sullivan Memorial Trophy which honor the athlete who best advanced the cause of sportsmanship during the year. America welcomed her return and honored her everywhere she went. She declined to participate in the 1964 Olympics saying that the best she could was return home with three gold medals. She decided to stick with the glory won, like Jesse Owens did in 1936, she was really one person who lived up to: "REFUSE TO LOSE" and "BE SECOND TO NONE."

Rafer Johnson, a superb athlete set records in school and while at UCLA dreamed of winning the decathlon of the world. In the 1058 "Little Olympics" in Mexico, he set a world decathlon record of 8,302 points, defeating Vasily Kuznetsor, Russia's "Man of Steel" by 505 points. In the 1960 Olympics in Rome Johnson finished with a fantastic 8,392 points setting a new world record. His dream had come true.

Some of our black record holders of track and field in the Olympic games are:

• Eulace Peacock of Temple University - one of the truly outstanding dash man of the 1930's

• John Borican from Virginia State College - twice defeated the mighty Glenn Cunningham at 1400 yards.

• Mai Whitfield at the 1948 Olympic games in London in the greatest individual performance since that of Jesse Owens in 1936. Whitfield set an Olympic record in the 800 meter race, in 1 minute and 49.2 seconds ran anchor on the winning 1,600 meter relay team; and took third in the 400 meter, his combined points were the highest individual scores of the 1848 games.

• Charles Dumas, United States high jump champion 1956, the first man to clear seven feet in the high jump.

• Milt Campbell of Indiana University won the decathlon gold medal at the 1956 Olympics in Melbourne, Australia.

In 1964 Dick Gregory, a black human rights activist, proposed a boycott of the Olympic games in Tokyo as a protest against unequal treatment of blacks in America. Early in 1965, black athletes selected to play in the American Football leagues East-West All Star classic threatened to boycott the New Orleans game because some of them had been refused admission to the city's social clubs. The Commissioner of the league reassigned the game to another city. Thus, the unity of these black athletes produced tangible results. When asked if the black athletes would boycott the Olympics games in Japan in 1968, Tommie Smith, a black student of San Jose State College in California stated that "it was a possibility in light of the racial injustices in America." A Human Rights Committee was formed to initiate some actions to address the racial problems, those on the Committee were: Dr. Louis Lomax, civil rights activist, Dr. Martin Luther King, Floyd McKissick, Director of the Congress of Racial Equality. Kenneth Noll was the chief organizer.

The goals of the proposed boycott were:

1. Restoration of Muhammad Ali's title and boxing license in America.

2. Removal from the International Olympics Committee of the Anti-Semitic and Anti-Black personality Avery Brundidge.

3. Curtailment of participation by all-white teams from South Africa, in Rhodesia and in the United States and the Olympic games and desegregation of New York Athletic Club.

Some major strides were accomplished with their involvement addressing these issues.

The 1963 Olympics in general was not that great, however, for black athletes, they as usual set the tone for excellence. Tommie Smith and Juan Carlos, followers of Professor Harry Edwards, spokesman for the Human Rights Olympic Committee, won the gold and bronze medals in the 200 meter dash. Smith's time 19.83 was an Olympic record. While on the victory stand, Smith and Carlos were presented with their medals, as the "Star-Spangled Banner" was played the two men raised black-gloved fists in the historic incident representing the "Black Power" salute and lowered their heads. This shocked the crowd. Smith and Carlos were suspended and evicted from the games and Mexico. These courageous men made a worldwide statement of the inhumane and unjust treatment of blacks in America.

Lee Evans, a friend of Tommie Smith set a record in the 400 meter race, time 43.8 seconds, he wore black socks to protest the ousting of Smith and Carlos. Evans, Ronald Freeman, Larry James and Vincent Matthews broke another record in their 400 meter in 2.561. The 100 meter relay squad of Charles Green, James Hines, Melvin Pender and Ronnie Ray Smith made Olympic history, establishing a new speed record of 38.19, Hines also won the gold medal for a record breaking 100 meter dash in 9.95.

On the distaff side in record breaking year, Wyomia Tyus repeated her gold medal performance in the 1964 games by winning 100 meter dash. In doing so she became the first athlete ever to win back to back Olympic gold medal victories. She teamed up later in the 100 meter relay with Barbara Ferrell, Margaret Bailes and Mildretta Nelter for another gold medal win.

In the Munich games of 1972 a very dramatic start, where terrorist attacked and killed eleven Israeli athletes, this horrible incident was a tremendous tragedy for the Olympics and the world at large. Despite the tragedy and turmoil, the games continued. Larry Black, Eddie Hart, Robert Taylor and Gerald Tinker won the gold in the 100 meter relay. Rod Milburne set a record of 13.24 in the 110 meter hurdles. In the Montreal games a remarkable reign of Edwin Moses in the 400 meter hurdles. A superbly trained and dedicated athlete, Moses set a new record of 47.64 which has yet to be surpassed in 1976. The games were boycotted in 1980 when the Soviets invaded Afghanistan. President Carter called for the boycott and was supported by fifty eight other nations.

It was fifty two years since the Olympic Games had been held in the United States in Los Angeles, once again it would be held in that host city in 1984. The opening and closing ceremonies were indeed a Hollywood spectacular, however, nothing could surpass the individual competitions that took place on that field, especially world records began to fall. Carl Lewis had announced he intended to respect Jesse Owens' 1936 win of four medals. Wilma Rudolph of the 1960 games was remembered when Valerie Brisco Hooks became the second woman in Olympic history to win three medals. It seemed all the focus was on Carl Lewis and Edwin Moses. Lewis was successful in duplicating Jesse Owens' feat, the only man to do so, with a long jump of 28 ft. 1/4 inch, ran a 100 meter dash in 9.99 seconds, and a record breaking 200 meters in 19.80, and he was anchorman in the 400 meter relay during the meet, Lewis nevertheless ran his anchor lap in a sparkling 8.94, his victorious teammates were Sam Graddy, Ron Brown and Calvin Smith. Edwin Moses won his second gold medal for the 400 meter hurdles in 47.75, eight long years after his first. That win was his 105th straight victory without a defeat. Simply remarkable, the greatest hurdler of all times in the history of track and field. I watched his historic performance on tape and I truly admired his commitment and will to win. That event was just amazing and lasting in my mind, especially whenever I think of all the blacks who got their chance to equally display their talents and skills before the greater audience of the world, other than being denied the opportunity to compete against a opponent who just did not think blacks were smart or white enough. Perhaps whites just did not have the confidence to compete against blacks here in America, the only thing blacks ever asked and even fought for was a fair chance to compete at whatever it may have been. That's why the Olympic games was so important to the black athlete, he competed against all races of people worldwide, was treated fairly and respected for what he brought to the game - courage and skills to compete - in the game of sports. In America it was about the color of your skin, to the world it was your skills and desires of which they respected and acknowledged. The great athletes are there, who accept all challenges and believe they are the best, and are willing to prove it to all who choose to play the game as well. The track and field games have been a tremendous vehicle to expand the worlds plan of Unity and Harmony of all races, creed or colors of our youth. They travel to different countries, seeing and meeting new cultures, ideologies, customs, learning a wealth of knowledge and friendship.

American whites always told their children that they were better than the black people, told them blacks were inferior, too dumb and ignorant to do anything. Believe me that was only because blacks were brought here unarmed and shackled, no means to defend themselves, we all have seen what happened when Nat Turner armed 20 black slaves, they burned and tortured and killed white people who owned five plantations, and destroyed the plantation as well. So it was only that blacks were not armed that they did not fight for themselves. When the opportunity presented itself, they did. Anybody who was chained, shackled, whipped, branded, can be controlled by the gun, rifle, or whip, of which made white people in their mind they were superior when in fact they were cowards. The superior man would have ensured after getting the slaves here, they found a way to get them to understand why they were brought here and that the only option was to work. Whites should have treated them as civil as possible and even allowed them to work for their own freedom over a certain period of time.

America was the only country that did not allow slaves to work for their freedom, they had stated slaves would be kept in servitude for life. While in Viet-Nam the Viet-Cong prisoners hated American soldiers however, we found a way to get them to work and do the details we wanted them to do. It was that or sit around and feel miserable all day. They worked and seemed to enjoy that activity. Just that as superior as whites claimed to be, they resorted to branding, raping, whipping and murder and all the strict laws of the Black Code to demoralize the children, old people with torture and horrendous abuse, these are not the traits and principles of a superior mind, it showed no creativity whatsoever, I write of sports, especially track and field just to reflect what Hitler and the Common Foe of America had in common, "Morbid Minds." Read your history, if you have not done so, it's very enlightening for those who have not the faintest inkling of what the nation projects to the world and the American Black people - they are definitely not the PRINCIPLES and VALUES America was founded upon.

chapter 34

Baseball

Baseball, one of America 's prestigious games, has had its share of racial problems, more so than any other sport, yet you see and enjoy the skills and play of hundreds of blacks over the years. From the very beginning when baseball was introduced to this country, the barriers were set in place to negate any black from playing, or participating in it The early period of the Civil War 1861-65 baseball spread into the north and south, prior to that the game was played by all white players. Slaves and black freemen probably played later in that period, in isolated areas. During the chaotic times of reconstruction, the black man was in destitute times. The "Black Code" body of laws which prohibited ex-slaves from giving testimony against whites in civil courts, existed. Among other things this Code controlled the social and economic rights of the black men, they were reduced to farming and doing domestic jobs. As a result of the Code, serious race riots occurred in the south during the summer of 1866. These riots, however, fueled the situation and empowered the whites to revise the code prohibiting blacks from being members of, and playing for the National Association of Baseball. The game was already being touted as the "All American" sport for "Red Blooded Americans" and that in no way included blacks. Baseball became a national symbol of patriotism; although blacks fought in the Revolutionary and Civil Wars with valor and patriotism yet they were not included nor allowed to play the game at all. In 1871 the Association's name was changed to "The National Association of Professional Baseball Players" where a "gentlemen's agreement" was created prohibiting the participation of black men in the organization.

One interesting thing resulted from this scenario, I think it was a great idea: blacks jointly sought creative ways to pursue excellence not only in sports, but also in all other avenues of life. Black people really have to find their own way of getting things done, if they are to be partaking in the economic growth of this country and we have to recreate for the welfare of our own. I've seen all other ethnic groups establish this, and continue to reap its rewards. Blacks in this country own very little in this regard, they are major consumers to all other groups, blacks have yet to learn how to create businesses to collectively recycle their revenue back into the black communities and business opportunities.

Blacks are sleeping while all others are gaining huge financial status and recognition in the business world. If in fact all of these barriers and roadblocks have been there since day one, why are we not capitalizing on these resources of the millions we are spending in the white business world? WAKE UP PEOPLE! Want to get out of poverty? Pool your finances, create black business where blacks can buy quality merchandize. Create jobs, take care of your own. The handwriting has been written all over this country for decades. If we had a black baseball league in the 1920's and '30's why not now? The people of Green Bay own that team. Black can make a corporation to achieve that same scenario and each city can do it, once established the fan fare will generate a larger scale to bring in the revenue. Place an ad for people interested in contributing money to generate a salary for these players that don't get the opportunity to play in the baseball or NFL, or arena football. There's talent out there, pay the players a set salary, play your games on college ball fields, make the tickets affordable to bring the children and family, and stop going down to these NFL games. Support your city team where things are affordable for all to enjoy, tickets $15.00, soda $1.50, hot dogs $2.00, no beer, parking $2.00 per car, just an idea. We have to be creative in this world of opportunity. There's plenty of talent out there, build your own corporation, hire the players at a set pay, maybe start with $75,000 each player, buy the equipment, uniform, and register in the city and have baseball competitions. The players will sign a Contract to play specific number of games. And the salary has to fall in that range because that's all you want them to do, play ball. It will take coordination, but it can be done. Just an idea for those of you that would like to expose your children to the game without paying damn near a hundred dollars, plus parking. Let's work our creative minds to get things done with pride and control of our own resources. There's plenty of people who would be willing to take on this idea, as revenue increase, the corporation grows to benefit the members - the community, the players, and our children. Like I stated, this is just a thought - a thought gave us ALL we see TODAY!

Let's get back to the subject at hand. We always seem to be cast aside at whatever the subject matter is, that's because it's still only black and white this country is concerned about, not the 12 million Mexicans that violated our border laws nor the Vietnamese, the Korean, the Indian, European, or any other ethnic people who have come here to live. Never heard of any other people being hung in this country, except the black man (other than the native Indian) discriminated from jobs and other entitlements, which the newly arrived immigrants enjoy. We go back to 1619 and today there's been very little change of attitude in spite all we have given. There's just no end to the sadistic white mind. It's imperative that we protect ourselves, unite and create progress. After all we have given and done here in the country of our birth, where we are still looked upon as a threat of all those white superiority thinkers, who never wanted us to play football. And when allowed, we were not intelligent enough to play as Quarterbacks, so they said. Then along came Doug Williams and shattered that mind set, he set in one game more records than many white quarterbacks ever thought obtainable. Couldn't play golf, it was for the elite until Tiger walked in, could not play tennis until Althea Gibson and the William sisters destroyed all standing records of the game, never wanted us to play basketball, yet some of the most amazing records belong to Chamberlain, Jordan, and many other black players. It goes on and on, is hate that deep for the Black Americans? It really is, when you look at it, it's ridiculous that it's still playing on their minds: hanging nooses and other racial incidents, is just mind boggling. All we ever asked for was equal freedom and justice, a job and education. There was a time when we could not avow to that, and it's not getting better at this point, after fighting the Revolutionary and Civil Wars. Blacks were murdered and lynched - and then they came up with a Code to shut out black players from the game. They were called "Red Bloodied" Be careful not to check the white's blood; there just might be a little black lineage in them, somehow. There was a rich white rancher who was notified he had some black relatives, they traced their blood line and sure enough, the black lady belonged to the same lineage, of his DNA. They met and to his credit he treated her as family, she spent about a week on his ranch and even traced others of their family members. So be careful of whom you call "Red Blooded" it just could find you a black relative somewhere. How ignorant the old Common Foe's mind could be. It has taken him even in sports. Now they are not comfortable with the name they have attached to themselves, "Superior," which in a lot of cases became "Inferior." They were afraid to compete against blacks in sports; it took a while before the old Negro League players got the opportunity to play the white team annually. And damn if those black players didn't win nearly all of those games. If there's such a thing as superior, then let me accept all challenges regardless of race, creed or color. If I am beat, let me improve to establish that I can be. The worst thing that ever happened in that scenario was that the whites had always told their children and each other that they were superior. Superior over who? The poor defenseless slaves in bondage? No weapons to defend themselves in a new and strange country, guarded by armed slave owners who whipped, branded and murdered innocent defenseless people. That did not make you superior, it only made you killers and bigots. Jack Johnson beating this country's great white hope in front of millions reduced such superiority into inferiority. Those white superior people even called their superior champion, who got beat by Johnson, a coward to their white race. Yet, I saw none willing to try to challenge Johnson. In fact they were just cowards themselves, so-called superior white people who were not superior enough to beat Johnson for nine years as champion. So that exposed such mind set to the whole world. What a shock for their children to see this supreme race of a superior class get exposed! No one is superior to anyone else, that's why we play the game to determine the outcome. He who wins today might just be the loser tomorrow. So from the early 1700's until recently those

"Codes" have been in place to bar blacks from equal opportunity to play in this country against the white American baseball teams. Blacks in the past found ways to have their own, why not now? During the black era of the black leagues, there was a large white crowd attending those games which were colorful. The skills of the black players were greatly displayed. In the North, black baseball players had a much greater degree of cohesiveness than the South, the games were exciting and affordable. We have to develop these sport teams, let's get it done!

New York produced not only the Baseball Hall of Fame, but also John W. "Bud" Fowler, the first black to be paid in organized baseball. In 1872 he joined a white team in New Castle, Pennsylvania. He was an all-around baseball player, playing any position, he played for 26 years primarily with white teams. The prejudices by his teammates and fans kept him constantly playing for other teams. He later organized a black team, called it the "All American Black Tourists" and put on a "Coon Show." The team played in top hats and tails, and the show was preceded by a parade, something similar to the Harlem Globetrotters, who still mesmerize the fans today with their overall game performance. Many blacks followed Fowler, there were thirty or more black players before the 1900's - it seemed that if a black player was really great, the bar was lowered a bit, as a need for good ballplayers was a must to keep the game at its utmost level There was Moses Fleetwood "Fleet" Walker, his brother Welday Walker, who were generally accepted by teammates and fans who, on many occasions, applauded their performance. They joined the league in 1884. Shortly racism raised its ugly head when the Common Foe started sending threatening notes and letters to the blacks. A letter was received by the Toledo manager, stating that if Fleet played, he would be mobbed, and there would be bloodshed. He never played in that game, he was released by the team shortly thereafter. He ended his career in 1889 with Syracuse in the International League. Upon his retirement from baseball, he became an author writing "Our Home Colony," a treatise on the past, present and future of the Negro Race in America. It was his belief that the only way to deal with racial prejudice in America would be for blacks to return to Africa.

The harassment perpetrated upon the few black men permitted to play in the early days of organized baseball never weakened their desire to play this "white man's game." They just showed up, played and got paid. Things really got worse when a highly-skilled black player named Frank Grant entered organized baseball in 1886. He had run into a white player named Adrian "Cap" Anson who was the first player to get 3,000 hits. Anson hated blacks with an unnatural vehemence, his main goal was to get blacks out of organized baseball. His efforts to rid the game of black players started in 1883, his protests against blacks did not go unheeded. He was very popular, and many whites agreed with him and joined his cause. More black players were now paid members of the baseball team, hence, the prejudice grew stronger. More so, baseball players were considered heroes by their fans, exemplifying the American way of life. The white public could not take it anymore and would not condone their children's admiration for black ballplayers. Money was not to be taken out of the hands of "red-blooded white Americans" and be given to descendants of ex-slaves.

On July 19, 1887 Cap Anson entered the ball field of the Little Giants and shouted: "Get the nigger off the field!" He was referring to George Stovey, ace pitcher in the field of organized baseball, for Newark and a black man. That cry was resounded until the blacks were no more. Those actions by Anson and his followers aggravated that hatred attitude to their children, whom they brought along to the see the public lynchings of black men, women and children in open parks. The exposure of young children to their evil, vicious and deplorable act explains why the hatred perpetrated throughout the centuries. Racist attitudes just got even severely intense, such children grew up hating blacks influenced by those sight of blacks hanging lifeless from the trees. This horrible sight gained total control of their minds during their formative years of childhood, fanned by their narrow-minded, ignorant parents' influence. Such images are forever embedded on the children's mind as expected of them to do. They may feel uncomfortable with it, but never get the courage to speak out to their parents, neither the fortitude to do so. The result? Feelings of superiority and hatred for blacks! Problem is, education thrives best in a diversified environment, in exposure to varied cultures, customs and traditions. Now their children remain racists and ignorant forever of blacks' rich cultural heritage and powerful legacy! Totally closing their eyes to the wonders of ancient black civilization, of a golden era, of cultural diversity - a plan perfected only by an Omnipotent Creator. Racial divide? You started it all! Superiority? Come on! Problems will never leave us until we take our blinders off! Your children will never forget the evil and injustice you spewed on them just as you still remember yours! You knew in your heart your parents did wrong and had done injustice, yet you held on to them as truths, all your life. Free yourselves from it, it's your life, why live it that way? By living the past and getting distracted from the beauty of all God's creation seen dimly from the racist's eyes. You know you have the power to do it, cause you will account for all truth and see justice in the end!

I say to you racists out there, it's not what was taught to you that was wrong, that got you in trouble. It's your actions and execution of them that did so, let the hatred go! There's a whole new world we live in – it's called Love and Unity, reclaim it, instead of the racial stressful place of which you dwell, enlighten yourselves of what your black culture has established in a rich past and present history. It's all there, taught to you. I've just touched on a few subjects, however, the list is long and has been hidden. Do not live through your life not ever knowing the truth, it will set your heart and souls free. I hope those who need this change will pursue it, and seek all there is to know, I found early on there's nothing special about whites or any other people. We are all born into this system of things, have the same fears, and die in so many years. When I was in boxing, I saw the fear in the opponent's eyes, on the battlefields I saw the fear and reactions to the various situations, no matter who the soldiers were, white, black or whoever. The fear was there! So in these pages, the only fear whites had was being outclassed, outplayed, embarrassed or defeated by a black person, women not so much, but for the white males – it's always been there, never get beat by a black person, if they did some would actually be ridiculed, called all kinds of names, to include coward. It went: "How could you even come home after losing to that nigger?" I was at a boxing match, the white kid was being really out-classed, his father was one of his trainers. After they lost, the kid damn near got lynched before he left the ring, his father just went crazy calling the fighter all kind of names I would not have called my dog. They finally got him calmed down and they all left the ring. I really felt bad for the kid, that's just not in their scenario, losing to a black man. And in these pages I write what I've read and things I have witnessed with my open eyes have revealed just how bad racism can be when a white father damn near beat his kid unmercifully before a public crowd. That kind of emotional outburst caused the father to be suspended for a period of time, and I never heard of the kid again. He had the potential, but when you enter into the sports arena, there's always the other guy who, too, has potential and is training just as hard as you do. And he's willing to show up and fight whoever, just to prove his heart and skills at whatever game they choose to play in life. So in all of these sports, we find blacks being isolated, until some genius saw how good they were playing in college and black leagues, exhibit-ing exceptional talent that they open up their thoughts to capital-ize on such talent they have seen over the last 60 years or so. Some of your major college programs would not have been as success-ful had it not been for the coaches recruiting the black athletes from various outstanding high schools. Blacks running back for over thousands of yards a season, receivers making hundreds of passes for touchdowns, those linemen making those tackles or opening holes, those superb and strong pitchers, base runners, hit-ters, field position players exhibiting excellent playing skills. In every sports blacks have been honored to the Hall of Fame, re-gardless of the setbacks, they still were a major asset to the sports. So, we are all born, have so many fears and die in so many years. There's no superior people, there's just white, black and other col-ored people we see excelling in all areas of life, all levels of sports, especially blacks who were denied the opportunity because some-one never liked the color of their skin. The skin color was okay when the whites trained them to fight their wars for them, Revo-lutionary, Civil, Indians, yet were not white enough to be allowed to play the Red Bloodied American games for hundreds of years.

Simply amazing, all other races never had those problems unless he was an American Indian, of course.

Things continued to prevent blacks from playing the game, so many formed black league teams, until a man who saw black talent and paid them to play on his team, his name, John McGraw. He was a white player who played for approximately 20 years before becoming manager of the New Giants in 1902. He marched to ten pennants in his first twenty one years there. During his thirty years with the Giants, he finished in second division only three times, and twenty one times in that period. The Giants were either first or second, a man they called "Little Napoleon" was of McGraw's caliber, who would defy the color barriers. He wanted to win, played to win, and wanted the best players possible. He did not care what color they were. Winning at any cost was credo. McGraw selected a black player he had seen playing on one of his black tennis teams and hired him. The player, Charlie Grant could pass on as a Cherokee Indian, thus they called him "Charlie Tokohama" but the President of the Chicago White Sox, Charlie Chomsky and others questioned his ethnicity and Charlie Grant never got to play the full season. There were other players who said they were Cuban or Indian. The problem got so bad that the team owners actually sent a representative to Cuba to check the player's identity, they got terminated from the white teams, and found work in the black league. McGraw had hired a black rubber or trainer, when he took over as manager for the Giants. One day a white player, Bill Terry came to him and told him that he did not want that black man putting his hands on him. A year later McGraw stepped down as manager in 1932. Bill Terry took over and the first thing he did was fire the black trainer. American teams would go to Cuba and play against the Cubans and black players there. In 1914 Ben Johnson, American League President stated: "We want no makeshift club calling themselves Athletes the black players, despite their skill and prowess in playing the game.

The black league kept improving and traveling to compete against each other in various towns and cities. Hotels and rest accommodations were often a no no, so sleeping in their cars and buses was the norm, one amazing thing however, was they always drew large white fans who watched their games. Suddenly a big black pitcher had come on the scene. He was Andrew Foster from Calvert, Texas, his reputation was all over the black leagues and whites as well. Wanting to become a professional ball player, he left school at eighth grade. Foster later found a black team Waco Yellow Jackets. After a few sessions, he was invited to join the Chicago Union Giants, at six feet four inches and weighing 200 pounds, he pitched a shutout in his first game. He was full of confidence, intelligence and instinctive baseball know-how, he refined his game and took on all comers. In 1902 Foster pitched an exhibition against a white team, the Philadelphia Athletics and their famous mound star Rube Waddel. Foster beat Waddel, and his teammates started calling him "Rube," a significant acknowledgement that he was the premier pitcher.

In 1905 Foster won fifty-five exhibition contests against major and minor league teams. Honus Wagner, the famous white shortstop of the Pittsburg Pirates said he was one of the greatest pitchers of all times. In 1911 blacks played for the first time in a major league ballpark, when John M. Schorling leased the grounds of the old White Sox and rebuilt the stadium to seat a capacity of nine thousand. Foster retired in 1917 and became manager of the Chicago American Giants.

After the riot of 1919 where twenty-three blacks and fifteen whites died as a result, the black owners formed the Negro National Baseball League. These teams of the Negro league found ways to keep developing teams, and played major games in Cuba, whenever the opportunity presented itself. There were approximately seventy-five clubs operating there and interestingly the blacks and whites played together on the same teams. Like they say: Racial hatred exists "Only in America."

Through the 20's, 30's and early 40's the Negro League produced some of the greatest baseball athletes ever to play the game. Foster, Alex Rompey, Tom Williams, Jimmy Lyons, George Dixon, Jim Brown, Lehory Grant, Jack Marshall, Cool Papa Bell, Satchel Paige, Oscar Charleston, Josh Gibson, Jimmy Crutchfield, Ted Paige, Leroy Greenlee and many more. Some of the teams were the Homestead Grays, Baltimore Black Stars, the Detroit Wolves, the Newark Browns, Eastern Cuban Stars, the Cleveland Stars. These black teams found a way to keep playing, something we need today, there's lots of talents out there coming out of these colleges that never get selected in the pro leagues, however, they could play and establish the National Black League again, something our black people could afford and attend. Creativity and pooling of resources gets it done. The area league utilized talent that did not make it to the NBL, only a select few were chosen, however the other talent is still there - to play for someone. Note: All the black superstars in baseball participated in the All Star Game in Chicago, 1933 there were 20,000 fans in attendance, 51,723 attended in 1943, and the white press came out in full force to record these magnificent display of black talent.

The Negro National League suffered many temptations. The Dominican Republic was crying for black ball players to go there. Mexico exploded with baseball madness, the money was good in these countries where blacks were welcomed as equals, there was no "separate but equal facilities." They could eat in the best restaurants and stay in first class hotels. Things really opened up for black baseball after World War II, attendance at games was phenomenal, and by 1945, it had reached new heights. Black players were being recognized for their skills and talent through the Negro League.

Suddenly a plan was orchestrated by a very clever man, to allow black players to enter and play in the National and American White Baseball Leagues. That man was Wesley Branch Rickey, a white man born in Stockdale, Ohio on December 20, 1881 to a very poor family that believed in the work and morale ethic of the Methodist Church. He did all kinds of jobs to save money for college, taught school for thirty five dollars a month. With that money he bought a bicycle, books on Latin rhetoric, higher mathematics, and saved seventy six dollars towards his college education. He later got involved with and ran the Brooklyn Dodgers, essayed on the racial problems in baseball and decided to do something about it. In college he played baseball and football. A broken leg ended any dreams of football, later after pursuing a baseball dream, he became ill with tuberculosis. After recovering he attended the University of Michigan, got a Law degree in 1911 and shortly was back in baseball. This time as a scout for St. Louis Browns, later becoming manager of that team. When he was a college coach, he had one black player, Charles Thomas. Ricky saw the devastating effects of racism when he took his team on the road where Thomas was refused a room in hotels. One time, he was able to talk the hotel manager to put a cot in his room so that Thomas would have a place to sleep. Another time when he was with the Cardinals, he protested the segregated seating arrangements in Sportsmen's Park. Blacks could sit in the bleachers and in the right field pavilion. As much as he tried, he could not get the owner of the Cardinals to change his position regarding segregation. Ricky, a strong believer, with religious convictions that man should not be judged by the color of his skin. One day a little kid recognized him and asked him for his autograph, and enquired if Negroes would ever play in the major leagues. Putting his arms around the boy, Ricky said: "Young man, one day you will live to see it happen!" In 1945 Ricky made his plans for the breakthrough of blacks in modern organized baseball. With the backing of the new Commissioner Chandler's sanctions, the bank's approval of the Dodgers Board of Directors, Ricky announced to press his desire to establish a Brooklyn Dodgers team.

Finally the door was open for Ricky to search out that one special black player to fulfill the role of being the first Black man to play in the Professional White Major League Baseball. Ricky formulated a team of professional scouts to canvass black talent within the ranks the Black League team. The scouts sent him a list of outstanding men with exceptional skills and talent, that black players list contained the names of Satchel Paige, Showboat Thomas, Josh Gibson, Sam Jethroe, Luke Easter and other black stars. But one name kept coming over and over, that of Jackie Robinson. He heard so much about Jackie, he made a special trip to California to check this young ballplayer's background. The man Ricky was looking for would have to be a man with enough pride and courage to take on "Jim Crow" abuses and derision from fans and other clubs, as well as from his teammates.

Robinson was a First Lieutenant in the army in 1944 and was denied to play on the post football or baseball teams at Ft. Riley,

Kansas. He spoke to the great Joe Louis, the Heavyweight Champion also stationed there. Racism was rampant in the service, even though whites and blacks were fighting and dying together on battlefields. Sgt Louis went up to the Brigadier General Donald Robinson and asked about all the racial discrimination in ball playing. Sgt. Louis told him: "Don't you know you've got one of the most outstanding players in the camp and he can't play on the Post team?" The General asked who he was talking about, Joe told him that by all means he wanted Robinson on the team, and any other qualified Negro to play on the team. This action by Joe Louis caused desegregation of baseball, football, and all facilities on military bases, especially those in the south.

The Meeting: On August 1945 Ricky and Robinson met. They had a lengthy discussion. Ricky was tremendously impressed with Robinson's character and composure. After explaining certain racial problems that may occur and the restrictions, to hold himself in check against the many pitfalls he may encounter, Robinson said: "Mr. Ricky, do you want a ballplayer who's afraid to fight back?" Ricky replied: "I want a ball player with guts enough not to fight!" They reached an agreement. Robinson would play for Montreal Royals for a season, and come to the Dodgers in '47. And the rest is baseball history. Jackie's first year was a mental challenge with the continuous racial slurs, not to mention the watermelons and shoeshine kits, placed outside the opposing team's dugouts, the verbal abuse of his manhood, his racial heritage. They likened him to jungle animals and talked about his family, the Philadelphia Phillies were the hardest on his psyche. Bob Carpenter, President of the Phillies stated that his team would not play if Robinson remained. The St. Louis Cardinals planned a protest strike against Robinson and tried to encourage all the teams in the National League to do likewise. The President of the National League proclaimed in writing to the Cardinals Organization:

"If you do this, you will be suspended from the league. You will find that the friends you think you have in the press box will not support you, that you will be outcasts. I do not care if the league strikes. Those who do it will encounter quick retribution. They will be suspended, and I don't care if it wrecks the National League for five years. This is the United States of America, and one citizen has as much rights to play as another. The National League will go down the line with Robinson whatever the consequences."

Robinson lived up to and surpassed the expectations of Ricky. He batted .297 and led the Dodgers in stolen bases with 29 and runs scored with 125. He was tied with the Dodgers home run leadership at 12 with Pee Wee Reese. For the first time since 1941, the Dodgers won the National League pennant, even Dixie Walker considered that Robinson had done a good job and was instrumental in bringing the flag to Brooklyn. The Yankees beat the Dodgers for the World Series that year, but Robinson was selected by Baseball Writers Association as National League Rookie of the Year. Robinson had a ten year hitting average of .311, in 1949, his last year, he led the League with a .348 average, and 37 stolen bases, scored 122 runs and drove in 124, he also won the National League's Most Valuable Player Award.

Branch Ricky was a very smart businessman who had talent, regardless of color or creed, and he knew that with all the great black talents, he had to be the first to establish their presence in the National Baseball League. After Jackie, came many great black players that became overnight superstars. They were that good, white players really had to be good to maintain their positions on a lot of teams, many were just not good enough.

The door to Baseball was wide open and the Black talents flowed in endlessly. Roy Campanella, Don NewComb, Hank Thompson, Monte Irvin, Willie Mays, Hank Aaron, Frank Robinson, Roberto Clemente, Reggie Jackson, Richie Allan, Maury Wills, Willie M. Covey, Bob Gibson, Joe Morgan, Ozzie Smith. The American League did not rush to sign up many black players, however, Larry Doby, Bobby Bonds were signed up in 1947, and the fabulous Satchel Paige who was past his prime but still a good pitcher and crowd pleaser signed up in '48, slugger Luke Easter in '49.

All these sports I just discussed reflected their really historical heritage, and believe me, it's worth reading about the price they paid, the struggles they overcame. These were the true pioneers of sports, they needed to prove themselves before the world and all negative barriers. They were our champions who refused to give up, stayed the course and earned their crowns in the game they chose to play. I encourage everyone, black, white or all others to read the rich history of blacks in sports. It's simply fabulous! Check it out and I have really enjoyed every page. My father boxed, told me to read about Jack Johnson who became my childhood hero, he never gave up, fought before thousands of white people, beating their great white hope, lived a life that was full. He enjoyed all people here and abroad. A people's champion who refused to accept or live by the double standards and refused to accept: "You can 't do this, you can't do that!" He just did and enjoyed them all despite the cowardly threats and senseless racist slurs, a champion even America could not dethrone, who set the journey for black people way back then. So read of all the fine human beings who just wanted to compete on an even playing field, it's what the Constitution states but has failed to represent what was written there, especially for the American black race. It's ironic that Cubans brown or darker than me could come here and play on white teams, however, American red blooded black man was not allowed to do so, that's really deep and downright insulting.

chapter 35

Football

January 21, 1988, Washington Redskins vs. Denver Broncos in Super Bowl XII in San Diego's Jack Murphy Stadium. Perfect day for this spectacular event, stadium packed, worldwide news coverage, teams ready to be introduced. Bronco's introduction first, next all awaited the Washington Redskins, this was a very monumental game in that it would feature a first, and that first was a special and talented athlete named Doug Williams, it was something that never happened in 21 years of Super Bowl competition. As the world watched and listened, they heard the words addressed to the stadium crowd and to the world at large: "Ladies and gentlemen, your starting quarterback for the Washington Redskins, Doug Williams." This was very meaningful to the superb football player, for his family, friends, loved ones, old school coaches, motivators, for himself and for the race of which he inherited his ethnic birth right. This man has shocked the world, a first, of which the sports world thought would never happen. It was stated that ever since the beginning this race of people were not intelligent enough, or even capable of orchestrating this very prestigious position. How could this happen ? It has been known for years that the white Old Boy, owners of those football teams never intended for anyone of his William's race to perform in a quarterback position. There were all kinds of barriers in place, what happened that one would actually prove to the world that we are all born equal, and if given the education and training, are all capable of getting the job done. However, we always had to prove it to the world, and especially here in America where we still continue to do so. On this day, the announcer introduced the first black man in football to start as quarterback. What a tribute to this man and the team coach, and the Washington Redskin's owner to allow this very first to happen. A major accomplishment for Williams who had to endure being underpaid, discriminated against, but still continued to persevere to excel in order to achieve his goal. And on this day, all who knew him, worked with him, played the game with him, encouraged and supported his efforts to prove he was Second to None, witnessed one of the most extraordinary performance that stands even until this day. He was voted top of his game, MVP of Super Bowl XXII, he set four Bowl records in the 42-10 victory over Denver: most yards passing in a game (340) most yards passing in a quarter (288), most touchdown passes and longest completion (80 yards), what an individual effort and tribute to his team players as well!

Doug spoke of the late Martin Luther King, Jr., of Jackie Robinson, and Jesse Owens who had to overcome major obstacles to gain some measure of respect in their profession and recognition for their achievement. He also spoke of terry Bradshaw, Joe Montana, Dan Fouts and many others in the NFL and also may I add that is another reason for this book, I speak of those who were brought here, not of their own free will, who suffered for their recognition for over 300 years, of proving themselves and as of yet has not received it. And I always start with Jack Johnson, for his individual effort to break down these obstacles we still endure today.

I read your book, I was on hand for that super day and recall those TDs, the catches, the runs, the team effort. I commend you for all you have achieved as well as the other blacks who had finally gotten the opportunity to play that position.

It's like whites are afraid that blacks may out-perform them in whatever endeavor they are competing for, and they are jealous or just might make them look not as superior as they were taught to think. Jesse Owens might not have won all of those medals if the games long jumper had not taught a new technique to his approach. He was the best, but took time to show Jesse a better way, which would give him more lift and distance. A white champion, confident in his abilities, showed a black man a way to improve himself. He had no hang ups, the moves he showed Jesse cost him his title that year. However, he saw the potential in Jesse, who was his only other competition, so he showed Jesse how to improve his game, for him to compete with Jesse at his best stance. They went on to challenge each other at two other trials, Jesse won both. It's like they put this label on blacks as being inferior and not smart enough, only to be embarrassed whenever a black man proves to the white world they are not as dumb as they were thought of. The first black who graduated from the West Point as I wrote earlier, was isolated from the other 100 classmates, there was no way they wanted him to graduate ahead of any of them, what would they tell their parents who would ask: "How in hell did you let that black man graduate higher than you?" I know it was embarrassing because the black man did just that, graduated among the top ten in his class. Some years ago, I went to apply for a job, met with the supervisor for the interview, he was in awe from the first he set his eyes on me, what was the result? I was overqualified, case closed. I was black, intelligent, well rounded, sharply dressed and of great presence and character,, and knowledgeable about the position I was applying for. It's as if they are very insecure, they have been for hundreds of years. So the bigotry and racism will be here forever, it's on in our jobs, in sports, and in our society. Reason I write to perhaps change some views and attitude to create harmony and balance, it just might resolve some of our social problems here in this country, and it affects blacks more than any other group.

I think of all the great black football players, the racism they endured, yet they stayed the course to become a major force in today's game, I wrote of Gale Sayers scoring those six touchdown runs, bet I could go on and on, the late Johnny Sample championship rings in both AFL and NFL. I could never sit here without thinking about the phenomenal Jim Brown, what he meant to the game, and the tremendous work he's doing with our youth and the prison system trying to keep these incarcerated blacks focused to pursue some other avenues than that which caused their confinement, perhaps a reach-out program for these individuals and I wish him all the success with it. In his day, I've seen him run over three or four guys, drag five or six guys fifteen - twenty yards before they could bring him down. The most explosive runner of the game, he led the NFL in rushing for eight years for a total of 12,312 yards, scored 126 touchdowns, 106 of them by rushing, three times voted MVP in the NFL, considered the greatest football player ever, Jim was elected to the Pro Football Hall of Fame in 1971.

Charles Follis was the first Black Professional Football player and the fans urged his teammates to put him out of the game, the team captain Jack Tattersoll addressed the crowd saying: "Don't call Follis a nigger. He is a gentleman and a clean player, and please don't call him that." Some of the people in the crowd applauded and Follis was not bothered anymore, he was once invited to a team party, only to be told that he was not welcome in the building, and would have to leave. So racism has been around in the games from its very beginning. Follis was followed by all of these legendary players Ray Kemp, James Turner, Jerome Brud Holland, Levi Jackson, Bobby Grier, Woody Strode, Kenny Washington, Bobby Mitchell, Marion Motley, Dick "Night Train" Lane, Rosey Brown, Lenny Moore, Jim Parker, Herb Adderley, Deacon Jones, Bobby Bell, Bobby Mitchell, Paul Warfield, Willie Davis, Charley Taylor, Joe Gellian, James Harris, Vince Evance, Toney Dorsett, Earl Campbell, Billy Sims, O.J. Simpson, Herschel Walker, Walter Payton, Lawrence "Lt" Taylor, Ed "Too Tall" Jones, Wilbert Montgomery, Drew Pearson, James Lifton, John Stallworth, Harold Carmichael, Charlie Joiner, Eric Dickerson, Franco Harris, Charlie Taylor, Lester Hayes, Terrill Owens, Irvin Fryer, Reggie White. I could go on and on forever, we hear some really great talented players out there today, who are just awesome at what they do, and they are definitely a tribute to the game and dedicated to continue a legacy of our great black players who have left their sweat, blood and tears on the many playing fields in our country, establishing a winning and lasting Tradition of those who preceded them. I say: "Continue to exhibit your skills before the world. REFUSE TO LOSE and BE SECOND TO NONE, at playing the game you chose to play. Continue to maintain a Winning Tradition for yourselves and our youth who are in need of role models, that speak to them of what it takes to be all they can be, to get their education, listen to their parents, upgrade their standards and character, let them know that Life is not an easy game to Play. We are looking for a few Good Men to enhance our children's attitudes whenever and wherever that may be:

STAY SHARP and Many more great Season!"

It's a shame the jobs are not being given equally to our people, causing poverty and hardship, more money spent in foreign countries than on our own soil, which means our black children's parents cannot afford to attend their local games. However, whenever you get the opportunity to be interviewed, ensure you give a shout out to those children that just may be watching; that special statement spoken to them could be a few cherished words that might make a difference. This is all an effort by us all to save our children and assist them in dealing with whatever they are seeing, hearing, the killings. It's all a Divine calling to reach out - speak to the whites as well as the Blacks, many white children are taught racism even today. So if the opportunity presents itself, address these issues. STAY SHARP AND GOD BLESS!

chapter 36

Golf

Here's a piece I wrote about "Tiger" in 1997 "THE MASTER OF HIS GAME AND THE DREAM"

Finally the door opened. Tiger walked in, and like the world's largest feline that his name identifies him with, he's handsome, young, graceful, proud, poised, confident, determined, respected, aggressive and tenacious. A smooth planner and operator of the hunt for his game, and as that Tiger, who's one of the worlds most fierce competitor ever to roam, the plains. Tiger relentlessly pursued his quest to conquer all and be master of the game.

These talents were evident during the three days of the PGA Master's Tournament For on these three days, Tiger demonstrated the beautifully coordinated movements in a superb and brilliant performance. His swings, follow through techniques, hand and body gestures, were pretty much in motion. Never has there been such an overwhelming and dominated force displayed in the history of the tournament. Tiger shattered all previous records and as the whole world watched, he established one of the most spectacular and extraordinary finishes ever recorded in the game of golf, certainly some of the most cherished and memorable moments in the world of sports. An advocate of: "REFUSE TO LOSE" and "BE SECOND TO NONE," Tiger truly became Master of the Game an his Father's Dream.

Tiger, a very intelligent and talented child, began to demonstrate a great deal of enthusiasm for the game, after observing his father practice his routine over a period of time. Blessed with two strong, knowledgeable, caring, loving parents, Earl and Kultida, he was nurtured and tutored not only for the game of golf but for the game of life as well. He paid his dues and as he grew, learned how to enhance his character and self-identity, to be strong, to persevere, how to deal with life's obstacles and challenges, they instilled a strong religious and spiritual foundation, they taught him how to be a winner.

On April 13, 1997, Tiger recorded his phenomenal masterpiece. He accomplished it all with discipline, class, style and dignity. He gave 110% of his God-given talent. His display of courage and skills were something to behold. He achieved excellence and earned that prestigious green Blazer, which is only worn by a select few in the world who have mastered the game.

Tiger, the youngest at 21, and the only American of African, and Thai heritage ever to accomplish this feat, he became a superstar, role model and hero of all people of the world, a legend in his own time. Tiger has not forgotten his parents, friends, and people who helped him get there, and those special pioneers of the game who paved the way, as he acknowledged them on his special day of victory.

He has become an idol for all and has reached out to the youth of the world to ensure that they keep focused on their dreams, that the Price of Victory is hard work and perseverance, let no one prepare harder or be more determined to win than you are at playing your game or excelling in life.

Tiger has made a major impact, a tremendous difference and powerful presence in our lives, and reminds the people of the world that it needs more Respect, Honesty and Love of all Mankind. Tiger, a name given him by his father, in honor of a very close friend, Nguyen Phong, has given us something very special, that gravitating smile that he has embrace the world with, he has given us The Master of The Game and The Dream. He's Simply the Greatest, he's done it all! Truly the best we will ever see for years to come! Playing golf is cool!

The game we know as Golf originated in Scotland, some may claim it was Holland, by 1440 the game was popular. In 1457 James II, ruler of Scotland at one point ruled the game unlawful because it took too much time away from practicing of the bow and arrow, which was the major weapon of warfare. With the Queen enjoying it so much, it was allowed to continue, the game flourished immensely and of course only the elite were playing members. The first tournament of record, there is 1860 at the Prestuick Course in Scotland, which later became known the British Open.

The game got its start here in America in 1885. Joseph Mickle Fox from Philadelphia took a trip to Scotland, was fascinated by the game. He founded the Foxburg Golf Club hear Philadelphia in 1887. The club is the oldest in America, still in existence. In Yonkers, New York, a Scotsman named John G Reid introduced the game to some friends in 1888, their enthusiasm for the game helped to spread the popularity across the United States. The United States Golf Association was established in 1894.

As you already know it was another of those sports of the elite and barred blacks, as we have seen in all other sports we have mentioned. Blacks however, did get involved, many of the caddies who worked on private courses were black. The expense of owning and maintaining the courses was prohibitive and certainly no black man would utilize valuable land for the purpose of playing golf Blacks however, because they would practice the game on the club grounds during their off periods, became very proficient that some clubs would hold "caddies' matches."

Suddenly there was a black man allowed to play pre-golf among the white elitist at the turn of the century, his name was John Shippen, an African American, the only black golf player, that was 1900, Shippen and his brother Cyrus were instructors at exclusive clubs in the East and on many occasions played exhibitions, entered the United States Open, it was the third year of the Open and objections came from everywhere, however, Theodore Haverman, the President of the USGA allowed him to participate. He finished his fifth overall. He retired from golf around 1930.

The 1920's were prosperous times and a number of golf clubs were organized by blacks throughout the nation under the United Golf Association - The black PGA. A national black tournament was established in 1926. John Shippen won that first year; Robert "Pat" Ball the title holder in 1927, 1929, 1934 and 1941. Howard Wheeler of Georgia was champion in 1933, 1938, 1946, 1947. The black clubs only had nine holes and were difficult to maintain because of the exorbitant cost to properly maintain them. The only time blacks got a chance to use the white courses was to wait for

"Caddy Day." There were segregated public courses, but inferior to the all-white public courses. Bill Spiller and Ted Rhodes qualified in the Los Angeles Open in 1947, but were barred from the Richmond, California Open by Horton Smith, President of the PGA, Rhodes who instructed Champion Joe Louis. Horton also sent a message to Joe Louis advising him not to show up for the tournament either, racism really turned up a notch, they barred the Heavyweight Champion.

By now World War II was over and the blacks were making fierce Civil Rights challenges, in 1948 blacks could only play on nine-hole courses that did not compare to white courses. A Baltimore lawyer John F. Law instituted a suit protesting the exclusion, of blacks, he won the case on July 13, 1948 and all municipal links were desegregated. On January of 1952, Louisville opened its courses to blacks and a pattern was formed. The Brown vs. Board of Education decision in 1954 culminated in desegregation of the schools, and in its aftermath affected the progress of blacks who wanted to play golf. Blacks showed up at restricted white courses demanding to play. The Supreme Court ruled that separate golf courses, which was often federally subsidized, were illegal. The wall came down, blacks could practice and easily participated in the United States Open and on April 1961 Charles Sifford became the first black to play in the Professional Association tournament in the South.

Lee Elder became the first black to play in the most prestigious even in Golf, the Masters Tournament, which takes place yearly in Augusta, Georgia. He was the first player in the Masters, the first black to earn more than $100,000 in a single session, first black golfer to play in the World Series of Golf and the first golfer to make the United States Ryder Cup Team. In 1968 Elders had the distinction of finishing second to golf's folk hero, Jack Nicklaus in the American Golf Classic at Akron, Ohio.

Calvin Peete in 1979 won the Milwaukee Open at the age of twenty-three, on March 31, 1985 he won the Twelfth Annual Tournament Players Championship by three strokes for the second largest purse, $162,000 in PSC history. It was Peete's tenth victory in his pro career and ninth since January 1982, giving more victories in that period than any other pro. His career earnings have topped the $1.5 million mark. Again we see the fierce competitors of the black players were restricted from exhibiting their skills against whites for a long period of time, only to play at the top of the games elite whenever given the opportunity. Now we will continually see Tiger, to rule the field of white competitors, the door was open just a bit in 1954, we got afoot in, Tiger got his paw in, and it's been wide open ever since. I commend those who continued to break the barriers down, also I salute John F. Law initiating the legal suit which definitely made a tremendous mark on the game we enjoy today, where we see and know, fairness to compete is all blacks ever asked for, they were denied over and over again, however the Universal Laws states to keep knocking and that door will somehow open to those who have the courage, perseverance and that inner force that responds to all who refuse to accept man-made discriminating and frivolous barriers, we should know by now, in this world, only the strong of character, heart, soul and faith fuel the courage to achieve all that your life desires. It comes from within, with the total belief that all things are possible when we utilize all of the avenues available to us, if we do we grasp that inner satisfaction, that says: "I am somebody, I am part of the Divine, who helps those who help themselves."

Use these elements and all of your dreams, desires and goals are yours to cherish and love forever. So, all of you who read and understand, continue to be all you want to be and remember there's no pot of gold at the end of any rainbow. Your treasure is within, you are the Treasure, all you do with it is reap the rewards and they are abundant!

chapter 37

Tennis

Yet another sport that blacks were not supposed to participate in, but we see they have achieved their accomplishments and excelled whenever afforded the opportunity to do so.

The origin of the game, some say come from the ancient city in the Nile Delta in Africa/Egypt. Wherever its origin, tennis was a game that was popular in royal courts of France and England. The game was played by men and women in all kinds of weather, indoors and out. 1874, Major Walter C. Wingfield, an Englishman devised and patented a new and improved portable court for playing the game. The name of the game was changed to Lawn Tennis and in June 1817 the first championship tournament, Wimbledon, was held. The popularity of the game spread, and on August 31, 1881 the first official championship of the United States, playing under English rules was held in Newport, Rhode Island. Tennis was considered a game for the elite, a sport for ladies and gentlemen to be played in exclusive clubs and on private courts. In 1881 the United States Lawn Tennis Association was formed and thoughts of blacks participating was an idea never ever remotely entertained, the Civil War was over, but the status of Blacks remained shaky. Blacks began to play tennis in the 1890's when it became popular in some of the black colleges. A few of the pioneering black champions were Emmett J. Scott, S.E. Courtney, Warren Logan and E.T. Atvell, all out of Tuskegee; there were also Charles Cook, Thomas Jefferson, W. W. Walker and Edward C. Brown out of various other universities. These men helped to popularize the game among blacks, and tennis courts for blacks were established all over the United States. Since blacks were barred from competition with white players, they organized their own American Tennis Organization in 1916. The first tournament was held in Baltimore at Druid Hill in 1917 won by Talley Holmes, he was also victorious again in 1918, 1921 and 1924. Another outstanding player was Reginald Weir of the City of New York College, he was captain of the school's Tennis Team and Singles Champion 1931,1932,1933,1037 and 1942.

In 1929 blacks sought entry into United States Tennis Association, they were rejected, the National Association for the advancement of color people sent a letter of protest. The answer received: "Answering your letter December 24, the policy of the United States Lawn Tennis Association has declined the entry of color players in our championship. We make no reflection upon the color race, but we believe that as a practical matter, the present method of separate Associations for administration of the affairs and championship of colored and white players should be continued. Signed. E.B.Moss, Executive Secretary. Various correspondence were exchanged between the black and white Associations, one of the statements made to the white association at the end was: "I am, and the country is shocked at your recent action in barring young Negro players, and can only say to you, in words of the late Booker T. Washington: "The only way to keep the Negro down is to stay down with him." Signed Arthur E. Francis, President, New York Tennis Association. In another response by the Board of Christian Service, it was stated that: "Moreover, inasmuch as you have made a racial issue of the matter, it seems to me manifestly unfair to white boys who have entered the tournament. It indicates that they are afraid of color competition and must be shielded if they are to win, whereas in reality the majority of white tennis players are very good sports and do not want the sort of victory that is even in part decided before the tournament starts by the elimination of excellent players." Signed by Secretary Spear Knebel. Is this not the fact in all endeavors where it seems the whites are shielded from competition, football, quarterback, baseball, at all positions, Lt. Flipper at West Point, no white wanted him to graduate ahead of them, golf blacks were barred, whites continually refused to compete against black competitors, Jack Johnson, eight years to get a championship title, and it goes on and on. And it always comes down to what Jack Johnson stated:

"Make the playing field even and blacks can achieve as all others do, or even better at whatever game of life it may be." That's why blacks who succeed are very good at whatever it is, because ever since that Constitution stated "All men are created equal with freedom and justice for everyone" blacks recognized that they did not receive that. These entitlements and statement were totally wrong, they never received equal treatment anywhere, so it was always for them to work twice as hard to be twice as good as any white man in this country. So when I hear these idiotic scientist saying that whites are smarter than blacks, it's a very comical racist comment. I've been on jobs where the white man had no business to be there, he only got the job because of discrimination or some friend or family member got them in the back door, with more than qualified black men turned away. So the handwriting has been on the wall for hundreds of years. I know a guy that was in a managerial position, could not complete all of the required paperwork, had it not been for his secretary, he would have been exposed or fired, just one who got in because his family members talked to someone who was in the position to hire him. I often wondered how in hell did he ever get in the door, let alone a managerial position. He finally got exposed when his secretary had to go on emergency leave of absence, he fell apart. So each one of these sports I write about has discriminated against blacks from the beginning. In baseball they had to create two leagues because of fierce competition and once a year the black league champion would play the white champion and would beat the white league most of the times that they played.

There's just so many amazing history to be read, especially about baseball, which I wrote a little of.

Reginal Weir waited twenty years until 1948 before he was allowed to compete in a JSCLTA tournament, at which he was well past his prime, he defeated Thomas Lewyn of Scarsdale 6-4, 6-2 but was defeated in the second round by Bill Trabergt. On the college level, late twenties, early thirties excellent black players came out of predominantly white schools, one such player was James McDaniel who became national champion of the American Tennis Association in 1940, 1941 and 1942. There were a number of prominent black women champions in ATA. Lucy Slove, 1917 followed by Isadora Chamels and flora Lomax, these women won the championship several times. Ora Washington of the Germantown YWCA, Philadelphia, was a particularly remarkable woman. In twelve years she played without being defeated, won 201 trophies, she won eight titles in nine years.

The black tennis world had to wait until the early 1950's for the arrival of the first black to compete at Wimbledon and Forrest Hills, that first black was a woman, Althea Gibson. Born on August 25,1927 in a small town, called Silver, in South Carolina. She was there when she went to live with her Aunt Sally in Harlem when she was eight, she then went to Philadelphia with her aunt Daisy finally in 1943 when her parents secured their own apartment on west 143rd street. Althea, being the only child, was reluctant to join them, she had enjoyed moving from place to place. From the beginning she hated school, she played hooky every chance she could, preferring to stay around the playgrounds where she could do what she liked best: stickball, basketball, baseball, football and paddle tennis, somehow she managed to graduate from junior high school, she was tough, streetwise, an arrogant teen-ager who could fight. Her father recognizing her athletic abilities started training her to be a woman boxer. The Police Athletic League on 143rd street, where she lived, into a play street and closed it to traffic. Althea became paddle tennis champion, playing against other Harlem play streets, she won a number of medals.

A young man named Buddy Walker, who worked with youth was a musician but worked with the PAL during the summer, was impressed with what he saw in Althea, he had the idea she might be able to play regular tennis real well. Walker bought the young girl two second hand tennis rackets and started her out hitting balls against the wall on the handball courts. She did exceeding well, he then brought her to Harlem River Tennis Courts to play a few sets with his friends, despite her inexperience, she did fantastically well. Juan Serrell saw her and offered to try to work out a way for her to play at the Cosmopolitan Tennis Club, which was on Sugar Hill. He signed her up and lessons were from Fred Johnson, a one-armed professional who taught her the basics of footwork and game strategy, and tried to instill on this rough diamond of a girl the polite manners that accompany the playing of the game.

One of the most impressive event at the cosmopolitan was the day Alice Marble played an exhibition match there of which Althea got a chance to watch her in action. Marble, from California, won the women's single's championship at Wimbledon in 1939. She won there in 1938, 1939 and 1940. Marble was the United States women's singles champion, watching her play the game, Althea gained insights she never imagined, Marble was powerful and aggressive, the effortlessness she seemingly portrayed inspired Althea. A year later after relentless practicing Althea entered the American Tennis Association. New York State Open championship being held at the Cosmopolitan in the girls singles, she entered and won. Later in the summer Althea entered the ATA nationals, she lost in the finals, 1943, she trained to improve her game. In 1944 and 1945 Althea won the ATA's nationals girls singles championship. It was later arranged for her to go live with a very wealthy black family, she was 18, she got her won room and received an allowance, just as Doctor Eaton's children did. For the first time in her life she really wanted to succeed in school, she practiced tennis regularly with Dr. Eaton, then joined the high school band and played the saxophone.

That first summer she played in nine tournaments and won the singles in each one of them. She won the ATA title for ten consecutive years and was proclaimed the best woman player in black tennis. She stopped entering to afford others the opportunities she had had. At twenty she was offered a tennis scholarship upon the advice of Walter Austin, the tennis coach. In 1950 she was invited to play in the Nationals Indoors -the first Black woman to be invited, but lost in the finals, even though she lost, this was a monumental achievement for blacks to even get to the Nationals.

Well, you knew it would raise its ugly head, racial discrimination always does. Althea had done so well that she would be invited to play in the summer grass court tournament, however, no invite was made to her by the USLTA, as far as they were concerned Gibson did not exist. Some newspapers though, began to question the obvious discriminatory practices of the USLTA, but the organization never budged. Out of nowhere God allowed Alice Marble, formerly one of the world's greatest tennis players, who wrote an editorial in July of 1950 issue of American Lawn Tennis magazine. She wrote: "On my current lecture tours, there are those who want to know if Althea Gibson will be permitted to play in this years Nationals, I could not answer that question, but I came back to New York determined to find out, I directed my question at the committee of long standing, the answer was: "Miss Gibson has not sufficiently proven herself. True enough but didn't 't I think the field was awfully poor, I did not. She stated it was her opinion that she performed beautifully under the circumstances, considering how little play she has had in top competition, her win over a seasoned veteran like Midge Buck seems to me a real triumph. She stated that if she is not invited to participate in them, as her committee member freely stated, then she obviously will be unable to prove anything at all, and it will be reluctant duty of the committee to reject her entry at Forest Hills. Miss Gibson is over a cunningly wrought barrel, and I can only hope to loosen a few of its staves with one lone opinion. I think it's time we face a few facts. If tennis is a game of ladies and gentlemen, it's also a time we act a little more like gentle people and less like sanctimonious hypocrites, she might be soundly beaten for a while, but she has a much better chance on the courts than in the inner sanctum of the committee where a different kind of game is played.

If the field of sports has got to pave the way for all of civilization, let's do it. At this moment, tennis is privileged to take its place among the pioneers for a true democracy, if it will accept the privilege. If it declines to do so, the honor will fall on the next generation, perhaps -but as inevitable as it has proven to be in baseball, in football, or in boxing; there is no denying so much talent. The committee at forest hills has the power to stifle the efforts of one Althea Gibson, who may or may not be the staff of which champions are made, but eventually she will be succeeded by others of her race who have equal or superior ability. They will knock at the door as she has done. Eventually, the tennis world will rise up in masse to protest the injustices ; perpetrated by our policy makers. Eventually why not now?" The committee still held fast to their decision.

Althea went on and played on the Eastern Circuit which had accepted her entry, got to the finals and was beaten by Doris Hart. Then Gibson quietly received word from the USLTA that an application for entrance into the Nationals at Forest Hills would be accepted. The day she was to play in the Nationals is beautifully depicted in her autobiography: "I always wanted to be Somebody." She won her first match with Barbara Knapp of England 6-2, 6-2, on the next day she was up against Louise Brough, Wimbledon Champion, the first set was won by Brough 6-1, Gibson took second set 6-3, she had a 7-6 lead on the third set, victory was nearly within her grasp when suddenly a storm erupted and the match had to be suspended until the next day. She lost her edge and was defeated when Brough won three straight games, but Gibson had won the battle, she was the first black woman to play in the Nationals at Forest Hills, undaunted. She made plans to play at the Wimbledon in spring of the following year, 1951. Under the auspices of the USLTA she went out to Hamtromock, Michigan for more tennis instructions with Jean Hoxie, a famed tennis teacher. She did not win in Wimbledon in 1951, '52, and '53. They were very disappointing years for her career. In the USLTA competition she was ranked number nine, 1952, number seven in 1953 and thirteen in 1954. She became very discouraged about her career in tennis, when suddenly she received an invitation from the State Department to make a tour of the Southeast Asia with a tennis team. It is interesting to note that the tour was conceived of shortly after Emmitt Till, a 13 year old black youth from Chicago visiting the South allegedly "eyed" a white woman and was murdered by her husband and friend. Gibson was prepped by her department and asked to remember she was representing her country, in 1956 the tour was over.

She went to play tournaments in Stockholm, Germany, and Egypt. By this time she had won sixteen out of eighteen tournaments and should be a cinch to win at Wimbledon. Before that she was the first black to win the French Open Title, with that under her belt she lost to Shirley Frey at Wimbledon and lost again at Forest Hills, newspapers were beginning to call her a "has been."

In 1957 the USLTA paid her way to Wimbledon, Althea won the Wimbledon title, beating Darlene Hard of San Diego, and she became the first black international tennis champion they had ever seen. After winning the singles crown, she teamed up with Darlene Hard and won the women's doubles at Wimbledon. 1958 she returned to Wimbledon and won the women's singles and teaming up with Maria Buenos of Brazil won the women's doubles. Upon returning to the United States in September, she won the women's singles finals at Forest Hills beating her old adversary, Louise Brough in straight sets. She was presented with the Wimbledon Cup by the Queen of England in the United States, then Vice-President Richard M. Nixon shook her hand and presented her with flowers; President Dwight D. Eisenhower wrote his "Congratulations!"

Althea went on to be a women's golf champion and a member of the New Jersey Boxing Commission, she was the director of a large New Jersey recreational park and camp, she was inducted into the International Tennis Hall of Fame in 1971. She was one tough competitor who lived up to her dreams that were expected of her, a very special and dedicated individual who was just fabulous in all of her life endeavors. I was very proud as a black man reading about this legendary black woman who had many firsts in her courageous career in spite of the racist barriers set forth to block her progress and what treasure! Alice Marble was in writing and supporting Althea to achieve her goals by addressing the racial discrimination in the sports world of their time. Just goes to show that respect of human beings can create togetherness, and must be reflected in today's racist attitudes to unify - rather than to separate, and reveal injustice which is everywhere before us. There's a need for white people to get this history I am trying to instill, that most of them are really not aware of, and I definitely need our black brothers and sisters to acknowledge and start appreciating what our past was about, and how we can find ways to create the unity, harmony, balance and leadership for our race today, there's got to be more togetherness among the ALL to create the WHOLE!

I must salute Arthur Ashe who broke into the game right after Althea Gibson's breakthrough, desegregation in tennis tournament had taken place, allowing him to exhibit his skills before the world and against some of the best trained players in the nation. By the time he was eighteen, the USLTA ranked him number twenty-eight. He accepted a tennis scholarship to UCLA, receiving excellent coaching from S.D. Morgan. He won the United States Amateur Championship at Longwood Cricket club in Brookline, Massachusetts in 1963 with a student, he was the first American black to be named to the Davis Cup team. Ashe became the first black man ever to win the United States Nationals and the first American male to win it.

By the end of 1968, he had won a total of thirty matches in a row and rated top tennis player in the country. Ashe had requested a South African visa to compete in South African Open, that country turned down his request, the country was devoted to segregation principles of apartheid in return for South Africa refusing to grant his request they were punished for their outrageous racial policies by being barred from participating in the 1970 Davis Cup competition. Ashe won the Australian Open title that same year. Arthur had a tremendous win in 1975 when he defeated Jimmy Connors in four sets for the Wimbledon men's singles title. He was the first black man to win that esteemed crown. Ashe retired in 1979 after undergoing quadruple by-pass surgery, after a massive heart attack.

He wrote a provocative message to black youth of America: "We have been on the same road - sports and entertainment - too long. We need to pull over, fill up at the library, speed away to Congress and the Supreme Court, the unions and the business world." New York Times, 1979.

chapter 38

Venus and Serena Williams

What a beautiful family affair. Richard and wife Aracene raised their two superstars in a close-knit family relationship, recognizing the vulnerabilities of pathways to fame and glory. Richard, seeing their early potential, removed them from public school and ensured they did not become distracted from their education, training and religious devotion. Seeing the barriers of racism in tennis, particularly when regarding blacks, the plan had to be masterminded to its fullest, very little outside force obstructing. As we have seen with Althea Gibson, broke through color barriers in 1949 - that color barrier which not only pertained to her, but to all black athletes, of both genders, before and after her. It's like Marley had written, the white athletes were shielded and not exposed to the excellent play of the nation's blacks. So all the necessary safeguards were in place to allow these girls to achieve their goals at each level, to mature under the constant tutelage in a family-structured setting. Richard became teacher, trainer and manager, along with their mother.

Venus and Serena have three older sisters, Yetunde, Isha and Lyndrea - who Richard also exposed to tennis. Richard had become inspired by seeing a women's tennis tournament, especially after seeing the winner being presented with a check for $30,000. He spoke to his wife about putting all the girls in tennis to become millionaires, and Venus and Serena did just that, the others Yetunde later pursued a medical career. Isha went to law school, Lyndrea preferred music. Richard took four and a half year old Venus to public tennis courts to practice, he had collected about 550 old tennis balls, he would toss to her, she would hit them back to him. Whenever he stopped, she would start crying, so he would wind up tossing all 550 balls to her, he took her to the East Compton Park

Tennis Court regularly. A year later four year old Serena began to join them, both girls had natural athletic talent, they had the ability to focus for long periods of time and strong desire to improve and excel. He encouraged them, praised them and always ensured they were having fun. What an amazing relationship they developed. It's really special when you nurture your children to believe in themselves, and trust in you as parents that you will always safeguard them, let them know how special they are, that they are your God-given treasures, to share your wisdom and knowledge with as you prepare them for life itself Richard was criticized for removing his children from public schools, to teach and raise them at home. What a great move that turned out to be, these two women are graceful in their demeanor, excellent role models, and beautifully spoken, highly intelligent, that reflects greatly the love and guidance of their parent's teachings and spiritual awareness. It's like the Jacksons and Woods families, they decided to get their children involved early on in life and I know that made a tremendous difference, they all became the best, at what they inherited early on from their parents. Afar cry from what we see today: children roaming the streets all hours of the night, not attending school, absolutely no control in many families today. So to succeed, we must be there early on to instill the love, for them to have that faith and confidence in you as parents. To ensure you have set some guidelines, you are always there, keeping them focused, allowing them to feel that love and security and above all that, nothing should come between that family harmony, pride and balance.

The women have achieved everything possible in the game they chose to play, absolutely phenomenal, they are fierce competitors, they have excelled above and beyond their father's dreams, and he dreamt big, for he told the world that one day his girls would be playing each other for the WTA, and they did. History was made in 1999 on March 28th when they played each other in the Women's Championship, this was the first time two black sisters competed for this prestigious title and the second time two sisters had ever played each other in 115 games, that first match was between 19 year old Maud Watson and her 21 year old sister Lilian Watson in 1884.

Zina Garrison, a world class black tennis player was asked a question about the sister's potential to break the racial barriers that continued to exist. She said: "Good Luck! "Well as we see these women have won the heart and soul of the tennis world, it was a tough road but truly they were prepared for it from the very beginning at five years of age and at four, where they had begun their legacy to the op of their journey, a journey that only proved their courage, heart and desire to 'REFUSE TO LOSE and BE SECOND TO NONE!'" even when it came playing each other. They were truly and duly prepared, it takes devotion, hard work and tenacity to exhibit your skills before the world, to be acknowledged the greatest among the greatest. Their names will forever be etched in the hall of fame and around the world, for their other business endeavors. I could go on and on about these two marvelous ladies, at least another two to three pages, it's been fun watching them, they have broken every conceivable record that there is, and established many of a first, extraordinary story of two Fabulous Women and a Father who can say: I Told You So.

Growing up in Philadelphia was a tremendous and rewarding experience, especially in the boxing game, if you were from Philly. The "hand game" was an essential part of our up bringing, and as I mentioned earlier, my step father taught me well. He taught me the "fast hands", balance, sparring techniques and the other fundamentals which are the building blocks of winning. I trained and fought in the many gyms in North Philadelphia, where every training session was a mental, as well as, a physical test of heart soul and desire.

There was 23rd Pal at 22nd and Columbia Avenue, where I encountered the sensational Gil Turner, who fought for the championship and other spectacular fights. Turner inspired most of us to venture forth in the pursuit of fame and glory. There was Sugar Hart, Charlie Scott, Dirty Red's, Gypsy Joe Harris, Phillip Thomas, Theodore Savage, where the great Joe Frazier got his start. The gym was built right in the heart of two rival gangs, The Valley and Norris Street. You talk about rumbling? Man we rumbled for recognition of gang pride! The blood, sweat and guts were left in the ring along with the "refuse to lose" attitude. Believe me, we earned one another's respect.

Then there was Champs Gym on 33rd and Ridge next to the great Pat's Steaks you could get your butt kicked, grab a steak sandwich and go on home. There you found the great Harold Johnson, the light weight champion, Sonny Liston and one of the greatest middle weights ever, Georgie Benton. I followed and knew Liston. He got a bad break from the police of Philadelphia who refused to allow the boxing fans to welcome him home after winning the championship from Floyd Patterson. The first time that it happened, it took a tremendous toll on him. It was very embarrassing for our city. I respected Liston for his boxing achievements for it was a fierce game in 'The City of Brotherly Love'. I remember the saying," If your brother is down kick him. That was the mind set of just about all who fought out of Philly. The Irish, Italian etc, they were all tough, and I still remember the fierce competitions.

There were great fighters all over the city as well as some great and committed trainers who molded the character and heart of many. They were the big brother or father figure to many a missing link of our era. We had Willie Reddish and Yank Durham who worked with Liston and Frazier. Yank took Joe to the Heavy Weight Championship. They were able to extract the very best from all who stuck with them. Not only did they train you to fight like a champion, they made you feel like one as well. I salute these men who encouraged us to get an education and carry ourselves like champions with dignity and respect. I train fighters periodically, and I too instill that "Refuse to Lose" and "Be Second to None" attitude. Consequently, I have had much success with my Winning Traditions Program where we focus our youth on the building blocks of life. I truly love the game. Fighting in Philly was one of my greatest experiences. I love the memories and I will always cherish the game, and all of those who made Philly known as the true proving ground of the game. To all of those who played a part in that era I say," Stay sharp! You were the greatest, and I can attest to that!"

chapter 39

Policing the Communities

I would like to salute the many fine police officers out there doing a tremendously professional and tactful job of law enforcement. It's a dangerous tedious job and always will be, especially in your major cities. I commend the mayor and people for the service they provided for the two policemen killed in the line of duty, really nice turn-out to honor them, the families have my sincere condolences, I sincerely hope things will turn around there. The commissioner seem abreast of the issues demonstrated by those who thought to be the judge and jury with the three black men 's unlawful beating in the streets there. I also would like to suggest if any citizen is mistakenly killed by a police officer that the same type of service be held to honor that person and his family as well, I've read of several cases where the officers fired because they thought someone had a gun when in fact there was none. The man killed in the house on New Year's eve when one of two officers fired 13 rounds in a crowded house where they were celebrating the coming in of the New Year, the second officer was not threatened enough to fire his, yet his partner shot and killed the man and wounded a little girl also. This was someone's loved one, son, husband or family member, there should be circumstances where some type of acknowledgement be made to that family, that type of incident is what keeps black people feeling they are all suspects and could be dragged out of their homes, or vehicles and beaten or killed. I was glad the new commissioner is stressing out training techniques of approach and arresting or apprehending people. We must always remember the Move incident where 14 innocent children, women and one man were killed in that inferno causing the burning down of two city community neighborhoods, firing over 10,000 rounds preventing those people from escaping that holocaust. I was wondering why even with the presence of one police commissioner and a fire commissioner on the scene they could not resolve the issue between them and the 14 unarmed people in that house, a tragic and disgusting show of law enforcement and fire department officer, who took an oath to protect and save lives. It never happened that day, what an incompetent lack of their professionalism and knowledge of which the world watched on national TV. 41st and park side avenue at approximately 11:30 pm that hot summer night, people were out on their porches when they heard police officers conduct a traffic stop, the officers approached the vehicle with one male occupant, next thing noted were the two police officers pulling the individual out of the car and started to beat the man, even when he fell to the ground he was still beaten. The witnesses watched in horror and even approached the scene, the beating stopped, the man was taken to the hospital where he died of head injuries. The family obtained an autopsy report, it was found out that the man had five fractures of the skull where he was beaten upon the face and head. Witnesses spoke at court trial, no one believed their version of the incident, a white lady showed up and testified, stated she lived up in northeast Philadelphia, saying she was driving by at that area and saw the young man jump out of his car and attacked the two officers, the case was then closed. I never knew they taught officers to beat people in the head during restraining them, they said he was high in PCP. Six months later a front page of the Philadelphia Enquirer where pictures of 12 police officers were posted headlined them as having cost the city of Philadelphia in lawsuits for physical assaults, falsification of police reports, misappropriation of evidences, and gross misconduct. Guess who's pictures were depicted there? One of them was the police officer involved in the death of that young man. So we see the Philadelphia police department dates way back in police brutality and negative law enforcement So when young people as well as old people see police officers following them or treating them like they were criminals on routine traffic stops, they have a right to distrust them and fear for their safety.

There's one thing I would like to recommend and that is putting the walking cops back into the neighborhoods, that accomplishes: 1.) A working relationship between parents, residents and children of the neighborhood. 2.) Establishes some trust on the police officers to have a better pulse on the community, getting the opportunity to interact with the people and children and have weekly get-togethers, and it would make senior citizens feel safer on the streets or blocks where they live. 3.) The police officers would get the opportunity to monitor nonresidents of their patrol areas. I also would like to give a word of praise for the 1000 men who have volunteered their time to walk the streets, again another plus for law enforcement, knowing these men could assist them in pointing out trouble-makers and just establishing a working relationship on both sides. I've also stressed a dress code and need for the parents to coordinate with the commanders of their area to address the stop frisk techniques to ensure that they, as well as their children understand the significance of such tactics, there's a lot of officers who are just too intimidating. I think building more confidence between the walking officers and community people would be a good thing, the whole scenario can have a tremendous effect on those wanderers of mass killing and I wish all parties the best in striving for a better relationship and positive decrease in murders and crimes, in that great city where I was raised.

chapter 40

Vision: Establishing a New Image of a Black Race

History when read and understood plays a major part in the development of things to come. Black history dates back to the very beginning of all things. The hidden treasures of knowledge, the role it played in the first civilizations of life on this planet has been the hidden truth denied us by the white man.

We as black people must know our history, it's the beginning of shedding your blinders to allow enlightenment, the beginning to understand the greatness of those who paved the way for things we see before our eyes today.

There's a passage in the scriptures that says: "Take my people in bondage to the land overshadowed by the wings of the eagle, where they will shed their blinders to give the nation the eyes to see." Very powerful and a predicament we find ourselves in today. In this, we were deprived of our birthright and indoctrinated into a system of terrorism, hate, discrimination, mental strife, rapes, murders, lynchings, this doctrine which they forced upon your ancestors left a depleted, confused and psychologically derailed people, they taught them they were not human, just 3/5th of a man, being inferior to their white captors, and were here to be slaves for life. Their children were confiscated and separated to deprive them from the older slaves stories about their origin, spirituality and of the days when their people were kings, queens and pharaohs of the land of the Nile, of their great cities, their universities that taught their ideologies, advanced technology of science, astrology, mathematics, physics, spirituality, universal magnetic and frequencies of the solar systems. They taught of celestial gods spirituality, the names and people mentioned differs greatly from the Bible that's been rewritten thousands of times with who's ever version reflect different races and characters to tell their story. Blacks taught the mathematical systems of the Great Pyramid, these astronomers taught the advanced knowledge in depth. The distance between the Sun and the Earth, the polar diameters of the earth and much more to other cultures of people attending their great universities, yes, the black Africans had established social organizations, medicine, operational procedures, architecture and engineering and it goes on and on, a greatness that has been hidden from the black and white Americans, this information must be read and taught in American school systems, to know life, you must know what every ethnic group has contributed to it.

We, as black people, must research and know our history which has been stolen from us here for 400 years, know your history, you understand and know thyself which in time will enlighten you of your purpose here.

One of the greatest harms inflicted upon the black race and the one most affecting us even today was their indoctrination of all the negatives that has the psychological mind encompassing and holding them to be part of the very nature of their thought process, thousands of blacks even after almost 400 years are demonstrating that timeless conditioning of their minds. It still affects them today, those everlasting elements are as they taught were "you are stupid, ignorant, not capable of learning, will never succeed, are slaves for life, cannot be trusted." They taught those house niggers to hate their other brothers and sisters, a divide that exists today, and told them that they were just not good enough or ever will be, to survive in his white world, he planted, it seems like a never-ending seed of self-doubt.

Self-doubt has made millions of blacks unable to utilize all of their God-given attributes, causing low self-esteem, embarrassment, mental stress and failure. That's why it's necessary to read your history and know the accomplishments of our forefathers before us. They were kings, pharaohs, teachers, scholars and builders of this very world we have lived in since the beginning of time, and if it holds true and it does, then all people have been taught by the very first people where the beginning of life and civilizations began. As I wrote before as the white men befriended the African men, learned from him, then came back to conquer and destroy all evidence of the facts, that he was instructed by the first people that existed, intellectual growth began with these first men.

The bible says we are all created equal so if I am already here when you come on the scene, then I must enlighten you of the knowledge of which I have, the universal laws of all things. I always say that he who discovers the treasures hides the truth. The American Indian was wiped out by the same white man, they taught him of this new land and the white man destroyed most of their history as well One thing that always happens is that truth will always be found if we search long and far enough.

The white man gained tremendous wealth of knowledge, from the black African, their philosophy, custom, spirituality and culture, then came back and burned all writings, confiscated all artifacts and anything of knowledge, even damaged the nose fixtures of the Sphinx because of its Negroid resemblance. However, they could not destroy the hieroglyphics which appeared on the walls of the pyramids after a lot of diggings in the ruins of the sand-covered grounds which, even without the writing and other materials they destroyed, told the truth when translated in time. All the knowledge proved that just as the Bible states, there's nothing new under the sun, all three of your great philosophers of European descent were taught in Africa, Socrates, Plato, Aristotle. Africa is a diverse land of cultures, beliefs and philosophies. It is a known fact that the ancient African continent is the birthplace of all humankind. A wealth of philosophical and spiritual concepts have emerged from North Africa. African philosophy views mankind simply as part of a harmonious whole, not as the exalted center of the universe or as a malignant accident of nature, and time was measured by sunrises, sunsets and changing of seasons. The philosophy is that there's no end in death, it is simply apart of life and a journey into a new phase or dimension of the spirit's existence. So while destroying this knowledge, they prevented any proof of a civilization that existed, yet they kept its wealth and treasures and hid the truth from the unfortunate people of the world, especially the American black slaves and other white people of this country who could care less in most cases. However, there are many who would love to share that wealth of knowledge, to them and all others, read, read, and ask. The Bible states: Seek and ye shall find!

Out Of My Darkness

"In my beginning there was Love, I never knew, there was darkness, I was there, but no one could see, only He knew I was there.

I began to grow from my infancy, no one knew, only He knew. He watched as I evolved from the unknown, through infinite time and space. I grew in the elements of his spiritual life giving substance, that only He could give.

In my darkness He expanded my mind of all universal harmony, I soared through the celestial spheres of boundless galaxies in the serenity among the twilight of the stars of heaven.

My extremities were formed in the image of Him, who created and held me so firmly in His divine grace. I grew in peace and love, that He continued to bless me with, in my darkness where only He had eyes to see.

I was there, I evolved in the cycle of His creation and manifested into a sacred child of his. I was there, I continued to develop. He nurtured me, gave me purity and provided me with those unique characteristics of my individuality.

He gave me all the essentials, my mind, my thought process, intellect and my oneness, which ties in with cosmic forces of life.

He entrusted me with the ability to receive and comprehend all things imaginable. I was there, they never knew, I continued to mature in my darkness. I began to move, then they knew I was there. I was conceived in their system of things. I heard their voices. I felt their vibrations and warmth, as we began to bond as one.

I felt their hands gently tracing my contours, as they moved over my body's housing space within. As I grew in size they became more excited of my presence and need to be nurtured, to be loved and cared for.

Then after a period of time as only He could do, He allowed this wondrous miracle, the greatest gift to mankind, the birth of a child into the world, to happen.

I emerged through the cradle of love, from my mother's womb into the light of humanity. I breathed the air, my eyes opened, I saw two beautiful and happy faces. I saw them in a state of joyous amazement. They were crying, I felt the warm teardrops, as they fell from their faces, onto my naked and trembling body.

I, too, was crying, I raised my arms and extended my fingers as I reached out to them. They cuddled me in their warm and tender embrace, I felt that love from whence I came, that love that only He could give, for us all to share, as one.

Yes, only He knew of my time of existence, only He knew when I would enter into this alien world of mortality.

As they held me my eyes began to wander across their faces, I saw man and woman, husband and wife, who became father and mother, after talking of me, thinking of and praying for me.

They bonded together in a blissful physical and emotional communion. Their thoughts of me entered into that universal and spiritual realm that connects to Him, who knows and controls all things. In return He answered their prayers and blessed them with this joyous birth of me, to them.

I also seem to understand that they knew that, He makes but one sacred demand, that demand is to take me, who in my tiny innocence, has been nurtured and blessed with a mind capable of receiving an unlimited abundance of knowledge of all things.

That they give of themselves spiritually and wholeheartedly without any equivocation of teaching and enlightening me with all the wisdom and knowledge they have acquired during their years.

That they show me right from wrong, educate me, so I can enhance my intelligence of life's principles, values and virtues to govern myself by. Teach me to be passionate and how to have compassion. How to love all people regardless of their race, creed or ethnic origin, to understand their cultures and ideologies. We are all part of his creation and master plan.

Teach me to have faith and accept the challenges I may encounter along the path of life, and above all else, to give my undying love and praise to the Father of all things.

Teach me to love mother earth, from where we receive our daily source of food and nutrients to sustain our growth and maintain our health. Show me how to be part of that globule and spiritual force that energizes our planet for the betterment of all mankind.

Teach me to enhance my spirituality and commit myself to his rules, as I walk in his light of life. Show me to prepare myself for the inevitable return back through darkness from whence I came, where, again, he will know I am there, where only He will have eyes to see, it's me.

I closed my eyes to sleep and I heard them pray, Our Father, who art in heaven, hollowed be thy name, thy kingdom come, thy will has been done in your joyful gift to mankind.... our child.

Yes, in my beginning Love was there and has always been there. In our total darkness Love created us in his sacred image. They called him Our Father, there's many names for him, from people of different theologies, I know him as Love, who's every-where in all of us to share, I also know him as, God, our Glorious King, whose only wish, is peace and happiness, for all mankind. Love, trust, honor and praise Him, have faith and glorify his name. God allowed us all to share that holy place of our darkness, where only He knew that we were there, where only He had eyes to see and create you and me.

Yes, we all come here fully prepared to embark on our life's journey, God gave us eyes to visualize the hatred, anger, injustices or the differences of the beauty in all good things, gave us ears to hear the blasphemies of violent words or the gentleness of which they could bring, lips to speak wisdom, knowledge and address the love and beauty of all things, a body housed with muscles, fiber, tendons and all the essential tissue structure to enable us to accom-plish all physical tasks with. We were born with love, even though at times we felt unloved and neglected, that universal love of us all that is always there, that power of love brought blacks through their bondage times. We will always be loved in good and troubled times and we fail to know that, however, it's the truth, things hap-pen for reasons, we learn that in our personal journey with God, there's many trials and the good as well as the bad to bring us our spiritual enlightenment.

We have strong hearts, the heart that the slaves showed when asked to fight a white man's war to establish their Independence, to have the courageous heart to unify this country, only the strong, brave and humble have hearts made of Gold.

The mind, the most powerful complex structure in the Universe, and when implanted with the positive thoughts can take you across a tight wire suspended hundreds of feet above the ground surface, they say wherever your mind goes the body will follow. Yet the white man tampered with it early on, making it a frightful thing just to think you could accomplish or excel at anything, we find early on where there's no positive thinking or efforts, there's no advancement, no trophy or any self-gratification ever to be proud of Millions have given up on their selves, unable to forgive their own failure, you must never give up because thousands of our ancestors have died to provide you with that opportunity to participate in the battle or challenge at hand and win, when you try.

Yes, God gave us everything we could possibly need to govern ourselves, to complete our journey. Mandingo's book tells us of all wonderful resources He has blessed each and everyone of his Treasures, birthed into this world regardless of race, creed or color, its only when we are not properly nurtured that we fail and give up on ourselves. So, as abducted and sold people we came to the country that's overshadowed by the wings of the eagle, to where we were mentally and physically deprived and denied the Universal Laws and system of things to take its course and were indoctrinated into mental darkness, not being ever told what we're capable of accomplishing. The Common Foe is a devious devilish soul who drafted up bonding codes to keep them in a black world of nothingness, mothers raped in front of their children and fathers, to present his power over all, the father helpless, the children traumatized with fear that they grew up with for hundreds of years, if their fathers could not protect them then who could, the psyche mind stabilized the inferior mind set of every thought, they could have, when in fact it always reflected: "I can't do that!"

They progressed through the years suffering before the white man, refusing to look him in the eye, bowing down to this white children, calling five to six years old children Master and Misses. The maltreatment continued, then one day a proud and strong black man found a way to put his God-given elements together to defeat the Foe. Jack Johnson exhibited all of the brawn, heart, desire, courage, dignity, class, character, willpower tenacity, will to fight and win in a white man's game and world. When he won that championship, the blinders dropped from the black man's eyes and allowed him to see change. On to Joe Louis, the great brown bomber, who refused to give boxing exhibitions unless the audience were equally represented, and challenged the military officials to correct a wrong, for servicemen fighting and dying for this country demonstrating the clear vision before his eyes, that a change was needed, he also used his God-given characteristics, he had eyes to see, a voice to be heard and a courageous heart to seek the unequal justice of which blacks fought for, they got what he asked for, change and equality, fair treatment on military facilities, bases, mess halls and God saw that it was good. Years later another great champion showed up and stated: "I am the greatest!" Muhammad Ali, America was in turmoil, rioting in the streets against a war that seemed to last forever, young ones of all ethnic groups being killed by the thousands. The military asked for him, he refused, they gave him a trial and he appealed the decision, they took his title, stripped him of the Championship. He went to God, who found a way for him to use his symbolism of greatness to speak out, using God's gifts of heart and fortitude to speak out, told the Military that he would not travel the world killing brown and black people just to make America look good, he emphasized that he had no quarrel with the Vietnamese people, that they never called him a nigger and that his fight was right here in America against the white racist people of this country. Again it took a huge heart to stand for his convictions, even stripped of his title, he gained world recognition that was worth more than the belt and crown taken from him. I often tell people it was not his boxing skills only that made him the greatest, it was the act of God that allowed him to be embraced and honored worldwide for his willingness to stand for justice and equal rights for black and poor people who were being discriminated against here in America, but was still being sent to Viet-Nam where they were being mocked by the enemy in many situations with "Why are you here fighting us, we never hung or lynched you, we never called you nigger?" Ali became the most recognized face around the world and today is still referred to as "The Greatest of All Times."

I had the honor of escorting Ali around military bases in Korea, after he fought a fight in Japan against their Heavyweight wrestling Champion, of which Ali won. A man I had searched for in his hometown of Louisville, when I was stationed in Kentucky. I finally got the chance to meet the Greatest; I love to tell this story. I was waiting for him to show up with a few officers I had selected in front of a really nice hotel there in Seoul, Korea, he had just flown to the country from Japan, we were standing there, when I heard this car drive up and stop behind us. I was in the process of turning around, when I heard someone yell: "Hey, Nigga, what the hell are you doing standing out here looking like the Heavyweight Champ? I am the Heavyweight Champ." He ran up pass the press who was covering his tour, started to throw a few punches at me. I stepped to an angle, threw a few jabs, slipped away from a right hand and countered with a left over the right, he jumped up, and yelled: "Hey, this Nigga can box too!" Everyone was in uproar, laughing, a large crowd gathered within minutes, the streets were crowded, we grabbed and embraced each other, I'll never forget that precious moment, I loved Ali he was my idol, I followed all of his fights after he beat another Champion I knew Charles Sonny Liston. I introduced myself, informed him of the places we were scheduled to visit, we jumped into our vehicle, he rode with me in the first car of the vehicle escort, at one point he asked to stop to stretch his legs in a small town area along the route, he got out and within five minutes at the most, there were wall-to-wall people, streets filled, that's how well-received and honored he was by those Korean people, luckily we had a Korean highway patrol for escort and added security, they finally got us out and we proceeded on our way. He definitely was a great guy, fun person, great presence of self character, carried himself with dignity and class, tall, handsome, ladies everywhere wanting to meet the champ. I had to turn them away by the dozens. I even offered myself but there were no takers ever, evidently everyone thought I was his manager. Every time someone wanted something, someone would say: "See that guy with the bald head..." We had a great time, I enjoyed this man immensely, he was truly the greatest I wrote apiece about him entitled: "Such a Man."

So through the hundreds of years here in this country being denied human and equal rights there's been these three great Heavyweight Champions who could just not defeat the Common Foe, so I write to all the wonderful people of our country to unify to take up the cause of human rights to step up to the challenge at hand, he's a strong formal character of deceit and deception, he may be everywhere, he's the racist cop, the racist governors, senators, judges, lawyers, discriminating housing people who refuse housings, the church clergymen who rape and abuse our children, he's the police commissioner, and fire chiefs who allow their men to fire 10,000 rounds in a house of unarmed children and women. He's the racist who continues to say we cannot accomplish anything, could not fly the airplanes, we're too stupid to fight as soldiers, he's the sheriff in Alabama who released those two Jewish and one black kid to be murdered in the back woods during their voting registration of blacks. They're the white men who bombed the church killing 4 innocent black girls, the racist soldiers who killed black soldiers who were helping them fight their enemies in the Revolutionary and Civil Wars, they're the racist bigots who hung and lynched blacks who returned from wars, in uniform, one was even burned alive, the whites who hung the nooses while the nation is sending our loved ones off to die, the 3 white officers who beat up that 67 year old black man in New Orleans, the cop who rammed a broomstick up a black man's rectum in the New York police station, the racist people who burned down the Tulsa, Oklahoma city, and the law enforcement officials who chose not to prosecute anymore, the corrupt corporate person stealing funds, the politicians taking bribe money. I could go on and on, however, there are some really nice people of all ethnic groups in this country, and I have mentioned some who have helped me turn my life around, those white abolitionists who fought slavery and racism since the very beginning and I truly applaud them. But we have our work cut out for us, if we seek the change to become the leader of the world, we must put our psychological racist ways behind us to unify this nation, we have the potential to accomplish this endeavor. We have made major strides in music, sports, dance, and wars, where we see blacks and whites come together with a winning tradition in unity, however, we cannot live in neighborhoods together, go to certain schools together or even work together. It's ludicrous that we here in America still have the white mind set being exhibited, that they are superior and it's just not so. Everywhere you look blacks have excelled in whatever field there is, this is not 1619 when slaves were brought naive to this country, this is 2008 where intellectually there's no superior race group. Blacks have closed the gap in spite of being denied access to a schooling system for 250 years, like the bible says: "We are all created equal" but of different blends of skin texture. "We are all God's treasures," so Og Mandino wrote. Thanks, my brother and I hope people continue to read your fabulous book.

chapter 41

Vision

In the past hundred years, we of white and black races have been seeing a different vision, however the one we are seeing today differs somewhat, blacks are seeing change in white standards. The white people are being laid off by the millions over the last five years, they are losing their homes, having their cars repossessed, they are complaining because the same problems the blacks have suffered through is affecting them now. Why is that? One thing for sure black people are not responsible for the fate you are suffering today, blacks never outsourced your jobs, or laid you off sending your jobs to various countries, causing your children to terminate college for lack of funds, black people didn't raise the price of gas, food and other essentials of living, black people never caused you to go out of business, black people didn't cause your sons and daughters to die in Viet-Nam where they were sent off to fight for 11 years, only to not win that conflict Blacks are not responsible for your one or two sons to be killed in Iraq, blacks are not the cause of your husband, wife, daughter or son suffering with PTSD or losing a leg or arm in Iraq. We are not responsible for fighting a war for over four years when you were told Mission Accomplished, no all of these situations are caused by your white leaders, yet you are hanging nooses, and discriminating against black people, blacks did not allow 12 million Mexicans to remain here taking jobs and moving in your neighborhoods where blacks could never think about living in. How can all these superior people be living in such circumstance today, we are seeing two different visions of our nation today, for blacks it's always been, but for white people it's a new awakening to actually have to be involved in these troubled times. The problem now is: Are we as a nation ready to identify our difficulties? Unite to heal that of which our nation is dealing with today, racial divide. If we, as a nation don't see the real problems of today, then we will fail as a nation, we have eyes to see, leadership needs to be changed, harmony needs to be established for the betterment and balance of our country, we are truly blessed to have these God-given assets to resolve these racist problems here and now.

The vision of Black people has not changed, it's just not been initiated by all of us. The vision is the principle, value and direction of our economic development to utilize the resources to be a more independent people, beginning with loving and educating our children and adults as well as how a capitalist system works. Part of that education is to begin right in the homes, parenting is the first step, reeling the black structure in and reestablishing basics of teaching, pride, dignity, character, principles and values. Neighborhood unity needs to be set up to ensure your living community is well-kept and clean, community function to establish that pride for where we live each day. Ensure that there's a law enforcement presence to prevent crime activity. These are the basic start of reform.

chapter 42

The Grace of Mom

We all are born into this world and part of that birth we all inherit is a very tiny space in the universal garden, this tiny space on earth is called the neighborhood, where we exist for years and in many cases people have never moved from or left that tiny dot embedded on this earth. It's where you call home for most of your adolescent years growing up attending school and maturing into this dimension of life. You learn to socialize with others preparing yourself for life's experiences, you learn these educational elements from home with your parents from the very beginning, then from your school system and lastly from the street, three different sources of learning. However, your main source is from your parents who are responsible for your growth and welfare, this home teaching is on-going and the basis of your enlightenment from your infancy. In this environment we learn one of the most powerful word, that word is Mother, however we call and refer to her as MOM. Yes, Mom is the most important person of your life at its very beginning, when we learn to feel secure in her hands. There's a reason babies cry so loud when the doctor remove them from their mother's womb, it's because they feel that the bond of God's love has been interfered with, that security was bonded for nine months. You have recognized her voice, because she has been talking to you daily, massaging her belly throughout the day and night, especially at the end of her pregnancy when you were moving and kicking, keeping her awake at night. Yes, Mom is your God-given treasure in this life. Whenever the doctor placed you back in her hands for the first time, you begin to stop hollering and screaming, because the bond is united again, and warmth of her hands and arms settles you down, where for the first time you look upon the beautiful and wonderful woman who you would begin to call Mom for the rest of your life. From the very beginning you learned to trust, to love and follow Mom everywhere, crawling after her, walking after her, holding onto her clothes, just like her inherited shadow. Yes, Mom is all you knew for a long period of time, your first teacher of this world. Mom's role is very significant because she has to nurture you of all things that she knows and has learned in her life to prepare you for your journey back to God from whence you came.

I write this because the birth of a child is a sacred miracle that only God allows to happen, in the beginning if you follow the period of Adam and Eve, God created Eve to be united with Adam, to become as one and to multiply with children of the earth. In this system of things we see women having children out of ignorance and lust, resulting in perilous times for the children they give birth to. There's the husband and wife, then there's the boyfriend, girlfriend scenario, then there's the one-night fling, the rapes, not utilizing condom, not knowing the baby's father. It goes on and on, these incidents have to be stopped. How many times have we seen a precious little baby depicted on a screen and the mother pointing to the features wherein she says identifies the baby with the guy sitting there on stage. She says: "You see the eyes, the nose, that's his baby" when in fact the DNA test results prove otherwise, or vice versa - the guy states it's not his, when in fact the test says it is his child. What a horrible travesty to place that poor innocent child on national TV, in one case the girl had identified five different guys and all proved not the baby's father. Unprotected sex, sleeping around with just about anyone, has a tremendous consequence, the total embarrassment to all parties concerned, including their loved ones, family and friends and the baby that should have never been put through such a disgraceful dilemma of its young life. In my time it was damn near a major crime to have a child out of wedlock, especially in white families, however, they found ways to not allow it to happen, by abortion. It worked for them but for the poor black girl, no money, so she had the child. This is a major problem within the last two years or so, not only blacks but all ethnic groups are confronted with these issues. So the word Mom I speak so proudly of in thousands of cases does not become that cherished title of those who know not how to be that of which they are addressed as, they carry the title however, without the pride, substance, knowledge, maturity or capability to raise and nurture such a God-given treasure presented to them. There's lots of work to be done, here and now. It takes the village to resolve and hopefully prevent these terrible troubled incidents of our youth, the parents, church, schools, relatives, friends and all others who truly care, speak out to these young people we owe so much of our time to them if we really care to make a difference, befriend a child who has no father around, you might just become a motivator and a molder of someone who just needed to be inspired to become all they can be. You will never know, seek these kids out, they seem to be everywhere, make somebody happy and they will be strong enough to succeed in their game of life. They are waiting for you out there, just turn the corner, that's where you will find them. Good luck, the rewards you receive are in the eyes of God who allows us to be the keeper of our young children, in the conditions of our cities, we can make a major difference in establishing that much-needed pride, dignity, principles, values and character.

chapter 43

The Love and Strength of Fathers

Another powerful word we all learn in our infancy is Father, because it ties in with the creation of all things, in religion they refer to God, as our Father, in the spirituality of our personal journeys, many call upon the Creator, Allah, Jehovah God who has millions of names throughout all universal system of things. So the title of man reflects the precious spiritual connection with the name he holds in the family structure of our world. Father, who becomes Dad to most of us here in America. In order to have the balance in the family, there must be a Father, he has a major responsibility for the harmony to provide the essential elements between man and wife and man and children. He's the major strength of the relationship, he exhibit's the confidence, he's the intellectual, faithful, responsible, caring, honest man with great moral values and principles, a man who takes time to nurture his children's character, he's their source of pride, dignity and lots of love and understanding. A father is a role model, who encourages the "BE SECOND TO NONE" attitude for the child to apply themselves wholeheartedly to accomplish each and every challenge. A father is the provider and is always there whatever the present circumstance is, with an undying love as the Father of which his name makes him a part of. There's no greater love than that of the Father for his children.

To all you Fathers out there, I give you a salute of love and appreciation for all you provide in the making of a loving, happy, and balanced family. I am totally impressed with the youth who demonstrates the character and pride of their loving and caring parents. The world is in terrible perilous times, especially for blacks, it's been so for hundreds of years and to see the parent's efforts to keep their children focused, to continue to make strides for change is just simply fabulous.

There's a lot of wanderers on our streets today, because of not being apart of the nurturing and caring parents, parenting never ends. My mother still calls each and everyday to impart some wisdom and encouragement to my life, and I am in my 60's. As I mentioned before, there's no substitute for raising our children, young girls not prepared to be Mothers and our young boys not ready to inherit the role as Father. We, as a people cannot allow our children not to be prepared for whatever is happening in our societies today. Never in the almost 400 years of our existence in this country was there a chance for all of us, especially blacks, to establish a new image. Martin Luther King, Jr. was knocking on your doors for change, instead, after his death we regressed. President Johnson signed into law some civil rights programs, we never took advantage of them and continued to divest ourselves of opportunities which were presented, Louis Farrakhan of the Nation of Islam preached till he was blue in the face at his million-man march in Washington D. C. and look at us now, one million men heard the message. Go back to your neighborhoods, clean them up, teach and nurture your children, protect your families, ensure they get educated, set new standards of dress, respect each other, create jobs, find a way to create a new image. Yet we have some of the filthiest neighborhoods, kids having babies, not going to schools, neighborhoods being run by drug dealers because the residents are afraid to take action against them, we are killing each other allowing police to terrorize your streets as well. If we continue this divide, then we, the blacks, are lost as a people here in America, after all we have fought for helping it establish itself among other wealthy countries, only to be kept discriminated upon for jobs, what's going to happen whenever new jobs are presented here in America? These jobs will go to the 12 million Mexicans here illegally instead of to the blacks and other ethnic groups who had their jobs outsourced. Nothing ever changes for the betterment of our black people, the jails are full of them, if we as a people don't start providing and helping each other we are lost, believe that, check your history. How can a country who has outsourced millions of American jobs, cause more people to be on welfare and poverty? By the way, all those millions whose jobs were outsourced were the same people who made that corporation or company. These rich companies turned around and stabbed them in the back totally disrespecting those poor people who busted their asses to make that company what it became. There was a company who laid off all their long-term workers years ago, approximately three months later, there was an ad in the job section for workers, they never hired the people they had laid off, they hired new people for lesser wages and little or no benefits at all. Then there was the supervisor who was asked to train two new management persons, but after their training they got rid of him, he was on the NBC TV presenting the circumstances of his termination, the people he trained took his job, they were from India. So the table is set, if in fact new jobs are created, people here illegally will get them first, how does a country in turmoil with no jobs allow 12 million people to stay here, it's ridiculous, and as I said early on most of your drugs are carried in across our border. Who knows if any terrorists were among those numbers. So much for our national security, it's established an outside threat is not our worry it's from within if it would happen yet 12 million are here illegally, simply amazing. So if these are not facts enough for you to unite and make change it will never happen at all. WAKE UP PEOPLE! The handwriting has been posted on the walls for hundreds of years, you must find your own way. That's why the time is now, our "Mothers- and- Fathers to be" must be aware of what's facing them here in the near future, so there's a need for everyone to do some soul searching to establish what we have been letting slip away. I listen to talk shows, hear people complaining, however they don't take any action, there's no leader stepping up to the challenge the negatives that are occurring, elected officials are not stepping up to ensure fairness and justice is done. Marvin Gaye said: "Save the Children" and that begins with change in that tiny little dot in the village garden of the world.

Millions of black people have fought and died for change. Why you have not done your part as a people, just look at your living areas, your school system, no black history taught there. What are you teaching at home? What are your plans for the betterment of your house and the neighborhood? Are your boys wearing those old need-to-be-discarded hooded jackets and old sloppy hanging pants at the crack of their asses? Check your daughters, are they looking like sexy young glamour girls going to school? You got to change these negatives to create the positives. It's your time, you have no recourse. I mentioned our Father, he's a loving and giving God, he has presented you with this time here and now to Change. God only help those who help themselves. He's never let us down, we have just failed in our attempts, but he who fails and tries again makes the difference in the will of the people. Here's a first step, have a meeting with all who live in your neighborhood, formulate a plan and initiate the action, I love you or I would not have asked our Father to allow this opportunity to write the words he has guided my hand to write, it's your life, your choice and your God-given decision, God allows you to make that choice, whatever it is, you and only you will have to live with it whatever it may be. I will continue to pray for you. This is my first attempt to write a book and I choose to write about our history, our cause and what we owe to all of our ancestors who have paved a way for us to make it better, we have paid the ultimate price and we need to reap the rewards of being the proud and beautiful people we can present ourselves to be to this country, world, and most of all to our Creator who has brought us here to give a nation the eyes to see, have the discipline and fortitude to create... THE BRIGHTER SIDE OF A DARK PAST WE ARE RESPONSIBLE FOR OUR FUTURE CHANGE.

Blacks who have suffered in struggles of America's wars and racism speak from wisdom and knowledge of lessons learned through all we have seen and experienced for 400 years, that accumulated understanding is that, elected officials, politicians, policy makers and the Common Foe in key places and positions fail to create the harmony, unity and balance of this nation, are causing a gross situation in the eyes of the world, who sees us as an undivided power with racial flaws all over it.

Our free slave labor enhanced the major banks and corporations to establish their wealth to what we see today, fought in two wars Revolutionary, Civil Wars, the key ones that freed the colonists to create an Independent nation, and the conflict between the league of Confederate states against the Union, where this country became the United States. In each of these crucial wars the black man was called upon to fight and die in defeating the foe, and yet with these major contributions we were still told that we would remain slaves, refused citizenship in a written Constitution, referred to as chattel and property, 3/5th of a man, not authorized to vote and told that this is a white man's world and even though thousands fought and died in each war, we had no rights and the lynchings and murders continued on up until the early 1900's. So, the game we see is hundreds of years old, nothing new, they conspired to give you no civil or human rights and we were only authorized to vote after two Jewish and one black registration team were killed down south in 1963 and that right has to be approved every 20 years. We the black free laborers for 250 years, the patriotic warriors who fought for their freedom to establish a democracy are the only human beings ever written in a Constitution as 3/5th of a man, called property or chattel, it's amazing how 3/5th of a man made the difference in two wars, and they made billions on buying and selling blacks worldwide and utilized them as properties in millions of bank transactions. They never loved you then, and they definitely do not love you today. This is not kindergarten, there's years of learning from our white racists. "We The People" must establish some rules and guidelines to embark on our journey of change and improvement of our image, character and awareness. Looking from afar, there's lots of work to be done in all levels of involvement

We the people must form a family gathering to address family problems: children, financial, health, and identify those young males and females that need to be told and advised just how dangerous times are today, to select their friends wisely, this will be a constant and on-going situation, especially with them, because of peer pressure on the street and at schools. I've seen numerous times where girl games are just as prevalent as the boys, also you need to address their attitudes, I know they can be angels at home and very devilish outside of it, it's always: "Oh, my daughter (or son) did not do that" when in fact he or she did. So establish that ongoing dialogue to ensure the continuity, if you as a family love your children, help save them. These family get togethers have to address the older people as well, they have all got to change their outlook, character and image if there are those who need them. There' nothing worse than seeing a grown man walking around, shoes not shined, clothes not pressed, needs a haircut, just general bad appearance. They have to contribute to these changes as well, it's a family affair, the elderly are also important to us, we are responsible for their well-being, if living in the household or otherwise.

You might want to address starting a family corporation of funds where all working members will put so much in every pay period and draw from it, as opposed to getting loan from the bank with the high interest rates, get rid of those credit cards which have most people in debt, I think one is enough if there is a need for it. Ensure someone checks on the seniors living alone. Take this opportunity to brief all the mothers and fathers to coordinate whatever there is that needs to be discussed and improved upon in the neighborhood. The Common Foe's game is still the same after hundreds of years. Should you be able to get repatriation better think twice, ever think the job market will change don't bet your house in it, if you still have one. After all the Blacks have given to this country, he is never going to be appreciated. The police are back to ethnic profiling, jobs are not given to blacks even if they are qualified, housing refused and racism and discrimination is everywhere. White people I hope will read some of these pages and maybe read about the history of those black slaves and what they endured and contributions they made to this country in all phases of its growth. The 65,000 George Washington allowed to fight and defeat the British, the 200,000 Lincoln allowed to fight against the south, there are millions of pages about black history untold to white people, and as long as it's not taught in our schools, you will never know it. Most whites never know the Tuskegee Airmen who protected some of your loved ones in their fighter escort of over 500 missions and never lost one plane or man, unbelievable, but it's true, if the movie had not been made, it would have been kept in the dark, we would not know that the first heart operation in this country was done by a black man at John Hopkins Hospital in Baltimore, who later trained 200 white surgeons to perform them; that Joe Louis, the Heavyweight Champion was called to the White House to meet with President Roosevelt who asked Joe to fight for the nation's pride, its people, a tremendous burden to ask of any man, however, Joe did his part, America has not lived up to theirs, when it comes to black people, however. I encourage all races of people to read about black history, especially those people from foreign countries who only reflect in many cases a white man's attitude that they are better than blacks, read your history. I make it a must to read about all ethnic people here in this country, and it's very enlightening when dealing with them. Trouble here is, that the black man was stripped of his culture and custom of his far away homeland upon him being transported to this country by a white Common Foe who separated the old and the young, where he caused a constant divide, refusing blacks to speak of their home, refusing them to learn to read and write, whipped each and everyone during horrific branding of our flesh, raped and sodomized our black women, fathering millions of mulatto children. He could not keep his hands off our black women, yet lynched and murdered black men, castrated them and stuffed their genitals in their mouth because they said he looked at a white woman. The fierce white man who became the serpent of this nation, and the oppressor of an innocent unarmed people, herded them to auction blocks, sold them to the highest bidder and branded them. He did not love you then, nor does he love you today, however, could not keep his lustful hands off or his penis out of our black women, a treacherous minded terrorist who beat the men and young boys unmercifully to create a psychological fear and superiority mental block in front of the black women and children. Our people constantly lived in fear of being killed or beaten and abused at random. The Common foe became the serpent of America and even developed a Black Code of how to break the spirit of his chattel herds of black flesh. Every now and then they will raise their ugly heads, snatch a black man, tie his feet to the bumper of a truck and drag him down an isolated gravel and rocky road until every ounce of his skin is stripped from his body in such a heinous crime against another abducted defenseless black man. A young 16-year old boy was hung in front of his grandmother's house with his hand tied behind his back and the sheriff investigating the crime called it a suicide, or the two white men who killed the 13 year old Emmit Teal, who was shot, castrated, ear cut off, eye gouged out and his body submerged with barbed wire around his neck, body attached to a 200 pound office fan in Mississippi. They beat the case in court and sold their story later to the Post Magazine of how they killed him, then continued to walk free. Or the black man who had the broomstick rammed up his rectum, the Rodney king incident seen on national TV, hanging nooses in police stations and job sites, when we as a nation are engaged in combat on two fronts, where the unity, harmony and balance of the land of the free and liberty and justice for all is not working. All of God's people are worthy to be respected until proven otherwise. Read whenever you can, we have established a rich heritage here. Blacks need to read it also to reestablish the pride and dignity of our people that was totally destroyed. Most people fight in only one battlefield, however, in the case of the black man, it's been two all the time since the year 1640. Blacks fought in the Revolutionary War, Civil War, World War I and World War II, and each time and each time after returning from the various battlefields, were lynched and murdered here, in uniform as part of the United States Armed Forces. So you see, there's lots to read and comprehend of the trials and tribulations of blacks, there's some really great contributions recorded in various elements of this nation, It's been one hell of a journey since the 1640 for black people, one of which reflects that they have earned the recognition to be respected for all they suffered through, all they fought for, and all their free labor, no other race can display such a horrid experiencing history nor the major contributions made on battlefields and the nation at large in spite of being an outcast and hated people here in this country where blacks have proved time and time again their patriotism and loyalty to the soil upon which we all stand today, and the fact of the matter is, if you don't seek this wealth of knowledge, you will never know who you are as a people, your roots, nor any of the historical contributions past or present to the overall development and heritage to America. It's not taught in schools, so seek out this literature in your library or online, you will see a totally different black man reflected than what the Common Foe presents today, don 't let this wealth of knowledge slip away. I was at Barnes and Nobles Bookstore, there were four large volumes covering each branch of the military services each book over 2001 pages and thousands of pictures, I only found about 15 pictures of black servicemen in them all, from the Revolutionary War until Iraq. There's a magnificent book called the "Africana," the encyclopedia of African American Experience by Kwame Anthony Appeal and Henry Louis Gates (1999), priced at $100.00 in the U.S. This phenomenal book of 3000 pages covers everything you can think of: medicine, wars, inventions, music, entertainment, sports, riots, renown people, the various states, Black accomplishments in every field of technology, literature, you name it, it's there. A wonderful volume of a chronicle history and achievements, the suffering and triumphs of Black Americans to include the rest of the world. Can be ordered form the internet ant www.perseusbooksgroup.com, a must piece of black history for all races to enjoy by Basic Avitas Books, a member of the Perseus Book Group.

The world has been indoctrinated by the racist white man of America, to reflect their mind set of black Americans, he also indoctrinated the black slaves to hate and disrespect each other causing a divide form the plantation until today, he's been very convincing in his pervasive effort in controlling the black lives and welfare in this country. Today the strong black people must turn this racial black divide around, learn to support them and help them and help them gain their confidence to achieve the unity needed if we are to take our place among the other races that have come here to cash in on the consumer dollars, there's a need to refocus the effort to establish our own and you must know that the black people of this country spend the largest amount of consumer dollars, without any recycling of their dollars back into their communities. Where's our creative vision, with some of these athletes in our families, you would think someone would influence them to invest in business ventures in black neighborhoods to create jobs for black people who are being discriminated against in the job market across the board. There are three job sites in Philadelphia with no

black workers, how is that so, especially if those contract bids are
city granted, no black then close the job site until that situation is
conducive for equal jobs for all involved, whites make the money,
send their children to colleges, make their house payments, where
blacks not afforded work, loses his home, cannot send his children
anywhere and continue to live in poverty, there's something about
the mayor making all things fair. I don't see it as of yet. Same thing
about all of these black townships running an all-white police
force. We The People have a voice in that situation, especially
when there's a drastic raise in crime in those places. The key here
today has got to be balance of representation. The mayor of Cam-
den, newly elected to office held a council meeting to assess the job
there, one of the areas addressed was the balance of law enforcement officers. Asked was how many blacks, Hispanics, and whites
were on the police force, the representative from the police gave his
figures. The city council president, after hearing the figures, stated
to the representative that in a predominantly black city, the total
make up of almost all white officers was not acceptable and informed him that in 30 days before the next council meeting he and
the mayor would want to see a balanced police force, and within a
few months the balance was made, that mayor made things fair,
and I recall that council meeting vividly, and these type of predominantly police officers have to be changed, especially when there's
an increase in crime because of it, there's lots of profiling again,
and at times when there's a white police officer hurt or killed, those
white police officers react at times in a witch hunt So if you live in
one of those townships, get to the mayor, governor or higher court
to have that situation balanced out. That's what happened in Texas
when the sixteen-year old black youth was found hanging from a
tree with his hands tied behind his back, a sheriff of an all-white
police department showed up and called it a suicide, who's to question his findings? The residents of the community are frightened of
the all-white police in a racist township. Law enforcement, if not
handled properly finds your jails overcrowded with blacks, because
of some of these prejudiced cops on witch hunts, and I know it's
there, I've been around law enforcement all my life. I just think no
balance in these police department creates a bad situation for the

community. I know damn well a white community could not tolerate an all-black police squad policing their neighborhoods.

Our journey has opened our eyes to many travesties we have learned to live with, however, many of us refuse to acknowledge the powers that still hold over us today. As we proceed day by day let these lessons of the past be our guideline to dealing and living in these cities and towns. Life and freedom are too precious not to be aware of what you are actually facing out here today. I was pulled over for over-speeding 10 miles over the posted speed limit, I was approached by a very hostile white police officer who I thought was very offensive, belligerent and intimidating. I complied with all requests made of me, after being issued a ticket, I requested to ask him a question I ask is this a regular traffic stop, he answered yes, well, I stated you have treated me as if I have just committed felony or major crime, I stated that I am probably one of millions who have been cited for speeding and as you say 10 miles over the 10 miles allowance due to speedometer reads, he asked if I thought he had given me a hard time, and my answer was I did. He told me to pay the ticket, then he got on his sedan and drove off. Be careful out there. Ensure you have your vehicle with current documents, all of your paperwork updated and above all remain calm and comply to all requested of you. You don't want any reason for them to take you or your car or apprehend you for the same actions the cop displayed towards me. You never know when he's the one molesting young girls and having sex with a horse which they convicted one cop of, a few weeks ago, as reported in the newspaper. I've heard of all sorts of crimes police officers commit, there are many on the forces that are actually worse than the criminals they lock up, they are just bad cops. Who knows how many people those two cops who had the Ku Klux Klan posters hanging in their squad wall lockers have locked up that they hated, because they hated blacks and Jews. The few or many are one of the reasons the image of the good officers got tarnished.

We the people have our work cut out for us and it's not just black people, it's all of We The People to work for the betterment and unity of our troubled streets. Communities and societies, our police officers, mayors, elected officials, politicians, priests, senators, governors, congressmen, and our President, even the Ku Klux Klan, We all make up the We The People, we are all part of the whole, our motto of: "All for one and one for all." We will need lots of tolerance as we move forward to reestablish that of which the forefathers set out to accomplish. This time however, all will start out equally, and if that $3/5^{th}$ of a man is still reflected in our Constitution then that's one of the initial concerns to be addressed by our top leaders. The leaders of this nation are not naive of the history of our country's black people, and if they don't act, how can they play a major role in sighting decades of racism and hatred in a country of which they govern.

Also the right to vote issue needs to be corrected. Everyone is calling for change, well change begins in the chambers of these individuals responsible for making it, and again I would think that all of these people are well aware what this document means to a black race of people who have paid their dues on the battlefields of which we call the United States of America, which these black ancestors caused to exist today. Is the nation strong enough in its character? If so, it can cash that cancelled check which was returned to Dr. Martin Luther King, Jr. with insufficient funds noted. I think that clause has affected the way the white race has held their superiority mind set from the very beginning. Once blacks become equal, they should gain respect nationwide. We The People will see how united or balanced we can become in the eyes of the world and if it's changed, I think it should be dedicated to King's name. He marched for We The People, brought millions to the steps of the White House, where there's been so many promises only to have no substance actually happen I will write to whoever becomes President of our nation in a personal effort to ensure that this one voice of We The People is heard regarding this issue. Actually We The People are requesting something from a Few Good People who we hope can handle and correct the truth as it should be. If we can spend billions on wars, then there should be sufficient funds to cash this check, which will entail no dollar, just the signature of a Few Good Men. Can they handle it? Is the question we shall see. If it does happen, the scripture at the bottom of the Martin Luther King, Jr. monument should reflect:

"We Have Overcome as a Nation"

The forefathers constructed the nation's most powerful documents ever written, the Constitution, Declaration of Independence and The Bill of Rights, to govern the country and its citizens. These established laws and rights are the guidelines that ensure fairness in legislative and judicial systems.

Very important beginning of the Declaration of Independence: In Congress, July 4, 1776 the Unanimous Declaration of the Thirteen United States of America: "When in the course of human events, it becomes necessary for one people to dissolve the political bonds which have connected them with another, and to assume among the powers of the earth the separate and equal station to which the Laws of Nature's God entitle them, a decent respect to the opinions of Mankind requires that they should declare the causes which impel them to the separation. We hold these truths to be self-evident, that all men are created equal, that they are endowed by their Creator with certain inalienable Rights, that among these are Life, Liberty and the pursuit of Happiness."

Beginning of the Constitution of the United States: "We the People of the United States, in order to form a more perfect Union, establish Justice, ensure domestic Tranquility, provide for the common defense, promote the general welfare and secure the Blessings of Liberty to ourselves and our Posterity, do ordain and establish this Constitution for the United States of America." Signed in Philadelphia on September 17, 1787.

chapter 44

The Bill of Rights

The Bill of Rights is a set of Amendments approved and became part of the established Articles of the Constitution. They represent a broader view of written rights that the government guarantees to its people, these written documents were ratified and implemented in 1791.

The documents mentioned above are essential read for all who are citizens of this country; they are involved in all court systems, although, in some cases an interpretation may differ from a small claims court, civil court or in the highest court of our nation, the Supreme Court where cases will be reviewed to ensure that the letter of the Law has been utilized in accordance with that of the Constitution. He who knows his laws knows his country. **Expand your mind!**

When I attended Grade School we had an assembly each morning where we would recite the Pledge of Allegiance to the American flag and nation, it went: "I pledge allegiance to the flag of the United States of America and to the Republic for which it stands, one nation indivisible under God with Liberty, Freedom and Justice for all."

Learn the laws of the country, read the Constitution and all other major documents that govern the people and the nation and above all else, how these legislative and judicial systems pertain to black people then and now. You must educate yourself of the white people's mentality, their prejudices whether they have changed any from the slavery period until now or whether they are just not as "open" and then we have to wonder, they lynched and abused anytime they felt like, now they still work in the shadows of all things. They refused housing to a black lady a month ago, major contractors refuse to hire blacks, they are hanging nooses all over the country, they are giving unfair sentences to black males in court systems. Thomas Cahill is releasing his new book, which covers the case where four teens killed a white man, the four youth, 3 blacks, 1 white, 1 black was sentenced to death, the other 2 blacks were charged with second degree murder, the white youth was not charged and was released. A very interesting book reflecting the white anger and hatred. The Common Foe is alive and working, it's as if in this early period of the Twenty-first Century we must still look over our shoulders for our safety in America, a country we as blacks were born in, fought in every war for and gave millions of black lives. When will it end? As I write this book there's a unity march scheduled for this Saturday at the United States Attorney General's Office in Washington DC in order to address racial issues.

As a black child I was indoctrinated into believing that the sacred principles of our nation were these Articles that would influence our unity, love and respect for each other and our country. Unfortunately I found out that these very powerful writings and quotes, as designed and instrumented into the principal structure to govern, did not apply to people of my skin pigmentation. I read books about slavery as my stepfather had instructed me. As I read, things were revealed to me, the horrid abductions of Africans, their journey to an unknown world to bondage, the journey which we, in our own wildest dreams, would never grasp nor imagine, the malicious cruelty those unscrupulous barbaric maniacs inflicted on those defenseless, distraught people, who were divested of their God-given humanity. How they were packed on those overcrowded vessels where thousands sacrificed themselves to the shark infested raging sea rather than to endure their death on board a ship integrated with sick, mutilated, and decaying dead bodies stuffed in the hull that became the slaves' living hell.

Reading about these slavery and racial problems gave me some insight and understanding why I lost my first white friend, Terry, and has made me aware of the demeanor of white people. I found myself asking why or how they could resort to such inhumane treatment of black people. In no books did I read where black people had invaded or attacked this nation in any way. I did however discover that black people had fought and died for America even before we had Presidents, even before the Constitution and Declaration of Independence were written. I ask myself still: "How did these atrocities against black people happen?" I could understand the war period with the Indians of this land. The Indians hated the white man's deceit, deception, and broken promises as they repeatedly took their land and "condensed" that space, and never honored treatises, neither furnished the Indians the money owed, neither did they deliver the supplies of food and clothing that they agreed to do. On the other hand, the black slave was a defenseless person in an unknown land, the Indians however knew the terrain, had horses, and were excellent warriors, with bow and arrow, in time the Indians went to war against the white men and his armies. As a kid watching the movies on Saturdays, I always saw the white soldier as the victor, however after reading of Sitting Bull and other courageous and brave warriors, the real truth came to light. I especially recall reading of the massacre of General Custer and his cavalry troops at the Little Big Horn and various other engagements where the whites were defeated. I learned to respect the Indians' bravery and the valor they displayed in fighting for their families, their pride, culture, heritage for this land. I also found out that the white men tried to use them again as slaves after they fought during the war, but now the whites could not control these Indians, so they brought in the new defenseless black men who had no experience in war, but who had to fight for their pride, dignity and heritage, in their new surroundings. He was ideal and advantaged of for hundreds of years. I never heard of any white President or leader of this country apologize for the illness and suffering blacks endured and overcame, no reparations given, however, reparations were paid to the Japanese when they were placed in concentration camp type compounds in California during World War II.

I continued to read about the hatred and discrimination, it seemed that all white ethnic croups hated or discriminated against blacks in general. The Irish resented us, the Italians reflected their racist's attitudes, the Jews only tolerated blacks because they controlled most of the commerce in their own neighborhoods, the Germans, Polish and others of white skin projected their annoyance whenever there was a need for blacks to pass through their neighborhoods. In numerous incidents we were chased. We fought with them as they showed their hostilities and negative reactions towards us blacks. I was searching for the liberty, justice, freedom and safety, these elements I never found in my youth, it was like this white world was against us, I was only 11 or 12 years of age, when I realized that the majority of the white world totally resented and hated black people. My divine birthright under God, born free and a citizen was violated and it seemed no one in the governed political system was enforcing or executing the laws, under all these beautifully written principles we were reciting, we were duped into believing it all as a child, the very same race elements that were in place upon blacks arrival to this country still exist today, in 2007.

Yes, the forefathers had the opportunity to make all things fair, they never did. Early on after the white man gained their Independence, some of the great political minds formulated a Committee to create the aforementioned documents of the nation. One of these statesmen was Benjamin Franklin, a scientist, publisher, designer of the city of Philadelphia, who played a major role in establishing the University of Pennsylvania and the only man to sign all four documents of the nation. A very important fact about Franklin, was that at the age of 82 he was elected President of the First Anti-Slavery Society in America, and only then did he actively speak out against the evils of the system. Franklin often brought his views to the Commander in Chief of the Revolutionary Army, Gen. George Washington, who had okay the blacks to serve in his military units, however, never addressed the option of freeing any of them. Washington at one point informed Franklin that he would not address the issue until 1780. Why the delay? Washington was the owner of approximately 219 slaves, who contributed a great deal of commerce and free labor on his many properties, once stating that to deprive himself of their labor would totally drain the financial gains and resources of his wealth and estates which he was committed to maintaining. In 1787, a Convention was held in Philadelphia wherein Washington was elected to preside over. The purpose of the Convention was to frame the Constitution for the United States. There were discussions pertaining to Slavery:

Whether slaves were just "property" or human beings as well. Should the slaves be counted the same as white people in representation of the States in Congress? If not, to what proportion?

Should the importation of slaves stop at once or if not, how long should it continue?

The outcome of these discussions to which Washington voted for was that slaves were to be considered property, that each five blacks should count as one white person, and that the slave trade should be allowed to continue for another twenty years until 1808.

In 1693 the Quakers and many other white groups had shown an interest in freeing the slaves in numerous public statements, also in an ongoing correspondence to Franklin. It was initially thought of that slaves would only be held in bondage for a short period of time and then freed, however, after Washington Convention years later, it was stated that slaves would be held in slavery forever. The embodiment of the North and South, upon sanctioning that slaves be classified as property also agreed to never freeing those already in bondage. In a letter to Washington by Franklin he stated;

"The unhappy man, who has long been treated as a brute, animal, too frequently sinks beneath the common standard of the human species. The Galling chains that bind his body do also fetter his intellectual faculties, and impair the social affections of his heart. Accustomed to move like mere machinery, by the will of the master, reflection is suspended; he has not the power of choice, and reason and conscience, he is chiefly governed by passion or fear. He is poor and friendless, perhaps worn out by extreme labor, age, and disease."

Mankind are all formed by the same Almighty Being, alike objects of his care and equally designed for the enjoyment of happiness. The Christian religion teaches us to believe this, and the Political Creed of Americans fully coincides with this position.

The forefathers delivered a vicious blow to the blacks, the slaves were working on their properties, in their fields, taking care of the white children and old family members, creating a tax-free economic wealth for them, unbelievable that the whites denied them the right to be called human beings in such documents, where all other ethnic groups were referred to as humans or citizens of this nation. Washington had accepted slaves in his continental army to fight the British, yet he denounced them when pressed for a decision on their freedom. A letter written to him by Col. Lauren: "The country is distressed and will be more so, unless further reinforcements are sent to its relief, had we arms for three thousands such black men as I could select in Carolina, I should have no doubt of success in driving the British out of Georgia and subduing east Florida before the end of July."

Washington's armies were being overwhelmed and many of his commanders were seeking to train and arm the slaves to save the nation.

Alexander Hamilton wrote Washington regarding his views on allowing the slaves to reinforce the military for the Americans to gain our Independence: "It appears to me, that an experiment of this kind, in the present state of Southern affairs, is the most rational that can be adopted... indeed I can see how a sufficient force can be, that the Negroes will make very excellent soldiers with proper management, and will venture to pronounce that they cannot be put in better hands than those of Col. Lauren's he has the zeal, intelligence, enterprise etc., etc... request to succeed. I hear it frequently objected to the scheme of embodying Negroes, that they are too stupid to make soldiers. This is so far from appearing to me a valid objection, that I think their want of cultivation (for their natural faculties are as good as ours.) Further he wrote: "I foresee that this project will have combat much opposition from prejudice and self-interest. The contempt we have been taught to entertain for the blacks makes us fancy many things that are founded neither in reason nor experience; and the unwillingness to part with property of so valuable kind will furnish a thousand arguments to show the implausibility, or pernicious tendency, of a scheme which requires such sacrifices. But it should be considered, that if we do not make use of them in this way, the enemy probably will; and that the best way to counteract the temptation they will hold out, will be to offer them their freedom with the swords. This will secure their fidelity, animate their courage, and I believe, will have a good influence upon those that remain, by opening a door to their emancipation. This circumstance, I confess, has no small weight in inducing me to wish the success of this project; for the dictates of humanity and true policy, equally interest me in favor of this unfortunate class of men..."

So we can see that not all people considered blacks stupid, and there were those in high places willing to accept and train them to save their country in their struggle with the British. The wealthy and ignorant opposed this plan because if they let their slaves be taken to fight they would have to do the dirty work to maintain their economic growth which the free slave labor provided, they would actually have to work and even then could not maintain resources the slaves provided. The plan was eventually approved, slaves were enlisted to save this nation's independence. Let it also be known that the slaves were sent to serve and die in place of their masters and sons; also slaves were enlisted with the promise of being freed at the end of the war. That never happened, after the war they were refused their freedom and soon were reclaimed by their former masters. The black man in this case rode up on the white horse to help save a nation of unappreciative white people who were cowards, not patriotic enough to defend this land, which they all claim to be theirs. The blacks died so these racists could keep their businesses and plantations, and I may also add that those blacks who were fortunate enough to survive and return home were often killed by these whites who forced them back into bondage. The slaves who fought so gallantly to restore their dignity, manhood and acceptance in this country never received them and the freedom promised was not forthcoming by another hundred years, and the racism and hatred continues today by that Common Foe we seek to exposes. As a young man I would marvel at the words of the Star Spangled Banner when I sing it or heard it, especially the words:

"And the rockets' red glare, and the bombs bursting in air Gave proof through the night that our flag was still there. O' say does that star-spangled banner yet wave Over the land of the free and the home of the brave."

Great song, written by Francis Scott and chosen to be the country's National Anthem. I enjoyed singing and hearing it sung at special events around the world. I think it's a national treasure, however, I fully realize that because of millions of black pieces of property, referred to the categorization written into the Constitution pertaining to slaves not human beings, but property who fought in numerous battles, giving their lives with valor and courage, played a major significant role, they allowed that flag to "Still Be There." The black man fought under that banner for the right for it to wave over this land of the free and home of the brave. Black men never got that freedom. Like in, a part of the great speech that Martin Luther King Jr. stated: "...When the forefathers signed those documents, they were signing a promissory note, the note promised that all men, even black men, would be guaranteed the rights of life, liberty, and the pursuit of happiness and most importantly their freedom."

America has defaulted on this promissory note, a note which came back marked "insufficient funds." Black men were exploited, many came home to be murdered, lynched and abused, many were reshackled back into slavery. Amazing they fought, survived, came home and were killed and abused fighting for the ignorant white ancestors who still had the hatred in their heads. These black men fought and established victory from the very beginning, hundred of years ago against the French and the British, never forget that. This land is not free because of the people here today, it is free because of our black heroes. Also let it be known that in the battle for the nation's Capitol, an all white American force of about five thousand troops ran, almost at once when the British soldiers advanced. President Madison watched this disgraceful rout, him, his wife, and some government officials who were forced to flee from the white house and the city. I think those black pieces of property who stood their ground are worthy to be praised for they exhibited the standards for which our flag represents as it continues to wave in the breeze, so strong an image, an image that reflects the Refuse to Lose and Second to None; those black troops accepted the challenge, lived up to Hamilton's expectations and became part of the millions who died for the land of the free and the home of the brave. In our Creator's eyes they will forever be part of the billions of human beings that He calls his greatest treasures to the world.

President John Adams contributed little on behalf of the slaves' situation. Like Pres. George Washington, he was content to allow slavery to go unattended, even though Washington had set a time period of 1808. Adams never gave it any consideration, other than to state that he had never owned a slave, even though many wealthy men had. That he had spent thousands to hire free men, that had he bought slaves which were very cheap, he could have saved a considerable amount.

Adams was very much engrossed in the slavery situation, he once told Jefferson, who favored it, that he had visions of a black cloud over the nation, there were armies of Negroes marching and countermarching in the air, in shining armor. Yet he knew not what to do in solving the nation's problem. He furthermore stated that he was terrified with this phenomenon: "I cannot comprehend this problem; I must leave it to you. What we are to see God knows, and I leave it to him and his agents in posterity." Again we have a fore-father who would not resolve or play a major role in whatever others would decide regarding it.

President Jefferson, early on in his political career spoke out against it, however, later, it was found out that he actually owned a great number of slaves and thought that it was a moral and political depravity; nonetheless refused to free his and gave no support to emancipation. Much of his writings and philosophical thoughts seemed to originate from European mind set. All men created equal, were the Negroes not entitled to theirs, along with liberty and the pursuit of happiness, as all others? How could Jefferson abide by his own words and still continue owning slaves himself? Interesting, Jefferson gave his reasons why the United States should not attempt to incorporate the blacks, he believed that the two races could never live peaceably together. The deep-rooted prejudices entertained by the whites, "as well as the ten thousands recollections by the blacks, and the injuries they have sustained.... distinctions which nature has made, and many other circumstances will divide races of people and produce convulsions, which will probably never end but in the extermination of one or the other's race." These words he wrote, hold true today, as the white hatred still is the cause of people hanging nooses, burn-

ing crosses on lawns, refusing housing to blacks, writing NIG-
GER on the front pavement of the small store, which two black
ladies opened on an all white strip of all white stores; refusing
jobs to blacks, creating the crime and poverty levels to escalate in
black neighborhoods. Jefferson furthermore addressed that the differences between the races first of course, is the color. "Whether
the black of the skin resides in the reticular membrane between the
skin and the scarf-skin, or in the scarf-skin itself; whether it pro-
ceeds from the color of the blood, the color of the bile, or from that
of some other secretion, the difference is fixed in nature, and is
real as if its seat and cause were better known to us." He states
that whites are more beautiful than the blacks. He asked whether
the blushes, those "fine mixtures of red and white which lends to
the expressions of the every passion in the white race are not superior to the eternal monotony... that immovable veil of black
which covers the emotions of the other race?" "We must recognize
that the whites besides having flowing hair and more elegant sym-
metry of form are considered by the blacks themselves as the more
beautiful. If then superior beauty, is thought worthy of attention in
propagation of our horses, does, and other domestic animals; why
not in that of man?" He further pointed put that other distinctive
differences include among these, "less hair on face and body, they
secrete less by the kidneys; and more by the glands of the skin,
which gives them a very strong and disagreeable odor. They require less sleep. They are at least as brave, and more adventuresome than whites. But this may, perhaps proceed from a want of
forethought. They are more ardent after their female; but love
seems to them to be more an eager desire, than a tender delicate
mixture of sentiment and sensation. Their griefs are transient. In
general, their existence appears to participate more of sensations
than reflection." Jefferson hesitated in putting the Negroes on the
level of white men, that they were inferior to whites both of body
and mind. Jefferson's views of the slave situations varied during
his two terms as President, he never signed into law the Emancipation fearing a grave conflict would erupt between the slave holders and their enormous economic and corporate partners. Great
loses would occur. However during his last years in office, did

sign various laws regarding slavery, he addressed the Congress, December 2, 1806 stating:

"I congratulate you, on the approval of the period at which you may interpose your authority constitutionally to withdraw the citizens of the United States from all further participation in those violations of human rights which have been so long continued on the unoffending inhabitants of Africa, and which the morality, the reputation and best interest of our country, have long been eager to proscribe." Here we see as was with Washington, Jefferson who was against slavery, but owned them, would not free the slaves, he wanted the political governing body to pave the way for it to be done. However, no one voiced against slavery more than he did in his old age and lost many southern friends by his constant fight to settle this evil situation. Jefferson later wrote: "The voice of a single individual ... would have prevented this abominable crime from spreading itself over the country." Thus we see the fate of millions unborn hanging in the tongue of one man and heaven was silent in that awful moment! But it is to be hoped it will not always be silent, and that friends to the right of human nature will in the end prevail. Like Washington, Jefferson hoped that "this abominable crime" could in some way be ended by legal measures, although he never thought out the details as to how this could be accomplished, he also believed that all slaves should be sent out of the country or back to Africa and declared a free and independent people.

Elected to President after Jefferson, James Madison wrote regarding urging him to present to Congress a petition requesting the slaves to be freed, there was a great flood of petitions and memorials for action pertaining to this problem. He wrote: "The futility of such attempt owing to the stand which representatives from the states had taken." He very diplomatically would refuse to present the petition. He stated that: "Those from whom I derive my office are known by me to be greatly interested in that species of property. It would seem that I might be chargeable at least with want of candor, if not fidelity were I... to become a volunteer in giving a public wound, as they would deem it, to an interest on which they set so great a value."

All through his tenure as president, Madison entertained ways of freeing the slaves, his biggest problem was how, and where would he relocate them, would it be deporting them back to Africa, or keeping them in America on isolated areas separate from whites. The other problem was financing such moves, also, how he was to obtain their release from the plantation owners who would demand replacement of their free laborers with white paid working forces, so over the years it got addressed but never activated in any way. So what Washington had left undone, Jefferson never addressed it to a definite plan, Madison reneged on implementing any Emancipation, he was just too conservative to take any direction in resolving it.

Abraham Lincoln, elected President on March 4, 1861 inherited the problem of which Washington, Adams, Jefferson, Madison passed on to 11 other presidents who failed to react to it from 1789 until 1861, some 72 years, during which period there were politicians, various prominent people and other whites who wanted to abolish slavery, however, no one in authority had the courage to do so. The slavery issue was the most important domestic problem other than the wars America was involved in. Lincoln, when asked about the situation made it clear that his major aim was to save the Union, he opposed slavery on humanitarian grounds, but he felt that the federal government had no right to prohibit slavery in the south. He stated that: "If I could save the Union without freeing any slaves, I would do it, and if I could save it by not freeing any slaves, I would do it." Lincoln made these comments shortly after his inauguration and many of the southern states were concerned with his views regarding the slaves. However, he promised not to interfere with slavery, but the southern states under Jefferson Davis was not convinced, some disagreements between Lincoln and Davis pertaining to the Constitution arose. Documents were submitted to the states for ratification. The south began leaving the Union which Lincoln opposed to, and stated that no state had the right to leave the Union, not fully trusting Lincoln, the Confederate States of America formed in February, 1861. Pulled out completely from the Union, the move was made after being sanctioned by Davis who was elected the President of the south. There were many differences, however, the major cause was over the slavery rights, which triggered the Civil War, being started in April of 1861. The war progressed into 1865, during this period the North and South waged the bloodiest war in American history, in three days of fighting 20,000 confederates were killed, wounded or captured. The Union army suffered 23,000 casualties. At the end of the gruesome war the North suffered approximately 364,511 killed or wounded, the South approximately 259,000 killed or wounded. The victory by the North meant that the country would remain one nation, the United States of America. Slavery was finally abolished in all parts of the country, and Blacks were declared citizens and given voting rights. Most people at the beginning of the Civil War thought it would be over in a few months. Yet as you see the Civil War turned out to be America's deadliest, and costliest of all time.

In reviewing this period, slavery has been a major problem from the very beginning of its establishment in America, from approximately 1640 to the election of the first President, it was considered a normal part of America's image in spite of numerous abolishments presented and neglected. We also see that from Washington thru to Lincoln, those who inherited the problem chose not to deal with it, a period of 74 years. I find that in all war conflicts of this nation, free blacks has fought in them all and made a tremendous impact with their courage and valor, especially in the Revolutionary and Civil Wars. The British had inflicted great casualties on Washington's forces to the extent that they were overwhelmed and could not engage or combat effectively because of insufficient manpower. Washington okay and accepted the training, arming, and recruitment of free black men and slaves as suggested by many of his subordinates, it was that or suffer a total defeat to the British.

Lincoln was advised by his military field generals of the major combat operations, and their manpower deficiencies, also on battlefield tactics against the south. Most of them requested utilizing the blacks, of which Lincoln was against doing, so the military suffered defeat for a period of time, until a very important individual, who would become one of Lincoln's most trusted adviser on slavery, entered into his life. This man, above all others, played a major vital importance in persuading him to finally free the slaves, bringing an end to a very evil and tragic period, to an inhumane treatment and abuse of a black race in the nation.

That one man, we know as Frederick Douglass, a black man who himself had been a slave that escaped from the chains that bound him, was a man who educated himself to become one of the most important and influential black leader of the nineteenth century. Lincoln had corresponded with Douglass, befriended him and valued his advice on matters involving the slave situation he was faced with. It's amazing how the Creator puts people in our lives to accomplish his goals and dreams in His master plan. It was by God's blessing this white President and this gifted and talented Black man joined together to carry out his will in the world.

Douglass was a writer, abolitionist, black leader, who fought against racism and discrimination, owner of a newspaper, orator, held several symbolically important part, United States Marshal, Recorder of Deeds for the District of Columbia, Charge d' Affairs, Santa Domingo and Minister to Haiti, joined the Anti-lynching Movement, addressed the U.S. Senate, the Congress and in 1852 gave an Independence Day Address. He was a spokesman for a Women's Suffrage and Liberation Movement Convention, New York, and writer of many great books of his era. A very powerful and respected man, he became a valuable asset to Lincoln during his troubled times of decision making regarding the war and slavery.

When the Civil War broke out Douglass came up with a slogan which was: "Union and Emancipation; Abolition or Destruction." He had written petitions to Lincoln and he also went to the White House to meet Lincoln after the President declared his goals were to save the Union even if it were necessary to retain slavery and color discrimination to do so. However, each time Douglass showed up at the White House, he continued to fight for the use of Negro soldiers until the need for them became extremely urgent, in order to save the Union army.

Lincoln later admitted, that Negroes furnished the balance of power which could decide the conflict in favor of the North, in a letter written to Charles G.D. Robison in early '63 he said:

"Drive back to the support of the rebellion the physical force that the colored people now give and promise us, and neither the present nor any coming administration can save the Union. Take from us and give to the very enemy the hundreds and thousands colored persons and we can no longer maintain the contest. The party who could elect a President on War and Slavery Restoration, would of necessity lose the colored force, and force being lost, it would be as powerless to save the Union as to do any other impossible thing."

Douglass fought stubbornly for Lincoln to utilize the Negroes. Lincoln later accepted his advise and signed the Emancipation Proclamation Declaration freeing the slaves. Douglass helped raise the 54th and 55th Black Massachusetts Regiments, his 2 sons were the first to enlist, there were about 200,000 Negroes enlisted or who volunteered in the Army that turned the tide of the war in favor of the Union.

Some 74 years later, Lincoln made the decision that took hundreds of young black men to do. He wrote great speeches, especially the Gettysburg Address. We can surely understand the rationale of freeing the slaves, however, Douglass had a much more difficult fight, that of making these free black men, citizens. Lincoln's main reason for freeing the slaves was to save the Union and unite America as a nation, but he was opposed to this idea, in a speech earlier at Charleston, Illinois, in September of 1859: "I am not, nor have ever been in favor of making voters or jurors of Negroes, nor of qualifying them to hold office." The Civil War perhaps modified his views on this very little. He, as other Presidents mentioned and believed in colonization of the blacks outside of the United States. Lincoln learned to appreciate Douglass for what he stood and fought for and constantly sent for him to seek his advice. He had he lived throughout his second term, it could have possibly happened that Douglass could have persuaded him to see otherwise. Both men one white, one black, came together in mutual respect for each other, both had their causes, one in keeping the Union as to create a United States, the other to free the Black man, brought here in slave bondage, suffering brutal, physical, emotional trauma and psychological abuse by racist fanatics for over 230 years. There's always hope that as our Creator allowed these two men to right a wrong in this country, we can look back on a very dark past for the blacks who labored, fought and died for to save this Union which we call America today and improve upon what they started. We are all God's creation, many races, creeds and colors with various ideas, cultures, and heritage of the different countries we all migrated from. With all of this said, it will require a great deal of tolerance to live among each other in harmony and peace, the Blacks who did not migrate here all others, were brought here by force for the purpose of slavery has endured a tragic period of atrocities from the beginning and yet the white race still find ways to violate their rights of which they have worked, fought and died for until this day. Most of the people are good of heart, however the Common Foe finds ways to degrade them which reflects and encourage other racial groups their ongoing hatred of the Black race. I ask you all to read your history, see what Blacks have endured, see what they have contributed to this country in spite of all the atrocities done to them, still they fought to save America. Know your history and know the true nature and character of the other people. As I wrote earlier Blacks are truly the reason we have survived the Revolutionary and Civil Wars, the additional manpower they provided in each conflict made a tremendous difference of victory or defeat. Reading of the suffering and abuse these Black men endured during these tragic times of peril, it amazed me that they accepted a role to fight and defend those who devastated their lives in so many gruesome and horrid ways. People are who they are because of the Love or Hate they hold in their hearts. I also understand that the black people are a very loving and forgiving race, and they exhibited that love, dying for the white race who inflicted so much pain, anguish and abuse upon them, that had to be the love that God instilled in us all at our very beginning of life itself. What a display of the blacks selflessness and character to project God's love to those who harmed them for 220 years. It goes to show that only God's love can conquer hate. I also commend those white people and Douglass for the perseverance for change he constantly fought for. Love unites and hates divides and in this violent period of world chaos and conflict, it's time for us as a nation to fuse that love to unify against the Common Foe divide, let's not allow the death of millions of our ancestors both black and white who died for the American Dream of which Martin Luther King Jr. presented to us in that memorial speech: "I Have A Dream." They died for that dream, and those of us who house God's love must continue to strive to eradicate the Racial Discrimination that's among us today. Love conquers all, surviving and enjoying life is making the right choices. The Creator has given us that option to do so, let's fight for all this country is supposed to represent: Freedom, Liberty, Pursuit of Happiness and Love for everyone throughout this land. Do the right thing and inherit the kingdom of God. I definitely want to be in that number. He who controls the mind of hatred and worldly intrusive thoughts inherits the key to the Love, Spirituality, and Salvation of his Heart. Read your history, we have all played a major role in the development of this country. Love and respect what we have nobly contributed! We need to accomplish our quest for UNITY AMONG US ALL! Let us leave a legacy for generations to come that we fought and overcame Racism and Discrimination in our world!

chapter 45

The Noose Game

Hanging nooses just goes to show us how far we as a nation have progressed in racial hatred. I was awakened this morning from a very troubling sleep due to dreams of the injustice in our country. Dreams of racial hatred and how this hatred of blacks has risen and escalated its ugly head across this land. White radicals who harbor discrimination and the superiority mind set allowed 4 white high school students to set the stage for them to show the malice to reflect the killing of blacks over a period of 365 years here in America, the last being a 16 year old black youth, having with his hands tied behind his back on the tree in front of his grandmother's house. A white sheriff investigating the incident called it a suicide and the fearful black community there was intimidated and accepted that decision as the cause of his murder. Reading into the story, the young promising college football player was dating a white girl on campus, the NAACP allegedly went there to determine what had happened, I never read of the outcome, other than he was allegedly dating the sheriffs daughter. The case was interesting to me due to the fact that it was called a "suicide." I've been involved with law enforcement for approximately 25 years and have never seen or heard of anyone hanging himself from a tree with his hands tied behind his back. To call that a suicide is just another lynching of a black person classified incorrectly, and killer or killers still on the loose. I can only blame the black people there however for accepting such a case to be closed without further due process of the sheriffs decision. Of all the lynchings of black men and women in America from 1640 to 2005 there's never been any white people convicted of them and there's been thousands. Where does that leave us at this point in time? It leaves us right where we started in 1640, when whites began lynching and murdering defenseless blacks in bondage, where the premise was that slaves were property and could be disposed of at the owner's discretion, they got away with it then, and they still get away with it today.

The "noose" has always been a symbol of intimidation to blacks, it was the tool for whites to express their true feelings of black people, that, and the whip, just about everyday a black person was being lynched by the noose or beaten to death or damn near, by the almighty whip on the hands of white racists. The noose game has never changed. White's hanging a black man from a tree in a noose was just about as common for them, as it was to having a family reunion, they always brought their families to these Nigger Cook outs, as they were called, where they all, young and old reflected their amusement at the site. A very true reflection of this is projected on the cover of Life Magazine (annually), it shows the little children there laughing with the grown people; there's even a cop in uniform in the crowd. These young children from the old era truly are the offspring of these haters we still encounter today.

As I previously mentioned, the burning of Rosewood, Greenwood and Brooklyn, where thousands of blacks were shot, murdered, hung by the noose, all of these mass killings by white people, again, none were ever charged. What a disregard for their young innocent children, taken to a place where there were one, two, or three black men hanging from a tree with nooses, castrated with their genitals stuffed in their mouths. I viewed a white racist supremacy family years ago on national television, they were telling the audience how they raised their children to hate blacks and Jews, a very interesting program, however I had to appreciate their courage to view their hatred. However, the incidents that have occurred over the years has not been done solely by these people, they are done by the general white racists' populace who are oftentimes incited by people telling bogus stories depicting blacks as the perpetrator. In Boston, years ago, a man told police that some blacks had killed his wife, the racist police went arresting any black male they encountered, to include invading private homes and dragging black males out at gun point without any lawful permission to do so, the next day the man finally confessed to killing his wife, although initially he had accused some blacks of doing such. A woman stated that her children were taken and killed by black males, incited the whites of neighborhood, and later on confessed she had drowned the 3 children herself. 3 white priests incited a crowd in New York when they stated that blacks should not be allowed to move in an empty project in their neighborhood, they rioted for 3 days killing hundreds of children and adults and caused mass destruction in that particular area of the city, no one was charged, it goes on and on. People have the right to hate, however, not the right to abuse or kill anyone. Our Creator said: "Thou shalt not kill." I wonder if these white haters thought He was talking to the rest of the world, because they damn sure didn't get the message here in America!

The churches of America is filled with "wall-to-wall" people on Sundays, holidays, etc. And never have I heard anyone telling these congregations to stop the hating of others, or if they are going to live Christ-like on Sundays, they should practice it also during the other 6 days of the week. Religion has been the cause of the majority of our world conflicts. Man has killed, maimed and destroyed civilizations because of religion. Knowing thyself and establishing your spirituality is where the difference is. When you discover who you are, what your purpose of life is, then there's the connection with your Creator who will assist you in making the right choices, doing God's will which is, as He stated: "I love you, so should you love one another." However, the Common Foe refuses to search within for his righteousness and salvation, so he remains the ill-guided villain who hates and kills God's creation upon this earth, Until you adhere to his word, you will remain the aimless wanderers of the world!

God also said: "Know thyself and you will find me." **Wake up people!** Life is too short and precious! Life is grand, or it will be whatever your feeble mind allows it to be! He who controls the mind controls himself, for the betterment of this country and the world. Find yourself, read, give that very sacred time of silence to the Creator where you can be spiritually enlightened of your true purpose in this system of things. **Expand your mind!** I find it hard to get caught up reading one book, especially after it has been rewritten for thousands of years, it's really simple, if you have the courage to take that journey within to find a brand new you, the you that will receive the wisdom and knowledge, that will allow you to make the right choices, that will expand your mind and extend yourself to help mankind, God will guide you to live within your heart, not in your mind. The mind is like the sea, it's calm it's raging, there's good thoughts and bad intrusive worldly thoughts, you have to discipline to create the balance to deal with life in the moment, there's no yesterday nor tomorrow, there's only the presence of now, only God knows when the arrow will pierce your heart, predicated on that why not live each day in giving, loving, respecting and making a difference for the betterment and harmony of the country. We must not allow fear to stand against this disgraceful hatred, discrimination and racial divide! We need a superior mind set to overcome this corruptness! We can't let ignorance and feebleness continue to destroy the standards of EXCELLENCE that our brave ethnic warriors have fought and died for, abroad and on this soil, to establish and maintain **FREEDOM!** Our ancestors shed their blood in many wars, as well as our loved ones today, who are still dying for honor and pride, blacks, whites and others, in order to preserve our long heritage - a heritage still marred mainly because of a select group that think they own this country. Many of them have never fought in any conflict, yet they are hanging nooses, burning crosses, those cowardly bigots. I remember them, because they called me Nigger while in a restaurant in South Carolina. I was wearing my military uniform enroute to Vietnam; they refused to serve me there! I fought the war, and returned, and now having these disgraceful incidents of ethnic intimidation. They are not intimidating the people of today, they are just cowards. If you want to make a statement, do so, don't hide your identity! They are the ones who state that their ancestors fought to free the slaves, that how smart they are, not knowing the history of this country and the circumstances slaves secured their freedom with; the ones who used to tell black children to go back to Africa where they came from, fact of the matter is, we all came here from somewhere else, the only difference is that black people were forced to this country in thousands hellish journeys to slave for the prominent white people. These historical facts should be taught to all white people who think they are the sole reason this country exists as America today. Korean and Vietnamese people asked the black American soldiers: "Why are you here, with all the racial problems in your country? Why are you here fighting us?" That was a very valid question. We fought, returned home, the Common Foe was still here, alive and well. There's a need to teach all of black history in all schools from 1640 until today. One of the biggest travesties was not allowing us black children to look on others to be our heroes and role models. If the white kids that hung those nooses knew the black history's significance, maybe they would have thought otherwise, however, I believe they are still taught to hate and divide.

There are 3 powerful books I would recommend for today's young and old alike:

God's Memorandum by Og Mandino

The Power of Now by Eckhart Tolle

Until Today by Iyanla Vangant

These are really great reads, literature that surely open eyes and hearts to a new beginning and how blessed we are to make a change in our life and this country when we realize that we are one of God's greatest treasures on this world.

As I continue to write, it seems there will never be an end to this racist madness. U.S.A. Today newspaper dated January 8, 2008, an article entitled: Anchor apologizes for "Lynch" Tiger remarks. Golf channel anchor Kelly Tilghman, who is white, on Thursday declined to comment publicly about suggesting on air Friday that young pro-golfers trying to catch up with Tiger Woods should "Lynch him in a black alley" Tilghman, the first woman to be a lead play by play announcer on PGA tour TV coverage issued a statement apologizing for her poorly chosen words. Tiger Woods' agent Mark Steinberg stated that Kelly and Tiger are friends and there were no ill feelings over her poor choice of words. The station said: "We regret if any viewers were offended by Kelly's remarks." Where has she been for the last 3 months? The school kids hanging nooses, another top talk show host in New York referred to black girls on a major University Basketball Team in New Jersey as "nappy-head hoes," was fired and rehired. He apologized on radio and at the University for those remarks. A black 23 year old girl was kidnapped, abused, raped, stabbed, and forced to eat human waste, she was held captive by 2 white females and 3 white males for 2 weeks, before being rescued by police. All 5 were arrested. A cross was burned on the front lawn of a black family's home after a child became involved in a fight with 2 white girls, in Cortlandt, New York, racial slurs and violence resulted from that incident, no arrest was made for the hate crime.

Three white Milwaukee cops were sentenced to long prison terms for beating Frank Jude Jr., a young black male. Officers Jon Barttell, Daniel Masarick and Andrew Spengler were convicted for the vicious beating that critically hospitalized Jude. He wrote in a court statement: "You and your fellow police officers, friends attempted to kill me and take my life." Mr. Barttell you are a disgrace to all police officers and every public official in the world. Officer Spengler was the only one of the 3 officers to show his emotions, wiping his tears and choking up during his statement to Jude. He said there was nothing he could say to erase what had happened, but that he has thought about it every day since. Philadelphia, a young black man shot and killed by undercover police officers who were dressed in regular clothes. They had monitored a drug transaction between two young blacks whom these officers approached, the black men took off running even when the undercover cops told them to stop. One man was caught, while the other kept running, and allegedly fired a weapon. During his flight, he was shot 2 times in the back, killing him instantly. There's a new Police Commissioner, hopefully some actions will be taken to help alleviate these police killings, 3 times in a week. These drug gangs out there warring over their turf, and when 2 people approach you at night on dark streets, who could determine who they were, dressed in regular street clothes? They could easily be thought of as the gang's street competitor, dressed as they were, without a way to identify them, in their plain clothes. Should he have been shot? Was that the proper attire for cops to wear? A dark street, the way these rival drug thugs shoot and kill each other. That could be the reason they ran away from the scene! The case is now under investigation. When a person gets shot in the back, how much of a threat was he?

The killings go on, the hate continues. A man was killed in his own house by a police officer who fired 11 shots in his home, killing him, wounding a child and another person. The other officer never fired his weapon. The officer who fired stated he was shot first by an unknown individual who ran into that house, so he fired back 11 shots into the crowded home, evidently the other cop never felt threatened after the individual ran into the house. At what point do you fire 11 shots into a crowded house and your partner never fires at all? They found the gun in the house however, never caught the man who fired it, but left behind 1 killed and 2 people wounded. Could death have been prevented?

A young black man was stopped at 42nd and Parkside Avenue in Philadelphia, PA, west section, at approximately 11:30 pm. Witnesses sitting on their porches said they saw the police pull the individual from the vehicle and beat him. The man died from that beating, an autopsy revealed his skull was fractured in 5 different areas. The officers said the man jumped out of the vehicle and attacked them, case went to trial, the black residents told their story which evidently was not believed in. A white lady stated she was at the time passing by the scene, and had observed this young black male jump out of his car and attack the police officer. Who was this mysterious witness, living in the northeast portion, who claimed to be in the area where the shooting happened? The Police Commissioner and judge closed the case predicated on the white lady's testimony, as opposed to the majority of eyewitnesses from the black community. The officers were found "not guilty."

A black youth was apprehended in North Philadelphia and handcuffed, was in the custody of at least 3 police officers, the subject was still being searched and was leaning over the trunk area of a vehicle when all of a sudden, another police officer drove up, ran over near the car and proceeded to punch the man in the face. It was caught on national TV at the evening news report. Later the cop stated he punched the subject because he had grabbed his genitals, which was preposterous, viewing the film. At no time was the officer behind the subject, he had approached the subject from the side. The assault was caught plainly on national TV news, seen by the viewers. These are the incidents that incite negative responses and non-support for these officers.

There are many good and excellent men and women serving in our police force, and many bad ones as well. Our communities look up to these good, noble law enforcement officers for their support, protection and professionalism. Police Officer's fortitude to cope with the sometimes unappreciated job of which the formulated, engaged and spoken. The poor choice of words has gotten thousands of black people lynched, murdered and damn near beaten to death in this white hatred world. Where does it end? When will our elected officials address this situation that created an immoral image of our country. The President sends our military of all ethnic groups to war, while the white racists here are allowed to hang nooses, burn crosses, blacks being killed, cops being killed, drugs everywhere, crime rate up, no jobs, schools closing, hospitals closings, gas prices as well as oil prices are up, people dying in unheated homes, bridges and infrastructure falling apart, students killing each other in high schools and colleges across the nation, poverty, "homeless" rate now is at an all time high, veterans returning home with all kinds of amputations, emotional and psychological trauma. A Mississippi based National Movement group is scheduled to march against Jena Six on Martin Luther King Jr. Day to protest the celebration honoring him and the support given to the 6 black Jena teens charged with beating up a white classmate, a spokesman for the group Richard Barrett stated the group has a court order that says the town of Jena cannot interfere with their march and that "we well be armed." Is that a form of intimidation to the law enforcement officials of the town, U.S. District Judge Dee Drell did not address the issue regarding the movement bringing weapons into the town.

This blatant statement was inciteful, disruptive and alarming to the other groups scheduled there to honor Martin Luther King. These type of threatening statements should not be taken lightly and every precaution should be taken by police and town officials

to either cancel the hate groups march or strictly monitor their behavior and above all else, that they comply with the town municipal laws regarding weapons to ensure the safety of all involved. It
should also be known to them they will be prosecuted to the fullest
extent of the law for any violation of any aggressive action initiated
by them.

I sit here thinking of our black war heroes fighting overseas
to protect our nation's banner, freedom and justice. I feel the pride
and valor they stand for, putting their lives on the line each and
every day, to safeguard our country. I think this hate group is trying to intimidate people here who are honoring one of our nation's black heroes, who spoke out about unity of all our people.
How unappreciative are these racist idiots, that Common Foe, to
tarnish the efforts of our fighting forces and what they are trying
to achieve.

These angry fanatics are a shameful deterrent to themselves
and our nation. These foes of our nation's unity have, by their
threats escalated the country's racial incidents to include invading
a town armed with weapons, to disrupt a holiday celebration for
King's birthday. What a travesty at this point in time from 1640 to
the late 1970's, blacks have been threatened, shot by the gun, disrespected, in spite of all they have contributed to this country.
These old terrorists tactics no longer apply, Blacks have fought for
their freedom, equality and justice here and around the world. They
will not be intimidated by some old hate group. Blacks have come
too far to regress to some cowardly bigot's terrorist threats, this is
not the old black defenseless slave, these are the young, strong-
willed people, aware of their rights and the price they have paid
from 1640 until today in Iraq and Afghanistan, where they are
shedding their blood and dying like all other Americans there. As
much as they have given, much has been taken away. They fully realize that there has always been two battlefields, one overseas and
the main one here in the land of their birth, defending against white
hate groups.

They liberated and freed others worldwide only to be continually abused and threatened to this day, so being threatened really
doesn't matter. They have come too far to yield to any derogatory

evil gestures from any of those ungodly narrow-minded individuals who refuse to allow freedom to ring across this country. You can mistreat and abuse a dog until one day it bites you in the behind. Blacks as no other group have endured over 350 years have overcome. Black men of the old era no longer exist. These blacks today have the fortitude to persevere against these racists who dwell here at home, these bigots are the worst blacks will ever have to deal with. As any other ethnic group of people they want to enjoy the freedom, justice and fairness. They have earned it!

Let us, who really care, find a way to live here in peace and harmony. The image of America has suffered tremendously worldwide because of what we project to others. They see homeless people, they see that jobs controversy has placed people in poverty situation, they see most poor Americans have no insurance. Our price of living has risen, the racial hatred projected against the blacks. They know more about our slavery years than our own people here know. We lost a lot of respect around the world - the world in the late 60's and early 70's during the Vietnam War era, so when we go to other countries to establish a democracy, it's fought again, they fight against it because it's not working here at home. We must make some positive changes of our image in the eyes of the world. It's imperative for all of us people. It's not like: white children are born to love and teach, while black children are born to abuse, hate and burned. Not so, we are all part of the **ONE,** all people together makes the nation, it's imperative that we make this happen. One day we will all discover this vital spiritual fact that we're all just part of the **ONE.** Unity, peace and respect creates the love for the family. Again, it's a family affair. It's imperative that we enlighten ourselves for the betterment of our family and the nation. We must have the spiritual enlightenment for togetherness. That's our true purpose in life. Let us make the difference **NOW.**

chapter 46

The Needed Awakening to Heal and Unite Our Nation

America, the great country has built a dynasty in our era, the most powerful nation in all factions, wealth, power, recognition and world influence. An empire that once ruled supreme among others. A country with a rich culture and heritage that truly amazes the world at large. The youngest nation, yet it has prospered and excelled in all phases of economic growth and development, made up of every race, creed and colors, the land of the free and home of the brave, predicated on freedom, liberty, justice, the pursuit of happiness and fortune, a country of my early years. I felt the pride and passion for all that I saw, as a young boy, this was America the beautiful!

Then there was that tragic and devastating day, I wrote earlier where my friend's father told him he could not play with any black NIGGER children, this incident exposed me to the racial problem, I was really heartbroken losing my best friend. After being told about the word NIGGER and being enlightened about racial discrimination and being told of at such a young age that white people referred to blacks as NIGGERS because they thought they were superior. My father told me however, all people did not feel that way, yet the damage was done, suddenly, America the beautiful was tarnished in my fragile subconscious mind. I would have to grow to understand this part of America's anger, hatred and prejudiced attitude, of these white people. My dad told me that I would encounter many barriers because I was black, Spoke of the desegregated army units, how these white soldiers caused racial problems in France, Germany and Italy, telling the people of these countries that blacks had tails, should not be allowed in their clubs, that white women should be kept away from blacks, and that they did not want blacks in their army or on the battlefields.

My father fought in Germany and Japan, and stated that the battles he fought was no match to the evil white American racist, which I would encounter within these United States of America, where our forefathers died for freedom and justice. Blacks made a major contribution in the Revolutionary and Civil Wars, as in Europe and Asian conflicts. He encouraged me to look into the black history books, found in major libraries, because the school system did not teach of our ancestors in our public schools. My Mother and Dad were very knowledgeable, and I praise them for all they made me aware of at such a young age, something that is not in most black homes.

WAKE UP BLACK PEOPLE! Especially parents, don't let your children depend on a white school system to teach them any black history, they only teach European history, and maybe a few token black figures at that. No African history, nothing of the contributions in technology and inventions, combat in wars, that Africa is the birthplace of the first people on this planet. They don't speak of the great Universities where the Greeks, Romans and other people were taught. If this information is to be taught, it will take a major orchestrated effort by "We The People" to get it approved at the city, state or congressional level, it's a must and need a concerted movement to accomplish. Our children must know that of which they have been deprived for over 300 years. Make sure your children know and understand their roots and all thereafter. If you are reading this book, act upon some of the suggestions here, it's imperative, if we are to break that indoctrinated mind set, in order to establish our pride and dignity. It all begins at home, children must know that they are "Second to None!" and that their ancestors were responsible for the lighting system, which we use each and every day, and so much more, it will truly establish just how great a race of people we always were and still are! We have let our children down in many ways, however as we move forward we must reach out and grasp that knowledge which has not been allowed to be brought forward. We are only as strong as the roots and knowledge of which we came from, which in our case was the Cradle of Life, Mother Africa, we will raise up our hidden culture, civilization and insight of the missing link of our race and people.

And if any whites are reading these pages, it's a wealth of knowledge for you as well, and I truly commend the white ancestors who also contributed to the alleviation of our struggles. The word NIGGER would forever be embedded in my heart and soul, the word NIGGER at that point in my life it destroyed a little innocent child in a wondrous world of joy and friendship, it created a new set of barrier in my mind, the word NIGGER ruined my youth at the age of 6 or 7. I had to advance beyond my childhood, years, to acknowledge that the word NIGGER was the most hateful, indignant, humiliating and disrespectful word I would ever hear in my life. My journey of life began with those sessions with my parents, who ensured that I was prepared to walk the path of life as it would present itself to me. My dad told me of returning from combat only to find blacks living here in America as second class citizens. (Remember Katrina, a few years ago, they referred to Blacks as Refugees) with no voting rights, freedom, liberty, justice, Jim Crow barriers and racism is the law of the land, not the Constitution, a document which, when read in its entirety, reflects that blacks were never included, although blacks responded... in spite of bondage and abuse, to fight for this land's independence, fought in the Civil War to save the Union. Yet, they were lynched, murdered, beaten, when they showed up to utilize their voting rights. There's no race of people more qualified to this voting system than the black race, who spilled blood, and died throughout this land. When you fight and die for something that a white government requests of you, then you are entitled to reap the rewards and enjoy all freedom, your blood has made you a beneficiary of all liberties, equal justice of the land, bar none. No other race of people provided the strength and power to these major endeavors. In the Civil War alone, blacks had 350,000 troops on hundreds of battlefields, they were called the freedom fighters, who liberated this country and their selves from bondage.

The Statue of Liberty stands where it is today because of blacks fighting on this land and gaining their liberty, something again hidden from the naive white people who think they are responsible for what we have in this country. Foreigners take advantage of what blacks and whites established. Blacks, white Union soldiers and Confederate troops are the only ones involved in one of the most devastating, cruel and savage war ever fought in this country, and yet 200 years later, blacks are still treated with undue disdain ignorance and conflict.

I adhered to my parents' wishes and continued my pursuit of truth, I grew up and began to read, found and understood that the game of life is not an easy game to play, especially if the pigment of your skin is black. Page after page in many of the books I've read, reflected the many barriers of racial discrimination, hatred, jealousy and a conspiracy to hide the real truth, and create the racial divide that has totally destroyed all that this country allegedly stands for. A nation that has taken away civil and human rights of the black people, where all are welcome, where only the black man is ostracized. Make no mistake about it, if you are black, America is becoming an increasingly dangerous place to live, unless you are some sort of entertainer, healthy and productive. We only have to look around to see the setbacks, nooses being hung all over the country, in parks, on school grounds, job sites, police locker rooms, Ku Klux Klan posters am police wall lockers, blacks being assaulted by racist white police officers who stomp and kick whenever apprehending or arresting suspects, acting as judge and jury on the scene. Nowhere in any Police Academy do they teach stomping and kicking, and when these type of officers resort to these kind of personal assault, then they should be relieved of their duties, sent to post traumatic syndrome evaluation, fired, or sued in civil court for their actions.

I was about eight years of age when two white cops sitting in their patrol car called me over to their vehicle. I was going to the store, the driver asked if I was staying out of trouble. I stated "I was," then he showed me a small hand held billy club called a flap jack, a steel bar about six inches long covered with heavy leather, with a flexible handle, when anyone is hit, the club continues to strike that spot due to the flexible handle. This racist cop hit me on my forehead in an intimidating psychological gesture. They both laughed as they pulled away, leaving me standing there, I felt violated, helpless, inadequate, to deal with my hurt and inner pride. I was abused, early on by a person sworn to protect, yet he chose to harm me, and embarrassed a kid that up until that point had looked up to them as role models and the good guys, only to have that respect turn into fearing the men entrusted to assist, protect, and help me at all cost. Yet he had turned into a racist bigot, hiding it all behind a blue uniform, badge and gun, so when I hear or see cops kicking and stomping as they did during the civil rights marches, I see these two racist cops assaulting a defenseless child, who on that day was totally humiliated, abused, and yet they got away with it. What a travesty, and we still have those type of individuals in our police force. Just imagine the innocent blacks in many cases locked up by these two, with the Klan signs in their lockers, who were reportedly on the force for eleven years. The racist cops join the police forces to do just that, falsify police reports, assault and lock up blacks in many of our cities today.

So let's not be led to believe that what se see in that police uniform is always an honest and clean police officer, and I commend the many brave and committed officers out there who truly uphold the established "SERVE AND PROTECT" professionalism, and I also know where there's law enforcement there's corruption within its ranks. So there's a need to scrutinize every arrest and procedure, just look at the increased jailed blacks and Hispanics. Again I say whoever made the decision to remove the presence of the walking neighborhood police officers, are partly to blame for the conditions we see in poverty stricken areas of our cities. I lived in north Philly and there were gangs everywhere, there was the Valley, the Exiles, the Village, the Tenderlion, Moroco, Norris Street and the Pandoras. The walking cops were respected, they knew the people, their families. I remember an old cop named Reed. We called him Reedy, he walked Columbia and Ridge Avenue, up around 22nd street, he would come up say "Let me have that corner!" And we respectfully moved on, Reedy did not play and there were lots of Reedies out there, that knew the fine points of policing, and there was always police presence in the neighborhood. I went to visit my cousin in West Philly, we sat out on his front porch from approximately 1:00 in the noon period, until 4 or 5:00. There was a church of which he was the Pastor of, across from there was a corner store. There must have been between 8 to 10 guys hanging on that corner the whole time we were out there. I even asked my cousin about that situation, he had no answer, so no police presence, no safety, especially for our children and senior citizens, unbelievable that no police ever came thru there for that period of time. When they removed the police, the drug traffic, robberies, assaults flowed in, then jails were built. What timing for all things to come together, the jails were not the answer, good police who knew their jobs were! The police commissioner and neighborhood residents will have to reestablish the safety and welfare of the communities for the betterment of the relationship between the police and the people. People are actually afraid of these cops, because of the controversial shootings, the manner in which they approach people - drawing their guns, assaulting individuals, hollering, or using abusive language, it's very intimidating not only to adults but to the young children as well. Hopefully things will change for the better, or you will see more of the same, and the jails will continue to consume our youth, where there's no future in sight for them. The more these youth are locked up, the more they are unable to compete for jobs or for anything else. Talk to your mayor and police commissioner. Police officers hold tremendous power over all citizens including the suspects and for a portion of them to violate such power is deadly. Individuals who possess this rule over people should be highly selected to become those who yield it. However, we know that even with a perfect selection, there are a few who get influenced to become corrupt, they are just ordinary humans and have their share of emotional and stressful problems: marital, financial, relationships, as all others have. There was the King incident where a racial comment was transmitted via the radio to other officers by the initial arresting officers, which led to 21 other officers to show up and beat him. Like they did, it was a witch hunt of racial police officers, it could have been a great night for the felons who were watching the rest of the city." Twenty-one cops responded to partake in that brutal beating, which cost that city ten million dollars in civil court. How about the cops that beat up a 67 year old black man during the Katrina disaster, or the cop who punched a man in the face on national television when the man asked the officer why he was arresting his son, parents have the right to know! There's all kinds of police officers, some good, others are unstable personnel, they arrested one for having sex with a horse not long ago, one officer got caught using steroids which made him highly emotional and abusive while arresting a suspect, there was a cop who rammed a broomstick up an individual's rectum while being detained in a New York police station. After two months investigation, they were brought forward. This can go on and on. Police management have a tendency to protect their own, and it's really sad that it's so! Cops should not disrespect the power and authority vested m them by the law and their commanders. If he does so, he jeopardizes his honor, that of his supervisors, the Police Commissioner, the Mayor, the people of the city and disrespects his comrades who uphold their values in the performance of their duties and responsibilities with tact and professionalism required of them. There's a price for making the wrong choices, and disciplinary action should be administered to them who violate their authority to the fullest extent of the law that govern them, as well as all others. I call to mind these incidents, because they cannot be allowed to proliferate, in dealing with our citizens who should not have fear of our law enforcement officers, there must be meetings between the community leaders and the police commanders of their respective districts, to include the commissioner, if he's available. Being a police officer is a tedious and unsung job at times, there's danger, long hours of court appearances, much documentation and reports, etc., however, this is what police officers do and they have committed themselves to this type of work. Fighting crime has always been emotional and stressful, where one has to be a knowledgeable and dedicated individual who knows notorious gang activities on the streets, thus the job requires strong mental and physical discipline, and the capability to demonstrate professional diplomacy or physical aggression when needed. Every black driver pulled over in a traffic stop is not a felon or a crime suspect, yet in many cases they are treated as such, including the passengers. The data on the vehicle computer already reflects the owner, tickets, summons, etc., so if there's no negative feedback for the officer, why are individuals required to show proof of their identity? At times they are even asked to exit the vehicle to be frisked even when he just ran the stop signal or driving too fast. Why is there a need to check all other car occupants, just seem like another harassment, unless alcohol, drugs, or weapons are noted. Police have such a bad image from all the TV coverage of beatings and abusing people both verbally and physically. There are lots of issues to cover at these meetings, however, I think it would start a working relationship between community and the police department.

chapter 47

Help the Plan

The plan to change starts at home, first with the parents, then the whole family, mothers and fathers must take a good look of what they are presenting to their children, have you been the ideal role model for them? Parenting is an on-going commitment, my mother is now 88 years of age, and she still manages to encourage and support my endeavors, and at times giving some good insight on various issues we discuss, still teaching. She's simply worthy to be praised, my guardian angel.

At this point in time, it's imperative that we begin to strengthen all phases of family structures, otherwise it will be hard for our children to compete for jobs whenever they become available for them. The 12 million Mexicans that are still here illegally will get them before blacks can, it's just a way to keep blacks second class citizens in poverty. Today our communities are infested with murderers, drug dealers, hustlers, bad cops, corrupt politicians, our children are constantly in harm's way, even in school environment where gangs are prevalent and despite the presence of cops in hallways. We really have to be involved, be visual, and concerned for our children, for all family members, and for the whole community. The country is in the worse chaotic state ever imaginable. Again, it begins at home, families who pray together stays together and prospers as a whole. There's a need to have family meetings at least once a week, families should eat meals together, where they discuss family and school related problems, and whatever needs to be addressed. Children should be required to talk of their school progress, and their homework should be discussed and later checked, parents should allow children to present their views on various situations, and problems they may be encountering at home, school, or in the neighborhood. They should be counseled about gangs, their behavior. Parents should know their children's friends and who they are affiliated with, and check on any negative activities they may see in their neighborhood and should immediately report such to the local police. Parents should ensure their children's clothes are appropriate for school, pressed pants and shirts, children need to be neat and clean, well-dressed and mannered. It is a must! Parents definitely have their work cut out for them, and our citizens should be involved in the process, as well. A clean home and wholesome neighborhood conditions are necessities. Areas where houses have been torn down by the city where there is weeds, trash and becoming a deplorable site should be reported to city officials to have them paved over and made presentable in that community. The residents of the blocks should ensure their areas are kept policed and clean, however, the city is responsible for those areas of which they destroyed and gutted out of those neighborhoods. Your children, as well as all who live there deserve a nice, clean block to live in, with pride and dignity! Police walking units should be requested in all neighborhoods to ensure gangs are not hanging on the corners and loitering along their streets. Also, there should be a request that police check the homes of senior citizens, there's been times in the past where elderly homes were invaded by drug dealers, and people taken advantaged of, held hostages, their place turned into drug houses.

Parents are encouraged to go out on trips with their families to museums, especially the Black museums in the Center City, or the planetarium, the zoo, and various other places. Children love activities which they share with the whole family where they enjoy a special bond of unity and togetherness. When parents are actively involved in their children's education, their school system, the teaching-learning experience, the children feel such concern for their welfare. Parents well-aware of their children's conditions in school, whether or not they are involved in gangs can better advice them to stay away from danger. The city has an obligation to assuage our children's safety, yet by the same token, helping your children to avoid bad company ensures discipline and safety. Another element is that parents should speak out to the city council and more so, to the mayor, to lobby that black history be taught in the school system, from grade schools on. Students have been deprived of this most valuable history of their lives, they must know of black contributions made in wars, especially the Revolutionary and Civil Wars. They have to increase their understanding of the impact the blacks made in winning the country's Independence and forming these United States, and the major inventions.

Again, parents are enjoined to teach on character, dignity and pride, these few essentials are definitely needed, ensure that the church is involved in the family structure, that God is the source of their Divine spirituality and its necessary for all family members to embark on their inner spiritual journey to know themselves, a personal commitment to our creator to find understanding to reveal the wisdom and knowledge of which we need to truly have, in harmony with all of God's people and creation. Where they will see that we are all our creator's treasures in this system of things. Yes, parents are the sole beginning of our first steps of knowledge and understanding, especially our mothers who are our first teachers. Again, I salute the single mothers raising children on their own, also the stepfathers, and I encourage the wayward fathers to make the connection with their children, the relationship may just set you free of the void created by leaving them, by divorcing, children need to know and relate with those who have the courage to make the connection, if it's feasible for all involved. Again, parenting is creating pride dignity and character.

Extend your hands, each and everyone, there's a need to expand our unity for the cause of establishing our pride and dignity for our race of people, we have been divided for hundreds of years, the indoctrination by the Common Foe has left us distrusting, hating, being jealous of each other, leading to drug addiction that kills our minds and souls, robbery, beatings and murders especially of the senior citizens and children, just totally dishonoring ourselves and the black race. It's been that way for over four hundred years, hating our black brothers, there's got to be an awakening to resolve our black issues to create the harmony and togetherness we need to establish peace, if we expect to find our way in a country we fought and died for only to be deprived of all there is. Divided we own nothing, divided we receive nothing, divided we suffer from poverty and economic degeneration, divided we fail in all our endeavors. Look at the nation, see the jails full of black people. Jobs going to all others other than the blacks. We are buyers of others products, what do we produce? Where do we stand among other races of people? We stand alone, it's been that way for hundred years. The Common Foe hates blacks so much, they discriminate against them, hang nooses, refuse housing rights, refuse to acknowledge a black man trying to right things of our past, Even we, as blacks, do not support a black candidate. They have poisoned black people's minds to just sit or stand around and wait for change, that will not happen, there will be more of the same. It never has changed, never will, unless we learn to unite, trust our fellow black people for the betterment of our race and culture. Every time we gave, they took it away, we fought wars, they killed us upon our return, even while in uniform, we fought again, returned and found more of the same. Fought again, returned and could not vote, killed while attempting to do so. Just more of the same, without our unity and togetherness, we will never change. Our fate is in our own hands, to change or remain stagnant, the choice is ours! Read your history, it's all there. I've tried to enlighten you, so it's your choice, make it positive or you will endure the negatives to the end.

chapter 48

Black White Issues

This country is deeply involved in financial and economic decline, jobs are not created and if so they will be given to illegal aliens from Mexico before blacks, know it will be more of the same, you can see that happening. There's city and state construction bids allocated to contractors who refuse to hire black people, it's always been blacks last since the very beginning, so don't look for any fairness at this point. Obama is your chance for change, if there is to be any, there have been corrupt policies put in place to deter blacks from getting into the economic growth programs, believe me, we need equality and fairness. When looking into his track records, it reflects he always upheld fairness not only for blacks, but for all others as well. If in fact he can just accomplish the feat of equality and fairness, then we, as a nation and people, shall have a major stepping stone to unity and some harmony. The choice is yours, let your vote count for the betterment of black people's interest for once in your life. Now, whites are seeing just how respected by the powerful brokers they are. Recent scenario proves if you are poor and white, you fit in the same predicament - poor and destitute blacks are. Again black people cannot be held responsible for the failure of your jobs, homes, savings and family values, your brothers have stripped your assets, just like they did with black second class citizens, whom you despised. Blacks have never harmed you, it's only the people you voted into office that ruined this country, so now you see when it comes to money, power and greed, blacks just don't count among those offenders, the select rich and famous.

Check your candidates' record, it will all be there to see, the people in power at this time have given you more of the same, that blacks have been dealing with, for hundreds of years. There are tremendous barriers against blacks, case in point, look at the progress made by black people who united and built one of the wealthiest and prosperous town, called the Black Wall Street of America, well, white Klan and Common Foe totally destroyed and burned it down, that city of Greenwood, district of Tulsa, Oklahoma, 1921, there has never been another black enterprise after that. So what we see is control of a race of people to prevent them from creating wealth. As I've stated before, he who discovers the treasures hides the assets and the truth. Without the truth, blacks cannot excel in economic growth. Again make your vote count, not for more of the same, but for the opportunity to break the bonds that negate progress of all people. I continued to read about this great black heavyweight Champion of all the racist harassment, Jim Crow, the threats on his life, the lynchings of about 100 black men on the night he beat the white Champion, racism was so bad in America that the country refused the film to be shown here, how embarrassed the superior minded white people were to see a black man beat a white in this country, that was not supposed to happen. The white men had told their wives and children that they were the best at all things and superior to blacks who were not considered humans but savages, monkeys, and only knew how to be slaves. The truth would have been the best thing to tell, how ignorant of them to tell their loved ones these lies. And these fabricated lies went even farther back, hundreds of years before that fight, that gave black people a role model of hope, that they could one day be recognized as somebody.

Johnson storybook took me farther back in time, that deeper past revealed the rest of the truth of which we as black people have been deprived of for hundreds of years here in bondage. I proceeded deeper and deeper, I crossed over the Civil War, the Revolutionary War and beyond, I learned that there has been an ongoing concerted effort of the white people in those eras, never intended to expose the amazing history of our forefathers in any of their history books, especially when you see that this country we inherit today exists only because of black men and women who fought and died to win its independence. They're all recorded in the archives of military wars, battles, dates, time, places, very important people who fought and won these key battles that turned the tide from defeat to victories, the hidden truth. The white man is embarrassed to tell it all after all of these years of deceit and deception. Their children and grandchildren still remain with their blinders on, however, the truth will be revealed in the near future, nothing remains hidden forever. Because of the black people who helped set you free, to claim independence, you racist people ought to realize that you must allow the truth to free your forefathers and ancestors, so they can be at peace in their graves, of which they lay. What heroes, what patriotism, what valor of these gallant black men who turned the tide, yet lay unappreciated and unacknowledged in their graves sites all over this nation! Your revelations will be heard in due time. PEACE BE UPON YOU!

I wrote of the Civil War, there's so much documentation reflecting times, dates and battles. To gain victory In numerous battles where the white Union troops were overrun, some of which even retreated, the white commanders called for the black slave units to re-enforce them. In one major fight, the white soldiers were nearly wiped out and could no longer handle the situation, so the commander called for blacks to continue the assault. The blacks lost 234 lives, fighting at Millikin's Bend using only bayonets, without cap bullets, yet they still overran the Confederates' position. They killed and secured the battlefield which is now a historic site today, read about the Fort Pillow, the New Market Heights, the Virginia battle, where the blacks achieved victories. In more than 449 battles until the South decided that it would swallow its pride and enlist blacks as soldiers, but it was too late. Read about Ft. Wagner, where more than 200 brave black men were slain, read about Ft. Sumter and some of the 449 battles fought and won. Read about the Statue of Liberty and why it was sent here. It was a gift in recognition of black soldiers who helped to win the Civil War uniting the United States, it was known worldwide that the black soldiers fought above and beyond expectation, and played the pivotal role in winning the war, ending African bondage in this country. The statue was the thought and creation of French historian Edward de Laboulage, Chairman of the French Anti-Slavery Society who, together with sculptor Frederic Auguste:

Bartholdi, proposed to the French government that the people of France present to the United States, through the American Abolitionist Society, the fact that the black soldiers won the Civil War in the United States, read of how the statue was rejected because of its Negroid features, however after three tries the United States accepted it, the Negroid features had been changed, but the shackles or chains on the statue's feet remained, this symbolized slavery. The truth goes and on, how grateful I am to my dad and to the people who kept honest records in high places, as it goes. Seek and you shall find, I found a great love and respect for my black forefathers, and praise the Divine Creator for allowing me to take my blinders off to see, as well as giving me the fortitude to continue into what millions of whites and blacks need, to read and enlighten themselves to its wealth. I have it, it's been revealed in every way and only gets richer and deeper. I go into my personal journey of God's awareness. To me our Creator says I give to you what you seek, in abundance, and God never renege on that of which he promised to us all! Lincoln was looking at the Union being defeated when he was talked into that Emancipation Act proclamation signing, to allow blacks to fight for the Union. Over 350,000 black combat slaves were enlisted, read of his speech regarding their patriotism and valor. I envision wars having been fought with such haunting atrocities of death and devastation! Those blacks who fought had it from three different sides they faced: the enemy they engaged in on their front side, the white Union racist soldiers beside them, in combat, who despised and killed them for fighting another white man, even if it was their enemy, and the third element were the white cowardly bigots who pushed the slaves into combat to save their lives, who killed, or lynched these blacks that survived the ravages of war. If captured black soldiers are never allowed to live, so death awaited those captured black soldiers: in the hands of their enemies, wounded, they would either be burned alive or nailed to the tree, or hands and ankles spread eagle style and nailed to the walls of a building, castrated, eyes gouged out, bodies severely mutilated. Despite facing death in war and even after supposedly surviving war, the black slaves joined the white man's war, winning it, saving them all, and you and I as well! So

when you look at the components of these wars, they were whites
and blacks, so how could blacks be hated after the war, after all is
said and done, did they not deserve a taste of promised freedom?
What they got was more death to their bodies and souls, hated and
despised! The whites hid the black soldier's fate from their children
and grandchildren, who knew nothing of their accomplishments in
war and in peace, thus racism against blacks proliferated, their sacrificed blood gained no voice in the succeeding white generations,
and even now still cry for peace and recognition! Viewing the pho-
tographs of lynchings, murder, torture of blacks have made me cry
many nights... even the search for truth has made me searching for
the salvation of whites who thrilled in committing such atrocities
against a race who made much sacrifice on their behalf! Can you
handle being called the Common Foe, for being a discredit even to
your own people, to the whole human race of which we all are
apart of!

There's a reason the rest of the world watches America, a
wealthy, historical, powerful nation who fought in more wars than
any other. The world knows about black history, they are reflected
all over their country, in churches, museums, the documents are
found worldwide since the beginning of time. The only place I
have been discriminated against, called a NIGGER, early on in
my life to make me feel inferior, that I had no culture or civilization, told me to go back to Africa, is here in America. Well, that
was okay then, but now that legacy that I uphold allows me to
stand tall, look any white racist in their eyes and state: "This is
my land, we fought and died for it, made a major contribution that
no other race of people can attest to. This nation is mine. And
when I think of the black men and women in this country whose
funeral services I had facilitated, as part of my task and responsibilities at West Point, and when I see their gravesites here and in
other countries like Germany, France and Italy, I hear and feel
their voices speaking to me, crying in anguish, for me to write of
these evil deeds, to vindicate their troubled souls and enlighten
the world of their plight.

That's my commitment to them like what millions of other
scholars have done in that era, and continue to do so today. Amer-

ica deserves this knowledge hidden within the confines of this earth to be revealed to set her free to enjoy the harmony and balance she needs to this very day. Mother earth is the keeper of the sacred blood spilt and embedded in her surface from north to south, east and west, she preserves it all for that special day when she will release this racism which has negatively clogged up the planet, making it hard for her to control the floods and hurricanes, she needs the power to release the anger, the hatred, she seeks the people's unity, knows that the whole truth rests in her bosom, blocking her arteries. We as a people owe our lives to Mother Earth, so we need to adhere to her voice for peace, for her to give us all her resources and restore the balance of all creation. Our malicious intrusive thoughts of hatred, racism, bigotry and discontent utterly disrupts the harmony and balance, positive vibrations and frequencies of the magnetic forces of the Universe causing chaotic conditions on Earth, who struggles to maintain equilibrium. Floods, hurricanes, tornadoes appear, disrupting our existence with their devastating effects! Marvin Gaye tells us in his song that "in such times of chaos, flowers won't grow and the world would be dying, what a sad way to live, there's far too many of you dying." We as people need to take care of what God has blessed us with. As I spoke of Adam and Eve, there's a price we pay for wars and destruction of lives, now it is in our hands to bring true understanding of our lives today, when we do so, knowledge and wisdom is upheld and unity of the Creator's plan is created. Peace, Love, Happiness transforms us all into peaceful, loving and joyful individuals. This harmonious change happens, and it's in our hands to do it, it's nothing new in this system. Rome, Greece, Africa, all great civilizations crumbled and met their demise because of angry, ugly racist people, people of greed and corruption in this world. Can we handle what all indicators are telling us? We cannot continue to be stupid minded people, because if we do so there will be more of the same, we have to save this world we live in, before we can ever expect our children to survive here. America has never been kind to its people, the outsourcing of jobs caused poverty in the land, first and foremost, jobs are crucial in a land of freedom and justice, without them people extremely suffer, and no one's to blame except We

The People who allowed this to happen before us, it's total chaos for the small people of the nation. We had those unjust wars where we lost our loved ones lives, to traumatic stress disorders, missing limbs, and a country in the worst state of every level. We are still fighting such wars. We need serious thoughts of our future, and not let it be taken by false promises which we hear today, especially in electing our new President. I must say, we who really care should listen intently and vote wisely, we wonder who would allow a country to be in such disarray? The major corporations and individuals who signed that open deal, where some of the people you voted into office, outsourced your jobs overseas, they never replaced you with any, why was that so? Some people stated they did not see it coming, now you, who really care, must decide. Is staying in Iraq to accomplish a victory more important than saving thousands of lives of our young fighting men and women? We stayed in Viet-Nam for eleven years, never got the V for victory, treated our returnees like outcasts, so we have some major decisions to make now. We went to war in Iraq without the major powers, Russia, France and Germany, who refused to send their troops on harm's way because they were not offered any bidding for construction and rebuilding of that country. I saw outside contractors make millions in Viet-Nam over the years. Same applies in Iraq, Haliburton and Becktel companies are the major contractors there, along with thousands of other smaller subcontractors. A lady in my neighborhood is moving into her son's house, he's in Iraq as a subcontractor, making approximately 250,000 dollars a year. Had these major companies given bids instead of us going to war with 130,000, they could have supplied us with another 390,000 of which 130,000 from each country could have been utilized to control the three different factions area instead of trying to do it all with the small forces the various small countries provided. One thing we know for sure is that war is hell! As to my journey, I must mention the last election. Had "We The People" stood up, giving of results might never have happened, due to the thousands of problems with those voting machines, it would have been better to allow the incumbent President to remain in office for approximately three to four months to fix the voting system and conduct another election. The people has power under the Constitution that governs us. When there's no cry from the people, other sources provide the outcome for us to live by, case closed, listen closely, you voters did not come here with yesterday's rain, you have been here for a while, however, when you don't know your rights and seize the power that you have, then everything gets orchestrated for you. I hope you are waking up and reminding your children and yourselves to read all the nation's documents involving We The People? Already it's reason to be concerned because a lot of governors and other people stated they would not vote for a black man, that's how far we have advanced from the past with racism, about two city blocks in 400 years. What type of mind set is it where we stand and deal with the issues, I know the Constitution did not include black people. But you would think after all we have given, it would reflect some change, however, even if it does, don't vote on skin color, vote for the best interest of your heart, everyone is saying we are a united country, however white people will not vote for a black man, how can they be so sure... only the people will speak, I'm sure.

The only thing that bothers me is whether or not this nation is strong enough to work off any negative influence some of these elected officials have created, we have made movements, before, the last one of which was with Martin Luther King, Jr., which lapsed back into obscurity after his death. With this up and coming election at hand, there must be a concerted effort and black support for Barack Obama by every person, the moment of NOW will never present itself again, hence we should grasp it wholeheartedly for, as a people we should not allow it to pass by, for one of our own who's ready, able and qualified as anyone else, to lead this country. First and foremost, we cannot judge, only thing we can do is vote. This man has been a leader all of his adult life, he's a people person with strong mental character, with passion and compassion, wise enough to seek the Divine Spiritual understanding that allows him to receive the Wisdom, Knowledge and Guidance from the God of all things who reminds us that when we do all things out of love and righteousness for the people, we shall do them in His name and he will give us guidance to lead well. Barack

Obama is blessed to have been anointed as were the kings, he has sincerely asked for God's guidance, and has accomplished much to where he stands today, let no one negate such, nor allow another person to prevent you from supporting and voting for him, nor deter you from pursuing the quest to vote for the first Black Democratic President of this country, we as black people who have fought the wars, were used and abused, discriminated against, suffered much, have made this country wealthy, so we need to vote for our own. We are responsible for its power and growth, yet we stand as the most disrespected people in this nation, we have been called anything under the sun, yet we continued with our struggle to rise above all we have dealt with, including lies and deception. This is the time we have been waiting for, what our ancestors died for, the time that Martin Luther King, Jr. stated he might not get there with us, this is the time the whole world has been waiting for, the reason the French government gave us the Statue of Liberty which stands to represent the Freedom of us all men and women irregardless of race, creed, or color, and especially to the blacks who were promised freedom from slavery. This is the time to come together as a people and nation. Obama will give the nation the eyes to see. There's lots of criticism for this man and I can see why, however, it's expected of individuals who run for presidency, a very prestigious office in our nation.

I can go back and criticize every President from the beginning, the Constitution records blacks as cattle, 3/5th of a man, yet neither the first 12 Presidents nor any other never corrected it, as blacks, you were entitled to vote, yet those Presidents never ensured you would go and exercise such rights, with the protection you needed doing so. A president allowed a little 13 year old kid's murderer to stand not guilty, when in fact the other two felons had already sold their story to the Post magazine, revealing the truth how the crime was committed, laughing and joking all throughout the confession, even as the whole world watched! That was indeed a total mockery of American justice, the president could have intervened, once the truth of the killing Emmitt Till was known. The child's mother requested that action be taken in the case, not knowing that all she needed to do was have the United States Attorney

General re-arrest the murderers and have them tried at the United States Federal Civil Court. It never happened, it goes on and on. There's always room to criticize, who's the President that allowed your jobs to be outsourced? Why are we in Iraq? Part of the problem is because we allowed these issues to go unnoticed, why was the last election approved, it should not have been allowed by "We The People!" Lost votes, electronic problems, miscounts in the poll, and yet it went forward, to plunge the whole world into what we are experiencing today!

Barack Obama has fought a controlled campaign up until this point in time, had to give in to various issues, however all that is behind him now, the battleground today is McCain Vs. Obama, this is where he will have his A Game! He can lay it all out, as I expect him to do, he has come too far to back out from whatever is thrown at him. Yes, we as blacks would like to hear what he's going to do for us, as a people. However, it does not work that way, he cannot stand up there and single out One ethnic group, it's We The People. He will represent all the people. Do we expect change for blacks? Yes, and you should hold him responsible for all he promised, I've never heard a presidential nominee say: "I am going to do this or that for any race of people!" However, once in the White House as President, that's when he is held accountable for concerns that affect all people, issues addressed for change to occur. I'm sure I'd love to see that black history be taught in our school system, we have a great American history established here since 1640 and our children should be privy to this right from the very beginning. It has never been done, and should be! The President has the obligation to make all things fair for all people, and I know there will be lots of resistance, but as long as he fights for the Change he has promised, it will happen and we will all move to support him as all others should! So, let's wish him success in all his endeavors! Fulfillment of all dreams! Victory for our Vision! He has to surround himself with sharp, brave, courageous and supportive people to carry him through his leadership towards Change!

Again we have heard many highly elected officials state that whites will not vote for Obama, these people are very influential, and for them to make that statement is just another way to enforce

that racism and divide. People who voted for the governors supported him wholeheartedly, and whenever they make these comments, they only fuel negative mind set against Obama. Blacks did
vote for white officials, why would they conclude on what they
think white people would do. No one can speak for other people,
black, white or any color, who have their individual mind set I've
heard some officials say that Obama is not experienced enough.
They say whites won't vote for him, yet they suddenly show up to
promote him to the oval office. Let's not get caught up in other
people's reflection of their philosophies!

Who really cares when your city bid contractor give the bids
to all white construction companies to bid there, there should be a
requirement to ensure fair employment throughout the city. Whites
get all the jobs, pay their mortgages, keep their homes, send their
children off to college and prosper, while blacks lose their homes,
can't afford to send their children anywhere, continue to live in
poverty because no one cares, the haves just ignore the double standards of the black and white divide. People are experiencing hard
times, inequality in employment in favor of the whites widens the
gap between them. What a travesty, showing corruption in the high
places of the government! The contractual office needs investigation and guilty officials need to be fired for their wrongdoings.
There should never be any city worksite that only employ white
workers, equal opportunity for all people should be adhered to.
People call, cry, and moan on radio shows because of the partial-
ity of employers to applicants, yet they do not support the courageous individuals who lobby or rally for their rights and
entitlements! They **have** no courage, faith to change their situation, to demonstrate at the jobsites! Why don't they do so, right a
wrong, end their suffering and not wallow in more of the same! It
will only get worse. You are losing a lot of black schoolteachers in
your school system, not only that, the academic curriculum con-
tains very little black history on it. As we stated before, we have
been learning European and American white history, which do not
reflect many of the major contributions, inventions, of war heroes
from the Revolution down to the Viet-Nam era, neither do they
teach about slavery, free labor, the patriotism of men that earned

this country's Independence or the difference they made in the Civil War...it goes on and on, we hear about scholars talking of Europe's greats, their knowledge, wisdom and understanding, then why not talk of the African great civilizations, if they teach of one, then they need to teach of all others, our children should not believe only of great people who do not look like them, it's this morbid mind that continues to deny black heritage and culture.

Again 'we are to defeat racism, we must be strong enough to reveal all that has been hidden, Divine Knowledge is allowing us to do that now, if not done in schools, be sure you, as a black men and women, do it in your homes. Let your children and the world know that your history, your roots, are sacred and that you will never allow your children not to be proud of our ancestors from time immemorial until now. It's everlasting knowledge that will have no end, it's recorded in the database of our minds, it has always been there to recollect, and that applies to all of our Creator's billions of immortal Souls, we have always been such, as we are everlasting. We are here to enlighten our brothers and sisters we, of all races and creeds are their keepers, as they are ours.

My journey was so crucial to me, because many white ignorant people who ruined my childhood psychologically caused me to hate at such an early age, that mind set instilled in my subconscious memory, making me struggle for years with my feelings of contempt against them. Then I got a job working for a very wealthy white man who, for some reason, became a very important figure in my life. He took me under his wing, was concerned about my life, talked to me, gave me a car to use, he owned a New Car dealership. I guess someone had told him I was Trying to be "up and coming" boxing contender. I could always go and talk to him about life and my boxing ambitions. He made sure I stayed out of trouble, introduced me to Frank Rizzo, another guy I admired, he even offered me a job once I had gotten out of service with the highway patrol. I also met one of my early idol in entertainment, Mr. Frank Sinatra. My boxing was really an out for me because I was really good. Whenever I met a white guy on the ring I not only fought to beat him, I took out all my bent up anger on them, never lost to any white fighter. Had I done so, I could never have lived with myself. I later enlisted in the Army, shipped to Ft. Jackson, South Carolina, and had ran into a middleweight contender, Candy McFarlane from Philly, I knew him at home, went over to the gym where they were conducting a boxing seminar. I was surprised to see him there, I was only at camp for three days. He asked if I wanted to participate, as there were four or five heavyweights there, all white. I gave an affirm, I beat up three of them within five minutes battered them they had to call me off. Candy told me: "Man, you came ready to rumble!" I just got on a grove, and it flowed. That ten minutes of boxing got me acknowledged all over Ft. Jackson. The other match which I have already written about, when I had a fight in the company area, where I would have been locked up in the stockade had the white soldiers not revealed the truth, then something changed, I've really respected those five or six guys that day, which changed my emotions towards white people, my anger was gone. I had finally encountered some strangers who held no racism in them, I was shocked, I became their hero in that Basic Training, they went everywhere with me, that day I left the inner malice I held for almost fifteen years, it was as if I had shaken a tremendous weight off my shoulders. I could not believe I was really so friendly with those white guys, it was truly amazing! I said goodbye to my racial imprisonment.

We must get over this racism, I did, and guess what? I met plenty of white people I respect and admire, especially those I fought with in Viet-Nam. Remember I wrote about Threadgill, the white boy from Tennessee who had his first time ever being around black people, the guy I wrote of who had been spitting tobacco all my feet while we were in formation, Stone Red Neck, you see what happens between two haters, we became the best of friends, and still are today! We just had to shed our blinders off, disregard our skin colors, and welcome each other into our world. Another thing the journey did for me, was make me a leader of men: white, red, brown and whatever, I molded them into some of the best soldiers and people you would ever want to associate with. We became our brother's keepers, we learned to see each others real character and established special relationships for one another knowing we are all special as God's children, where we sometimes become teachers in some capacity. We learned to totally respect and trust each other, especially on the battlefields during our service, where blacks equally shared responsibility, along with other people of different colors of skin, shapes, and form. We all shed the same tears, and felt the agony and pain for those who did not make it and we all carried that loss within, which remained a part of the whole!

Today, after fighting the war in Viet-Nam, why are there major U.S. corporations established in that country? There's Wal-Mart and many other American enterprises, commercial complexes." Why are there no businesses like those established in Africa? Or Haiti, where poverty exists? No jobs, no development, if America is to be the leader of the world, they must also establish economic growth in those countries as well, yet there are sanctions and discriminations against Haiti, a small country, ever since it won its independence from the French government in early 1700's. The United states suspended 3.4 million dollars in economic aid in December 1995, making it one of the poorest independent nation in this vicinity.

chapter 49

Change

Change is the keyword to be used in this election. The divine knowledge tells us everything must change, nothing remains the same. The young becomes the old with many treasured memories to be told, he who was first shall become the last, the revolution of all universal elements continue in a never ending cycle "We The People" must ensure this time around the cycle will not be more of the same!

This time around we must make the pieces fit, all the people shall pursue their inner journeys as well, in order to obtain the strength, faith, and courage to implement peace among the races, find a way to respect and if possible, love all people, create the Unity for the common cause, for all to prosper and achieve economic growth of our nation. We must ensure we as adults teach our children of our ancestors great civilization and culture. There should be a school debating team between all ethnic students to learn more of their culture and exchange ideas with each other, so that all shall have gained knowledge and better understanding of topics they bring to the table, of their race historical background, areas needing incorporation into the academic curricula, through proper endorsement and support of the City Council and the Mayor. I traveled the world and found out about people's civilization and culture. We The People must make this apriority!

Barack Obama is the man to take us as a nation where it needs to be, to have Unity, Pride and Character! I see him as a smart, intelligent man, dedicated to human and civil rights, who knows his purpose and direction the country needs to go into. He's wise enough to know and understand matters in order to accomplish his goals. He needs to be surrounded with seasoned, sharp, proficient Cabinet who can support his endeavors, as he upholds his ideals of service and accountability to this country and to the whole world. He's a man willing to listen and defend the people of America's best interest, a man who has worked diligently to keep himself abreast with White House policies and protocol as President of the United States of America, preparing himself to successfully perform the enormous task of leading the most powerful nation in the world as her Commander-in-Chief. He's well grounded in his life experiences, a man who will seek God's guidance with Understanding, Wisdom and Knowledge. The Creator says whenever we do things in his name his presence and blessing will be in abundance, especially in leading a nation comprising all God's children, wherever God is, there's never a battle lost! This is the most challenging battle for anyone! There's been corruption in all avenues of this political system, along with negligence leading our economy into a quick chaotic downfall with the exuberant costs of the war in Iraq, the skyrocketing prices of gas, mortgage foreclosures, the Wall Street scene that has plunged the world in a global crisis, the $700 billion bail-out proposal submitted needing only one person's approval, how such a thing happen? Yes, this is a critical period in this nation's history! Yet, Republican Presidential/Vice Presidential candidates can afford to be giving scripted speeches, addressing a beleaguered nation, where's their experience and expertise in public speaking? Obama to me revealed his sincerity by speaking to the people directly from his heart and soul, pure, honest and equipped with the knowledge and understanding of the whole scenario vis-à-vis the present socio-political genre, reflecting his preparedness to lead the nation. This election is gigantic task for all American people, especially the whites who exposes racism by saying: "1 cannot vote for a black man." If they knew the hidden truth, they possibly would think otherwise, in most cases. If these racist' people make statements like this, then they are like the ones who are still totally in the dark, who really can't love this country, these were the little children way back then who were brought by their parents to those lynching parties, taught into believing that blacks were inferior, were properties, and 3/5th of a human being, and yet these parents never told them about the courageous men and women of valor who fought for their inde-

pendence, which they enjoy today!
This is the biggest battle of our nation! This is the next step to
Martin Luther King, Jr.'s dream, he gave us a VISION, Obama
will accomplish that goal wherein all men shall become "We The
People". He's wise enough to know weapons, bombs, and missiles do not rule the world, they only destroy it, all great world
powers had them, yet they are no longer powerful today. God's
love, wisdom and knowledge has always reigned supreme in the
creation of all things. Obama knows that a good harmonious relationship with the Congress and Senate, with leaders of other nations, with the United Nations Council is where peace lies.
Leaders and representatives in this assembly will find a way to
address all problems, and finally come up with the solutions. He
knows keeping abreast with the economy here at home is the utmost concern at this point in time: creation of jobs, mortgage concerns - rendering a sound, structured program to alleviate issues,
of people caught up in some fraudulent scams. Another significant point to handle is racism, which I know he will resolutely
and vigorously resolve, to unite the many cultures and races of
people here, especially black and white issues dividing these two
factions, there will surely be difficulties in addressing the ridiculous white superiority over blacks. Black history being taught in
schools will increase the people's understanding of everything
blacks have contributed to the development of America's wealth
and economy through free slave labor, victories in war, whites will
gain more knowledge of their rich cultural heritage and powerful
African civilization, their enlightenment of such truth allows them
to reevaluate their racist's attitude at its core. Blessed with the
union of parents of both cultures, Obama has achieved a track
record of commitment and dedication to people of all races, of the
whites who possessed the wealth, and the blacks who manifested
such, through their enduring struggles on their behalf Is superiority a causal or resultant product of such historic transformation?
Does racism create perfection? History proved otherwise on many
battlefields, victory loomed in the hands of these oppressed "inferiors." Such that despite the Common Foe's display of racism,
physical abuse, hatred, murder and for lynchings, the blacks still

showed courage to forgive, patriotism and valor fighting his war, understanding, wisdom, knowledge, patience and fortitude for hundreds of years during their struggles to overcome, these were the real virtues of a man. Even with the infliction of more of the same by the whites, terrorism, physical and mental abuse, total disregard for human and civil rights for those held captives, denial of proper education.

Obama, as a leader will call for Unity between blacks and whites, and all others, for them to join hands in order to fulfill the vision of Martin Luther King, Jr., and the hopes of our ancestors. He will establish a more productive cultural group for the future of our youth, and the realization of tomorrow's New Dream! The dream of Challenge and Change by Barack Obama, who will surely give the nation the eyes to see, that we as a people can right the wrong of the past, unite to bring forth harmony and change, and enlighten the world that "We The People" will break the bonds that kept us separated and allowed the chaotic downfall of our vision, that disrupted positive approaches, and created the negative ideas that caused our country to falter under a crumbling leadership which made preposterous decisions, indulged in a unnecessary war, plunged into financial crisis that totally embarrassed the people just as much as racism still continues to do. America will have to be strong enough under this new leadership to show the world we, as a people, will stand together to restore our place among the great nations, and uphold peace and unity, instead of changing the whole world to fit our purpose! We shall begin here in our country, that has been abandoned by its governing elected officials, who made heinous decisions on world policies affecting us all, causing economic and social ills, who else could be blamed but they who plummeted us to this recession, they must be held accountable for all their actions, especially on the outsourcing of jobs, depriving us of our livelihood that is the mainstay of our family.

America is faced with a tremendous challenge, and I believe that if we can mend our racism and unite for the common goal of establishing the real standards of which America stands for, then we can make the pieces fit together, it's going to take the joint effort of all our citizens, to keep the tenacity and fortitude to rebuild

America. Together we shall pursue the journey upholding the virtues, principles, values of sacrifice and hard work to overcome and transcend this devastating environment

I started this book to call our nation together to defeat the racist Common Foe who has caused hatred, discrimination and racial divide for over 400 years. There's millions of people of all walks of life, creed and color who are willing to stand side by side to Change our country, to respect each other's character and not discriminate others with a different color of skin. We see how this regime has affected all of us, we must never again fall prey to another misdirected government, let us unite, bond and unify our Voice to powerfully reflect that "We The People" are ready for Change. We must embark on our future starting here at home, not oversees beyond our territorial jurisdiction, for the betterment of us all! Blacks, whites, and all others need to enlighten themselves of the black history for better understanding of our roots and contributions to this country, their struggles for 250 years of slavery, yet they held countless achievements with honor and patriotism, eventually creating a wealthy America, created financial corporations, banks and businesses around the world. Awareness of these strong achievements bridges gaps and generate peace among the people and all nations. We helped in gaining the independence, winning the Civil War, we know of the 350,000 blacks who turned the tide of the nation's future, we live our prosperous lives of technology largely due to thousands of inventions of blacks, read about the great civilization of Mother Africa, the roots and beginnings of mankind. I enjoyed writing this first book of mine, it was indeed a great Spiritual enlightenment for me, a journey of which I am still seeking the truth of all things, it will be somewhat controversial because it reveals the hidden truth of all things we, as blacks have struggled with as a people, yet we have been strong enough to overcome. The history is all there, and I encourage all to seek and find, there will be totally different outlooks on the black race, who has been unacknowledged, unappreciated, yet continues to remain forgiving, strong, intelligent, and caring, as a race of people!

The TIME is NOW! Voting time is set, and the Challenge is yours, to respond for this very powerful election, get registered, cast that sacred vote, for which our ancestors struggled and died for. We as a black people have paid the price to ensure we all get it right this time!

I read once a passage that stated:

> "Take my people in bondage, to the land
> Overshadowed by the wings of the Eagle
> Where when they take their blinders off
> Will give that Nation the
> Eyes to See.....

All things are a continuous circle, and all things must "CHANGE" nothing remains the same, and always the truth shall be revealed, in due time, this is the time for new knowledge, wisdom, leadership and direction for our people and nation now!

Peace be unto you all from all parts of this world of which we live, and especially to this country, and the birthplace of our New President, Barack Obama! Seek the spiritual guidance of our Creator and the Truth will set you Free!

chapter 50

African American Major Contributions to America: The Myth of White Intellectuality and Superiority.

Vivian Thomas: Formulator of First Open Heart Surgery Procedure: 1910 - 1985

John Hopkins Hospital, 1944 November 29, one of the greatest operations was performed, the operation was the first of its kind. There was a serious heart condition referred as the "Blue Baby Syndrome." This condition is where a baby is born without the heart operating properly, causing a low oxygen rate which causes the baby to have blue lips, eyelids, fingernails and toes, instead of the normal color of pink. It hurts the baby to breathe, these babies, when older would have to be isolated from all others because of the stress on them physically, not being able to move without the needed oxygen. In a short period of time this condition could be the cause of their death. If this procedure were not created, thousands would have died because no medical scientist or doctors knew how to perform such a delicate procedure. This operation had to be done while the heart was functioning.

On this day in that hospital, the whole medical team of surgeons, as well as heart specialists were to perform a successful surgery that would change the medical genre, in saving babies' lives - as the whole world awaited for the results!

Even before the operation, word was out about this attempted miraculous procedure, the world mass media: radio, newspapers, television reporters were all on hand for the coverage of this extraordinary event! This innovative procedure which took months to develop was created by one of the doctor's staff, a person who worked long and extended hours in the laboratory, perfecting numerous operating techniques on dogs. He knew that the procedure on the baby was safe. He had given the dogs medicine to alleviate their pain, and that each operation that failed taught him a new way to operate. He made special tools to be utilized that could cut and sew in tiny and limited spaces. After almost 200 operations, the quiet, careful scientist operated on a dog named Anna. This little dog survived, blood flowed through her lungs, giving the oxygen her body needed. His cutting and stitching was perfect, the doctor who performed the operation stated: "They seemed to be something the Lord made!"

Eileen Saxon, the "Blue Baby," first patient ever to have this surgery, was fifteen months old. She weighed only nine pounds, her lips were blue, her face had a soft blue color because her heart was not functioning well - pumping blood into her lungs, they way it normally needed to do.

Dr. Blalock, the heart surgeon, had hired the young man as his medical assistant, working in his research laboratory. This man had formerly been a carpenter, cautious, doing his measurements twice each time in order to make an accurate result, thereby cutting just once, never wasted wood, nor time. He saved money to fulfill his dream of becoming a doctor. The nation was in hard times then, companies lost money, the stock market crashed, his bank went out of business that he lost every dollar he had saved for his future. Thus, he was so fortunate to have this job that the heart surgeon gave him, through the introduction of a friend. This brilliant and powerful doctor he worked with was a great teacher, however, he was radical, too, ranting and raving at him at times. Approximately a year after working with this doctor the young man could no longer endure his ordeal, so he ran out. The doctor managed to bring him back, promising never to yell at him again. And he never did!

Times got increasingly tough for this tenacious and dedicated young man, who was doing difficult experiments, perfecting his surgical skills by operating on animals, while struggling to feed his family with his meager salary. The doctor did not raise his pay as he promised causing him to find other jobs to make ends meet. Finally, he told the doctor he was quitting. Responding to the situation the doctor accessed the young man to a financial assistance with some scholarship which helped him get through his studies.

In 1940 Dr. Blalock accepted a very important position at John Hopkins Hospital in Baltimore, Maryland, so he asked the young man to come with him and be part of his team. The young man accepted, despite the meager pay, he got a job as a bartender to cover his family's financial needs. In 1943 Dr. Helen Tussig requested to meet with Dr. Blalock and the young man, she showed them the sick "Blue Babies" who would not live long. Dr. Tussig knew that heart surgery had never been envisioned done with the human heart, however she requested the two men to find a way and do it, to save the children's lives. Other doctors warned "nobody should operate on someone's beating heart" which was then the basic rule in the medical field, with emphatic word that "it should not be broken." However, Dr. Blalock and his confident assistant did not listen. As stated at the beginning, this young man had already operated on two hundred dogs before coming up with a successful procedure which he shared with Dr. Blalock, who gave his final decision to do the surgery on the little baby Eileen.

The operating room was all prepared for the operation, the tools and instruments ready, all the surgical team were in place, the nurses ready to hand Dr. Blalock his instruments. You could hear a pin drop, the doctor hesitated, looked puzzled, looked over his shoulder and suddenly hollered out an order to get his young assistant. The nurses ran looking for the young man through the research laboratories, they finally found him working there as though it was just another day. It was not!

The young assistant raced to the operating room, washed up and put on surgical gloves and mask. The doctor pointed to a wooden stool adjacent to his right shoulder, so the assistant could have a clear view and could confer with him throughout the procedure. This time the doctor took the instrument and began, step by step this young assistant instructed him and talked the doctor through all phases of the delicate surgery. The first artery, the clamps that the young man made stopped the bleeding. All in the room saw two men become one fantastic operating team, one was the Chief Surgeon of the famous hospital, the other a thirty-four year old black medical researcher who was not a doctor at all, but who was directing the doctors of every move in that successful open heart surgery. This man that developed and formulated this pioneering procedure that would save millions of lives later was Vivien Thomas, a black man!

The surgeon sewed the artery in place, it took three hours the operation, they saved a baby, so small that its arm was only a bit larger than the doctor's index finger. Vivien Thomas stepped down and went back to the laboratory. The hospital and all watching them was glowing with excitement. Within two weeks the baby was a healthy pink, a day that they would never forget! The multi-media - newspapers, radio, TV carried such an astounding news all over the world, indeed a marvelous, auspicious milestone in medical history! Thomas assisted Dr. Blalock on the first hundred operations, people brought their babies from all over the world.

Here's the tragic ending to the whole story, newspapers all over the United States and around the world never mentioned the main person who was responsible for guiding, orchestrating and overseeing that successful surgical procedure, their stories only mentioned Dr. Blalock and Dr. Tussig in their articles along with their pictures. And quiet as it was kept, the doctor even had to be stopped and corrected from making an error, the very first minutes of the surgery, wanting to make the initial incision on the wrong place! That was why he needed Vivien at his side, he never knew the full procedure or technique to accomplish it alone! He had to confer with Thomas on every move. The articles and pictures stayed on the headlines of every newspaper for about a week, however, it was always giving their names and pictures, but missing that of the one man responsible for saving millions of lives here in America.

Dr. Blalock worked had worked with Thomas for many years, he depended on his genius for surgery, but never invited him to the celebration party, the Doctor could not overcome being raised to believe that one race was better than another. It took a long time for Americans to see the person inside and not the color of the outside, and believe me, all of those racists who took their wives and children to see white people killing black men and women, are responsible for the hatred attitude that exist today. This ungrateful racist doctor showed his true color at the end!

I visited John Hopkins's Hospital when I was stationed at Aberdeen Proving Grounds in Maryland in 1970, I walked in the main lobby entrance, the first thing I saw was a very large picture of Vivien Thomas. Doctor Denton Cooley, who had been a part of the team that performed the first operation described Thomas's work stating: "There wasn't a false move, not a wasted motion when he operated." He remembered it was Vivien who worked it all out in the laboratory, there were no heart experts then, that was the beginning that changed the world of heart surgery, there's been millions of such operation not just on these children here, but on all other countries as well.

Dr. Blalock died in 1964, Vivien Thomas was fifty-four years old then, he would go on running the laboratory for another fifteen years. The man who could not afford medical school later trained hundreds of surgeons. John Hopkin's Hospital made him an honorary Doctor of Laws in 1976, although he was teaching students for years, he was officially appointed as an instructor of Surgery, his picture was painted and placed in the same hall as that of Dr. Blalock, along with a picture of the dog Anna whom Thomas successfully operated on first.

The carpenter who became a scientist, had proved to the world that surgery on a beating heart could be done safely. He retired from the Hospital in 1979. Vivien was born on August 29, 1910 in New Iberia, Louisiana, his father William was a carpenter, his mother Mary was so sure that her next child would be a girl she named it Vivian before it was born, when boy number five arrived, she kept the name, but changed it to Vivien to make it into a boy's name. He died on 26 November 1985.

So when you Common foe racist people out there who ever had an open heart surgery done, just know it was a Black man who created that procedure saved you and your loved ones, isn't that amazing? When whites were killing blacks, a black man's creation was saving millions of whites. Ever since blacks arrived in this country, they have been contributing to white's welfare and wealth, read your history and open your eyes to this hidden knowledge.

DR. DANIEL HALE WILLIAMS
HEART SURGEON

On July 1893 Dr. Daniel Hale Williams made history at Chicago's Provident Hospital by performing the first successful open heart surgery operating on James Cornish who was brought into the emergency room with a stab wound to the heart. The attending doctors sewed up the external wound, however Cornish's condition began to deteriorate. They concluded that he had internal bleeding. Dr. Williams was informed of his condition by the attending medical physicians. Williams took it upon himself to perform his own procedure on Cornish. Other doctors tried this delicate procedure on previous patients, but none of them survived.

Dr. Williams opened the chest cavity, finding the knife had slashed an artery and tissue around the heart, he used catgut thread to sew up the internal wounds, the operation was the first of its kind to be successfully done. Cornish lived for another 20 years after that, the first open heart surgery ever performed in America.

He is remembered as a great black surgeon and founder of one of the first interracial hospitals which was training African American nurses and doctors in the United States, founded in 1891 they provided care for all colors. During his long career Williams also served as chief surgeon at Howard University's Freeman Hospital in Washington D.C, he was also the first African American to be appointed associate attending surgeon at St. Luke's Hospital in Chicago. He retired in 1920.

DR. LOUIS T. WRIGHT
SURGEON / PHYSICIAN

Dr. Louis T. Wright achieved many firsts during his long career as a surgeon and physician. A true pioneer of medicine, he was the first Black to be appointed to the Staff of a New York municipal hospital, the first Black to experiment with antibiotic aureomycin on humans and the first black physician to head a public interracial hospital. Louis also specialized in surgery, associated with head injuries and fractures, he devised a neck brace for neck injuries, which is still being used today.

BENJAMIN BANNEKER
ASTRONOMER 1731-1806

In 1761 he carved a wooden clock by hand, using only two models, a pocket watch and an old picture of a clock. The clock kept nearly perfect time for 50 years. A solar eclipse happens when the moon passes between the sun and the earth, casting a shadow on the earth. As an astronomer, he correctly predicted that a solar eclipse would occur in 1789. A few years later he published an almanac more accurate than the one published by Benjamin Franklin. Banneker also helped survey the site for Washington, D.C., the nation's capital. When Major Pierre - Charles L' Enfant of England, the man President George Washington selected to design the new capital resigned and went to France, Benneker ensured that the surveys continued, hence the nation's capital was eventually built.

GEORGE W. CARVER
BOTANIST 1864 -1943

When George Washington Carver died on 5 January 1943, he was one of America's most honored scientist. From his modest laboratory at the Tuskegee Institute in Alabama, he rescued a dying agricultural economy in the south by helping to institute methods to replenish the soil, thereby increasing crop production. He discovered hundreds of products that could be made from the peanut, the sweet potato, the pecan, and he became an authority on plant's diseases.

Born on a plantation in Diamond Grove, Missouri in 1860, him, his mother, and sister were kidnapped by a band of night raiders. The plantation owner got George back in exchange of a race horse, however, he never saw his mother and sister again. A university in Kansas offered him a scholarship but when the President saw that he was Black, he turned him away. Finally, Simpson

College in Iowa accepted George as the school's first black student. He also became the first Black student to attend the Iowa State College of Agriculture and Mechanical Arts.

BESSIE COLEMAN
AVIATOR 1893 -1926

Bessie Coleman was the first Black woman to fly an airplane. She was also the first African American to earn an international pilot's license. Bessie was determined to fly at a young age, she applied to a number of aviation schools, but everyone rejected her because of her skin color. A friend told her to learn to speak French and apply to a school in France, she did, and was accepted.

From 1922 to 1926 Bessie performed flying exhibitions at air shows were she executed daredevil maneuvers. She gave lectures on aviation, she wanted to inspire young African Americans to enter the field of flying. In April of 1926 during a practice flight, the woman they called the world's greatest flyer was mysteriously killed when the plane developed an engine malfunction, and she was thrown from the plane.

LLOYD AUGUSTUS HALL
CHEMIST 1894 -1971

During his long career, Hall was granted more than 100 patents in the United States and abroad. Hi knowledge and innovations in food chemistry earned him numerous honors, appointments and seats on the boards of prominent organizations. 1916 Lloyd earned a degree in pharmaceuticals chemistry, he went on to earn a graduate degree from the University of Chicago and the University of Illinois. He had impressed a personnel officer during a telephone interview. But when he went to the office in person, the personnel officer, seeing Lloyd was African American, told the energetic young man: "We don't take niggers." He later developed a new meat preserving process, he created sterilization techniques for foods and spices, and even patented a process that reduced the time needed to cure bacon.

GUION BLUFORD JR.
AEROSPACE ENGINEER 1942-

During the early morning hours of August 30, 1983 the space shuttle Challenger blasted off for its third flight into space. Among the five-man crew was Lieutenant Colonel Guion S. Bluford Jr. For "Guy" this was a dream come true, as a child growing up in Philadelphia, he would always close his eyes and visualize himself on a spaceship headed into the solar system. As a youth he built model airplanes and studied their movement, he spent countless hours trying to understand the dynamics of flight. In 1960 Guy entered Pennsylvania State University to study Aerospace Engineering, four years later earning distinguished Air Force ROTC honors, he received his pilot wings. During the Viet-Nam war, he flew 144 combat missions, while assigned to the 557th Tactical F Fighter Squadron. His years as a fighter pilot were challenging, however, he never lost his desire to explore space.

In January, 1978 Guy was selected as a candidate for the astronaut program, now he had the chance to become an astronaut and fly into space. After successfully completing the rigorous NASA Training program, he was chosen to be an astronaut on August of 1979. On August 30, 1983 Guy's dream came true, the Challenger blasted off, giving the dark sky an enormous illumination for miles across the land, night powerfully turned to day for a moment in time! Inside the spacecraft Guy must have thought "Mission Accomplished!" Once in space, he helped launch a $45 Million satellite. President Reagan called from earth below saying to Bluford: "You are paving the way for many others and making it plain that we are in an era of brotherhood here in our land!" Bluford told the President that he was only part of a Team and that he was pleased to be a participant. Later he would say: "My flight on the shuttle represented another step forward!" Opportunities do exist for black youngsters, if they work hard and strive to take advantage of those opportunities. PEOPLE, TAKE NOTE OF THAT!

RONALD MCNAIR
PHYSICIST - ASTRONAUT 1950 -1986

The excitement could be felt everywhere, only a few more minutes and the shuttle called Challenger would take off for a six day flight through outer space, this would be McNair's second flight mission. On February 1984 he also served as Mission Specialist on an eight-day flight aboard Mission 41 - B. Ronald was the second Black astronaut in space. On his day in January 1986 a tragic accident happened. McNair and six other astronauts on board died in an explosion just 73 seconds after the spaceship's launching at Cape Canaveral, Florida.

MAE JEMISON
ASTRONAUT 1956-

In August 1987 Dr. Mae Jemison was in between patients when she received at phone call at a hospital in Los Angeles, California from a representative of the National Aeronautics and Space Administration (NASA), she was told that she had been chosen as an astronaut candidate. She could become the first Black African American woman to travel in space! Mae was a very multi-talented woman with notable accomplishments. She received her Bachelor of Science degree in Chemical Engineering and a Bachelor of Arts degree in African and Afro-American Studies from Stanford. From there she enrolled at Cornell University Medical College. She traveled to Cuba, Kenya and Thailand, working in Medical Training programs. She also worked in Africa with the Peace Corps. She had applied to NASA, and out of the 2000 applicants, she came out one of the 15 selected for the training class. In 1988 Mae completed one year of training and evaluation, in August 1992 she traveled into space on the Space Lab J, becoming the first Black woman astronaut to do so, a now much sought after speaker and consultant.

ROBERT H. LAWRENCE
ASTRONAUT

Air Force Major Lawrence became the first Black astronaut on June 30,1967, he completed his training and was to become one of the pilots in America's Manned Orbiting Laboratory Program. However he was killed during the landing of his F 104 Star fighter on 8 December 1967 at the age of 32, he never got the opportunity to venture into space.

THURGOOD MARSHALL
SUPREME COURT JUSTICE
1908 -1993

When Thurgood Marshall died in 1993 he was the second Justice to lie in state at the Supreme court's Chambers. This honor capped the outpouring of praise for the Court's first Black Justice. His tenure as Chief Counsel for the National Association for the Advancement of Color People (NAACP) and founder of its Legal Defense and Educational Fund, made him one of America's most influential and best known lawyers.

Marshall once said that his father told him: "If anyone calls you nigger, you not only have my permission to fight him, you got my orders to do so!" He was one of our nation's greatest lawyer, yet he had been turned down admission to the University of Maryland before, an all -white law school, an institution whose segregation he later challenged and defeated in Murray v. Maryland (1936). He then entered the law school at Harvard University. Marshall would become the architect of new strategies that increasingly attacked segregation itself. Plessy v. Fergusson (1896), a case involving segregated public railroads in Louisiana had decreed segregation to be constitutional as long as facilities for both races were equal. In a series of cases concerning graduate education, Marshall and the NAACP began asking whether separate could ever be equal. Each victory in Murray and other law school cases as Gaines v. Missouri and Sweath v. Painter brought the Supreme Court closer to toppling Plessy's "separate but equal" formula.

The case that finally ended legal segregation in America was Brown v. Board of Education. Drawing on psychological and sociological evidence Marshall argued that the mere fact of racial separation even without gross inequality, irrevocably harmed African American children. The Court unanimously agreed. Marshall brought 32 cases before the Supreme Court, he won 29 of them. The Constitution which degraded blacks as property, chattel and 3/5th of a man was in time corrected by a Black man with Divine guidance. Without the black man fighting and dying to secure the nation's Independence from the British, there would never have been a Constitution. And those who totally disregarded these black men's courage and patriotism, orchestrating such Document, finally felt the hand of justice establishing that those brave black men did not die in vain! Marshall, a true fighter for equal justice prevailed. He died January 24, 1993 in Bethesda, Maryland. An advocate of "the right of every American to an equal start in life" which the racist Common Foe totally disregarded for hundreds of years.

DR. RALPH BUNCHE
AMERICAN DIPLOMAT AND POLITICAL SCIENTIST
NOBEL PEACE PRIZE WINNER, 1950, 1904 -1971

At the age of 13 Ralph was orphaned and was sent to live with his grandmother, Lucy Johnson in Los Angeles. Early on Lucy not only insisted she would ensure that Ralph was self-reliant and proud of his race, but that he, a high school valedictorian, go to college. Bunche enrolled at the University of California and graduated in 1927, he went on to graduate school at Harvard University where he became the first Black American to earn a Ph. D. in Political Science from an American university. And this is also where he won the prize for his Outstanding Doctoral Thesis on Social Sciences in 1934. He conducted his postdoctoral research on African colonialism at Northwestern University, the London School of Economics and University of Cape Town, where he defied the South African government's objections to housing a black scholar. Bunche expressed his commitment to racial integration and to economic improvement for workers in civil rights protest and in establishing the National Negro Congress in 1936. He was the first black American to run a departmental division of the federal government, and still continued to work on African Colonial issues.

Bunche first made his name as a peace-maker in 1949 when defying all expectations, he negotiated the truce that ended the first Arab-Israeli War. Originally sent to Jerusalem in 1948 as the Assistant to the United Nations mediator Count Folke Bernadotte, Bunche stepped in when Bernadotte was assassinated and worked almost single handedly to bring Israel and the Arab states to an agreement, for his efforts Bunch was awarded the Nobel Price for Peace in 1950.

BARBARA CHARLINE JORDAN
AFRICAN AMERICAN TEXAS STATE SENATOR
1936 -1996

Barbara Jordan was the first African American political pioneer of her time since 1883, the first woman ever to be elected to the Texas Senate and the first Southern Black woman to serve in the U.S. Congress, a spellbinding orator. She may be best remembered for the speech she gave as a member of the House Judiciary Committee which in 1974 determined the impeachment of President Richard Nixon. She stated that although the U.S. Constitution's clause: "We the people..." had not originally included her as an African American, and as a woman, yet she had faith in the Constitution and refused to be "an idle spectator to its subversion" by the President.

Jordan attended Phillis Wheatley High School, was an exemplary student. As a member of the debating team she won numerous awards, including the National Ushers Oratorical Prize in 1953. Determined to be a lawyer she enrolled at the historically Black Texas Southern University (TSU). She majored in Government and, with the guidance of debating coach Tom Freeman, polished her oratorical skills. She persuaded Freeman to include her in an all-male traveling debating team, despite his policy of never taking women on national tours, he conceded. Blacks were customarily excluded from white debating contests. After a period of time, she began going around the United States to debate white teams, and became one of the first African American to equal white debaters from Harvard. She stated: "I woke to the necessity that someone had to push integration along in a private way if it were ever going to happen." She went on to attend Boston University Law School. Eyeing a political career, she volunteered on the Kennedy Johnson campaign, her public speaking talents were noted and she was put on public speaking circuit for Harris County Democrats. Barbara's first bid for a seat on the Texas State Senate in 1962 - '64, she lost. Running again in 1966 after the Civil Rights Act, she won against a very popular white liberal by a two to one margin. She was instrumental in setting up the first Texas Minimum Wage Bill and she sponsored much of the state's environmental legislation. In 1972 she was elected to the U.S. House of Representatives, where she became a member of the Judiciary Committee and won national recognition for her moving indictment of President Richard Nixon during the Watergate hearings. In 1978 she would run for Governor or for the U.S. Senate, she was also mentioned as a possible candidate for the U.S. Supreme Court, but in 1979 she retired from Congress, afflicted with multiple sclerosis, a neuro-muscular disease. She garnered the Eleanor Roosevelt Humanities Award in 1984 for her achievements, and earned more than twenty Honorary Doctorates from leading U.S. Universities. A woman I admired tremendously as a person and for her work for civil rights and justice within the system. This she demonstrated in "The Nixon Indictment." Where's the Barbara Jordan of today? That determined force for correctness is truly needed today! A strong and powerful voice was heard throughout our nation, and its result and impact caused the downfall of a President for deceiving "We The People."

NEIL DEGRASSE TYSON
ASTROPHYSICIST 1948

One of my favorite astrophysicist is Mr. Tyson, a well - renown spokesman for our solar system wonderment. I bought one of his books entitled: "Origins, Fourteen Billion Years of Cosmic Evolution." He's an extraordinary man and teacher of the treasures of our universal system of things. As a young kid growing up in Philadelphia I was introduced to the city's planetarium in Center City, it was absolutely amazing, sitting in this very large darkened room, with all the embodiment of the solar system revolving all around me. It was awesome! I often visited that planetarium and found it fascinating each and every time. Whenever I see him on one of the television programs, it is still mind boggling, the enlightenment he projects to his audiences and he only gets better each and every time I tune in.

Neil received a Bachelor's degree in Physics from Harvard University, a Master's degree in Astronomy from the University of Texas, and a Doctorate degree in Astrophysics from Columbia University. After his childhood dream of becoming an astrophysicist, he was one of the limited few blacks on that field. He was selected to a research position at Princeton University. Neil, after a number of years of research was appointed and became one of the youngest Directors ever in one of the world's largest and most significant planetarium: "The American Museum of Natural History" in New York.

He has written a number of books and articles, including his Biography. "The Sky is Not the Limit" is another masterpiece like "The Origin" I mentioned above, which explains the soul stirring leap in our understanding of the Universe.

In my personal journey during meditation, I am in those celestial boundless zones and structures of galaxies, and dimensions of Creation where only my Divine and Spiritual enlightenment allows me to become part of the Manifester of all Things and Times, where I feel the love I need in this world of which we exist!

OPRAH GAIL WINFREY
ACADEMY AWARD NOMINATED ACTRESS
AFRICAN AMERICAN TALK SHOW HOST
PRODUCER OF THE SYNDICATED
"OPRAH WINFREY SHOW"
January 1954

What can I say about Oprah? She's been a beacon of light and power for us all! After a troubled period in her youth, her mother sent her to live with her father, a barber and businessman in Nashville, Tennessee. While with her father, it seemed that things began to fall in place, under his guidance. She excelled academically and in public speaking as well. At the age of sixteen, she got the first place in a Public Speaking Contest, the price being partial scholarship to Tennessee State University. This was sponsored by the Elk's Club. As a freshman she worked briefly as a radio newscaster before winning two local beauty pageants which helped her to land a news anchor position at WTVF - TV in Nashville. In 1976, only a few months shy of her Bachelors Degree at the University, she was given a job as a reporter and the evening news co - anchor at WJZ in Baltimore. Her station manager realized that she would be better suited to co-host WJZ's morning talk show "People Are Talking." Oprah helped turned the show into a raving success with her appealing personality, interviewing style and charismatic presence. After eight years as the co-host, she was offered a job as the host of A.M. Chicago Talk Show, that aired opposite of Phil Donahue's very popular morning show. In one month Winfrey equaled Donahue's and in three months surpassed his rating. Donahue acknowledged her rating supremacy and moved his show.

New York in 1985, also in such a year the A.M. Chicago Show was renamed "The Oprah Winfrey Show" and was syndicated in 1986. It became the highest rated talk show in television history. By 1997 fifteen to twenty million viewers watched it daily in the United States, as well as her fans in more than 132 countries as well! The show has received twenty five Emmy Awards, six of them for Best Host! She was named one of the most influential people in the world. I loved the part she played in "Color Purple."

In 1986 she founded HARPO Productions, becoming only the third woman to own her own television and film studios, where she also produces dramatic mini TV series: "TheWoman of Brewster Place" (1988), "The Wedding" (1998). In addition to supporting African American Literature through her television movies, she presents an on-air book club that has brought new readers to various unknown writers. An entertainer, political activist, she was instrumental in the passage of the "National Child Protection Act" in 1991. In 1993 President Bill Clinton signed Oprah's Bill into law. In her many ventures she donates time and money to efforts aimed at protecting children and establishing academic scholarships. A wonderful and very talented woman who has given so much of herself to America and the world at large, in the pursuit of Unity, Peace and Enlightenment to the millions who tune in.

ASA PHILLIP RANDOLPH
FOUNDER AND RESIDENT OF "THE BROTHERHOOD OF SLEEPING CAR PORTERS"
ARCHITECT OF THE "MARCH ON WASHINGTON MOVEMENT FOR ESTABLISHING THE FAIR EMPLOYMENT PRACTICES COMMITTEE" in 1941
ARCHITECT of the "MARCH ON WASHINGTON" in 1963

Randolph, a civil rights leader, spent most of his time as a labor leader working to bring more and better jobs to African Americans. After a long, successful battle to win representation for the nation's Pullman porters, Randolph was instrumental in forming the FEPC which protected African Americans against job discrimination in the army and defense industries. In addition, he co-founded and edited "The Messenger," the socialist black magazine.

Randolph grew up in Jacksonville, Florida, graduated from the Cookman Institute in 1907 and was valedictorian of his class. He found menial jobs until he moved to New York City, worked as an elevator operator and took classes at the City College of New York and New York University. In 1914 he met Chandler Owen, whose progressive politics and interest in socialism matched his own. They founded "The Messenger," where editorials strongly opposed the United States entry into World War I saying that: "no intelligent Negro is willing to lay down his life for the United States as it now exists." The magazine offered a more radical voice than that of W.E. Du Bois conventional New York Age. The Messenger, with its advocacy on labor crimes, was especially popular among the Pullman porters, all of whom were black, serving white railroad passengers in luxurious sleeping cars. The Pullman Company was the largest employer of African Americans after the Civil War.

Many of the Pullman porters were college graduates who enjoyed great respect within the communities, but at work they were subject to unfair and discriminatory practices. A relentless fighter for fair employment, he was instrumental in opening opportunities for blacks in the defense industries. President Roosevelt issued Executive Order 8002 which outlawed such discrimination and also established the FEPC to investigate any breaches of the order.

Randolph also fought for desegregation of the Armed Force of which President Truman signed in July 1948. Truman signed Executive Order 9981, finally ending the historical segregation of African American Soldiers. A man who accomplished his many goals for the betterment of African Americans.

ELIJAH MUHAMMAD
1897-1975
LEADER AND FOUNDER OF THE NATION OF ISLAM

Elijah's grandfather named him after the biblical Elijah, and all through his young life, he was teasingly referred to as "The Prophet" He was exposed to the ministry at an early age by his father who was a church pastor. He took an avid interest in Christian Theology, but later on broke away from it because of his father's fire and brimstone sermons, causing him to question the gloomy interpretations of its spirituality. His father also introduced him to Islam.

As a young boy of about ten years old, he left school to work with his sister chopping firewood to help provide economically in the family's financial problems. As a child, he was sheltered somewhat from the brutal racism of the area in which he lived. Then the racist Common Foe raised his ugly head, he witnessed the lynching of an 18 year old friend, then another incident occurred while he was walking home from work, a white man taunted him with the severed ears of a black person. These horrible incidents caused him to seek an escape, he was quoted: "I had seen enough of the white man's brutality in Georgia to last me for 26,000 years. A few years later after numerous jobs, he moved to Detroit, got married, and fathered two children. It was at this time that his father began to speak to him about the Islamic Movement.

In 1931 Elijah attended his first meeting where he met Wallace D. Fard, he became fully immersed in its teachings, causing him to abandon his "Slave Owner" surname. He was initially called Karriem, and later Muhammad. He made rapid advancement and became Fard's top assistant. Later he was named Supreme Minister, with full administrative power. Under the police hostilities, he moved the Nation to Chicago, where it prospered and evolved.

Under Elijah they started to invest in radios and modern farm equipment. In order for black separation to succeed, he believed total economic in depended was crucial. In 1945 the Nation purchased 140 acres of farmland in Michigan, two years later a Nation-owned grocery store. The Nation's influence spread throughout various black communities around the United States. As a leader in quest for black nationalism, he was considered a hostile force by the United States government. He served a jail sentence for draft evasion during World War II and was wired by the FBI for more than two decades. Nevertheless, he continued his dream of independence from white supremacy in America. When blacks were refused jobs and education he started his own businesses and schools. The spiritual mosque made the white Common Foe feel threatened for some reason. They did not provide for black people, here was a black man who showed black people you can achieve your own if united, and he did a magnificent job as we all see today! These people of the Nation of Islam are very articulate, well-mannered, intelligent and well-dressed. I am truly impressed with their accomplishment to this day. Muhammad's emphasis on black self-sufficiency later turned a lot of government heads, so much so that the Mayor of Chicago, Richard Daley in 1974 declared March 29 "Honorable Elijah Muhammad Day" in Chicago. This man was truly an achiever of his dream, we as black people should have followed his lead, instead of being refused jobs, education, discriminated against in sports and other fields of the business world, we should have found a way to be self-sufficient in this racist white man's world, where he thinks he rules supreme! So now we see the Nation of Islam still maintains its own business and honorable lifestyle. A Man worthy to be Praised for his accomplishments and what the Nation still stand for, under the leadership of **Louis Abdul Farrakhan**, who orchestrated the Million Man March in Washington D.C. in March of 1995. It goes to show while we as black race ran around hating and killing each other, a man who had a dream showed his followers how to unite, use their skills and intellect to create their own. What the Common Foe had wanted to prove was that blacks are not smart enough to achieve any of this or do that! Islam Nation has been on its own since 1941, while the majority of blacks are not employed, yet they are prospering, having their own schools, which are not some racially gang-infested institutions now where whites are hanging nooses, and telling blacks what part of the school grounds they cannot utilize, where there's cops in every hallway, teachers having problems controlling classrooms, children showing up with pants hanging off their butts, girls with mini dresses with lots of sex appeal, how much are our children learning in our public schools? So it's a price we pay for not managing our children, and that of parents as well, we as black people have failed our children tremendously, and have lost their respect as well.

I look at **Richard Williams**, father of **Venus** and **Serena**, who took his girls out of public schools, taught them at home and look at the achievements these young, intelligent, beautiful girls have accomplished for at least the last 15 years, and still winning the goal, must I say more other than WAKE UP PEOPLE! The handwriting has been on the wall since the white business was allowed to send your jobs overseas, and endorsed by your government officials to do so. We are the highest consumer of all items in America, yet we have nothing to show for it. Elijah Muhammad used his wisdom and built what everyone else thought could not happen. When there's unity, sincere togetherness and commitment we can do it all! I salute Elijah and Farrakhan for their achievements. Are we sharp enough to follow their lead?

I could sit here and write of thousands of black men and women who have made a tremendous difference in the lives of the American people of all ethnic groups. It's noted, however, throughout history of this country, that black people are ignorant, not intelligent, incapable of that, not capable of this, which is totally absurd. Yet the white racist have implanted this ludicrous notion in the minds of their gullible-minded white followers, who as of this day still think they are superior, only to find out at this point in time, that they have been duped by their own racist bigoted brothers!

As I've mentioned throughout these pages, find me a white superior person and I'll find a black man to talk circles around him, at whatever he thinks he's superior in. The knowledge the outer forces stole out of Africa still have them puzzled as to how the African civilization possessed this advanced knowledge or how they obtained it. All knowledge begins with the African cultures.

Professor **Peter Schmidt** and Professor of Engineering **Donald Avery** of Brown University announced to the world that between 1,500 - 2,000 years ago, Africans living on the western shores of Lake Victoria, Tanzania had produced "carbon steel," this announcement was made in 1978. They stated the Africans had done this preheated forced-draft furnaces, a method that was technologically more sophisticated than any developed in Europe until the mid 18th Century, how was this so, or how can it be, perhaps the most superior minds were those of the first black civilizations possessed. Schmidt and Avery unearthed 13 Iron Age furnaces, they were all of the same composition of steel. The temperature achieved in the blast furnace of these African steel smelting machine was higher than achieved in an European machine until modern times. It was approximately 1.800*C, some 200 to 400*C higher than the highest reached in European cold blast bloomers. The African superiority was due to the fact that they preheated the air blast by inserting blowpipes into the base of the furnace.

American scientists **B.M. Lynch** *and* **L.H. Robbins** uncovered an astronomical laboratory in Kenya, it was dated 300 years before Christ, found on the edge of Lake Turkana. It was in the river of an African Stonehenge with huge pillars of basalt like the stumps of petrified trees lying at angles on the ground. Not far from the area were stones standing in circles around graves. But these huge stone pillars at Namoratunga II were different from ones found earlier, there were nineteen of them, arranged in rows and set at such angles that the sense of an order, precise and significant, immediately struck the observers.

It was known that the modern Cushites in Eastern Africa had a calendar based on the rising of certain stars and constellations. Upon evaluating they found the prehistoric beginnings of one of the most accurate pre Christian calendar. They found that each stone was aligned with a star as it rose in 300 B.C. Each stone lined up in accordance with the solar system, the star Bellatrix lined up with Stone 17, the constellation Orion with Stone 16, the star Sirius with Stone 15, Saiph with Stone 14, all fell in order except for one, the exception was a stone too small to be a line of sight. They concluded: "attests to the complexity of pre historic cultural developments in sub Saharan Africa. It strongly suggests that an accurate and complex calendar system based on astronomical reckoning was developed by the first millennium B.C. in eastern Africa.

Far more than the megalithic observatory found in Kenya before Christ was the discovery of an extremely complex knowledge of astronomy among a people in West Africa known as the Dogon. They live in a mountainous area of the Republic of Mali, approximately 200 miles from where the legendary university of Timbuktu once was. The astronomer priests of the Dogon had for centuries, it seems, a very modern view of our solar system and the universe, the rings of Saturn, the moons of Jupiter, the spiral billions of worlds in space, like the circulation of blood within the body of God. They knew that the moon was a "barren world," they said it was "dry and dead like dried blood." They also knew things far advance of their time, intricate details about a star which no one can see except the most powerful of telescopes. They observed and studied its mass and its nature. They not only saw it, they plotted and orchestrated its orbit almost until the year 2000. And they did all these between five and seven hundred years ago.

Hunter Adams III, a scientist at the Argonne National Laboratory (Argonne I), wrote in: "African observers of the Universe: The Sirius Question," has thrown the most recent light on the scientific breakthrough of these Africans. He not only summarized the work done by anthropologists on the Dogon but he poses the gross prejudices of Eurocentric scientists who try to explain away what the Dogons have done, who would not accept that African astronomer priests could have developed a science of the heavens so advanced that it could yield knowledge which until the 20th Century escaped European observation.

Two French anthropologists, **Marcel Griaule** and **Germaine Dieterlen** lived with and studied the Dogon people from 1931 to 1956, watched and recorded everything, even drew diagrams of the evocative architecture of their village, which was patterned after the human body. These two actually were initiated into the tribe. Griaule became so loved and trusted that when he died, quarter of a million Africans turned up at his funeral. Yet, in spite of this relationship, they had to pass through stage after stage on the highest ladder of their knowledge, this stage was known as the "the clear word."

Among the revelation of this stage was the Dogon's intimate knowledge of a star within the Sirius star system. They had a ceremony to Sirius every sixty years, when the orbit of Jupiter and Saturn converge. The thing about it though, was, although Sirius is the brightest star in the sky, the ceremony was not for Sirius but for its companion Sirius B, a star so small, so dense, so difficult to perceive. It is truly amazing that any medieval science was more aware of it, the Dogons were not only aware of it, but saw it as the basis of that star system while Sirius A, the big, bright star we know so well, was simply the point around which this unusual little star orbited. To the Dogons, this dwarf was the most important star in the sky, to them it was "the egg of the world." They also knew that this star, although invisible to the naked eye took 50 years to complete its orbit around Sirius A. Modern science confirms this orbit. The Dogons drew a diagram showing the course and trajectory of this star up until the year 1990, again modern astronomical projections are identical with this. They also stated that this tiny star is composed of a material brighter than iron and that if all men on earth were a single lifting force, they could not budge it. Again modern science confirms that this is the nature of that type of star.

To provide such detail about something that only the most advance observatories can detect today and to do it ahead of them has set Shockwaves throughout the scientific world. Yet the black man is supposed to be ignorant of these intellectual knowledge that the whole world, to include modern scientists of America and Europe, are researching on. How could that be, how were they able to develop and keep such knowledge, laid hidden for thousands of years! **Kenneth Brecker** of the Massachusetts Institute of Technology, for example, said quite bluntly in an article: "They (the Dogons) have no business knowing any of these!) He suggested that perhaps a Jesuit priest told them about it. **Robert Temple**, a member of the Royal Astronomical Society of Great Britain in a highly acclaimed book: "The Sirius Mystery" speculates that space beings from Sirius star system must have brought this marvelous knowledge down to the Africans. Again the black man was the first teacher of Astronomy, and we found two scientists who gave their lives learning the secret of the eight steps of the ladder of "Clear Knowledge," however, they died just after twenty years or so after reaching the first step. The outside world is still spellbound to the Dogon's knowledge which the whites stole and tried to claim as their own. All those advance knowledge, that modern scientists are still trying to unravel, the construction formula of the pyramids throughout Africa. Yet blacks, as whites say had no civilization and could not have possibly built the complex structure. When you read your history, you will find out from the real scientists, the astronomers and anthropologists who devoted their whole lives to the truth, and reveal in fact that the black people of such era of great ancient civilizations, built all those that we see today! That's why there was a destruction of African black civilizations, while destroying they kept all of the valuable artifacts you now see in European, Asian, and all major world countries museums filled with the stolen legendary history which tells it all! So we are seeing an unequaled race of intellectual black people who were far more advanced than those who conquered and changed the writings of that exceptional knowledge and technology, to reflect their own story, and take the credit for all stolen legacy. Most of your white Europeans were taught in every field of intellectual endeavor by those black African scholars in their Motherland. Check and read the history, the truth will set you Free!

Mathematics, Architecture, Engineering, Agricultural Science, Medicine, Navigation, Writing Systems and all the functions of intellectual learning were taught by our stolen African Civilizations. Black men and women have lead great dynasties for thousands of years and the proof is forthcoming. No nation or group of people will ever be able to surpass what our Creator has put in place on this earth. We are some of the wisest and wealthiest people of our time, not only in monies but in understanding, wisdom and knowledge. We have accomplished everything imaginable, we ruled, we created and we even enlightened the people who stole our learning and teaching philosophies. In spite of being enslaved here and divested of our African culture and heritage, not allowed to be educated, murdered, lynched, branded, whipped, abused and disrespected as human beings, we still overcame to be some of the brightest and knowledgeable people in this country today. Just think, we were kept in bondage where we were not able to get good education in any school system for over 20 years. Yet we are among the selected few who are indeed highly educated, as I stated, find me white so called intellectual and I'll find a black person to talk circles around him. We were all created equal even if the Common White racist foe refuses to acknowledge such a very important fact of life. It really doesn't matter now, we have mastered all things and the only thing that really counts is that we truly understand such equality. We know that God created us all equal! We as African Americans intend to stand and take our rightful place with dignity and respect, even as we too reach out to all other ethnic groups of America! We vow to help assist in uniting our Country with togetherness, to create the balance of which this Country stands for, to tear down the racial divide that exists where we, once again can show the world that this country is capable of righting its wrong and become the leader upon the world's body of humanity. And the true beginning of our future is resolving racism, the black, white issues that has been going on for 500 years. I have strongly encouraged white people, as well as all blacks, to read past Black history of our African ancestors, which will allow our children, as well as adults, to know what we as black people have contributed to this universe. We all bring something of our past to this country, once enlightened, there will be total appreciative outlook on the black people, the role they played in the African Civilization, the major contributions they made to help establish America where we all should share the entitlements and resources on fair and equal terms.

chapter 51

African American Inventions/Accomplishments

Here are some inventions that blacks have been able to register through the years, like stated blacks were not viewed as human beings, so a lot of inventions were credited to the white people or bought, registered and patented them. There's been thousands of inventions stolen from the originator of their creative works. The same applied of the stolen ancestral ideologies and artifacts, I have ventured into European museums and saw these valuable treasures which the white man stole and took credit for:

1787	The Free African Society of Philadelphia, organized by Richard Allen and Absalom Jones, is formed.
1790	The first United States Patent Act is enacted.
1792	Benjamin Banneker becomes the first African American to publish an almanac.
1806	The African Meeting House in Boston, Massachusetts, is the first major building in Boston, constructed solely by African Americans.
1827	Freedom's Journal, the first Black newspaper is published.
1832	Hyram S. Thomas. A Saratoga; the ice cream of Augustus Jackson, a Philadelphia confectioner known as "the man who invented ice cream."
1843	Norbert Rellieux patents his vacuum evaporation system, which revolutionizes the sugar industry and food production in general.
1853	William Wells Brown becomes America's first African-American novelist when his book "Clotel, Or, The President's Daughter: A Narrative of Slave Life in the United States," is published in England.

1864   Rebecca Cole and Rebecca Lee are the first African-American women in the United States to receive medical degrees.

1868   John Mercer Langston founds and organizes the Law Department at Howard University, which is founded in Washington, D.C.

1870   Hiram M. Revels becomes the first African American United States Senator when he is elected by the state of Mississippi.

1872   P. B. S. Pinchback of Louisiana becomes the first African American to serve as governor of a state.

1878   Meharry Medical College is founded in Nashville, Tennessee.
            Tuskegee Institute is founded.

1881   Lewis H. Latimer patents the first co-efficient method of producing carbon filaments for electric lights.
            Jan Matzeliger patents the first successful shoe lasting machine.

1888-1958   Archie Alexander, Design and Construction Engineer, built bridges, freeways, airfields, railroads and power plants, obtained an Engineering degree in 1912 from the Iowa State University.

1891   Ida B. Wells starts her crusade against the lynching of African Americans. She later helps to found the NAACP.

1893   Dr. Daniel Hale Williams becomes the first person to perform a heart operation successfully.

1896   George Washington Carver accepts a position as professor at Tuskegee Institute.
            Mary Church Terrell is elected President of the National Association of Colored Women.
            In Plessy v. Ferguson, the United States Supreme Court upholds legal segregation.

1897   Andrew J. Beard patents a coupling device for railroad cars.

1899	Mary Eliza Mahoney is the first African American woman to graduate from a professional White nursing school.
	Maggie Lena Walker establishes the St. Luke Penny Savings Bank, which becomes the St. Luke Bank and Trust Company. She becomes America's first Black woman bank president.
	Mary McLeod Bethune establishes a school now known as Bethune-Cookman University.
1908	Jack Johnson becomes the first African American heavyweight champion when he knocks out Tommy Burns in the fourteenth round. The National Association for Colored Graduate Nurses is founded.
1910	Madame C. J. Walker opens her own beauty care factory. She becomes America's first Black self-made millionaire. 1920's The Nineteenth Amendment to the Constitution guarantees women the right to vote.
	Bessie Coleman, the first Black American female pilot performs her air show in Chicago.
	Garrett A. Morgan patents a three-way automatic traffic signal.
1926	Negro History Week, now Black History Month, is begun by Carter G Woodson.
1928	The Edgecombe Sanitarium is established in Harlem by Dr. Wiley Wilson and associates.
1935	The National Council of Negro Women is formed.
1940	Frederick McKinley Jones patents a practical refrigeration system for trucks and railroad cars.
	Dr. Charles Richard Drew is the first person to set up a blood bank. Dr. Drew found that blood plasma could be used in transfusions rather than whole blood.
1942	Ernest Coleman directed high energy physics at three Federal Agencies: the Atomic Energy Commission, Energy Research and Development Ad-

ministration, and the Department of Energy. He
was awarded the Distinguished Service Award of
the American Association of Physics Teachers. A
graduate of the University of Michigan.

1954   The United States Supreme Court rules in Brown
v. Board of Education of Topeka, Kansas, that
segregation is unconstitutional.

1959   Lorraine Hansberry's play "A Raisin in the Sun"
wins the New York Drama Critics Award.

1968   Arthur Ashe becomes the first African American
male to win a major tennis tournament when he
captures the singles title at the United States Lawn
Tennis Association Open Tournament.

1988   Jesse Jackson becomes the firsts African American to mount a serious run for the Presidency of
the United States.

1993   Toni Morrison becomes the first African Ameri-
can to win the Nobel Prize in Literature.
Dr. Jocelyn Elders is sworn in as United States
Surgeon General.

1995   Shirley Ann Jackson becomes head of the Nuclear
Regulatory Commission.

1998   Dr. Patricia Bath receives patent for laser method
and apparatus for removing cataracts.

In writing about major contributions by African Americans,
there's so much more to convey, however, that's for those truly interested in educating their children and themselves, and that will
take your personal research. It's been a cruel circumstance of what
we have endured here, as well as our ancestors from whence we
came. The ancestors have provided the whole world with their advance knowledge only to be robbed of that credibility with stolen
truths. Just a case in point, the world's major professors, architects,
anthropologists and so-called powerful minds are still in wonderment of the advanced culture and technology of our people. They
have yet to figure out the ways and means of how the ancestors
structured and built the pyramids of ancient Africa, or find the der-

ivation, origin and development of the mathematical formula as regards the alignment of the solar system's magnetic force field and frequency? So threatened by the pyramids, and especially the Sphinx's Negroid features, they chopped off the nose from its face! It's a necessity to learn of the mind set that has contributed to white's being so racist against our ancestors' achievements and the American black people here as well. What we see here and especially in Europe is that black people throughout the world are not intelligent enough to have the skills or technical knowledge to have built this complex system of science, mathematics, writings, astronomy, philosophies, etc. Instead of giving appreciative views of the black people's accomplishments, and acknowledging their human capabilities to contribute immensely to world culture and civilization, the whites painted all black people as dumb, ignorant, uneducated, fit only to be slaves for life here in America! Today, blacks have equaled or even have surpassed their white counterpart in many fields of endeavor. Given a level playing field we have awesomely proved our prowess and excellence at all levels we pursued! Stand with pride among our peers! We, as blacks must uphold the values, principles and legacy of our ancestors of Africa, the brave black American soldiers who fought and died on these white man's battlefields and in the whole world at large! They did not die in vain! To you our beloved ancestors we say: "We stand here today among the elite of the society because of the struggles and strife you have overcome to allow us to pursue our real hallowed spot in this nation, for freedom and justice for all! Your sacrifices, enslavement and blood has made us ONE in Peace and Unity, committed to achieving the highest standards of life to prove to all that we were once KINGS in this world!

chapter 52

The Dream

MARTIN LUTHER KING, JR.
1929 -1968
Clergyman, Nobel Prize Winner
Civil Rights Leader, Advocate of Non-violent Protest
Fought against Racial Discrimination
1950- 60's; Assassinated in 1968 Seeking racial justice.

On the 28th of August, 1963, one of the most powerful speeches ever spoken in America was heard at the Lincoln Memorial place in Washington D.C. given by a young, strong, courageous fighter against racial discrimination. He stated: "I have a dream that one day this nation will rise up and live out the true meaning of its Creed: We hold these truths to be self-evident, that all men are created equal... I have a dream that my four little children will one day live in a nation where they will not be judged by the color of their skin, but by the content of their character..." The orator of this unforgettable, mesmerizing speech whose name still rings across the country, where we are still awaiting for the ultimate realization of his dream, was Martin Luther King, Jr.

From the halls of the Memorial, his divine message still echoes the cry for Unity, Peace and Justice! His speech allowed millions of Americans from all walks of life, of every ethnicity, to come to the "promise land," the White House, where so many of our politicians have made millions through them over the 400 years, only not to allow their dreams to materialize, after stealing their votes! These people struggled, died for, and trusted such deceitful individuals who eventually rejected and disrespected them! Martin Luther King, Jr. led them there, where they took off their blinders, and observed the beautiful multitude of colors - people represented at such an auspicious gathering, where the magnitude of people spoke volumes of the quest of the leader to unify our nation. They grasped this moment to share in his relentless cry for this nation's sole purpose under God's plan, which is Love and Togetherness, to show the world that despite the racial hatred and discrimination of black people in bondage for hundreds of years, racism could truly be defeated! Luther preached of God's peace and happiness throughout the land, for all mankind, and in fact we are the keepers of the garden and its people. We also noted over the years that our Creator's name is bogusly disrespected in the context of the Constitution, where it reflects Black human beings as cattle, 3/5th of a man, and property. How could such supposedly superior people of that time use the most sacred name throughout the world, other than what God, who represents the Divine Oneness of all things where the bible of which has been rewritten thousands of time over still holds a quote from the Creator of us all which states: "I AM THE LORD THY GOD!" To me, that means God of all things addressing the beings birthed into this system of things of which we live. It's time for the powers that be to correct this nation's highest Document, the Constitution, that reflects the standards of which it stands for: "One nation indivisible under God with justice and freedom for all." As it stands now, it's a total travesty that keeps the racial divide, for whites to think they are God's only creation. I could write on and on regarding the rewriting of the Bible that reflects their story. Well, if we are to change, then that's definitely the first step. When there's greed, lust for power and control, eventually it catches up with the deceivers of any great empire or dynasty! Read your history and you will find that America is at that point of demise of its greatness and leadership around the world, the change must occur if we are to prosper under God's divine guidance of which we must truly seek at this point in time. Bombs, missiles and all war materials are not the way of power, this crucial element will always in time, crumble under Understanding, Wisdom, Knowledge, and the Divine guidance of the Creator. It has happened for thousands of years. What God has put in place, no one will put asunder. The first passage I read some years ago about Adam and Eve was very meaningful to me: "God gave them everything they could ever want," however, He gave them only one restriction and when it was violated, they lost their souls, same thing applies now as it did then. That's the divine guidance and nature of this all, never try to be all things to all people or countries, no one nation rules all others, at least, not with weapons of mass destruction. We are the most powerful country in this world, yet from Viet-Nam until now, we have lost our way. The powers that will reestablish our role in this system of things will accomplish this. The word of God will guide us and "We shall overcome!" We the People hold in our hand the worst image this powerful and wealthy country has ever had, now we must stand together, where we all can share the same fundamental principles and values of that sacred Unity and Justice, to reach new Heights to set the standards for all to see, as the world is watching to see how all things will unfold. We still have a purpose, all we need now is to formulate the plan for this nation, where each and every nationality of mankind is to the world "We the People."

On Martin Luther's Day in D.C. all the people were present, it was a glorious sight to behold! They were holding hands, embracing one another for the common cause of what his purpose was. On that day we truly stood with faith and hope, I will always remember his speech and the nation's reaction, it will always live in my soul! Then in just a short period of time all that hope we walked away with, began to deteriorate, we went back to where we once were. The racist Common Foe was back in action, there were riots in Selma, Alabama from whites protesting the rights of blacks to vote, police beat and tear-gassed black marchers there, that day was televised worldwide and became known as bloody Sunday. Another march was orchestrated by King to speak to the people of Montgomery, Alabama, where he addressed more than 20,000 people in front of the capitol building. This march created support for the Voting Rights Act of 1965 signed by President Lyndon Johnson. This Act suspended the use of literacy test and other voter qualifications that were used. King also spoke out against the Viet-Nam war so strongly that many whites shifted their activism from civil rights to anti-war movement. His struggles with civil rights continued on until he went to Memphis, Tennessee to support striking black garbage workers, he was assassinated by a sniper on April 4th. The world was shocked and there were riots in more than 100 cities in the days to follow.

In the investigation on his death conducted by historians researching his life, they found out that the Federal Bureau of Investigation often tapped King's phone line and reported on his private life to the President and other government agencies. King's historical importance was immortalized at the Martin Luther King, Jr. Center for Social Justice in Atlanta, and at the King's Center where his tomb is located. Perhaps the most important memorial is the National Holiday in his honor designated by Congress in 1983 and observed on the 3rd Monday in January, a day that falls on or near his birthday on January 15th.

Luther told us that he had reached the mountain top and seen the "Glory of the Coming of the Lord." He had seen the promise land and told us that although he might not get there with us, but wanted us all to join hands and thank God Almighty for all he was allowed to accomplish and all he shared with us, as a Nation!

"WE THE PEOPLE" THIS TIME MIGHT JUST MAKE THE PIECES FIT TO FULFILL HIS AND OUR DREAM!

chapter 53

The Greatest Sound They Ever Heard

The plantation owner had just observed one of his slave drivers flog one of them for being sickly and not keeping up with the set quota of the day, after the whipping he started out to the big house, when suddenly a sound he had never heard before was flowing with the wind. It was all around him, he could not distinguish this unusual sound, what was it? He was mesmerized and totally in awe of what his ears where experiencing, what was its source, why had he not heard it before, the sound got louder and louder, it was actually overwhelming in its beautiful and powerful tone, that vibrated all around and in him. Suddenly he turned and looked to where those amazing rhythmical sounds could be originating from, to his surprise, this wonderful harmonizing spiritual tones were coming from the slaves who had gathered around their abused and suffering brother, who lay bleeding on the ground.

They were actually chanting and humming these never-before heard of sounds, he stood there, engulfed in what he was hearing and experiencing, some of the most wonderful and powerful sounds ever heard by him. He looked at the slaves and thought of all these poor black bastards were enduring, still they actually had the energy to make these phenomenal sounds, to get them through their time of pain and sorrow, and he felt a sense of respect for these slaves he had purchased and owned for many years. And he tried to figure out why he had not heard them make this sounds before. He stood there until they had finished, then he slowly turned and continued on to the big house, saying softly to himself, what splendid voices they had, and How Sweet the Sound.

One of the most wonderful gifts our Creator has given to us all are the ears to hear, what a creative God we all have.

Ears to hear the chirping of the birds, the sounds of the wind, the howling of the wolf, the crying of our babies, the purring of the cat, the raindrops pounding our window sills, the sound of the water waves, the ringing of the bells, sounds of the drums, the horns, piano, the sound of our lovers as they whisper in our ears, the sound of the mother's voice as she says goodnight, and the roaring sound of fathers when we have done something wrong, the sound of the tree limbs as they are blown to and fro in the strong current of the wind, the sound of laughter, the sound of the elephants asking for peanuts, the roaring sound of the lion who we call the king of the jungle, sound of the caged birds, sounds of the monkeys playing on the trees, the sound of the almighty eagle soaring miles above the earth, sounds of the great dolphins and whales in their communication system of the oceans, the sound of the stars as the glitter in the night, the sound of the rainbow so beautifully displaying its miraculous blend of magnificent colors, the sound of the thunder as it flexes it power and energy.

Every element of life has a sound which is tied into voices of our world, and on this day, the plantation owner heard some of the most powerful creative sounds ever in his life, the sounds of a far distant continent, they were the most extraordinary sound of the black voices which would, in time turn the white man's ears to all their voices were saying to the white man's world of hate and vileness - the sound of sorrow, of love and spiritual awakening all through the land they call America.

The sound of the Black voice with its capabilities to reach phenomenal range at all levels has become renown all over the world, in the gospel, the billions of rock and roll songs, the love sounds, the spiritual music, Broadway, opera. Black songwriters were phenomenal at producing and orchestrating millions of songs. Black music took over America, not only did they have the sound, they had the stage performances, second to none. The black music became the soul sound and whites even tried to ban them from the music stores, in order to sell them to the producers, who featured white models on the covers of the albums, however, after it got revealed all over the country, there was, as they said: "There ain 't no stopping us now." Black singers put their sound in the heart of all

Americans and the world. Our Creator is worthy to be praised, the sound will forever embrace us all. The sounds of our black people is beauty in its frequencies and vibrations throughout our world. When you see Doo-wop on television that originated when blacks would hang on the corners and sing the songs to the exact sounds of the performances themselves, even the white groups sang it like the blacks did, and became pretty good at it. I was really good at lead for the song "In the Still of the Night," even sang it in a club in Spain and in France, where I was stationed for two years. You come from Philly, you could definitely sing, dance, dress and rumble.

The Great Black Actors of Our Time

A tribute to those actors and actresses, playrights and producers who projected the major struggle and accomplishments of our people and nation to our crying eyes. Those extraordinary people who inspired hope and gave us a sense of pride and dignity.

They gave us *Roots, Rosewood Burning, Color Purple, The Tuskegee Airmen, The Charlie Parker Story, Mendela, Shaft, In the Heat of the Night, Risen Is The Sun, Independence Day, Malcolm X, The Great White Hope, The Buffalo Soldiers, Lady Sings the Blues, A Lady Called Moses, The Ray Charles Story*, and many more memorable films and performances.

The magnificent Hollywood Players: Morgan Freeman, Sidney Poitier, Danny Glover, James Earl Jones, Jamie Foxx, Will Smith, Denzel Washington, Lawrence Fishbourne, Spike Lee, Halle Berry, Whoopi Goldburg, Diana Ross, Whitney Houston, Lena Horne, Angela Basset, and Queen Latifah. The list goes on and on of these accomplished and special players of the movie industry, we applaud them for their wonderful and lasting memories.

chapter 54

The Birth of America's Black Entertainment

The plantation owner was so excited about the singing of his slaves, that he encouraged them to sing on Sundays of which he gave them off, he had even invited his fellow plantation owners over, to hear this amazing music he was speaking of. Even though they were not allowed to read or write, the owner had a few to learn to read the bible about the slaves and their servitude recorded in several books in the scriptures for them to retain that superiority mental block over their slaves. So the plantation had a black preacher and a choir at which the plantation owner and his guest would attend. The preachers became really soul speakers and got them raved up, that even the owner and guest knew it was quite different from their white church services, it seemed it had more spirituality on the plantation and the encouraging singing became really something special, so for the first time in 1640 the black man became the entertainer for the white man, of which he has been enjoying for over 400 years. The had singing, preaching, and fighting on the plantations, the owner always wanted to own the best of the slaves, they even had champion black studs, they groomed them like they groomed and studded their horses. So we see the white man was entertained, which is what we see today. Back in the day, there was Nat King Cole, Paul Robeson, Sam Cook, Ella Fitzgerald, Jackie Wilson, Sammy Davis, Billy Holiday, Pearl Bailey, Sarah Vaughn, Nancy Wilson, Diana Ross and the Supremes, Ruth Brown, Aretha Franklin, you as a black man would not be able to get a seat at their performance, tickets all sold out to the white people wanting to see them, the sounds of the black voice was in demand, and that's just a few of the thousands of performers I could name. Then you come forward along, talking about Ray Charles, James Brown, Marvin Gaye, Smokey Robinson, Jerry

Butler, Teddy Pendergrass, the Four Tops, the Dells, Flamingos, Temptations, the Spinners, the Blue notes, Moon Glows, Cool and the Gang, Isaac Hayes, the Defonics, Curtis Mayfield, Stevie Wonder, Michael Jackson, Little Jimmy Scott, King Pleasure, Dakota Staton, Isley Brothers, Arthur Prysock, Earth Wind and Fire, Gil Scott Heron, Luther Vandeross, Al Jarreau, Billie Paul, Barry White, Dionne Warwick, Blue Magic, Roy Hamilton, SADE, Dinah Washington, this list can go on and on of what the sound of black voices have given to this country and the world.

I remember when I was a young kid they used to have a show on TV called the Band Stand, hosted by Dick Clark, it allowed no black children on the program, however, it featured primarily all black artists to perform on it. It took approximately two years of protesting that they finally allowed the black children on, and it was really comical, because all of the white kids looked so awkward dancing on the show, as soon as the blacks came on, the white kids started to show some rhythm in their dance as they were copying the dance steps of the blacks on the show. How discriminating was that, to feature almost all black artists, yet blacks could not participate in its nationally viewed TV show. There are albums I cherish that really speak of the times of the day: Marvin Gayes "What's going on?" Curtis Mayfield's "Superfly" Stevie Wonder's "Visions" Roy Hamilton's "You'll Never Walk Alone"Nina Simone's "I Love you Porgy" and Gil Scott Heron's "Reflections." As I mentioned I could go on and on and who could ever top Ray Charles singing "America" or "Georgia On My Mind." And I must salute Mrs. Eleanor Roosevelt, the nation's First Lady who resigned from the Daughters of the American Revolution, DAR, an all-white group because they denied Marian Anderson's request to perform at the Constitution Hall in Washington DC in 1939 because she was black. Mrs. Roosevelt's protest against the DAR inspired the then Secretary of the Interior, Harold Licks to arrange an open-air concert at the Lincoln Memorial on Easter Sunday, which was attended by 75,000 people. Marian sang once more on the Memorial, as part of the March on Washington in 1963, a key event in the Civil Rights Movement. Anderson was the first Black American to perform at the Metropolitan Opera house, in 1958 President Dwight D. Eisenhower appointed her to the United States Delegation to the United Nations, where she spoke on behalf of African independence. Anderson received the highest award conferred by the National Association for the Advancement of Colored People in 1941. She sang at President Eisenhower's Inauguration in 1977. President Carter presented her with a Congressional Gold Medal bearing her profile. An amazing woman and how sweet the sound. I witnessed Ray Charles singing "America the Beautiful" and "Georgia on my Mind" the theatre was packed to its full capacity with white people, and damn near everyone of them was crying during his performance. What a travesty and my heart grieves of this nation that has not the character nor the courage to right a wrong done to these patriotic and loving people, although blacks have forgiven all, they have not received their just dues as of yet. They have earned them in every way despite the bigots and continuous discrimination. I applaud the Wachovia bank industry for acknowledging a wrong during the slavery period, with saying they were sorry for the actions of the whites who took advantage of slaves, utilizing and selling them in thousands of banking transactions as property. They set up a trust fund for black scholarship programs. And those Common Foe racists with their continuous hatred are in my mind just as ignorant and calloused as the feeble-minded villains we see shooting, hanging nooses and killing blacks today. They are the white people of yesteryears who hung, murdered, and lynched blacks, their blood is on your hands by your racist' action, you continue to clandestinely orchestrate like the cowards that you are, they say what goes around comes around. You continue to be part of the problems happening to black people who fought, died and worked freely, deprived of their human rights and were taken advantage of, who were denied their freedom of this country, their education for hundreds of years, the continued lynching of black men, the raping of black women and all the atrocities your kind orchestrated and caused over the 100 years. I will never forget the time I was called a nigger in a white restaurant in full United States Army uniform en route oversees to fight and protect this nation's freedom. It is still etched in my mind, you are simply despicable. Let me say I retract my ill-feelings as stated above, I almost got caught up in your racist world, and I ask God to forgive me for even thinking such malicious thoughts against anyone, but I am only human, and I know God will understand my thoughts at that moment, as I try to live my life in the image of my Creator who's the source of love and forgiveness. And believe me that takes faith and courage to retract my inner feelings however, I've learned on my spiritual journey within to find understanding which allows me to obtain the wisdom and knowledge to see the full and total understanding of being one with God, who says humble thyself and forgive them for they know not what they do. How sweet the sound and feeling, so I pray for you world righteous people, so to speak, to seek God who's within you and discard those negatives that has caused so much suffering and death, all along the pathway of their lives, who tried to extend their love, appreciation, their patriotism for this country and its white family. Peace and blessing be upon your soul, as well as mine. Love will always conquer hate in due time, God bless, life is really too short not to live it and let others live it to their fullest. There's enough of America for all equally, don't leave here without doing all we can to create the harmony, balance and unity for our country, our fellowmen and ourselves. There's a recording by Pharaoh Sanders entitled: "The Creator has a Master Plan"... where there's peace and happiness thru all the land, the Creator has the master plan, peace and happiness for every man, really good listening. Ronnie Liston Smith says to extend your hand to help the plan, millions of songs given to us to help the people and nation to change, to establish the pride and image that our Creator is seeking from us, one nation under God of which we stand. God is truly waiting, he sees the nation, however, it has not learned to stand as one under his name, and until we live up to the standards of which we utilized his name, we will continue to be lost in chaotic state until we find the courage to do so. The Bible states that God says everything you do, do it in my name, we have placed his name on a document and have failed to meet the promise in God's name, we cannot have insufficient funds for this check, this only requires the faith of each and everyone to fulfill that obligation which has been documented since the 4th of July, 1776, it's over 330 years old and we have not had the courage to live by it.

Two very important insertions therein:

When in the course of human events, it becomes necessary for ONE people to dissolve the political bonds which have connected them with another, and assume among the powers of the earth the separate and equal station, to which the laws of nature and of nature's God entitle them.

The most famous phrase, the Basic Rights of all men:

We hold these truths to be self-evident, that all men are created equal, that they are endowed by their Creator with certain inalienable rights, that among these are life, liberty and the pursuit of happiness, deriving their just powers from the consent of the governed.

Studying the demise of all great empires and nations, there has been one common element of their fall from grace of the world and our Creator, and that is the treatment of the little people who fight the wars to protect their dynasties. Our Constitution further states that whenever any form of government becomes destructive of these ends, it is in the light of the people to alter or abolish it, and to institute a new government laying its foundation on such principles to effect their safety and happiness. Interesting read, I say know your Constitution, Declaration of Independence and Bill of Rights. They all contain an unheard of sound for many.

chapter 55

The Jazz Masters

Blacks have been making these amazing sound for over a great period of time, not only in singing but in the jazz world as well. I've been listening to jazz since 1953 as a young kid coming home after a hard work at the boxing gym or from an equally hard work-out at the job. I had to keep strong cutting trees down around the city, I would return home, lay back and listen to jazz and fall right to sleep. The old heads of the neighborhood got me into jazz, listening to Charlie Parker, The Bird, the jazz master of his day, from him there came those who tried to reach that plateau and many certainly did. John Coltrane, Cannonball Adderly, Sonny Stitt. Blacks excelled in all instruments, again creating some amazing unheard of sound, how mellow those sounds were. We gave white people and the world Horace Silvers, the legendary Miles Davis, Jimmy Smith, Ronny Liston Smith, Pharaoh Sanders, the phenomenal Eubie Blake, saw in concert at 90 years old, awesome performance. Others include: Louis Armstrong, Gene Ammons, Art Blakely, Donald Bird, Billy Eckstine, Duke Ellington, Jim Hendrix, Lena Horne, Tina Turner, Quincy Jones, Ramsey Louis, Abbey Lincoln, Wynton Marsalis, Wes Montgomery, James Moody, Lee Morgan, Oscar Peterson, Grover Washington, Charlie Earland, Kevin Eubanks, Dexter Gordon, Johnny Hammond, Milt Jackson, The Four Sounds, Earl Klugh, Stanley Turrentine, George Benson, Ahmad Jamel, Lou Rawls, King Pleasure. These were some renown artists who perfected the sound of jazz and mostly every time I attended their concerts, the white audience was wall-to-wall, if they loved the black artists and people the way they loved the music they played, we would definitely have a better relationship of our races, and just think if all the innocent blacks killed who never got to see if in fact they could become whatever they could have been, if their lives were not taken from them.

So 1 reflect of these amazing artists who, as well as the artists of 1640 were entertaining the white plantation owners and their guests, how sweet the sound! Truly man is created equal, only in the eyes of the racist they are not, and that's very sad.

For me the greatest and most powerful voice of sound ever spoken to me, I have never heard, yet I acknowledge its every word. I felt it, the sound that was part of every living existence and object, all in ONE from the very beginning of time, and I only felt this tremendous feeling when in my silence of my darkness, its flowed from the depths of the unknown, traveled across the many galaxies of the total twilight spheres of billions of periods of all things, it graced the solar systems of the planets and stars of universal dimensions to engulf this place we call earth, it's the power source of the miraculous form of the rainbow, creating the ultraviolet of radiant blend of colors, the cause of the raging sea, it's the power that creates the thunderstorm, the energy that allows the rain to drench Mother Earth, the silent whisper that causes the eclipse of the moon, that of which allows the sun to radiate the warmth that energizes the cycle of new birth of life. Its origin we will never know, that silent sound that causes our stars to shine upon cosmic structure of the universe and all the formations of all evolutions of this limitless boundaries and timeless elements, all at once. This silent voice that somehow whispers to me in my total state of unworldly things and I have only been able to have the most extraordinary beautiful sound when I found my true purpose of me in this system of things, after ending my journey of divesting all worldly negatives to gain that ultimate, which is the true understanding, that understanding which allows me to know that the wisdom and knowledge of which I seek, is from the most powerful source of all things. I found wisdom and knowledge is God, who has enlightened me of which I seek,

I am only one of billions, unique in my oneness, my purpose to love all mankind, to give myself freely and unequivocally for the betterment and harmony of life on this earth, to assist in all endeavors and seek guidance and do all things in God's name, that is part of the wisdom and knowledge embracing my silent voice whispering in my heart and soul, I have felt the presence of that majestic flow throughout my existence, which has become one with the Manifester of the All. We are all a part of the All and the All is the Whole that balances and controls all things. I always say I am just part of Thee I am, and even though I have never heard the sound or the voice, I heard every word God has spoken to me. How glorifying, spiritual and beautiful.

THE SOUND...

It keeps saying that we are all created equal, however, there are those out there that are totally blind and evidently refuse to hear or acknowledge... how sweet the Sound that says WE ARE!

All praise and glory to God for allowing me to reach out to our Nation. I also pray for our President who has a tremendous task of righting and reestablishing the pride and image of Country's symbols that we reflect to the world. He is also dealing with power and corrupt minded elected politicians, who not only have failed to support him, but have vowed to destroy his every effort, truly they reflect their ignorant and biased racist personalities, during one of the most devastating struggle of our nation's history. They have incited and deceived American people to denouncing our President at orchestrated weapon carrying Tea Party Rallies with hateful rhetoric which many have employed these same sentiments to national leaders of other countries. These elected politicians were selected to assist in supporting issues for the betterment of "We The People." They are constantly calling to take their country back; this country they speak of, is the country of every American person that exist on this soil, it's the land that our heroic patriotic veterans, men and women of all ethnicity have died for and still are defending our way of life. When the rockets' red glare and the bombs bursting in air, gave proof thru the night that our star spangle banner was still there, on the battle field here and abroad, this is our country and they are fortunate to sit in an elected seat to govern, which many have made to mockery of, calling the President a liar before the world is a most disgraceful jus-

tice, he might as well, throw his shoe, it's not about the President, it's about resolving issues in the settlement of We The People and Nation. I also asked God and the people of our great Country to not adhere to these malicious comments of these people who are not ready to support a Black man. They reflect just how much we progressed only to regress back to racial prejudice and divide, we all must unite with God's given understanding, wisdom and knowledge to overcome and reach that of what we have been striving to achieve Racial Harmony of America, that's what a Democracy is to me.

The question I asked early on was: Are you strong and courageous enough to unite for the betterment of Our Nation against its Racial Divide, one of the most important challenges and issues of our era? We must establish pride, dignity, and respect for those Symbols by which we as people have fought and died for since its beginning. That's why I wrote this book.

I hope the answer is "I AM."

Love and respect to all. God Bless.

Reference Index

Freedom's Journey

African American Voices of the Civil War
. . . . by Donald Yacovone, Lawrence Hill Books

We the People
. . . . by Thomas E. Patterson

History of Black Athletes
. . . . by Double Day and Co Books

Africana Encyclopedia of African and African American Experience, Basic Civitas Books
. . . . by Kwame Anthony Appiah and Henry Louis Gates, Jr.

African American History
. . . . by Melba J. Duncan, Alpha Books

Racial and Ethnic Relations in America
. . . . by Dale McLemore, Allyn and Bacon Books

The Destruction of Black Civilization
. . . . by Chancellor Williams, Third World Press Books

The African American Bookshelf
. . . . by Clifford Mason, Citadel Press Books

Quest for Liberty
. . . . by Chapin/McHugh/Gross, Addison Wesley Books

We Shall Overcome
. . . . by Herb Boyd, Source Books

The Power of Now
. . . . by Eckhart Jolle, Nameste Publishing

African Contribution to Civilization

.... by A.K. Osei, Inprint Edition
World Great Men of Color
.... by J.A. Rogers
100 Amazing Facts About the Negro with Proof
.... by Helga M. Rogers
The Journey of the Songhai People
.... by Dr. Molefi Asante, Dept. Head of African Studies,
    Temple University, Philadelphia, PA, Foundational Book
Come Home America, It's GOD's last call
.... by David E. Johnson
Ethiopia and the Origin of Civilization
.... by John G. Jackson, Black Classic Press
My Life in Search of Africa
.... by John Herrick Clarks
Early American Views on Negro Slavery
.... by Matthew T. Mellon
The Bill of Rights
... by Eugene W. Hickok, Jr., University Press of Virginia Books
The Community of Self
.... by Dr. Na'Im Akbar, Mind Productions
The Black Man in America (1877-1905)
.... by Florence Jackson, Franklin Watts Library Edition
The Community
.... by Time - Life Books, New York

The Negro in the Making of America
.... by Benjamin Quarles
The Book of Coming Forth by Day
.... by Dr. Muata Agnaya Ashley, Egyptian Series
The Old Man, John Brown at Harper's Ferry
.... by Truman/Nelson/Holt/Rinehart/Winston